Nutrition and Behavior

New Perspectives

Robin B. Kanarek
Robin Marks-Kaufman

Tufts University
Medford, Massachusetts

An **avi** Book
Published by Van Nostrand Reinhold
New York

An AVI book.
(AVI is an imprint of Van Nostrand Reinhold)

Copyright © 1991 by Van Nostrand Reinhold

Library of Congress Catalog Card Number 90-13072
ISBN 0-442-23398-1

Printed in the United States of America.

Van Nostrand Reinhold
115 Fifth Avenue
New York, New York 10003

Chapman and Hall
2-6 Boundary Row
London, SE1 8HN, England

Thomas Nelson Australia
102 Dodds Street
South Melbourne 3205
Victoria, Australia

Nelson Canada
1120 Birchmount Road
Scarborough, Ontario MIK 5G4, Canada

16   15   14   13   12   11   10   9   8   7   6   5   4   3   2   1

Library of Congress Cataloging-in-Publication Data

Kanarek, Robin B.
    Nutrition and behavior : new perspectives / Robin B. Kanarek and Robin Marks-Kaufman.
        p.   cm.
    "An AVI book."
    Includes bibliographical references and index.
    ISBN 0-442-23398-1
    1. Nutrition.   2. Nutritionally induced diseases.   3. Dietary supplements—Psychological aspects.   4. Food additives— Psychological aspects.   5. Neuropsychology.   I. Marks-Kaufman, Robin.   II. Title.
    [DNLM: 1. Behavior—drug effects.   2. Behavior—physiology.
    3. Diet—adverse effects.   4. Nutrition.   5. Nutrition Disorders— etiology.   6. Nutrition Disorders—physiopathology.   QU 145 K155n]
QP141.K285   1991
616.3'9—dc20
DNLM/DLC
for Library of Congress   90-13072
                                                                          CIP

To
John, Daniel, and Jacob (RBK)
and
Richard, Melissa, and Jennifer (RMK)

Contents

Preface

Within the past decade there has been a veritable explosion of interest in the relationship between food and human behavior. It seems that there is an insatiable desire to find connections between what we eat and what we do. A clear example of this is the proliferation of books, magazine and newspaper articles, and television and radio programs devoted to the topic. More important, however, is the increased attention the scientific community is giving to the study of nutrition and behavior as evidenced by the growth of research, the development of undergraduate and graduate programs, and the number of scientific conferences addressing the problems in this area. The burgeoning scientific interest in this field makes it a very appropriate time for this book.

The principal goal of *Nutrition and Behavior: New Perspectives* is to provide a comprehensive examination of the scientific evidence dealing with relationships between nutritional variables and behavior. Although findings in research using experimental animals will be introduced, the primary emphasis will be on investigating the nutrition–behavior relationship in our own species.

The first chapter provides a historical introduction to the area and examines the techniques used in the scientific assessment of nutrition and behavior. This material gives the reader the necessary background to place recent research on nutrition and behavior within a wider perspective and to evaluate its reliability and validity.

Chapters 2–6 focus on the behavioral effects of nutritional deficiencies and excesses. Individual chapters review the consequences of protein-calorie malnutrition, vitamin deficiencies, and mineral deficiencies on brain functioning and behavior, and evaluate the effects of excess intake of vitamins and minerals with particular attention to the use of megadoses of these micronutrients in the treatment of psychological disorders. The last chapter in this group describes the detrimental neurological and behavioral effects of heavy-metal contamination in our food.

The third portion of this book examines the significance of commonly consumed food constituents and behavior. The physiological and psychological consequences of the intake of food additives, caffeine, sugar, and artificial sweeteners are surveyed in chapters 7 through 10. Chapter 11 addresses the problem of excess alcohol intake and its effects on the brain and behavior in adults and on fetal development.

The final portion explores research on human feeding behavior. Chapter 12 examines recent scientific findings on the effects of the macronutrient content in the diet on brain chemistry and behavior. The final two chapters survey the physiological and psychological aspects of obesity and eating disorders.

Because the nature of research in nutrition and behavior is interdisciplinary, this book will be of interest to individuals from a variety of backgrounds including nutrition, dietetics, food science, biochemistry, psychology, medicine, and anthropology. This book will be of use to students, researchers, and clinicians. For students, it will bring together, in a cohesive manner, the scientific information that is currently available on the relationship between nutrition and behavior. For researchers, it will serve as a valuable source of references for future investigations. For clinicians who must decipher and relay the vast quantities of information to the worried consumer, this book will put into perspective many of the most recent concerns about nutrition and behavior.

Acknowledgments

We would like to acknowledge the valuable help we have received in the preparation of this book. In particular, we would like to thank John Tovrov for his careful and thoughtful editing of the original manuscript, Robin Lin for his artistic contribution to the drawings in the text, and Madeline Amico for her assistance with many of the practical aspects of completing this book. Additionally, we would like to express our appreciation to Eleanor Riemer, Vincent Janoski, and the other members of the staff of Van Nostrand Reinhold who have helped in the development and production of *Nutrition and Behavior: New Perspectives*.

Introduction

In groups as different as Neanderthal hunters and twentieth-century Americans, people have consistently believed that the food they eat has powerful effects on their behavior. Some foods have been blamed for both physical and mental ills, and others have been valued for their curative or magic powers. Beliefs about food play an important role in our efforts to maintain health and happiness, and can influence scientific inquiry on nutrition and behavior in subtle ways.

This chapter presents a selective historical chronicle of ideas about the interaction of food and behavior that will lead to an examination of some contemporary beliefs. We will end with a discussion of current research methods used in studying relationships between nutrients and observable behavior.

HISTORICAL PERSPECTIVE

The idea that particular foods are crucial in determining character, behavior, and achievement was perhaps best summarized over 160 years ago by the French philosopher and gourmand Jean Anthelme Brillat-Savarin, who wrote in his treatise, *The Physiology of Taste,* "Tell me what you eat, and I will tell you what you are" (Drayton 1970). The notion that "you are what you eat," however, did not originate with Brillat-Savarin. Ancient documents and artwork demonstrate that beliefs about the power of food had a prominent place in early medicine.

Recognition of the potential effects of food upon health and disease can be traced to earliest recorded history. According to the Bible, Adam and Eve fell into sin and brought disease and death upon the world by eating forbidden fruit. To ensure good health, the ancient Egyptians espoused a complex system of dietary medicine. With respect to behavior, they held that onions could induce sleep, almonds and cabbage could prevent the undesirable consequences of excessive alcohol consumption, lemons could protect against the evil eye, and salt could stimulate passion.

The ancient Greeks also staunchly believed that diet was an integral part of the treatment of both physical and psychological ills. Their beliefs were based on the doctrine that the human body was made up of four basic "humors" to which the characteristics of heat, cold, moisture, and dryness were intrinsic. Imbalances in these humors were thought to result in variations in temperament. Because the characteristics of heat and cold, moisture and dryness, were also considered to be inherent properties of food, the consumption of particular dietary items could correct humoral imbalances (Darby 1977; Farb and Armelagos 1980; Cosman 1983; Messer 1984).

The use of food as medicine reached its zenith during the Middle Ages. The typical medieval view was that there was a unity between food and health. Good diet helped the body heal itself. Maimonides, the great twelfth-century philosopher and physician, declared that any illness that was curable by diet alone should not otherwise be treated.

The effects of food on behavior were championed not only by medieval practitioners, but also by their patients. People of all social classes respected particular foods for stimulating or tranquilizing their erotic impulses. As finely described by Cosman (1983), medieval men and women used food to both encourage and restrain sensuality. Rare roast beef in saffron pastry, roast venison with garlic, suckling pig, boiled crab, quail with pomegranate sauce, turnips, leeks with honey, truffles, figs, savory, and mustard were all endowed with the ability to excite the sexual passions. On the other hand, although far less numerous, erotic tranquilizers including lettuce, cooked capers, rue, and hemlock juice in a dilute solution with mild wine also were identified in the medieval medical arsenal.

Beliefs that certain foods could regulate behavior did not end with the Middle Ages. Brillat-Savarin postulated a number of direct relationships between diet and action. He was one of the first to document the stimulant actions of caffeine, and he believed that a variety of foods—including milk, lettuce, and a rennet apple eaten before bedtime—could gently induce sleep. If dreaming were desired, Brillat-Savarin recommended a dinner containing red meat, hare, pigeon, duck, asparagus, celery, truffles, or vanilla (Drayton 1970).

The conviction that food affected behavior was an integral part of the nineteenth-century health reform movement in the United States. Diet was believed to determine physical and mental health, spirituality, intelligence, and sexual prowess. The health reform movement produced persuasive leaders who charmed their followers with their oratory skills and their own brand of proselytism. Two of the most prominent leaders of this movement, Sylvester Graham (remembered best for the graham cracker) and John Harvey Kellogg (recognized for the introduction of breakfast cereals) lectured widely throughout the country, promoting the use of natural foods and decrying the ingestion of meat, which they believed would lead to the deterioration of mental functioning and arouse animal passions. Kellogg further concluded that the breakdown products of meat acted as dangerous toxins that, when absorbed from the colon, produced a myriad of symptoms including depression, fatigue, headache, aggression, and mental illness. Indeed, Kellogg wrote that "the secret of nine-tenths of all chronic ills from which civilized human beings suffer" ranging from "national inefficiency" to "moral and social maladies" could be traced to the meat eater's sluggish bowels (Kellogg 1919). In keeping with his puritanical background, Kellogg warned his followers that spicy or rich foods would lead to moral deterioration and acts of violence (Kellogg 1882, 1919; Whorton 1982).

What is important to realize about these early convictions about the interaction of nutrition and behavior is that they are not merely of historical significance, but continue to be prevalent today.

FOOD FADDISM

During the last 20 years there has been an explosion of interest in the field of nutrition and behavior. The current obsession with health and fitness, as well as the desire to use food as a panacea, has led to a myriad of self-help books, magazine articles, and "nutritional therapies," all claiming that simply altering one's diet will lead to both physical and mental health. For example, it has been claimed that refined carbohydrates can cause psychological problems ranging from depression and criminal behavior to schizophrenia (e.g., Duffy 1975), while artificial food additives have been implicated as a primary cause of migraine headaches in adults and hyperactivity in children (Feingold 1975). On the other hand, a number of foods have been promoted for their ability to improve mental health. Bee pollen has been advocated as a means to enhance athletic prowess, garlic for curing sleep disorders, ginger root as a remedy for motion sickness, ginseng root to increase the capacity for both physical and mental work, and vitamins and minerals taken in excess of the recommended daily allowance as a panacea for everything from schizophrenia to cancer (Jarvis 1983; Dubick 1986; Herbert and Barrett 1986; Yetiv 1986; White and Mondeika 1988). In some instances there is some basis for these claims; however, in other situations they are based on anecdotal evidence, insufficient observations, or misinterpretation of scientific findings.

In extreme situations, claims about the consequences of consuming particular foods can lead to food faddism, which can be defined as an exaggerated belief in the impact of nutrition on health and disease. Food faddists maintain that nutrition is more significant than science has established. Such thinking frequently leads people to overestimate the beneficial effects of some foods (e.g., organic foods, raw foods, and whole grains) and condemn others (e.g., sugar and white flour).

Apprehension about particular foods or food components (e.g., sugar, food additives, and caffeine) or about food manufacturing processes has led many people to adopt alternative food practices and to seek nonconventional approaches to nutrition. In many instances these practices are harmless, but this is not always the case. Food faddism can have serious consequences. For example, a variety of nutritional deficiencies have been observed in the children of parents who follow a strict vegetarian diet (Dwyer et al. 1979; Olson 1979; Zmora, Gorodischer, and Bar-ziv 1979). Conversely, overuse of particular nutrients can also have adverse effects; over the past several years, reports of toxic reactions resulting from excessive intake of a number of vitamins (e.g., vitamins A and B_6) have steadily increased (see chapter 3).

Food faddism is also expensive. Because of lower sales volumes and higher distribution costs, foods promoted as "organic" or "natural" generally demand premium prices. Moreover, food faddism is often espoused by pseudopractitioners who use unproven forms of diet therapy to treat their patients and charge significant amounts for their services. The following are ways in which these practitioners can be recognized (Jarvis 1983; Herbert and Barrett 1986):

1. Promises rapid, dramatic, and miraculous cures.

2. Supports nutritional claims with reports of personal experiences and testimonials.

3. Displays credentials and degrees from schools that are not academically accredited.

4. Uses nonstandardized tests to convince people of their nutritional needs.

5. Tells you not to trust your physician or that the medical community is suppressing his or her work.

6. Prescribes questionable substances, such as megadoses of vitamins and minerals, herbs, enzymes, or extracts from the glands or brains of animals.

7. Has something to sell via direct sales to the public or magazine advertisements, rather than through a physician or pharmacy.

RESEARCH STRATEGIES

The only way to establish the validity of claims about nutrition and behavior is to use established scientific methods. Three research strategies have been prominently employed to assess these claims. These methods, as well as their benefits and pitfalls, are described in the next sections.

Correlational Studies

Correlational studies are used to generate hypotheses about nutrition–behavior relationships. Their primary objective is to define a link between dietary intake and behavior, with the specific expectation that statistical associations will be derived between the two variables. This type of research can provide important insights for experimental evaluation of the connection between diet and behavior.

There are several conditions that must be met before we can accept the validity of a nutrient-behavior connection. First, reliable and valid measures of nutrient intake must be made. One of the most widely used approaches for measuring dietary intake is the 24-hour recall, in which subjects are asked to record everything they have consumed during the preceding day. There are wide day-to-day variations in any individual's food intake; however, a 24-hour record does not always provide an accurate determination of average daily food intake. Consequently, it has been suggested that a minimum of seven 24-hour records be used in correlational studies (Anderson and Hrboticky 1986).

Second, proper subject sampling techniques must be used to minimize extraneous variables that might affect the behavioral outcome. In general, a larger number of subjects is preferred. If the number is too small, the probability of observing relationships between a dietary component and behavior is reduced, and a false negative relationship may be concluded. On the other hand, correlational studies using large numbers of subjects risk the possibility of finding false positive associations. For example, when correlations are made between several dietary variables and a behavioral measure, the chance of achieving statistically significant results increases with the number of subjects and with the number of correlations made. When large numbers of subjects are used, small correlations also can become statistically significant, making it necessary for the researcher to decide on the clinical or physiological importance of such findings (Anderson and Hrboticky 1986).

Finally, it must be stressed that it is impossible to establish cause-and-effect relationships from correlational data. For example, positive correlations have been found between sugar intake and hyperactive behavior in children. These results have been interpreted by some (especially the popular media) as demonstrating that sugar causes hyperactivity. However, it is just as possible that high levels of activity increase sugar intake, or that a third unidentified variable influences both sugar intake and hyperactivity.

Experimental Studies

In contrast to correlational studies, experimental studies have the potential of identifying causal links between diet and behavior. If the manipulation of a specific dietary component (the independent variable) significantly alters the occurrence of a behavioral measure (the dependent variable), a causal relationship can be postulated. Before discussing these experimental paradigms, a number of methodological issues need to be considered.

One of the more difficult problems encountered in research on diet and behavior is how to separate nutritional from nonnutritional factors. Because food is intimately involved with so many aspects of daily life, it contains much more significance than its obvious nutritional value. Food is an intrinsic part of social relationships, religious observations, and cultural practices. Since food is a "loaded" variable, both experimenters and subjects may harbor biases about expected research outcomes.

To minimize the confounding effects of research bias, experiments should be conducted under *double-blind* conditions. In such an experiment, neither the researcher nor the subject knows whether the subject is receiving the test substance (i.e., the nutrient) or a placebo. This procedure can be readily incorporated into experiments investigating the behavioral consequences of individual nutrients, such as vitamins and minerals, by using pills that are indistinguishable from the placebo.

It is more difficult to use double-blind procedures when experiments involve the total diet. A change in diet can be easily recognized by the subject and by those in close contact with the subject. For example, because of substantial differences between diets containing food additives and additive-free diets, it has been difficult to adequately test the hypothesis that food additives lead to hyperactive behavior in children. The improvements in hyperactivity that have been reported to accrue from an additive-free diet may as easily have been the result of changes in the dynamics of families as they attempted to adhere to this new diet (see chapter 7).

When possible, *dose-response* procedures should be used in studies of nutrition and behavior. Because a low dose (amount) of a dietary variable may have different behavioral consequences than a higher one, several doses of the dietary variable should be tested whenever feasible. When different doses are used, researchers can determine if there is a systematic relationship between the dietary variable and behavior. The lack of a systematic effect is a danger sign; either the apparent effect is spurious or the variability is greater than expected.

The duration of treatment must also be considered. Although short-term (acute) studies permit the evaluation of the immediate effects of a dietary variable, they cannot provide information about long-term (chronic) exposure. Since the behavioral effects of dietary components (e.g., food additives) may only appear with extended exposure, both acute and chronic studies should be used to assess the nutrition–behavior interaction.

The time of day a nutrient is tested may also influence its behavioral effects. For example, Kanarek and Swinney (1990) observed that a snack (candy bar or yogurt) significantly improved subjects' ability to pay attention to relevant stimuli when it was eaten in the late afternoon, but not when it was eaten in the late morning.

Prior nutritional status is another potential source of variation in short-term studies. The types and amounts of foods previously consumed can affect how the test nutrient is metabolized. Standardizing dietary intake prior to testing the behavioral consequences of a nutrient can eliminate this source of variation.

The greater nutritional context of any dietary manipulation must also be considered when evaluating research. Experimental alteration of one dietary variable frequently alters the intake of others. For example, a concomitant of eliminating food additives from the diet is a reduction in sucrose intake (see chapter 9).

A final challenge in conducting nutrition and behavior experiments is choosing appropriate subjects. Differences in nutritional history, socio-economic background, and other environmental factors create subject heterogeneity which poses a threat to the internal validity of the research. Internal validity concerns the ability to conclude that a causal relationship exists between an independent and dependent variable. Because of subject heterogeneity, alternative explanations may exist for the observed effects, which lowers internal validity. For example, research on the dietary treatment of hyperactive children has shown that the home environment can affect results. Children from an unsupportive home environment show much less improvement with dietary treatment than children from more supportive homes (Rumsey and Rapoport 1983).

Standardized selection procedures for subjects (inclusion and exclusion criteria) help to eliminate the possibility of extraneous variables influencing the results of experimental research. The use of within-subjects designs in which each subject experiences all treatment conditions can be used to limit the potentially confounding effects of extraneous variables. Since order of dietary treatment may affect behavioral outcomes, however, it is important to vary the sequence of treatments among subjects (Anderson and Hrboticky 1986; Kruesi and Rapoport 1986; Kanarek and Orthen-Gambill 1986; Hirsch 1987).

Two major paradigms have been used in experimental studies of nutrition and behavior. In *dietary replacement studies,* the behavioral effects of two diets, one containing the food component of interest (experimental diet), and the other as similar as possible to the experimental diet but not containing the food component (control diet), are compared over a period of time (e.g., two or three weeks). If appropriate double-blind conditions and sampling methods are employed, differences in behavior between the two groups can be assumed to be the result of the dietary manipulation.

One obvious advantage of dietary replacement studies is that chronic dietary effects can be examined. A clear disadvantage is that the difficulty of making two diets equivalent in all factors except for the food component being studied makes the use of double-blind techniques difficult to employ successfully. Another limitation is that it is not feasible to test more than one dose of the dietary variable. Finally, replacement studies are generally very expensive as well as time-consuming.

Dietary challenge studies have been used to evaluate the acute effects of dietary components. In these experiments, behavior is usually evaluated for several hours after an individual has consumed either the substance being studied or a placebo. One advantage of these studies is that double-blind procedures are relatively simple to implement. The food component and placebo can be packaged so that neither the subjects nor the experimenters can detect which is being presented. Moreover, to control for potential order effects, a crossover procedure can be utilized in which half of the subjects are given the food component on the first day of testing and the placebo on the second, while the remaining subjects are given the placebo on the first day and the food component on the second. Although not frequently done, more than one dose of the dietary variable could also easily be tested.

One obvious drawback of challenge studies is that they do not provide information on the possible cumulative effects of a food component.

CONCLUSION

As shall be seen in the following chapters, both correlational and experimental studies have been employed to assess the behavioral consequences of a large of number of dietary components. Vitamins, minerals, heavy metals, food additives, sugars, and artificial sweeteners have all been studied in an effort to square superstitions with current scientific knowledge and shed light on the real, but often misunderstood, relationships between what we eat and how we behave.

REFERENCES

Anderson, G. H. and N. Hrboticky. 1986. Approaches to assessing the dietary component of the diet-behavior connection. *Nutrition Reviews* 44 (Suppl. 1): 42–50.

Cosman, M. P. 1983. A feast for Aesculapius: Historical diets for asthma and sexual pleasure. *Annual Review of Nutrition* 3:1–33.

Darby, W. J. 1977. *Food: The Gift of Osiris*. New York: Plenum.

Drayton, A. 1970. *The Philosopher in the Kitchen* (trans. of J. A. Brillat-Savarin, *La Physiologie du gout*, first published 1825). New York: Penguin.

Dubick, M. A. 1986. Historical perspective on the use of herbal preparations to promote health. *Journal of Nutrition* 116:1348–1354.

Duffy, W. 1975. *Sugar Blues* New York: Warner Books.

Dwyer, J. T., W. H. Dietz, G. Hass, and R. Suskind. 1979. Risk of nutritional rickets among vegetarian children. *American Journal of Diseases of Children* 133:134–140.

Farb, P. and G. Armelagos. 1980. *Consuming Passions: The Anthropology of Eating*. Boston: Houghton Mifflin.

Feingold, B. 1975. Hyperkinesis and learning disabilities linked to artificial food flavors and colors. *American Journal of Nursing* 75:797–803.

Herbert, V. and S. Barrett. 1986. Twenty-one ways to spot a quack. *Nutrition Forum Newsletter,* September:65–68.

Hirsch, E. 1987. Sweetness and performance. In *Sweetness,* ed. J. Dobbing, pp. 205–223. New York: Springer-Verlag.

Jarvis, W. T. 1983. Food faddism, cultism and quackery. *Annual Review of Nutrition* 3:35–52.

Kanarek, R. B. and N. Orthen-Gambill. 1986. Complex interactions affecting nutrition-behavior research. *Nutrition Reviews* 44 (Suppl. 1):172–175.

Kanarek, R. B. and D. Swinney. 1990. Effects of food snacks on cognitive performance in male college students. *Appetite* 14:15–27.

Kellogg, J. H. 1888. *Plain Facts for Old and Young*. Burlington, IA.: Segner.

Kellogg, J. H. 1919. *The Itinerary of Breakfast*. New York: Funk & Wagnalls.

Kruesi, M. J. P. and J. L. Rapoport. 1986. Diet and human behavior: How much do they affect each other? *Annual Review of Nutrition* 6:113–130.

Messer, E. 1984. Sociocultural aspects of nutrient intake and behavioral responses to nutrition. In *Human Nutrition, Nutrition and Behavior,* vol. 5, ed. J. Galler, pp. 417–471. New York: Plenum.

Olson, R. E. 1979. Vitamin B_{12} deficiency in the breast-fed infant of a strict vegetarian. *Nutrition Review* 37:142–144.

Rumsey, J. M. and J. L. Rapoport. 1983. Assessing behavioral and cognitive effects of diet in pediatric populations. In *Nutrition and the Brain,* vol. 6, ed. R. J. Wurtman and J. J. Wurtman, pp. 101–162. New York: Raven Press.

White, P. L. and T. D. Mondeika. 1988. Food fads and faddism. In *Modern Nutrition in Health and Disease,* ed. M. E. Shils and V. R. Young, pp. 666–671. Philadelphia: Lea & Febiger.

Whorton, J. C. 1982. *Crusaders for Fitness: The History of the American Health Reforms*. Princeton, NJ: Princeton University Press.

Yetiv, J. Z. 1986. *Popular Nutritional Practices: A Scientific Appraisal*. Toledo, OH: Popular Medicine Press.

Zmora, E., R. Gorodischer, and I. Bar-ziv. 1979. Multiple nutritional deficiencies in infants from a strict vegetarian community. *American Journal of Diseases of Children* 133:141–144.

2

Protein-Calorie Malnutrition, The Central Nervous System, and Behavior

Malnutrition is a major health problem throughout the world. Although we usually associate malnutrition with conditions of poverty in under-developed countries, recent reports have clearly demonstrated that modern nations, including the United States, are not immune to this problem. Malnutrition may have an impact on as many as a half-million children in this country. Low birth weight, growth failure, weakened resistance to infection, increased vulnerability to environmental toxins such as lead, and other consequences of nutritional deficiency are not infrequent among low-income pediatric populations in this country (Physicians' Task Force on Hunger in America 1985; Brown 1987).

In this and the following two chapters, the behavioral consequences of protein-calorie malnutrition and deficiencies of essential vitamins and minerals are assessed. Because alterations in behavior are ultimately the result of changes in the functioning of the nervous system, we will begin with a brief description of the normal structure and development of the central nervous system.

STRUCTURE AND DEVELOPMENT OF THE CENTRAL NERVOUS SYSTEM

Structural Components

NEURONS

Neurons (nerve cells) are the fundamental building blocks of the brain. These cells serve as the information processing and transmitting elements of the nervous system. The capacity of neurons to process and transmit information depends on two properties: their abilities to generate and conduct electrical signals, and to manufacture and secrete chemical messengers or neurotransmitters.

Neurons possess the structural elements of most of the other cells in the body, for example, a nucleus, mitochondria, endoplasmic reticulum, and Golgi apparatus. They also have special properties that allow them to function as components of a rapid communication network, such as the capacity to form and maintain intimate structural connections with other specific cells over very long distances. Another significant property of neurons within the adult central nervous system (CNS) is that they do not undergo cell division. If a neuron is fatally damaged, it is gone forever.

It is estimated that the adult human brain contains 10^{11} neurons. No two of these neurons are identical, but most share certain structural features that make it possible to distinguish three regions of the cell: the cell body, the dendrites, and the axon (see Figure 2-1).

The *cell body* or *soma* contains the nucleus of the neuron, as well as much of the biochemical machinery for synthesizing enzymes and other molecules necessary for the life of the cell.

The *dendrites* (from the Greek word "dendron," meaning tree) are fine extensions that branch out to form an elaborate treelike structure around the cell body. Dendrites serve as the main physical surface on which the neuron receives incoming information from other nerve cells. Microscopic examination along the surface of the dendrites reveals outgrowths known as dendritic spines, which give dendrites a rough or corrugated surface (Figure 2-2). It is at these spines that chemical messages are conveyed to the dendrite.

Each dendrite typically receives messages from hundreds of other cells. These messages affect the activity of the neuron, which as a result may or may not transmit information down its single axon to other nerve cells. The

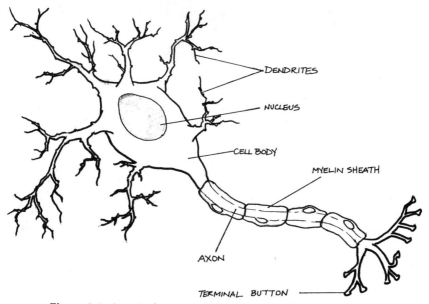

Figure 2-1. A typical neuron within the central nervous system.

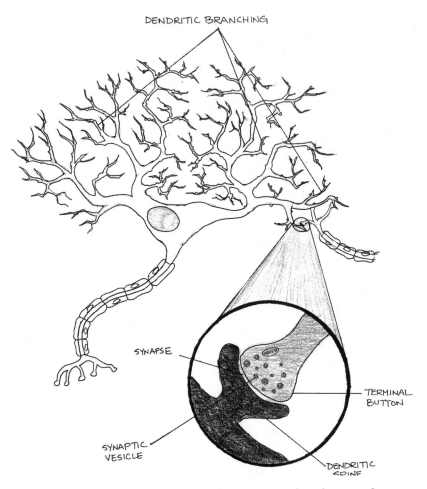

Figure 2-2. Enlargement of dendrites of a neuron within the central nervous system. Note branching of dendrite and dendritic spine.

axon extends from the cell body and provides the pathway over which signals travel from the cell body to other neurons. Most axons are thinner and longer than dendrites and exhibit a different type of branching pattern. Thus, while the branches of the dendrites tend to occur near the cell body, the branches of the axons occur predominantly at the end of the fiber where the axon communicates with other neurons (Figure 2-3).

The point at which information is transferred from one cell to another is called the synapse (from the Greek word "sunaptein," meaning "to join together"). A typical neuron has from 1,000 to 10,000 synapses and receives information from 1,000 other nerve cells. Most synapses are made between the axon of one cell and the dendrite of another; however, axons may also synapse on the cell body or axon of other neurons.

At the synapse, the end of the axon is enlarged to form a *terminal button* containing many small spherical structures, synaptic vesicles, that hold the chemical messenger of the cell, the neurotransmitter (see Figure 2-3). When a nerve impulse reaches the terminal button, some of the vesicles release their contents into the narrow space (synaptic cleft) that separates the terminal button from the dendritic spine of another neuron. The release of neurotransmitters from the synaptic vesicle can either excite or inhibit the receiving cell, and thus helps determine whether this cell will send a message to other cells with which it communicates.

SUPPORTING CELLS

Neurons constitute approximately half of the volume of the brain. The remainder consists of a variety of supporting cells, the most important of which are the *glial cells,* or *glia* (from the Latin word for glue). It has been estimated that there are 10^{12} glial cells within the CNS. The glia occupy essentially all of the space in the nervous system not taken up by the

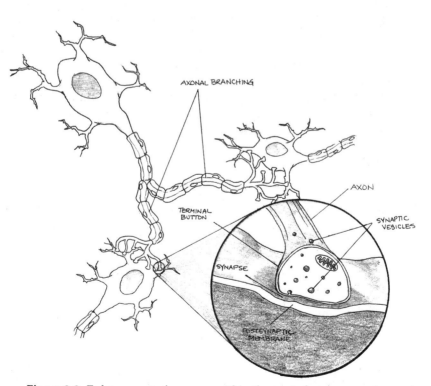

Figure 2-3. Enlargement of an axon within the central nervous system.

neurons. Several different types of glial cells, each with a special role, are found in the brain.

Astrocytes, or *astroglia,* were named on the basis of their starlike shape. The largest of the glial cells, they provide physical and nutritional support to neurons. Some of the extensions of the astrocytes are wrapped around blood vessels, and others are wrapped around the somatic and dendritic portions of the neuron. It has been hypothesized that this arrangement allows the astrocytes to supply neurons with nutrients from the blood. Astrocytes also surround synapses, and thus limit the dispersion of neurotransmitters that are released into the synaptic cleft from the terminal button. In other words, these cells isolate synapses from each other and prevent "cross talk" among neurons that may be performing different functions. Finally, certain types of astrocytes act as phagocytes ("eating cells") and have the task of cleaning up the debris resulting from neuronal death caused by head injury, infection, or stroke.

Oligodendroglia provide support for axons and coat axons in the brain and spinal cord with myelin. Myelin, which is made of lipid (70–80%) and protein (20–30%), insulates axons from one another. Myelin is produced by the oligodendrocytes in the form of a tube surrounding the axon. The tube does not form a continuous sheath, but rather consists of a series of segments, with a small portion of uncoated axon between each segment (node of Ranvier). Myelin isolates axons from each other and conserves the neuron's metabolic energy. In general, myelinated nerve fibers conduct nerve impulses faster than unmyelinated fibers.

A third type of glia, the *microglia,* are extremely small cells that remain dormant until damage occurs in the nervous system. They are then transformed into phagocytes, which move through the brain searching for and cleaning up the debris left by dead neurons.

Development

PRENATAL

A single fertilized egg gives rise to all of the cells in the body. During its second week, the human embryo develops three distinct cell layers which are the beginnings of all the tissues of the body. The nervous system develops from the outer layer, the ectoderm. During the third week of embryonic life, a pear-shaped neural plate arises from the dorsal ectoderm. All of the cells that are destined to be neurons develop from the neural plate. Shortly after formation, the neural plate raises a pair of bilateral ridges that later join together to form the neural tube. This tube, containing approximately 125,000 cells, forms the basis of the nervous system.

If neurulation is defective and the neural tube does not close properly, one of several possible anomalies can result. These include anencephaly, in which the forebrain fails to develop correctly because the anterior portion of the neural tube does not close, and spina bifida, which results from failure of the posterior portion of the neural tube to close.

Once the neural tube is closed, which occurs during the fourth week of gestation, nerve cells begin to proliferate rapidly. At birth, the human brain contains approximately 100 billion neurons. Based on an average 270-day gestation period, this means that new neurons must be produced at the rate of about 250,000 per minute during prenatal development. With few exceptions, neurons in the human nervous system stop forming before or shortly after birth. The period of proliferation varies for different populations of cells. In general, proliferation of larger neurons, which tend to serve long-distance functions within the nervous system, precedes proliferation of smaller cells which are destined primarily for "local circuits" within the brain.

Before they differentiate into their final form, neurons are referred to as neuroblasts. When neuroblasts have finished dividing, they migrate to their ultimate location within the brain. One type of glial cell, the radial glia, which is only present during prenatal development and disappears shortly before birth, plays a prominent role in directing neuronal migration. These cells extend from the inner to outer surfaces of the emerging nervous system and appear to act as guide wires on which the migrating neuroblasts crawl toward their destinations (Rakic 1981). Some later-forming neuroblasts migrate in a different manner. These cells are attracted to the surfaces of neurons and migrate along the axons of earlier formed nerve cells (Rakic 1981).

After a neuroblast has migrated to its final location, it must orient itself properly and become associated with other cells of a similar kind. This process, called aggregation, is important for the development of functional units within the nervous system (e.g., layers of the cortex; thalamic nuclei). Molecules on the neuronal surface, called neural cell adhesion molecules, promote the aggregation of neurons destined to have similar functions (Hoffman and Edelman 1983).

Neuroblasts initially bear no more resemblance to mature nerve cells than to other cells in the body. However, once a neuroblast has arrived at its destination, it begins to acquire the distinctive appearance of neurons characteristic of its particular location. During this process of differentiation, each neuron develops its own specific dendritic pattern, axonal structure, and distinctive chemical transmitter.

Once cells have began to differentiate, they must make appropriate connections with other neurons. Connections between neurons occur at synapses, where one neuron releases a neurotransmitter that affects the activity of the receiving neuron. While the formation of synapses (synaptogenesis) begins during prenatal development, it is not confined to this period. In fact, the formation of most synapses in the human neocortex occurs after birth. A variety of environmental factors, including nutrition, can alter postnatal synaptogenesis.

Many more nerve cells are produced than actually are found in the brain at birth. Extensive cell death is a crucial phase of brain development. Depending on the area of the brain, 15% to 85% of neurons die during fetal development. One possible reason for the survival of some neurons and the death of others is competition for the life-maintaining factors they receive from their proper synaptic targets. Thus, neurons that do not make appropriate synaptic connections are mostly likely to die. Like synaptogenesis, cell death continues after birth. Indeed, it has been suggested that functional or behavioral maturity results not from synaptic formation after birth, but rather from the elimination of excess connections and the increasing efficiency of those that remain (Bloom and Lazerson 1988; Kimble 1988).

POSTNATAL

At birth, the human brain weighs between 300 and 350 grams. It grows rapidly during early development, reaching approximately 80% of its adult weight of 1,250 to 1,500 grams by approximately 4 years of age. Four types of changes are important in postnatal growth of the brain.

First, is the proliferation of glial cells. Glial cells begin to rapidly proliferate at about 30 weeks of gestation. Unlike neurons, however, glial cells continue to develop throughout life. In many mammalian species, including humans, the most intense phase of glial production occurs shortly after birth.

Coupled with the development of glial cells is the development of the myelin sheath around axons. This process, called myelination, greatly alters the rate at which axons conduct messages. In humans, rapid myelination begins shortly after birth and continues into the third and fourth years of life. The first nerve tracts in the human nervous system to become myelinated are in the spinal cord. Myelination then spreads into the hindbrain, midbrain, and finally the forebrain. Within the cerebral cortex, sensory neurons become myelinated before motor neurons, and correspondingly, sensory functions mature before motor functions.

As previously mentioned, synaptogenesis continues after birth. This process represents the largest change in brain cells between birth and maturity.

Finally, recent work has indicated that some neurons may develop postnatally. There are a few areas around the brain ventricles in which proliferation of nerve cells remains evident after birth. Small neurons derived from these areas may be added to portions of the brain, including the hippocampus and the olfactory bulbs, throughout the first several years of life (Spreen et al. 1984; Rosenzweig and Leiman 1989).

DEFINITION AND PREVALENCE OF PROTEIN-CALORIE MALNUTRITION

Protein-calorie malnutrition (PCM) results from an inadequate supply of protein, calories, or a combination of the two. Although the problem of malnutrition has long been recognized, it has yet to be solved. Malnutrition represents one of the world's major health problems. It is estimated that from 0.5 to 20.0% of the world's population suffers from severe PCM, and up to 50% is afflicted with milder forms of the disease. PCM occurs most frequently and has its most devastating consequences in early childhood.

Severe malnutrition in children has been traditionally classified as either *marasmus* or *kwashiorkor* (Table 2-1). Marasmus results from extremely low intake of both protein and calories. In comparison, victims of kwashiorkor usually consume sufficient calories, but protein intake is insufficient to meet the body's needs. Marasmus and kwashiorkor are thought to represent the extremes of a continuum describing severe PCM. The majority of severely malnourished children lie at some point between these two extremes, exhibiting symptoms of both conditions or alternately displaying symptoms of one, then the other. This combined or alternating condition has been called *marasmic kwashiorkor*. It is important to realize that for every child hospitalized with severe PCM, there are 99 children with milder forms of the disease (Pollitt and Thomson 1977; Gurney 1979; Reddy 1981).

The primary cause of PCM is a lack of sufficient nutrients. The problem of malnutrition, however, cannot be viewed in isolation from other envi-

TABLE 2-1. Comparison of Some Features of Marasmus and Kwashiorkor

Feature	Marasmus	Kwashiorkor
Age of onset	Below 1 year of age	2–3 years of age
Growth failure	Severe	Present, but less severe than in marasmus
Muscle wasting	Always	Always
Subcutaneous fat	Absent	Present
Edema	Absent	Always
Skin changes	Rare	Frequent
Hair changes	Frequent	Very frequent
Liver enlargement	Rare	Frequent
Appetite	Ravenous	Anorectic
Diarrhea	Frequent	Frequent
Anemia	Frequent	Always
Serum proteins	Normal	Low
Pancreatic and intestinal hormones	Normal	Low
Psychological profile	Irritable, apathetic	Irritable; apathetic; loss of interest in environment; whimpering cry

ronmental conditions. Children suffering from PCM most often come from the lowest socioeconomic strata of their societies, and therefore overcrowded living conditions, family instability, a high probability of infectious disease, inadequate health facilities, and limited educational opportunities must also be considered when assessing the consequences of PCM.

Marasmus

Marasmus, which is due to insufficient energy intake, typically accompanies early weaning and thus is most often observed in children under one year of age. Frequently, the formula that is substituted for breast milk is overdiluted by economically disadvantaged parents trying to make the most of limited resources, and contaminated by dirty water or unclean preparation, leading to bacterial infection. The child then suffers repeated gastrointestinal infections, during which time the mother may withhold food in an attempt to cure him or her. Little or no food, coupled with recurrent infections, eventually lead to marasmus.

One of the primary clinical features of marasmus is marked growth failure; the child is often less than 60% of normal weight for age, and body length is substantially reduced. The marasmic child is reduced to "skin and bones" because of an almost total absence of adipose tissue (Figure 2-4). The skin is usually dry and baggy, and hangs in wrinkles around the buttocks and thighs. The face of the child with marasmus has been called "monkeylike" because of sunken cheeks and the loss of subcutaneous fat. The hair is sparse, thin, and dry; has lost its normal sheen; and can easily be pulled out. Repeated episodes of gastroenteritis can result in diarrhea, dehydration, and anemia. Heart rate, blood pressure, and body temperature may be low.

Behaviorally, the marasmic child is commonly irritable, but may also appear weak and apathetic. The child may also be ravenously hungry, but can seldom tolerate large amounts of food and vomits easily (Pollitt and Thomson 1977; Gurney 1979; Galler 1984; Torún and Viteri 1988).

Kwashiorkor

The term kwashiorkor, which comes from the Ga language and means "the sickness the older child gets when the next baby is born," was first used in the medical literature in 1935 by Dr. Cicely Williams, who was working with the Ga tribe in Ghana. Williams described the progressive nature of kwashiorkor, which typically develops between the ages of 1 and 3 years, when the child is weaned from the breast following the birth of the next sibling and fed the high-carbohydrate, low-protein diet of the family. Although this diet may provide adequate protein for an adult, it is insufficient to meet the needs of a rapidly growing child. As the child begins to

Figure 2-4. Marasmic child displaying growth failure, muscle wasting, and loss of subcutaneous fat. (Dr. Stanley Gershoff, private collection.)

explore his or her environment, there is also an increased opportunity for bacterial and viral infections which can exacerbate the consequences of a low-protein diet (Torún and Viteri 1988).

The consequences of kwashiorkor are quite different from those of marasmus. The classic symptom of kwashiorkor is edema (an excess of extracellular water), which usually begins in the extremities and then progresses to the legs and trunk. It is edema of the trunk that gives the child with kwashiorkor its characteristic swollen belly. Like the child with marasmus, a child with kwashiorkor experiences growth failure and muscle wasting. In contrast to the marasmic child, however, the child with kwashiorkor may retain some subcutaneous fat.

Distinctive changes in the skin and hair are also common in kwashiorkor. The skin may become depigmented and may become dry and crack. "Flaky paint" dermatosis, in which dry flakes of skin may peel, leaving hypopigmented skin beneath, is frequently observed on the legs and arms. Additionally, raw, moist ulcerated areas of skin at flexures, such as on the groin and on the buttocks, is not uncommon. The hair of a child with kwashiorkor is typically dry, thin, depigmented, and easily separated from the scalp.

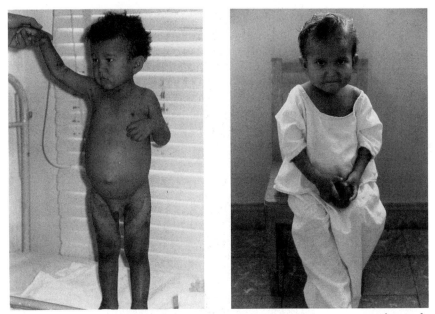

Figure 2-5. A 4-year-old child with kwashiorkor. (a) Note the presence of growth failure; edema of the trunk; sparse, thin hair; and dermatosis. (b) The same child after nutritional rehabilitation has been initiated. Note that the child is smiling, one of the first characteristics of recovery from kwashiorkor. (Dr. Stanley Gershoff, private collection.)

Enlargement and fatty infiltration of the liver is estimated to occur in over 30% of children with kwashiorkor. Diarrhea and anemia, decreases in pancreatic and intestinal hormones, and reductions in serum protein levels are also observed in a substantial proportion of children with the disease.

The behavioral characteristics of kwashiorkor are striking and include listless apathy, irritability, and a lack of interest in the environment. The child cries easily and frequently displays an expression of misery and sadness (Figure 2-5). Anorexia, sometimes necessitating intragastric tube feeding, is also common (Winick 1976; Gurney 1979; Galler 1984; Torún and Viteri 1988).

CONSEQUENCES OF MALNUTRITION ON BRAIN DEVELOPMENT

As shall be seen in this and subsequent chapters of this book, nutrition plays an important role in normal brain development. Nutritional factors can affect brain development by modifying

Neuronal number

Neuronal size

Position of neurons in the central nervous system

Development of dendrites and axons

Development of synaptic connections

Production of neurotransmitters

Development of glial cells

Myelination of axons.

The potentially detrimental effects of early protein-calorie malnutrition on brain development have been demonstrated in neuroanatomical and neurochemical studies in experimental animals. Results of these studies have indicated that the brain is most vulnerable to malnutrition during certain critical periods of rapid growth, which vary for different animals. In humans, the period of fastest brain growth, and thus maximum vulnerability to malnutrition, occurs in late pregnancy and the first several months of postnatal life (Dobbing 1976).

Prenatal and Early Postnatal Period

During the last 25 years, increasing attention has been paid to the developmental effects of undernutrition in utero. It was formerly believed that because of its "protected" relationship with the mother, the fetus was spared the adverse consequences of maternal malnutrition. The fetus, does, in fact, have two buffers against inadequate nutrition: direct nutrition from the mother's intake of food and placental transfer of nutrients stored by the mother. If maternal malnutrition is severe, however, these two buffers are insufficient to maintain normal fetal development.

Severe malnutrition early in development typically results in a failure to maintain embryonic implantation, or spontaneous abortion. Moderate malnutrition throughout pregnancy or more severe deficiencies later in gestation generally permit continued fetal development, but lead to changes in the growth of both the placenta and fetus. In experimental animals, low maternal energy or protein malnutrition have been associated with low birth weight, decreases in brain weight, and reductions in numbers of both neurons and glial cells, as well as insufficient myelination and impairments in dendritic development. Nutritional rehabilitation later in life does little to reverse these alterations in brain development (Zamenhof, Van Marthens, and Margolis 1968; Winick 1976; Nowak and Munro 1977; Shoemaker and Bloom 1977; Resnick et al. 1982; Spreen et al. 1984).

In human infants, a marked reduction in cranial circumference provides the first indication that malnutrition, particularly during gestation and the first two years of life, has resulted in permanent brain damage. Because of the younger age at which marasmus typically develops, the marasmic child is more likely to have a reduced cranial circumference than the child with kwashiorkor (Winick 1976).

Studies of the consequences of early malnutrition on the cellular growth of the human brain have been limited. Winick and Rosso (1969) observed significant reductions in the brain weight, total protein, and total DNA and RNA content in infants who died of marasmus during the first year of life. Children with particularly low birth weights, indicative of prenatal malnutrition, had a lower brain DNA content than malnourished infants with higher birth weights. The reduction of DNA represents decreases in the number of both neurons and glia. Additionally, as in experimental animals, early malnutrition in humans is associated with impaired myelination of the CNS (Winick 1976).

Late Postnatal Period

Experimental evidence concerning the role of malnutrition on postnatal brain development has generally been consistent with the hypothesis that development is most impaired in those cell types and regions that are demonstrating maximal growth at the time of the nutritional deficiency. Thus, postnatal malnutrition is generally not associated with a reduction in the number of neurons, but rather the number of glial cells may be permanently decreased. The primary effect of postnatal malnutrition is a reduction in the size of both neurons and glial cells. Additionally, synaptogenesis and myelination of axons may be inhibited. Some degree of recovery from the effects of postnatal malnutrition docs occur if an adequate diet is fed later in life (Nowak and Munro 1977; Spreen et al. 1984).

Kwashiorkor, because it occurs later in life, has fewer permanent effects on brain development than marasmus. For example, kwashiorkor does not lead to a marked reduction in neuronal number. Children who died of kwashiorkor during their second year of life had only minor deficits in total brain DNA levels. The brain weight : DNA ratio was decreased, however, indicating a reduction in brain cell size (Winick 1976).

BEHAVIORAL CONSEQUENCES OF MALNUTRITION

Effects in Adults

Relatively little is known about the behavioral effects of malnutrition in adults. Reports of individuals surviving conditions of extreme privation in concentration camps and during periods of severe famine suggest that undernutrition is associated with apathy, lethargy, social isolation, and impairments in memory. It is impossible, however, to determine if these behavioral changes are directly related to deficits in energy intake, or to other devastating aspects of these environments (Winick 1979; Widdowson 1985).

The most extensive information on the behavioral effects of malnutrition in adults comes from the work conducted by Keys and colleagues at the University of Minnesota during World War II (Keys et al. 1950). This study, which examined both the physiological and psychological effects of moderate malnutrition in healthy young men, was undertaken to provide a basis for nutritional rehabilitation programs in Europe after the war. The 32 subjects, who were conscientious objectors, were told the purpose of the study and initially were willing volunteers. They were housed at the university and permitted to participate in classes and other activities. Following a baseline period, during which time daily caloric intake averaged 3,500 kcals, daily energy intake was reduced by more than half to 1,570 kcals for 6 months. The psychological consequences of undernutrition were assessed qualitatively by personal interviews, and quantitatively using questionnaires and psychological inventories.

At the beginning of the study, subjects displayed a keen interest in the training program. With the passage of time and the loss of body weight, however, their interest waned. One of the first noticeable changes in the men was a decline in social initiative. They became reluctant to plan activities, make decisions, or participate in group activities. Their earlier interest in having a voice in making the policies and rules for the conduct of the nonscientific aspects of the study dwindled. They spent more and more time alone and reported that it was "too much trouble" or "too tiring" to have to contend with other people. Subjects who had begun taking classes at the university dropped out. Results of psychological inventories revealed decreases in activity, sex drive, mental alertness, self-discipline, and motivation, and increases in moodiness, irritability, and apathy. Although responsiveness to the social environment and motivation were reduced, the subjects' capacity for learning, as measured by an extensive battery of intelligence tests, was not impaired.

One of the most interesting changes in behavior was the subjects' constriction of cognitive interests. As intellectual, cultural, and political issues lost their appeal, interest in food increased. It became the principal subject of conversations, reading, and daydreams for almost all of the subjects. Cookbooks, menus, and information bulletins on food production became a primary interest of many of the men. Moreover, mealtimes became extended with the men slowly consuming and adding spices and condiments to their limited rations (Keys et al. 1950).

Nutritional rehabilitation led to a reversal of the majority of behavioral changes that were observed in the study. Anecdotal reports, however, suggest that the heightened interest in food experienced by many of the subjects continued even after complete rehabilitation.

The results of this study demonstrate that undernutrition can profoundly alter behavior in adults. These alterations were most notable in social interactions. Intellectual abilities, however, were not affected by malnutrition in these circumstances.

Effects in Children

As previously discussed, both marasmus and kwashiorkor are associated with distinctive alterations in behavior. Behavioral symptoms of marasmus include irritability and apathy, and those of kwashiorkor include anorexia, apathy, withdrawal, and irritability often accompanied by a whimpering, monotonous cry. Of all of the behavioral symptoms associated with marasmus and kwashiorkor, reduced activity and lethargy are the most commonly observed. It has been hypothesized that this reduction in activity may functionally isolate malnourished children from their environment, and thus delay behavioral development (Galler 1984).

A number of researchers have experimentally investigated the effects of current malnutrition on behavioral development. Using several different quantitative scales of behavioral development (e.g., the Bayley Scale, Griffiths Scale, and Gesell Developmental Schedule), these researchers have documented that regardless of the type of malnutrition, the development of malnourished children is significantly delayed. In general, language and verbal development are most affected by malnutrition (e.g., Cravioto and Robles 1965; Cravioto and DeLicardie 1972; Guthrie, Masangkay, and Guthrie 1976; Cravioto 1979).

One problem with this research is that children with severe malnutrition were usually studied during hospitalization, and their behavior was compared to nonhospitalized children, making it difficult to separate the effects of malnutrition from those of hospitalization. To overcome this difficulty, Grantham-McGregor and colleagues (1978) compared behavioral development in hospitalized malnourished children with that of children hospitalized for other reasons. They found that although development was delayed in both groups of children, developmental delays were more severe in malnourished children than in children with other illnesses.

Noncognitive aspects of behavior are also altered in malnourished children. Infants with a history of malnutrition have low activity levels, difficulty tolerating frustration, reduced social responsiveness, and a lack of initiative and independence. Low birthweight infants, who presumably also suffered from prenatal malnutrition, display little vigor of movement, move more slowly into higher states of arousal, and have difficulty orienting themselves toward visual stimuli, as compared with normal weight infants (Brazelton et al. 1977; Barrett 1984).

Current malnutrition in children has also been associated with abnormalities in cerebral functioning as measured by electroencephalograms

(EEGs) and psychophysiological tests of arousal. For example, Lester and colleagues (1975) used heart rate deceleration to novel stimuli to measure arousal processes in malnourished male infants. Heart rate deceleration occurs when a novel stimulus is presented. When the infant becomes accustomed to the stimulus, habituation occurs and cardiac deceleration is reduced. Heart rate deceleration thus provides a measure of responsiveness to the environment. In the studies of Lester and colleagues, well-nourished infants evidenced heart rate deceleration in response to a novel auditory stimulus, and subsequent habituation of the response to repeated stimuli. In contrast, malnourished infants displayed no alterations in heart rate when a novel auditory stimulus was presented. These data suggest that severe malnutrition leads to a diminished responsiveness to environmental signals and therefore to a reduction in the organism's capacity for information processing. These deficits in information processing may persist even after nutritional rehabilitation has occurred (Pollitt and Thomson 1977; Cravioto 1979; Galler 1984).

Finally, malnutrition can alter mother–infant interactions. Malnourished infants spend significantly more time nursing and have more physical contact with their mothers than well-nourished infants. These changes may interfere with behavioral development by making the child more dependent on the mother and reinforcing the child's isolation from the environment (Galler et al. 1984).

Taken together, the effects of concurrent malnutrition can be seen as limiting the child's interaction with its physical and social environment. These limitations may have profound effects on later intellectual and behavioral functioning.

LONG-TERM EFFECTS OF EARLY MALNUTRITION

In children with marasmus and kwashiorkor, many of the effects of malnutrition can be reversed by an adequate diet and proper medical care. Certain metabolic consequences of malnutrition rapidly recover, whereas other consequences, such as physical growth and behavior, may only slowly improve over extended periods, and may never reach normal levels (Galler 1984).

Investigators in many different countries have attempted to assess the effects of early malnutrition on subsequent behavior. The majority of these studies have focused on measuring intellectual performance, because testing procedures are readily available and the demonstration of permanent intellectual deficits would have obvious social impact.

Before reviewing research on early malnutrition and later behavior, it is important to note the difficulties of directly isolating early malnutrition as the cause of alterations in mental functioning. Malnourished children invariably come from lower socioeconomic strata and more deprived environments than even the most carefully matched control groups. Cravioto and colleagues (Cravioto and DeLicardie 1976; Cravioto 1979) also have reported than even when socioeconomic status is equated, there are distinct differences between the home environment of malnourished and well-nourished children. These researchers observed that there was less stimulation in the homes of children who became malnourished than in homes of children who did not develop malnutrition. The mothers of malnourished children were less interested in their children's performance, sensitive to their children's needs, verbally communicative, and emotionally involved than mothers of well-nourished children. Subsequent studies have also indicated that children with histories of severe malnutrition often come from homes with decreased levels of intellectual stimulation. These children may be read to less (i.e., when literate), take fewer excursions away from home, and generally have less interaction with adults than better nourished children (Galler et al. 1984).

Several different types of studies have been used to investigate the role of early malnutrition on behavior. In *retrospective studies,* prior nutritional deprivation is assumed from present anthropomorphic data. In some studies, behavior of children with short height for weight and/or age has been compared to that of children with normal height. Results of these studies generally suggest that early malnutrition is associated with later deficits in intellectual performance. There are, however, significant limitations with this type of research that make it difficult to substantiate a direct relationship between early malnutrition and later behavior. The primary limitation of retrospective studies is that the early history of these children, including birth weight, age at which the child became malnourished, degree and duration of malnutrition, medical data, and parent–child interactions, is usually not available. Other factors that could influence development, such as the mother's age at birth, number of siblings, and genetics, also often are not taken into account. Thus, it is difficult to draw conclusions about the direct effects of malnutrition on behavior.

Intervention studies measure the effects of nutritional supplements, with or without environmental enrichment programs, on the behavior of malnourished children. Typically, one group of mothers and children receive a nutritional supplement, and a second group of mothers and children, matched as closely as possible for age, sex, socioeconomic background, maternal education, and other relevant factors, are not given the supplement. One advantage of such studies is that with careful matching of groups, the supplemented and nonsupplemented groups are less likely to be different from each other in ways that could affect later behavioral and mental development. Another benefit is that these studies provide potential models for the amelioration of deficits that might follow from nutritional deprivation. Thus, intervention studies can serve the dual function of increasing our understanding about the role of malnutrition in behavioral development, and of providing models for effective intervention programs to prevent malnutrition and its consequences (Rush 1984).

The results of intervention studies have not been consistent. Several factors may account for this. First, the nutritional value of supplements has varied substantially across studies. Some have used high-protein supplements, and others low-protein or protein-free supplements. Second, timing of nutritional supplementation has differed. In some studies, nutritional supplementation has taken place during both the prenatal and postnatal periods, while in others, supplementation has been more limited. Third, the type of behavioral measures used and the age at which behavior was measured have not been consistent.

In *longitudinal studies,* the behavior of children with an early incidence of either marasmus or kwashiorkor is compared at some later point in time to that of children living under similar circumstances but not subjected to nutritional deprivation. Compared to retrospective studies, longitudinal studies have several potential advantages: detailed information about the episode of malnutrition may be available, it is possible to collect data about the families' background both when malnutrition occurred and at the time of behavioral testing, and the behavioral consequences of malnutrition can be measured at several different times. The disadvantages of longitudinal studies are that they can be very costly in time and money, and as in retrospective studies, subtle differences in the home environments of malnourished and well-nourished children may confound results.

With the caveat that significant problems exist in strategies for exploring the consequences of early malnutrition on later behavior, most studies clearly suggest that previously malnourished children have impairments in a variety of behavioral tasks. Most notable among these deficits are problems of attention and short-term memory. Additionally, deficits in IQ and school performance have frequently been observed (Richardson et al. 1972; Pollitt and Thomson 1977; Cravioto 1979; Galler et al. 1983a, 1983b). For example, Cravioto and colleagues found that in comparison to their nonmalnourished siblings, twice as many children who experienced severe malnourishment before 3 years of age and with 2 years or more of recovery had IQs below 70 (Cravioto, DeLicardie, and Birch 1966; Cravioto and DeLicardie 1972; Cravioto 1979). These researchers additionally reported that early episodes of malnutrition were associated with deficits in intersensory integration, or the ability to correlate information entering the brain from different sensory modalities, which has been associated with reading and writing disabilities.

Results of intervention studies have indicated that nutritional supplements can increase activity and attention span. What is perhaps provocative about many of these studies however, is that nutritional supplementation has little effect on behavior if it is not combined with cognitive stimulation. This finding suggests that behavioral deficits associated with malnutrition are not solely the result of protein or energy deprivation, but rather are the consequence of a combination of nutritional, social, intellectual, and emotional deprivation (Rush 1984).

Over the past two decades, one of the best longitudinal studies of the behavioral consequences of early malnutrition has been conducted in Barbados by Galler and colleagues (Galler et al. 1983a, 1983b, 1983c; Galler 1984; Galler and Ramsey 1985). In this study, the behavior of 129 children hospitalized with marasmus during the first year of life has been compared with 129 classmates of similar social and economic backgrounds with no histories of malnutrition. The several advantages of this study over previous work are:

- The delivery and documentation of health care in Barbados are good, with records of obstetric care readily available; education is widespread, and comprehensive school records are available; and the population is relatively stable, with little immigration or emigration, and largely homogeneous with respect to ethnicity and socioeconomic level.

- Extensive information on the home environment of each child was collected; a large sample of both boys and girls was studied; a variety of behavioral measures were examined including IQ scores, academic performance, classroom behavior, and attention; and behavior was studied at several different points in time.

As in previous studies, Galler and co-workers found that despite careful matching of malnourished children with controls, differences in the home environments of the two groups existed at the time of behavioral testing. Children with histories of malnutrition lived in homes with fewer modern conveniences and fewer rooms than the control children. Fathers of the malnourished children held less skilled jobs, and the mothers of these children had less education, than the control children's mothers. Mothers of previously malnourished children also socialized less and were more depressed relative to the mothers of controls. Although these aspects of the home environment were not measured prior to or at the time of the episode of severe malnutrition, it can be presumed that these conditions were present (Galler 1984; Galler and Ramsey 1985).

Taking the effects of the home environment into account using multivariate statistical procedures, Galler and colleagues found that a history of malnutrition still had a strong association with behavioral problems. For example, IQ scores measured between the ages of 5 and 11 years were consistently lower in previously malnourished children than in controls. Nearly 50% of the previously malnourished children had IQ scores of 90 or lower, but only 17% of the control children scored at or below 90. As might be expected on the basis of IQ scores, children with a history of malnutrition had significantly lower grades in school than nonmalnourished classmates.

Previously malnourished children also exhibited impairments in a number of classroom behaviors. These children were more likely to display a reduced attention span, poor memory, distractibility, lack of cooperativeness, restlessness, and emotional instability than controls. Approximately 60% of the children with histories of malnutrition demonstrated symptoms of attention-deficit disorder as compared to 15% of controls.

Follow-up studies of the same children when they reached the ages of 9 and 15 years have revealed that intellectual performance and fine motor skills of previously malnourished children continued to be impaired during early adolescence. Children who experienced marasmus during the first year of life had significantly lower IQ scores than nonmalnourished children. Approximately 50% of the previously malnourished children had IQ scores of 70 or less contrasted with under 15% of the control group. IQ scores measured between the ages of 9 and 15 years were significantly correlated with scores measured four years earlier, clearly suggesting that the deficits associated with early malnutrition were not alleviated in adolescence (Galler, Ramsey, and Solimano 1985; Galler, Ramsey, and Forde 1986).

Taken together, the results of studies examining the long-term behavioral effects of early malnutrition suggest that malnutrition can have detrimental consequences on later psychomotor development, intellectual abilities, and classroom performance. However, it is important to remember that environmental and social factors, such as the presence of modern conveniences in the home and parents' interest and support of their children occurring concurrently with the episode of malnutrition, can also play a role in determining later behavior. Surveys prior to onset and at the time of malnutrition are needed to clarify the interaction between malnutrition and social factors on subsequent behavior.

CONSEQUENCES OF SHORT-TERM NUTRITIONAL DEFICITS

The vast majority of studies on the consequences of malnutrition have concentrated on the effects of severe episodes of marasmus or kwashiorkor on current or subsequent psychomotor performance, intellectual capabilities, or academic behavior. However, there are several studies that suggest even short-term nutritional deprivation, such as skipping breakfast, can have detrimental effects on behavior. For example, Pollitt and associates clearly demonstrated that skipping breakfast had a deleterious effect on children's late morning problem-solving performance, and that this effect could be related to their metabolic status. Children who skipped breakfast made more errors on a matching test and concomitantly had lower glucose and insulin levels than children who had consumed breakfast (Pollitt, Leibel, and Greenfield 1981; Pollitt et al. 1982–1983). Similar results were obtained by Conners and Blouin (1982) who reported that children who did not consume breakfast made significantly more errors in arithmetic tasks than those who had eaten breakfast. Moreover, the difference in cognitive performance became more pronounced as the morning progressed.

In a recent series of studies, Sampson and colleagues examined the effect of a school breakfast program on school performance (Meyers et al. 1989; Sampson 1989). The changes in scores on a standardized achievement test and in attendance rates before and after the implementation of the school breakfast program for children participating in the program were compared with those of children who also qualified but did not participate in the program. Those who participated in the program demonstrated significantly greater improvements in achievement test scores and a significant decline in tardiness and absence rates when compared with children who did not participate.

These results indicate that even short-term nutritional deficits can have significant consequences on academic performance, as well as important implications for policies aimed at reducing educational disparities between poor and nonpoor children. Adequate nutrition for the entire population is necessary to maximize intellectual potential.

CONCLUSION

It is clear that malnutrition does not occur in a vacuum, but rather is a single part of a complex social structure that includes poverty, disease, and the lack of appropriate support systems. It can be concluded, with this complex structure in mind, that malnutrition has adverse behavioral consequences. In adults, malnutrition can lead to alterations in daily functioning including decreases in motivation, mental alertness, and social interactions and increases in moodiness and irritability. Malnutrition also can profoundly affect brain growth and functioning in the developing child. Children who have suffered from an early episode of marasmus or kwashiorkor may be permanently marked by a reduction in brain weight, impairments in myelination, and decreased synaptogenesis. These alterations in the central nervous system may later translate into behavior problems including decreased intellectual abilities, reduced attention span, poor memory, and emotional instability.

A nation's economic and social development relies heavily on the trained brain power of its citizens. If a substantial proportion of a nation's population endures the consequences of malnutrition, the potential for progress of that nation can be severely limited. Thus, it becomes apparent that reversing the conditions that lead to malnutrition should be one of the primary objectives for the 1990s.

REFERENCES

Barrett, D. E. 1984. Malnutrition and child behavior: Conceptualization, assessment and an empirical study of social-emotional functioning. In *Malnutrition and Behavior: Critical Assessment of Key Issues,* ed. J. Brozek and B. Schurch, pp. 280–306. Lausanne, Switzerland: Nestlé Foundation.

Bloom, R. E. and A. Lazerson. 1988. *Brain, Mind, and Behavior.* New York: W. H. Freeman.

Brazelton, T. B., E. Tronick, A. Lechtig, R. E. Lasky, and R. E. Klein. 1977. The behavior of nutritionally deprived Guatemalan infants. *Developmental Medical Child Neurology* 19:364–372.

Brown, J. L. 1987. Hunger in the United States. *Scientific American,* pp. 37–41.

Conners, C. K. and A. G. Blouin. 1982. Nutritional effects on behavior of children. In *Research Strategies for Assessing the Behavioral Effects of Foods and Nutrients,* proceedings of a conference held at Massachusetts Institute of Technology, November 9, 1982, pp. 177–193.

Cravioto, J. 1979. Malnutrition, environment, and child development. In *Malnutrition, Behavior and Development,* ed. D. A. Levitsky, pp. 28–38. Ithaca, NY: Cornell University Press.

Cravioto, J. and E. R. DeLicardie. 1972. Environmental correlates of severe clinical malnutrition and language development in survivors of kwashiorkor or marasmus. In *Nutrition, the Nervous System and Behavior,* pp. 73–94. PAHO Publication.

Cravioto, J. and E. R. DeLicardie. 1976. Microenvironmental factors in severe protein-energy malnutrition. In *Nutrition and Agricultural Development: Significance and Potential for the Tropics,* ed. N. S. Scrimshaw and M. Behar, pp. 25–35. New York: Plenum.

Cravioto, J., E. R. DeLicardie, and H. G. Birch. 1966. Nutrition, growth and neurointegrative development: An experimental and ecological study. *Pediatrics* 38:319–372.

Cravioto, J. and B. Robles. 1965. Evolution of adaptive and motor behavior during rehabilitation from kwashiorkor. *American Journal of Orthopsychiatry* 35:449–464.

Dobbing, J. 1976. Vulnerable periods in brain growth and somatic growth. In *The Biology of Human Fetal Growth,* ed. D. F. Roberts and A. M. Thompson, pp. 137–147. London: Taylor and Francis.

Galler, J. R. 1984. Behavioral consequences of malnutrition in early life. In *Nutrition and Behavior,* ed. J. R. Galler, pp. 63–117. New York: Plenum.

Galler, J. R. and F. Ramsey. 1985. The influence of early malnutrition on subsequent behavioral development: The role of the microenvironment of the household. *Nutrition and Behavior* 2:161–173.

Galler, J. R., F. Ramsey, and V. Forde. 1986. A follow-up study of the influence of early malnutrition on subsequent development: Intellectual performance during adolescence. *Nutrition and Behavior* 3:211–222.

Galler, J. R., F. Ramsey, and G. Solimano. 1985. A follow-up study of the influence of early malnutrition on subsequent development: Fine motor skills in adolescence. *Pediatric Research* 19:524–527.

Galler, J. R., F. Ramsey, G. Solimano, W. E. Lowell, and E. Mason. 1983a. The influence of early malnutrition on subsequent behavioral development: Degree of impairment in intellectual performance. *Journal of Child Psychiatry* 22:8–15.

Galler, J. R., F. Ramsey, G. Solimano, and W. E. Lowell. 1983b. The influences of early malnutrition on subsequent behavioral development: Classroom behavior. *Journal of Child Psychiatry* 22:16–22.

Galler, J. R., F. Ramsey, G. Solimano, and K. Propert. 1983c. Sex differences in the growth of Barbadian school children with early malnutrition. *Nutrition Reports International* 27:503–517.

Galler, J. R., H. N. Ricciuti, M. A. Crawford, and L. T. Kucharski. 1984. The role of the mother–infant interaction in nutritional disorders. In *Nutrition and Behavior,* ed. J. R. Galler, pp. 269–304. New York: Plenum.

Grantham-McGregor, S. M., M. E. Stewart, and P. Desaix. 1978. A new look at the assessment of mental development in young children recovering from severe malnutrition. *Developmental Medical Child Neurology* 20:773–778.

Gurney, J. M. 1979. The young child: Protein-energy malnutrition. In *Nutrition and Growth,* ed. D. B. Jelliffe and E. F. P. Jelliffe, pp. 185–216. New York: Plenum.

Guthrie, G. M., A. Masangkay, and H. A. Guthrie. 1976. Behavior, malnutrition and mental development. *Crosscultural Psychology* 7:169–180.

Hoffman, S. and G. M. Edelman. 1983. Kinetics of homophilic binding by embryonic and adult forms of the neural cell. *Proceedings of the National Academy of Sciences* 80:5762–5766.

Keys, A., J. Brozek, A. Henschel, O. Mickelsen, and H. L. Taylor. 1950. *The Biology of Human Starvation,* vols. 1 and 2. Minneapolis: University of Minnesota Press.

Kimble, D. P. 1988. *Biological Psychology,* New York: Holt, Rinehart and Winston.

Lester, B. M. 1975. Cardiac habituation of the orienting response to an auditory signal in infants of varying nutritional status. *Developmental Psychology* 11:432–442.

Lester, B. M., R. E. Klein, and S. J. Martinez. 1975. The use of habituation in the study of the effects of infantile malnutrition. *Developmental Psychobiology* 8:541–546.

Meyers, A. F., A. E. Sampson, M. Weitzman, B. L. Rogers, and H. Kayne. 1989. School breakfast program and school performance. *American Journal of Diseases of Children* 143:1234–1239.

Nowak, T. S. and H. N. Munro. 1977. Effects of protein-calorie malnutrition on biochemical aspects of brain development. In *Nutrition and the Brain,* vol. 2, ed. R. J. Wurtman and J. J. Wurtman, pp. 194–260. New York: Raven Press.

Physicians' Task Force on Hunger in America. 1985. *Hunger in America, The Growing Epidemic.* Boston: Harvard University School of Public Health.

Pollitt, E. and C. Thomson. 1977. Protein-calorie malnutrition and behavior: A view from psychology. In *Nutrition and the Brain,* vol. 2, ed. R. J. Wurtman and J. J. Wurtman, pp. 261–306. New York: Raven Press.

Pollitt, E., R. L. Liebel, and D. Greenfield. 1981. Brief fasting, stress, and cognition in children. *American Journal of Clinical Nutrition* 34:1526–1533.

Pollitt, E., N. L. Lewis, C. Garza, and R. J. Shulman. 1982–1983. Fasting and cognitive function. *Journal of Psychiatric Research* 17:169–174.

Rakic, P. 1981. Developmental events leading to laminar and areal organization of the neocortex. In *The Organization of the Cerebral Cortex,* ed. F. O. Schmidt, pp. 7–28. Cambridge, MA: MIT Press.

Reddy, V. 1981. Protein-energy malnutrition: An overview. In *Nutrition in Health and Disease and International Development,* ed. A. E. Harper and G. K. Davis, pp. 227–235. New York: Alan R. Liss.

Resnick, O., P. J. Morgane, R. Hasson, and M. Miller. 1982. Overt and hidden forms of chronic malnutrition in the rat and their relevance to man. *Neuroscience and Biobehavioral Reviews* 6:55–75.

Richardson, S. A., H. G. Birch, E. Grabie, and K. Yoder. 1972. The behavior of children in school who were severely malnourished in the first two years of life. *Journal of Health and Social Behavior* 13:276–284.

Rosenzweig, M. R. and A. L. Leiman. 1989. *Physiological Psychology,* New York: Random House.

Rush, D. 1984. The behavioral consequences of protein-energy deprivation and supplementation in early life: An epidemiological perspective. In *Nutrition and Behavior,* ed. J. R. Galler, pp. 119–157. New York: Plenum.

Sampson, A. E. 1989. The Lawrence Breakfast Studies. Doctoral dissertation, Tufts University.

Shoemaker, W. J. and F. E. Bloom. 1977. Effect of undernutrition on brain morphology. In *Nutrition and the Brain,* vol. 2, ed. R. J. Wurtman and J. J. Wurtman, pp. 147–192. New York: Raven Press.

Spreen, O., D. Tupper, A. Risser, H. Tuokko, and D. Edgell. 1984. *Human Developmental Neuropsychology.* New York: Oxford University Press.

Torún, B. and Viteri, F. E. 1988. Protein-energy malnutrition. In *Modern Nutrition in Health and Disease,* ed. M. E. Shils and V. R. Young, pp. 746–773. Philadelphia: Lea & Febiger.

Widdowson, E. M. 1985. Responses to deficits of dietary energy. In *Nutritional*

Adaptation in Man, ed. K. Blaxter and J. C. Waterlow, pp. 97–104. London: John Libby.

Winick, M. 1976. *Malnutrition and Brain Development.* New York: Oxford University Press.

Winick, M. 1979. *Hunger Disease: Studies by Jewish Physicians in the Warsaw Ghetto.* New York: Wiley.

Winick, M. and P. Rosso. 1969. The effect of severe early malnutrition on cellular growth of the human brain. *Pediatric Research* 3:181–184.

Zamenhof, S., E. van Marthens, and F. L. Margolis. 1968. DNA (cell number) and protein in the neonatal brain: Alterations by maternal dietary protein restrictions. *Science* 160:322–323.

3

Vitamins, the Central Nervous System, and Behavior

Vitamins constitute a group of 13 organic compounds that are essential for the metabolism of other nutrients and the maintenance of a variety of physiological functions. As a virtue of being organic compounds, all vitamins contain the element carbon. However, the 13 vitamins vary greatly in chemical composition and in the roles they play in the body. Vitamins, in contrast to the macronutrients, protein, fat, and carbohydrate, are required in relatively small amounts in the diet and are not a source of energy. The primary function of many vitamins is catalytic; they often serve as coenzymes which facilitate the actions of enzymes involved in essential metabolic reactions.

The significance of vitamins for human health was first recognized as a result of the deficiency diseases which are associated with the lack of these nutrients in the diet. Research conducted primarily at the turn of this century led to the hypothesis that certain diseases such as scurvy, rickets, pellagra, and beriberi were caused by the lack of an essential substance in the diet and cured by adding this substance back. In 1912, Casimir Funk coined the term "vitamine," "vita" for life and "amine" because the substance contained nitrogen. Later work demonstrated that there was not one, but many, of these vital substances and that only a few were amines, and so the final "e" was dropped, leading to the term vitamin.

There are a variety of causes for vitamin deficiencies. Some individuals, due to genetic abnormalities or disease conditions, have a decreased ability to absorb vitamins provided in food. For example, chronic alcoholism can impair the absorption of thiamin from the gastrointestinal tract. A second cause of vitamin deficiency is the increased need for a vitamin, leading to deficiency symptoms on an intake that would normally be adequate. Increased need for vitamins can occur during pregnancy or lactation, or as a result of drug intake. Patients with tuberculosis given the drug isoniazid, for example, demonstrate an increased need for vitamin B_6. The most common cause of vitamin deficiencies, however, is inadequate intake. In many parts of the world, inadequate amounts or varieties of food continue to be the rule, and deficiency diseases remain common.

A number of vitamins—thiamin, niacin, pyridoxine, cobalamin, and folic acid—play important roles in the functioning of the central nervous system, and in human behavior and development.

THIAMIN (VITAMIN B₁)

The symptoms of inadequate thiamin intake that constitute the disease known as beriberi were described by the Chinese as early as the seventh century, but the disease was relatively uncommon until the Industrial Revolution when the consumption of refined cereal grains increased dramatically. Indeed, in areas where people obtained over 80% of their calories from cereals such as rice and refined wheat, beriberi became a major health problem during the late 1800s.

The increasing prevalence of beriberi in the 1800s led to the development of many theories about the causes of the disease. The first hint that it was the result of a nutritional deficiency was provided by Takaki, who found that the prevalence of beriberi was decreased in Japanese sailors when they were fed a diet that included dry milk and meat. Studies in the late 1800s by Eijkman contributed further support for the idea that beriberi resulted from a nutritional deficiency. Eijkman demonstrated that chickens fed a diet consisting primarily of polished rice developed neurological symptoms similar to those associated with beriberi. Adding the bran or outer coating of rice to the animals' diet rapidly cured these symptoms. It was subsequently shown that rice bran extract was also effective in curing beriberi. In 1926, an anti-beriberi factor was isolated from rice bran, and in 1936, this factor, named thiamin, was chemically identified and synthesized (Haas 1988; McCormick 1988a; Guthrie 1989).

Requirements and Dietary Sources

Thiamin is a component of the coenzyme thiamin pyrophosphate (TPP) which is necessary for the metabolism of carbohydrate (Figure 3-1). Three steps in carbohydrate metabolism are critically dependent upon the presence of TPP. First, TPP is required for the oxidative decarboxylation of pyruvic acid and the subsequent formation of acetyl coenzyme A, which in turn enters the Krebs cycle. A second and similar role for TPP occurs in the Krebs cycle when alpha-ketoglutarate, an intermediary product of both carbohydrate and fat metabolism, is decarboxylated to succinyl-CoA. The oxidative decarboxylation of pyruvate and alpha-ketoglutarate are essential for normal energy metabolism. The third important role for TPP in carbohydrate metabolism is activation of the enzyme transketolase, which is necessary for the metabolism of glucose in all cells in the body, with the exception of those in the skeletal system.

THIAMIN

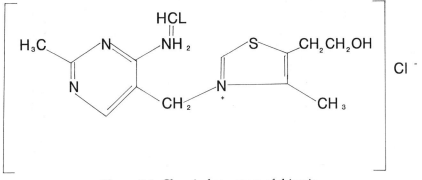

Figure 3-1. Chemical structure of thiamin.

Recent work suggests that in addition to its coenzyme function, thiamin is important for neurotransmitter synthesis and release, and for normal conduction of electrical impulses in the nervous system (Robinson and Lawler 1982; Witt 1985; Haas 1988; Guthrie 1989; Tucker et al. 1990).

Because thiamin is necessary for normal carbohydrate and energy metabolism, the recommended intakes for the vitamin are proportionate to the carbohydrate and caloric content of the diet. The Food and Nutrition Board recommends a thiamin intake of 0.5 mg/1000 kcals for adults, or between 1.0 and 1.5 mg per day (see Table 3-1). The richest dietary sources of thiamin are pork, organ meats, yeast, lean meats, eggs, green leafy vegetables, whole grain or enriched cereals, nuts, and legumes (Table 3-2). Cereal grains contain substantial amounts of thiamin, but the commercial milling processes used in most Western countries remove the outer portions of the grain which are the richest sources of the vitamin. As a result, white flour and polished white rice have little if any thiamin (Burton and Foster 1988; Guthrie 1989; Food and Nutrition Board 1989).

Despite awareness of the dietary sources of thiamin and the availability of synthetic thiamin, beriberi continues to be a serious health problem in parts of the world where high-carbohydrate diets are common and rice and wheat are not enriched as a common practice. In Southeast Asia, where the diet of the poorer segment of the population consists primarily of polished rice, beriberi is prevalent. Additionally, the predominance of carbohydrate in the diet raises the metabolic requirement for the vitamin and may precipitate the disease. Infantile beriberi frequently occurs when pregnancy and lactation raise the mother's requirement for thiamin. Breast-fed infants develop the disease when the milk of malnourished mothers is deficient in the vitamin. In the Philippines, beriberi accounts for

TABLE 3-1. Recommended Dietary Allowances

Category	Age (years) or Condition	Thiamin (mg)	Niacin (mg NE)	Vitamin B₆ (mg)	Vitamin B (mg)
Infants	0.0–0.5	0.3	5	0.3	0.3
	0.5–1.0	0.4	6	0.6	0.5
Children	1–3	0.7	9	1.0	0.7
	4–6	0.9	12	1.1	1.0
	7–10	1.0	13	1.4	1.4
Males	11–14	1.3	17	1.7	2.0
	15–18	1.5	20	2.0	2.0
	19–24	1.5	19	2.0	2.0
	25–50	1.5	19	2.0	2.0
	51+	1.2	15	2.0	2.0
Females	11–14	1.1	15	1.4	2.0
	15–18	1.1	15	1.5	2.0
	19–24	1.1	15	1.6	2.0
	25–50	1.1	15	1.6	2.0
	51+	1.0	13	1.6	2.0
Pregnant women	—	1.5	17	2.2	2.2
Lactating women	—	1.6	20	2.1	2.6

From Food and Nutrition Board, National Academy of Sciences Research Council 1989.

TABLE 3-2. Thiamine Content of Selected Foods (100 g edible portion)

Food	Thiamin (mg)
Canadian bacon (raw)	0.91
Ham, cured, cooked	0.54
Pork luncheon meat	0.32
Brazil nuts, shelled	0.86
Peanuts, roasted	0.30
Wheat-flake cereal	0.56
Bran-flake cereal	0.46
Cornflakes	0.41
Green peas, cooked	0.25
Whole-wheat bread, enriched	0.30
Frankfurter, cooked	0.16
Lima beans, cooked	0.14
Asparagus, cooked	0.13
Lamb chop, cooked	0.14
Hamburger, cooked	0.08
Milk, whole or low-fat	0.04

75 infant deaths per 100,000 births. Finally, a number of foods including some freshwater fish, shrimp, tea leaves, and betel nuts contain compounds that act as thiamin antagonists that decrease the availability of thiamin. Individuals living on marginal diets and consuming large amounts of these foods have an increased risk of developing thiamin deficiency (Robinson and Lawler 1982; Burton and Foster 1988; Guthrie 1989).

In the United States, thiamin deficiency occurs almost exclusively in alcoholics, primarily due to poor diet with inadequate vitamin intake. Alcohol consumption also contributes to thiamin deficiency because it leads to degeneration of the intestinal wall and thus impairs absorption of the vitamin.

Thiamin Deficiency

Because thiamin deficiency in humans usually occurs in conjunction with decreased intake of other B vitamins, it is often difficult to attribute symptoms specifically to a lack of thiamin. However, specific symptoms of beriberi have been identified. Two distinct forms of beriberi, wet and dry, have been described. Wet beriberi is characterized by abnormalities of the cardiovascular system including enlargement of the heart, heartbeat irregularities, systemic venous hypertension, edema, and congestive heart failure. The development of wet beriberi is typically associated with severe thiamin deficiency and is favored by high carbohydrate intake and high levels of physical activity.

Malnutrition and low levels of activity favor the development of dry beriberi, which principally affects the nervous system. Early clinical signs of dry beriberi include decreased initiative, increased irritability, inability to concentrate, fatigue, and depression. As the disease progresses, peripheral neurological symptoms become evident. This neuropathy is characterized by bilateral symmetrical impairment of sensory, motor, and reflex functions that first affects the longest nerve pathways, and thus the most distal parts of the lower extremities. Paresthesias ("pins and needles") of the toes, followed by a burning sensation in the feet, are common manifestations of dry beriberi. If the disease is not treated, the symptoms progress to include decreased perception of light touch, loss of vibratory sense and normal reflexes, and eventually motor weakness and secondary muscle atrophy. Initially, these symptoms affect the most distal portion of the legs and then advance proximally until the hands and arms are also affected.

The exact role of thiamin in peripheral nerve conduction is not known. The vitamin is found in nerve cell membranes and mitochondria, and in the form of the coenzyme TPP may play a fundamental role in the control of sodium conductance at axonal membranes. Additionally, thiamin deficiency leads to the degeneration of axons of neurons in the peripheral nervous system, which contributes to the symptoms of neuropathy characteristic of dry beriberi (Tanphaichitr and Wood 1984; Burton and Foster 1988; Haas 1988).

WERNICKE-KORSAKOFF SYNDROME

Wernicke-Korsakoff syndrome is characterized by a wide range of neurological and psychological deficits as well as a specific constellation of neuropathological damage. Although sometimes associated with alcohol toxicity, Wernicke-Korsakoff syndrome is a direct result of thiamin deficiency. The first indication of central nervous system damage following thiamin deficiency has been termed Wernicke's encephalopathy. The clinical features of this condition include anorexia, nystagmus (involuntary rapid eye movements), ophthalmoplegia (paralysis of the eye muscles), and ataxia (difficulty maintaining balance while walking), along with apathy, inattentiveness, confusion, drowsiness, and decreased spontaneity of speech. Following administration of thiamin, the mental symptoms of Wernicke's encephalopathy rapidly improve; however, the psychomotor aspects of the disease including nystagmus, ophthalmoplegia, and ataxia may become more apparent as the patient becomes more testable.

If the deficiency remains untreated, Korsakoff's psychosis may develop, which is characterized by an inability to learn and to form new memories (anterograde amnesia), unpredictable loss of past memories, hallucinations, and confabulation. Korsakoff's psychosis is only minimally or slowly responsive to thiamin administration. The rapidity of the response to thiamin depends upon the conversion of the vitamin to its active form in the liver. Thus, patients with advanced liver disease, such as cirrhosis, have a delayed response to vitamin therapy.

Most frequently Wernicke-Korsakoff syndrome is seen in chronic alcoholics who also present with clinical symptoms of malnutrition. However, the syndrome can occur as a complication of disorders characterized by nutritional depletion and/or metabolic stress affecting thiamin metabolism, such as carcinoma of the stomach, chronic gastritis, gastric stapling for morbid obesity, hyperemesis, the prolonged use of diuretic agents, anorexia nervosa, and food faddism.

CNS ALTERATIONS AS A FUNCTION OF THIAMIN DEFICIENCY

Post-mortem examination of the brains of patients with Wernicke-Korsakoff syndrome and research on thiamin deficiency in experimental animals have revealed distinct neuropathological alterations. In all species, thiamin deficiency is associated with bilaterally symmetrical lesions throughout the brain, particularly in the thalamus, the hypothalamus, the mammillary bodies, the midbrain, the brain stem, and the cerebellum. Damage to the cerebellum and brain stem, both involved in the control of movement, are the probable basis for the ataxia and ophthalmoplegia characteristic of Wernicke's encephalopathy. Atrophy of the mammillary bodies and damage to thalamic nuclei are commonly observed and are hypothesized to be the primary cause of the memory deficits seen in the disorder. Atrophy of the cerebral cortex, abnormalities of cerebellar structure, enlargement of the cerebral ventricles, and alterations in the myelin sheath surrounding neurons are also typical of Wernicke-Korsakoff syndrome (Witt and Goldman-Rakic 1983a; Witt 1985; Haas 1988).

Research on the effects of intermittent thiamin deficiency in rhesus monkeys by Witt and Goldman-Rakic (1983a) has demonstrated that the number of damaged central nervous system structures increases with successive periods of thiamin deficiency. Additionally, these researchers have observed significant correlations between the severity of neurological symptoms and the extent of neuroanatomical damage. Animals with the most widespread neuropathological lesions exhibited the most severe clinical symptoms. The best correlation between location of anatomical damage and symptoms was found in the visual system. These results indicate that the effects of thiamin deficiency are cumulative in the sense that clinical symptoms appear sooner with repetitions of the deficiency, and that the number of damaged central nervous system structures tends to increase with increasing periods of deficiency. These results emphasize the importance of early detection and treatment of thiamin deficiency.

Experimental studies of thiamin deficiency have also demonstrated alterations in neurotransmitters in the central nervous system, suggesting that the vitamin is important for normal neurotransmitter functioning. Cholinergic systems are sensitive to thiamin deficiency, as they are to other conditions that impair carbohydrate metabolism. Thiamin deficiency leads to a reduction in the turnover of acetylcholine and thus alters the functioning of cholinergic neurons. It has been suggested that alterations in some forms of motor coordination in thiamin-deficient animals may be the result of damage to central cholinergic systems (Barclay, Gibson, and Blass 1981).

Both whole brain and regional concentrations of the three amino acid neurotransmitters, gamma-aminobutyric acid (GABA), glutamate, and aspartate, are decreased in the thiamin-deficient rat. Thiamin deficiency also has been associated with a loss of glutamate and GABA-containing nerve terminals, particularly in the regions of the cerebellum and brain stem.

Thiamin deficiency also reduces serotonin metabolism within the central nervous system. The generation of neurological symptoms, particularly ataxia, thermoregulatory abnormalities, and memory loss, have been attributed to changes in the functioning of serotonergic neurons in the cerebellum, brain stem, and diencephalic structures. Studies have indicated that following intermittent thiamin deficiency in monkeys, brain stem lesions are found predominantly in areas containing serotonergic neurons. Because these animals display a pattern of memory loss similar to that seen in patients with Wernicke-Korsakoff syndrome, it has been proposed that amnesia in these patients results from a loss of serotonin-containing neurons (Witt and Goldman-Rakic 1983b). In support of this proposal, cerebrospinal fluid levels of the primary metabolite of serotonin, 5-hydroxyindoleacetic acid, were found to be reduced in patients with Wernicke-Korsakoff syndrome.

Norepinephrine levels are also reduced in thiamin-deficient animals. Disturbances in norepinephrine turnover in thiamin-deficient rats have been associated with pronounced hypotension and bradycardia which were reversed by the administration of the vitamin. Reductions in levels of the norepinephrine metabolite, 3-methoxy, 4-hydroxy phenylglycol, have been observed in cerebrospinal fluid of patients with Korsakoff's syndrome. Reductions in the levels of norepinephrine and its metabolite have been correlated with measures of memory impairment. In addition, administration of clonidine, a drug that increases norepinephrine activity, has been associated with improvements in memory. It therefore has been suggested that the memory deficits of Korsakoff's syndrome may partly result from damage to noradrenergic systems within the central nervous system (Witt 1985).

In conclusion, thiamin deficiency alters the activity of six neurotransmitter systems in the mammalian central nervous system. However, the association between these alterations in neurotransmitters and the histological damage found in the brains of thiamin-deficient individuals remains unknown. Four of these neurotransmitters, acetylcholine, GABA, glutamate, and aspartate, are related to glucose metabolism in the brain. It has been suggested that the alterations in these four neurotransmitters are the result of a reduction in TPP-dependent enzyme activity or membrane transport mechanisms. Alternatively, the loss of neurons and axons associated with thiamin deficiency may lead to alterations in neurotransmitters within the central nervous system (Witt and Goldman-Rakic 1983a, 1983b; Witt 1985; Dreyfus 1988; Haas 1988; Blass 1989).

NIACIN (VITAMIN B$_3$)

At the turn of the century, large numbers of people in the southern portion of the United States suffered from a disease characterized by skin lesions, severe gastrointestinal disturbances, and mental disabilities. The disease occurred predominantly among the poor and those in institutions where extremely limited diets were common. In severe cases, the prognosis was always unfavorable: death within two to three weeks.

It was soon recognized that although new to North America, this disease had long been known in Europe. Don Gaspar Casal, a physician in the Spanish court, first described the disease in 1735 as "mal de la rosa" (sickness of the rose) because of a characteristic redness of the skin that worsened when patients were exposed to the sun. In 1770, the disease was noted in Italy and given the name "pellagra," meaning rough skin. As in the United States, the disease in Europe was particularly common among the poor, whose dietary staple was corn.

During the early part of this century, pellagra was identified as a major public health problem in the United States, particularly in the South where it affected more than 200,000 people per year. The endemic nature of the disease resulted in it becoming the focus of extensive investigations by the Public Health Service (PHS). Initial work concentrated on the possibility that an infectious agent or toxic substance in spoiled corn caused the disease. However, on the basis of studies demonstrating that pellagra could be produced by dietary restriction, and later work showing that it could be cured by the addition of yeast to the diet, Dr. Joseph Goldberger of the PHS hypothesized that the disease was the result of the lack of a critical dietary component. Due to the absence of an appropriate animal model for the disease, however, the dietary factor responsible for preventing or curing pellagra was not identified for 20 years. In 1937, Elvehjem, working at the University of Wisconsin, found that nicotinic acid was effective in curing black tongue, a condition in dogs similar to pellagra. Treatment of pellagra with nicotinic acid quickly led to dramatic improvements, with the number of pellagra victims in southern hospitals and mental institutions rapidly decreasing toward zero (Etheridge 1972).

Today, pellagra is relatively rare in this country, occurring primarily in alcoholics or individuals suffering from pancreatic disease. However, it continues to be a problem in many parts of the world, and is still encountered among the Bantus of South Africa; in Romania, Yugoslavia, and Egypt where corn is a dietary staple; and in areas of India where sorghum is extensively consumed. Pellagra is not found in South America, although corn forms a major portion of the diet. In this part of the world, the traditional preparation of corn with alkalis (e.g., soda lime) liberates the niacin bound to protein, making it more available for absorption (Rao and Gopalan 1984; Guthrie 1989).

Requirements and Dietary Sources

Nicotinic acid and nicotinamide are organic compounds with relatively simple chemical structures and equivalent biological activity (Figure 3-2). Niacin is the generic term that includes both forms of the vitamin. Niacin is required by all living cells. The vitamin is a component of the coenzymes nicotinamide adenine dinucleotide (NAD), which is crucial for the metabo-

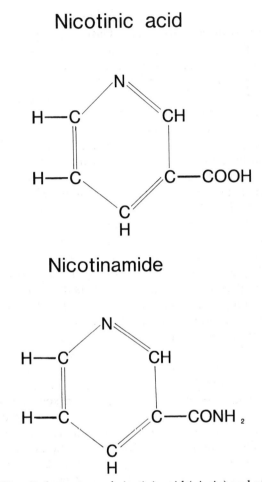

Figure 3-2. Chemical structure of nicotinic acid (niacin) and nicotinamide.

lism of fat, carbohydrate, and amino acids, and nicotinamide adenine dinucleotide phosphate (NADP), which plays an important role in the synthesis of fats and steroids.

Niacin is widely distributed in food (Table 3-3). Meat, liver, poultry, cereals, legumes, and peanut butter are rich sources of the vitamin. Additionally, the amino acid tryptophan serves as a precursor for niacin. Most dietary proteins contain about 1% tryptophan, with approximately 60 mg of tryptophan yielding 1 mg of niacin or one niacin equivalent (NE). Thus, 6 g of protein would provide 60 mg of tryptophan or 1 NE.

Dietary requirements for niacin are expressed as niacin equivalents representing niacin itself plus that obtained from tryptophan. Since niacin

TABLE 3-3. Niacin Content of Selected Foods (100 g edible portion)

Food	Niacin (mg)
Peanuts, roasted	16.2
Calves liver, raw	16.1
Chicken liver	11.8
Tuna fish, canned	12.8
Swordfish, cooked	10.3
Bran-flake cereal	8.7
Puffed wheat cereal, enriched	6.4
Veal cutlet, cooked	6.1
Lamb chop, cooked	5.6
Dried peaches, uncooked	5.4
Hamburger, cooked	4.8
Brown rice	4.6
Ham, cured and cooked	4.2
Whole-wheat bread	3.0
Cornflakes enriched	2.2
Asparagus, cooked	1.2
Broccoli, cooked	1.1
Dried prunes	1.7

is critical for the release of energy from nutrients, the RDA is based on caloric intake. The recommended daily allowance for niacin for adults is 6.6 NE/1,000 kcal (Table 3-1). Regardless of caloric intake, a minimum daily intake of 13 NE is advised (Rao and Gopalan 1984; Guthrie 1989; Food and Nutrition Board 1989).

Niacin Deficiency

CLINICAL MANIFESTATIONS

Pellagra affects the skin, gastrointestinal tract, and central nervous system. Early signs of the disease include fatigue, listlessness, headache, backache, loss of weight, and general poor health. As the disease progresses, soreness of the tongue, mouth, and throat become evident followed by inflammation of the gastrointestinal tract, nausea, vomiting, and severe diarrhea. A characteristic symmetrical dermatitis that is sharply separated from the surrounding healthy skin then appears, especially on areas of the body exposed to sunlight such as hands, forearms, elbows, feet, neck, and face. Initially, the skin becomes red, somewhat swollen, and tender, resembling a mild sunburn. If the condition remains untreated, the skin becomes rough, cracked, and scaly with exposure to sunlight and heat exacerbating the dermatitis.

Chronic, severe niacin deficiency leads to alterations in the functioning of the nervous system. Indications that the peripheral nervous system is affected by niacin deficiency include weakness, tremor, loss of the ability to detect the position of one's limbs in space, spasticity, exaggerated tendon reflexes, and paresthesia. Initial manifestations of CNS abnormalities include irritability, sleeplessness, dizziness, loss of memory, confusion, and signs of emotional instability. In advanced cases, hallucinations, delusions of persecution, severe depression, and catatonia are observed. These latter symptoms are similar to those of schizophrenia. Indeed, many individuals diagnosed as schizophrenic and placed in mental institutions in this country at the turn of the century were probably suffering from pellagra (Etheridge 1972; Robinson and Lawler 1982; Rao and Gopalan 1984).

Niacin therapy leads to a rapid reversal of the symptoms of pellagra. Nausea, vomiting, and diarrhea may stop within 24 hours. The appetite improves, and mental symptoms are quickly relieved; confused patients become mentally clear, and those who are agitated become calm. The effects of niacin are so specific in this regard that it can be used as a diagnostic agent in patients with frank psychoses but with questionable evidence of pellagra.

PHYSIOLOGICAL AND BIOCHEMICAL CORRELATES

Many attempts have been made to relate the neurological and psychological symptoms of pellagra to specific biochemical or physiological alterations within the nervous system, but none of these has been completely satisfactory. Examination of the brains of chronic pellagra victims has revealed degeneration, especially in the large neurons of the motor cortex, brain stem, and anterior horn of the spinal cord. Similar alterations have been found in the brains of dogs suffering from black tongue, which is also caused by niacin deficiency. These findings suggest that chronic niacin deficiency leads to permanent structural changes within the central nervous system (McIlwain and Bachelard 1985).

Experimental pellagra has been induced in a variety of animals by feeding them diets low in niacin and tryptophan, or by the administration of the niacin antimetabolite 6-aminonicotinamide (6-AN). Several hours after the administration of 6-AN, mice exhibit paralysis and loss of motor control. Chronic treatment with 6-AN leads to degeneration of neurons and glial cells in adult animals. Studies with experimental animals have also revealed that niacin deficiency is associated with a reduction in brain levels of NAD and NADP. The reductions in these coenzymes that are critical for normal nutrient metabolism may contribute to the alterations in nervous system function associated with niacin deficiency (Lipton, Mailman, and Nemeroff 1979; McIlwain and Bachelard 1985).

PYRIDOXINE (VITAMIN B$_6$)

The terms pyridoxine or vitamin B$_6$ are used to denote a group of three related compounds, pyridoxine, pyridoxal, and pyridoxamine. The active form of this vitamin is the coenzyme pyridoxal phosphate (PLP) which can be formed from any of the three compounds. PLP is the coenzyme for a large number of enzyme systems, most of which are involved in protein metabolism. For example, PLP is essential for the process of transamination in which the amino group (NH$_2$) from one amino acid is transferred to another substance, and for deamination, in which an amino group is removed so that protein which is not necessary for growth can be used as a source of energy. PLP is also required for decarboxylation, or the removal of carboxyl groups (COOH) from amino acids, which is a necessary step in the synthesis of several neurotransmitters including GABA, serotonin, norepinephrine, and histamine. Further, pyridoxine is involved in several biochemical steps in the conversion of the amino acid tryptophan to niacin.

Because pyridoxine is essential for almost all aspects of protein metabolism, the requirement for the vitamin is proportionate to the amount of protein in the diet. Thus, the daily requirement of individuals eating a high-protein diet is greater than that of individuals eating a low-protein diet. The 1989 recommended dietary allowances are 2.0 mg/day for men and 1.6 mg/day for women (Table 3-1).

Requirements and Dietary Sources

Pyridoxine is widely distributed in both plant and animal foods. Good sources are liver, white meats (chicken and fish), whole-grain cereals, soybeans, peanuts, egg yolks, bananas, and potatoes (Table 3-4). Freezing can lead to a 15 to 70% decrease in the pyridoxine content of vegetables, and as much as 50 to 90% of the vitamin is lost in the milling of grains. A number of drugs, including oral contraceptives, agents used in the treatment of tuberculosis, and penicillamine, can alter the metabolism of vitamin B$_6$ and lead to a deficiency of the vitamin (Robinson and Lawler 1982; Burton and Foster 1988; McCormick 1988b; Guthrie 1989; Food and Nutrition Board 1989).

Pyridoxine Deficiency

Given its role in protein metabolism, it is not surprising that pyridoxine deficiency is associated with a large number of abnormalities in amino acid and protein metabolism. In experimental animals, newborns are more sensitive to this dietary deficiency than weanlings. Pups born to rats deficient in pyridoxine display neuropathological damage including hypomyelination and decreased levels of brain serotonin. Alterations in central

TABLE 3-4. Vitamin B$_6$ Content of Selected Foods (per serving)

Food	Serving	Vitamin B$_6$ (mg)
Banana	1 medium	0.63
Cornflakes, enriched	1 cup	0.54
Roast beef	3 oz	0.47
Tuna fish	3 oz	0.42
Chicken	3 oz	0.40
Ground beef	3 oz	0.32
Frozen spinach	4 oz	0.28
Baked potato	1 medium	0.22
Corn, canned	4 oz	0.20
Cantaloupe	one-half	0.15
Milk, 2% fat	8 oz	0.10
Whole-wheat bread	1 slice	0.04

nervous system functioning also occur in adult animals suffering from pyridoxine deficiency. Dogs and rats fed a pyridoxine-deficient diet initially display impairments in learning abilities followed by irritability, ataxia (difficulties in walking), and seizures. The ataxia is believed to be the result of demyelination in motor pathways and peripheral nerves, while the intensity of the seizures correlates with a decrease in levels of the enzyme glutamic acid decarboxylase which is necessary for the formation of the neurotransmitter GABA. (Lipton, Mailman, and Nemeroff 1979; Blass 1989)

As in experimental animals, human infants are more sensitive to B$_6$ deficiency than adults. Convincing evidence of the necessity of the vitamin was shown in 1952 when infants were inadvertently fed an autoclaved commercial formula in which the B$_6$ content was not properly preserved. These infants were normal at birth and in good health until 8 to 16 weeks of age when they suddenly displayed nervous irritability and convulsive seizures. These symptoms, which were noted in more than 300 infants, were eliminated by pyridoxine treatment. Confirmation of a role for pyridoxine in CNS functioning comes from observations of infants suffering from pyridoxine-dependency syndrome. In this very rare syndrome, seizures usually begin within the first days of life and consist of severe generalized convulsions, accompanied by hyperirritability and hyperacusis. Mental retardation is a common outcome. Post-mortem examinations of the brains of infants afflicted with this syndrome have revealed diffuse neuronal degeneration. Infants with pyridoxine-dependency syndrome have a persistent increased need for vitamin B$_6$. Daily administration of 10 to 50 mg of the vitamin prevents irritability and convulsions in these infants (Lipton, Mailman, and Nemeroff 1979; Henderson 1984; Blass 1989).

Uncomplicated primary B$_6$ deficiency is rarely encountered in adults, since ingestion of diets with insufficient amounts of the vitamin would likely also lack adequate amounts of other B-complex vitamins. However, two drugs used in the treatment of tuberculosis, isoniazid and cycloserine, can result in vitamin B$_6$ deficiency. These drugs form compounds with the vitamin that lead to a decrease in the activity of several enzymes for which pyridoxal phosphate is a coenzyme. Reported complications associated with the use of these drugs usually involve the central nervous system. Neurological symptoms include headache, tremor, somnolence, dysarthria, abnormal electroencephalogram, and convulsions. Additionally, patients may experience depression, loss of self-control, suicidal thoughts, suspiciousness, and paranoia. Administration of large doses of B$_6$ reduces many of the neurological symptoms associated with drug treatment, but is less effective in ameliorating the psychiatric symptoms (Lipton, Mailman, and Nemeroff 1979; McCormick 1988b).

The use of oral contraceptives containing high levels of estrogen may also lead to vitamin B$_6$ deficiency. There is evidence that estrogens and other steroid hormones compete with pyridoxal phosphate for binding sites, leading to an increased need for B$_6$. One consequence of B$_6$ deficiency is lower levels of a number of neurotransmitters including serotonin. A reduction in serotonin levels in the central nervous system has been implicated as a possible cause of depression. It has been suggested that depression as a common side effect of oral contraceptive use is the result of B$_6$ deficiency. In support of this suggestion, administration of B$_6$ can lead to improvement in depressive symptoms in some women taking oral contraceptives. It also has been suggested that supplemental intake of B$_6$ may be a useful adjunct in the treatment of the symptoms of premenstrual syndrome; however, the data supporting this conclusion are contradictory (Lipton, Mailman, and Nemeroff 1979; see chapter 5).

Potential Toxicity

During the past decade, pyridoxine has gained public acceptance as a component of body-building regimens and as a palliative for premenstrual syndrome. Tablets containing 50 to 500 mg of the vitamin are widely available. It is generally believed that intake of water-soluble vitamins including pyridoxine does not have harmful consequences. However, recent reports demonstrate that daily intake of large amounts of pyridoxine can lead to sensory neuropathy. In 1983, Dr. Herbert Schaumburg and his colleagues reported on seven adult patients consuming 2 to 6 g of pyridoxine a day for periods ranging from 2 to 40 months. All seven individuals initially experienced an unstable gait and numb feet. Numbness and clumsiness of the hands followed within several months. All patients had a "stocking glove" distribution of sensory loss affecting all modalities (i.e., light touch, temperature, pinprick). Studies of nerve conduction indicated dysfunction of the distal portions of the sensory nerves, and nerve biopsies in two patients revealed widespread nonspecific axonal degeneration. Neurological disabilities gradually improved once the patients stopped taking pyridoxine.

Further evidence supporting the hypothesis that the mammalian peripheral nervous system is vulnerable to sustained megavitamin doses of pyridoxine comes from studies in which rats and dogs receiving high doses of the vitamin progressively developed unsteady gait. Examination of the peripheral nervous system in these animals revealed degeneration of the spinal cord, sensory neurons, and nerve fibers extending from these neurons. These data, in conjunction with data on the consequences of excess pyridoxine intake in humans, make it clear that long-term treatment with large doses of pyridoxine is not safe. Vitamin B_6 therapy for behavioral or other disorders should not be undertaken until the value of such treatment has been established through controlled experiments (Schaumburg et al. 1983).

COBALAMIN (VITAMIN B_{12})

Until the 1920s pernicious anemia was a fatal disease of unknown origin with no known cure. In 1926, however, Minot and Murphy reported that feeding patients large amounts of liver (approximately a pound a day) could cure the anemia and prevent the neurological symptoms that accompanied the disease. In the same year, Castle set forth the hypothesis that an antipernicious anemia substance was formed by the combination of an extrinsic factor in food and an intrinsic factor in normal gastric secretion. It is now known that the extrinsic and intrinsic factors do not combine to form an antipernicious anemia substance, but rather that the intrinsic factor is necessary for intestinal absorption of the extrinsic factor. The search for the active substance in liver culminated in 1948 when scientists in the United States and England isolated a few micrograms of a red crystalline substance that was dramatically effective in the treatment of pernicious anemia. This substance, which was designated vitamin B_{12}, was found to be a complex molecule containing the mineral cobalt in its center. The presence of cobalt in the vitamin led to the term "cobalamin."

Requirements and Dietary Sources

The need for cobalamin is small as compared with the other B vitamins; the recommended dietary allowance is 2.0 ug a day for normal adults (Table 3-1). All vitamin B_{12} found in food is made by microorganisms. The vita-

**TABLE 3-5. Cobalamin Content in Selected
Foods (per serving)**

Food	Serving	Cobalamin (ug)
Liver	3 oz	87.0
Oysters	3 oz	16.2
Tuna fish	3 oz	2.2
Roast beef	3 oz	1.5
Milk, whole	8 oz	0.9
Egg, fried	1 large	0.6
Chicken	3 oz	0.3
Cheddar cheese	1 oz	0.2

min is absent in plants except where they are contaminated by microorganisms (e.g., nodules on roots of legumes). Thus, B$_{12}$ is obtained almost exclusively from foods of animal origin. Liver and kidney are excellent sources, while muscle meat and fish supply it in moderate amounts, and whole milk in smaller quantities (Table 3-5).

Because the body can store B$_{12}$, deficiencies develop slowly even on a diet completely lacking the vitamin. It takes a number of years for B$_{12}$ deficiency to develop in adults who are strict vegetarians consuming no dairy products or eggs, as well as no meat. Children following strict vegetarian diets become B$_{12}$-deficient within two to three years because they have no stores of the vitamin. It is recommended that strict vegetarians take vitamin B$_{12}$ supplements.

Vitamin B$_{12}$ is involved in DNA synthesis and is necessary for normal growth, carbohydrate and lipid metabolism, normal blood formation, and the proper functioning of the nervous system (Food and Nutrition Board 1989).

Cobalamin Deficiency

Cobalamin deficiency in human beings is almost exclusively the result of limited intake and/or inadequate absorption. Pernicious anemia, which is the classic example of B$_{12}$ deficiency, usually develops because of decreased absorption of the vitamin due to a lack of the intrinsic factor, complete or partial removal of the stomach, or a lack of the protein in the blood that binds cobalamin. In pernicious anemia, red blood cells are large but not properly developed, which interferes with the ability of hemoglobin to carry oxygen to cells in the body. Clinically, the disease is characterized by pallor, prolonged bleeding time, anorexia, weight loss, abdominal discomfort, and glossitis (Herbert 1984; Herbert and Colman 1988; Guthrie 1989).

Cobalamin deficiency also has profound effects on the nervous system. One of the first signs of nerve damage is demyelination of peripheral nerves. With continued B_{12} deficiency, demyelination progresses centrally to involve the posterior and lateral columns of the spinal cord and eventually the brain. The neurological signs of cobalamin deficiency begin with paresthesia, especially numbness and tingling in the hands and feet, diminution of vibratory sensations, unsteadiness, poor muscular coordination, and ataxia. As the disease progresses to include damage to the central nervous system, moodiness, mental slowness, memory deficits, confusion, agitation, depression, delusions, hallucinations, and overt psychosis may occur (Herbert and Colman 1988).

Symptoms involving the central nervous system tend to improve rapidly following treatment with B_{12}. However, the neurological symptoms resulting from demyelination take longer to improve. Because the axon underneath the deteriorated myelin is also damaged, healing is related to the speed of regeneration of damaged axons, which is approximately 0.1 mm per day (Herbert and Colman 1988).

Until recently, it was thought that patients with cobalamin deficiency who presented with neurological symptoms but without megaloblastic anemia were rare. The neurological sequelae were typically believed to be late manifestations of B_{12} deficiency which occurred following the development of anemia. Within the last several years, however, it has been suggested that the neuropsychiatric disorders caused by B_{12} deficiency can frequently occur in the absence of anemia. For example, Lindenbaum and colleagues found that 40 of 141 patients suffering from B_{12} deficiency displayed neuropsychiatric abnormalities without anemia (Lindenbaum et al. 1988). In these patients, impaired vibratory sensation and paresthesia of the extremities were the most common symptoms, followed by impaired touch or pain perception, ataxia, weakness of the limbs, and decreased reflexes. Indications of central nervous system damage were also evident, with a number of patients displaying memory loss, hallucinations, and changes in personality or mood. Evidence that vitamin B_{12} deficiency was the primary cause of these symptoms came from measures of serum cobalamin levels and observations of the patients' responses to the vitamin. Treatment with cobalamin produced neurological improvement in all patients. Although objective improvement was seen in clinical signs, some residual neurological abnormalities, particularly deficits in vibratory senses, were not eliminated even years after initiation of cobalamin treatment.

FOLIC ACID

Folic acid (folacin) was originally discovered in the 1930s during the search for the factor in liver responsible for its effectiveness in curing pernicious anemia. It was subsequently discovered that although folacin cures megaloblastic anemia by stimulating the regeneration of red blood cells and hemoglobin, it is ineffective in relieving the neurological symptoms of pernicious anemia. Thus, it was concluded that folacin was not the true antipernicious anemia factor. Subsequent work, however, has established that folic acid is necessary for the synthesis of essential nulceic acids, which in turn are required for normal cell division and replication.

The daily requirements for folic acid in humans have not been definitively established. It has been estimated that 3 ug/kg of body weight meets the needs of most adults. The minimum requirement for folic acid may be influenced by a variety of factors including body size; increased consumption of alcohol, which interferes with absorption; and any condition that leads to an increase in metabolism of 1-carbon units, such as hyperthyroidism, hemolytic anemia, pregnancy, and the use of certain drugs. As a result of these factors, as well as differences in the availability of the vitamin from various food sources and the assumption that only 25 to 50% of the vitamin is absorbed, the Food and Nutrition Board has allowed a wide range of safety in setting the RDAs for folic acid (Table 5-1).

Substantial amounts of folic acid are found in liver, wheat germ, wholegrain cereals, asparagus, broccoli, lima beans, spinach, lemons, bananas, oranges, and cantaloupes. Although the vitamin is found in a wide variety of foods, cooking and storage can lead to significant losses of the vitamin, and thus it is difficult to determine the actual amount consumed in the diet.

Folic acid deficiency is common in gastrointestinal disease and in alcoholism, and among the elderly and poor whose intake of fresh fruits and vegetables is limited. As oral contraceptives and anticonvulsant agents can interfere with the utilization of the vitamin, individuals taking these drugs also have an increased need for folic acid. It has been suggested that folic acid deficiency may be the most common vitamin deficiency in the United States. It is associated with a macrocytic anemia that resembles pernicious anemia without the nervous system involvement. Gastrointestinal lesions, diarrhea, glossitis (inflammation of the tongue), and intestinal malabsorption may accompany the anemia (Wagner 1984; Burton and Foster 1988; Guthrie 1989).

Recent work has suggested that folic acid deficiency may also have significant effects on behavior. A number of studies, for example, have indicated that anticonvulsant-induced folate deficiency is associated with a higher than usual incidence of psychiatric symptoms including depression and psychotic behavior. It is impossible, however, to establish a cause-and-effect relationship from this association. Indeed, higher intakes of anticonvulsant medications, which cause greater inhibition of folate absorption, may be the cause of some symptoms.

Other studies have found that in medical patients with folic acid deficiency, psychiatric symptoms including irritability, hostility, and paranoia occur more frequently. In psychiatric patients, the same symptoms are more severe than in those with normal levels of the vitamin (Bell et al. 1990).

Finally, some studies have suggested that folic acid may lead to improvements in neuropsychological functioning and in symptoms of affective disorder. Godfrey and colleagues (1990) in a double-blind, placebo-controlled study found that treatment with methylfolate significantly improved the clinical and social recovery of both depressed and schizophrenic patients. In keeping with the view that the response of the nervous system to folate may occur slowly, the benefits of the vitamin over the placebo increased with time. Improvements in psychological functioning have not been universally documented, however, particularly when high doses of the vitamin have been used.

It should be noted that although folic acid corrects the hematological changes associated with pernicious anemia, it not only fails to alleviate the degeneration of nervous tissue but may accentuate the changes. Thus, the use of folic acid as a treatment for pernicious anemia may be potentially dangerous, allowing irreversible nervous system symptoms to progress undetected. In addition, high doses of the vitamin may have toxic consequences including irritability, excitability, sleep disturbances, and gastrointestinal upsets. Taken together, these findings indicate that care must be exercised in prescribing folic acid for the treatment of behavioral problems. Large doses can exacerbate the neurological consequences of pernicious anemia and may prove toxic (Herbert and Colman 1988; Young and Ghadirian 1989).

CONCLUSION

It is clear that vitamins play a significant role in the functioning of the nervous system and behavior. Vitamins are important in the synthesis of neurotransmitters, maintenance of neuronal integrity, myelination of neurons, and conduction of electrical potentials. Vitamin deficiencies can result in neurological and psychological problems ranging from impairments of sensory and motor functioning to overt psychotic behavior. Observations that vitamin deficiencies are associated with alterations in the central nervous system and behavior that can be reversed by vitamin administration have led to the idea that increased intake may be useful in the treatment of a variety of psychological disorders. However, as will be seen in chapter 5 on megavitamin therapy for the treatment of behavioral illnesses, the evidence for this idea is controversial.

REFERENCES

Barclay, L. L., G. E. Gibson, and J. P. Blass. 1981. The string test: An early behavioral change in thiamine deficiency. *Pharmacology, Biochemistry and Behavior* 14:153–157.

Bell, I. R., J. S. Edman, D. W. Marby, A. Satlin, T. Dreier, B. Liptzin, and J. O. Cole. 1990. Vitamin B$_{12}$ and folate status in acute geropsychiatric inpatients:

affective and cognitive characteristics of a vitamin nondeficient population. *Biological Psychiatry* 27:125–137.

Blass, J. P. 1989. Vitamin and nutritional deficiencies. In *Basic Neurochemistry: Molecular, Cellular, and Medical Aspects,* 4th ed., edited by G. J. Siegel et al., pp. 671–684. New York: Raven Press.

Burton, B. T. and W. R. Foster. 1988. *Human Nutrition.* New York: McGraw-Hill.

Dreyfus, P. M. 1988. Vitamins and neurological dysfunction. In *Nutritional Modulation of Neural Function,* edited by J. E. Morley, M. B. Sterman, and J. H. Walsh, pp. 155–164. New York: Academic Press.

Etheridge, E. W. 1972. *The Butterfly Caste: A Social History of Pellagra in the South.* Westport, CT: Greenwood.

Food and Nutrition Board, Commission on Life Sciences, National Research Council, 1989. *Recommended Dietary Allowances,* 10th ed. Washington, D.C.: National Academy Press.

Godfrey, P. S. A., B. K. Toone, M. W. P. Carney, T. G. Flynn, T. Bottiglieri, M. Laundy, J. Chanarin, and E. H. Reynolds. 1990. Enhancement of recovery from psychiatric illness by methylfolate. *Lancet* 336:392–395.

Guthrie, H. A. 1989. *Introductory Nutrition.* Boston: Times Mirror/Mosby.

Haas, R. H. 1988. Thiamin and the brain. *Annual Review of Nutrition* 8:483–515.

Henderson, L. M. 1984. Vitamin B_6. In *Present Knowledge in Nutrition,* edited by R. E. Olson et al., pp. 303–317. Washington, D.C.: Nutrition Foundation.

Herbert, V. 1984. Vitamin B_{12}. In *Present Knowledge in Nutrition,* edited by R. E. Olson et al., pp. 347–364. Washington, D.C.: Nutrition Foundation.

Herbert V. and N. Colman. 1988. Folic acid and vitamin B_{12}. In *Modern Nutrition in Health and Disease,* 7th ed., edited by M. E. Shils and V. R. Young, pp. 388–416. Philadelphia: Lea & Febiger.

Lindenbaum, J. E., B. Healton, D. G. Savage, J. C. M. Brust, T. J. Garrett, E. R. Podell, P. S. Marcell, S. P. Stabler, and R. H. Allen. 1988. Neuropsychiatric disorders caused by cobalamin deficiency in the absence of anemia or macrocytosis. *New England Journal of Medicine* 318:1720–1728.

Lipton, M. A., R. B. Mailman, and C. B. Nemeroff. 1979. Vitamins, megavitamin therapy, and the nervous system. In *Nutrition and the Brain,* vol. 3, edited by R. J. Wurtman and J. J. Wurtman, pp. 183–264. New York: Raven Press.

McCormick, D. B. 1988a. Thiamin. In *Modern Nutrition in Health and Disease,* 7th ed, edited by M. E. Shils and V. R. Young, pp. 355–361. Philadelphia: Lea & Febiger.

McCormick, D. B. 1988b. Vitamin B_6. In *Modern Nutrition in Health and Disease,* 7th ed., edited by M. E. Shils and V. R. Young, pp. 376–382. Philadelphia: Lea & Febiger.

McIlwain, H. and H. B. Bachelard. 1985. *Biochemistry and the Central Nervous System.* New York: Churchill Livingstone.

Rao, B. S. N. and C. Gopalan. 1984. Niacin. In *Present Knowledge in Nutrition,* edited by R. E. Olson et al., pp. 319–331. Washington, D.C.: Nutrition Foundation.

Robinson, C. H. and M. R. Lawler. 1982. *Normal and Therapeutic Nutrition*. New York: Macmillian.

Schaumburg, H., J. Kaplan, A. Windebank, N. Vice, S. Rasmus, D. Pleasure, and M. J. Brown. 1983. Neuropathy from pyrudoxine abuse: a new megavitamin syndrome. *New England Journal of Medicine* 309:445–448.

Tanphaichitr, V. and B. Wood. 1984. Thiamin. In *Present Knowledge in Nutrition,* edited by R. E. Olson et al., pp. 273–284. Washington, D.C.: Nutrition Foundation.

Tucker, D. M., J. G. Penland, H. H. Sandstead, D. B. Milne, D. G. Heck, and L. M. Klevay. 1990. Nutrition status and brain functioning in aging. *American Journal of Clinical Nutrition* 52:93–102.

Wagner, C. 1984. Folic acid. In *Present Knowledge in Nutrition,* edited by R. E. Olson et al., pp. 332–346, Washington, D.C.: Nutrition Foundation.

Witt, E. D. 1985. Neuroanatomical consequences of thiamine deficiency: A comparative analysis. *Alcohol and Alcoholism* 20:201–221.

Witt, E. D. and P. S. Goldman-Rakic. 1983a. Intermittent thiamine deficiency in the rhesus monkey: Part I. Progression of neurological signs and neuroanatomical lesions. *Annals of Neurology* 13:376–395.

Witt, E. D. and P. S. Goldman-Rakic. 1983b. Intermittent thiamine deficiency in the rhesus monkey: Part II. Evidence for memory loss. *Annals of Neurology* 13:396–401.

Young, S. N. and A. M. Ghadirian. 1989. Folic acid and psychopathology. *Progress in Neuro-psychopharmacology and Biological Psychiatry* 13:841–863.

4

Trace Minerals, the Central Nervous System, and Behavior

Awareness that small amounts of inorganic compounds are imperative for normal growth began over a century ago when it was recognized that iron, copper, and zinc were essential for the maturation of plants and microorganisms. Further evidence of the importance of these minerals for animal nutrition was subsequently derived from two major sources: basic studies on the effects of specially formulated diets, low or high in a specific mineral, on growth and reproduction in animals; and the realization that a number of endemic diseases of man and animals resulted from mineral deficiencies.

A large number of mineral elements are found in living cells; however, only 22 of these are considered essential. Essential minerals participate in functions that are vital for life, growth, or reproduction. When an essential mineral is removed from the diet, a deficiency syndrome develops. Improvement in growth or health occurs when these minerals are included in the diet. Normal functioning does not occur if the mineral is replaced with something else.

Essential minerals have been divided into macronutrient elements, which are present in relatively high amounts in animal tissues (greater than 0.005% body weight), and micronutrients or trace elements, which are present in extremely small amounts (less than 0.005% body weight). For humans, the essential macronutrient elements, in order of the amounts found in the body, are calcium, phosphorous, potassium, sulfur, sodium, chlorine, and magnesium. Fifteen trace elements, including iron, iodine, copper, zinc, manganese, and cobalt, presently are recognized as necessary.

Biological Functions of Minerals

Minerals serve a variety of critical functions. They are necessary constituents of a number of enzymes, such as iron in the catalases and cytochromes; of hormones, such as iodine in thyroxine; of vitamins, such as cobalt in vitamin B_{12}; and of body tissues, such as calcium and phosphorous in bone and teeth. Minerals act as catalysts or cofactors for biological reactions, they are necessary for the absorption of nutrients from the gastrointestinal tract and the uptake of nutrients by cells, and they help to maintain the acid–base balance in the body.

Minerals and the Central Nervous System

Minerals are vital for the normal functioning of the nervous system. The conduction of nerve impulses along nerve fibers depends upon the presence of sodium and potassium. As a nerve impulse travels along a nerve fiber, the permeability of the neural membrane is altered, allowing sodium to enter the cell and potassium to leave it, which leads to a temporary change in the electrical charge on the cell membrane. This charge then alters the permeability of the next portion of the nerve, which in turn changes the electrical charge. Thus, the nerve impulse is passed down the fiber. Anything that modifies the concentration of sodium and potassium in the fluids surrounding nerve cells can interfere with the transmission of nerve impulses.

When a nerve impulse reaches the axon or end terminal of the nerve fiber, it triggers the release of a chemical substance or neurotransmitter which is necessary for the transmission of information from one nerve cell to another. The release of neurotransmitter is regulated by another mineral, calcium. A decrease in calcium in the medium surrounding the axon is associated with a reduction in neurotransmitter release.

Neither sodium, potassium, nor calcium deficiency are common nutritional problems. However, sodium deficiency or hyponatremia can occur in chronic wasting diseases, such as cancer, liver disease, semistarvation, and ulcerative colitis; following major surgical treatment or extensive trauma; as a result of abnormal external loss of sodium without adequate replacement including gastrointestinal losses due to diarrhea or vomiting, and excessive sweating; and as the result of severe dietary restriction. Potassium deficiency or hypokalemia is often associated with abnormal food intake such as occurs in severe malnutrition, anorexia nervosa, chronic alcoholism, and low carbohydrate diets for weight reduction. Additionally, surgical trauma or any condition that reduces the availability of nutrients for absorption, such as prolonged vomiting and diarrhea, can lead to potassium depletion. Hypokalemia can have profound effects on neural functioning and alter neuronal connections to both smooth and cardiac muscles. Calcium deficiency or hypocalcemia has been associated with hypoparathyroidisim, diabetes, chronic renal failure, and the intake of certain drugs such as tetracycline antibiotics, which bind calcium and make it unavailable for use. Symptoms of hypocalcemia include neuromuscular irritability, seizures, intermittent paresthesias of the extremities, and choreiform movements (Robinson and Lawler 1982; Randall 1988; Avioli 1988).

It has been well established that the trace elements iron, iodine, and zinc are important for normal functioning of the nervous system. Deficiencies of these micronutritients alter central nervous system functioning and are associated with significant changes in behavior. As detailed in the following sections, iron deficiency can lead to fatigue, decreased capacity for physical activity, and deficits in cognitive performance. Both zinc and iodine deficiencies are accompanied by changes in behavior including increased irritability, fatigue, and depression. These two minerals also are crucial for normal growth of the nervous system. Deficiencies of zinc and iodine during neonatal development result in permanent alterations in neuronal structure and functioning which have been associated with severe mental retardation.

IRON

Iron is found in all cells and is crucial for many biochemical reactions in the body. Its primary role is to facilitate the transfer of oxygen and carbon dioxide from one tissue to another. Most of the body's iron is found in hemoglobin, the principal component of red blood cells. Hemoglobin combines with oxygen in the lungs and releases oxygen in the tissues whenever a need exists. Hemoglobin also aids in the return of carbon dioxide from tissues to the lungs. In muscle tissue, oxygen is taken up by another iron-protein complex, myoglobin, which serves as a temporary oxygen acceptor and reservoir. In addition to its role in oxygen transport, iron is a structural component of or a cofactor for a number of enzymes essential in oxidative metabolism, DNA synthesis, and neurotransmitter synthesis and degradation (Hallberg 1984; Fairbanks and Beutler 1988; Burton and Foster 1988; Guthrie 1989).

Requirements and Dietary Sources

The total amount of iron in the body varies as a function of a number of factors including gender, weight, hemoglobin concentration, and size of the organs that store iron. The average body content of iron in adult males is approximately 50 mg per kilogram of body weight, or a total of 3,500 mg; and in adult females, 35 mg per kilogram of body weight, or a total of 2,300 mg. Over two-thirds of the iron in the body is essential for normal body functioning and is contained either in hemoglobin, myoglobin, and tissue enzymes or in blood (bound to the protein transferrin). The remaining one-third is stored in the liver, spleen, and bone marrow as ferritin, a soluble iron complex, or hemosiderin, an insoluble iron-protein complex (Hallberg 1984; Fairbanks and Beutler 1988; Guthrie 1989).

It has been estimated that the normal adult male must assimilate about 1 mg of iron a day to balance the natural losses that occur via the gastrointestinal tract, urinary system, and skin. As a result of the blood lost in menstruation, women must absorb from 1.4 to 2.2 mg of iron a day. Since approximately 10% of the iron in food is absorbed, the desired daily iron intake for adult men and women ranges from 10 to 20 mg (Table 4-1).

Pregnant women require supplemental iron to make up for normal losses, the increased demand due to the enlargement in red cell mass that accompanies pregnancy, and the requirements of the fetus and placenta. These increased needs develop primarily during the last half of pregnancy, when the fetus is growing most rapidly and iron requirements can reach 7 to 8 mg a day. As this amount cannot be supplied by diet alone, iron stores in the body are used to prevent the development of iron deficiency. Total iron requirements during pregnancy are estimated to be approximately 1,000 mg; that is, 800 mg from dietary sources and 200 mg from body stores. The recommended daily allowance for iron during pregnancy is 30 mg per day.

Liver is the best dietary source for iron: however, it is not a popular food

TABLE 4-1. Daily Recommended Dietary Allowances for Iron, Zinc, and Iodine

Category	Age (years) or Condition	Iron (mg)	Zinc (mg)	Iodine (ug)
Infants	0.0–0.5	6	5	40
	0.5–1.0	10	5	50
Children	1–3	10	10	70
	4–6	10	10	90
	7–10	10	10	120
Males	11–14	12	15	150
	15–18	12	15	150
	19–24	10	15	150
	25–50	10	15	150
	51+	10	15	150
Females	11–14	15	12	150
	15–18	15	12	150
	19–24	15	12	150
	25–50	15	12	150
	51+	10	12	150
Pregnant women		30	15	175
Lactating women	First 6 months	15	19	200
	Second 6 months	15	16	200

Food and Nutrition Board; National Research Council (1989).

TABLE 4-2. Iron Content of Selected Foods (per serving)

Food	Serving	Iron (mg)
Beef liver	3 oz	5.3
Ground beef	3 oz	2.8
Cornflakes	8 oz	1.8
Baked potato	1 medium	1.8
Tuna fish	3 oz	1.6
Green peas	4 oz	1.2
Whole-wheat bread	1 slice	1.0
Egg, fried	1 medium	1.0
Rice	1 oz, dried	0.9
Chicken	3 oz	0.9
Green beans	4 oz	0.8
Raisins	1 oz	0.6
Tomatoes	1 medium	0.6
Cheddar cheese	1 oz	0.2

for most Americans and has recently fallen into disfavor because of its high cholesterol content. Other reasonable sources of iron include lean meats, shellfish, poultry, egg yolks, green leafy vegetables, whole-grain cereals, and fruits (Table 4-2).

The absorption of iron from food is influenced by a variety of factors, and thus the iron content of a food does not always provide a true picture of the mineral's availability. For example, absorption of iron is enhanced when it takes place in an acidic solution. For example, ascorbic acid, by forming a soluble complex with iron, also results in enhanced absorption of the micronutrient. Additionally, absorption of iron from foods of plant origin (e.g., wheat, corn, beans) is more efficient when these foods are consumed with meats than when eaten alone. Conversely, excesses of fiber, phytic acid (an organic acid found in some whole-grain cereals), or oxalic acid (an organic acid found in some leafy green vegetables, such as spinach and kale) impair iron absorption because they combine with iron to form insoluble compounds that pass through the intestinal tract without being absorbed. Drinking tea or coffee with a meal decreases iron absorption due to the presence of iron-binding substances called polyphenols in these beverages.

Cooking procedures also influence iron availability. Iron is lost from foods if they are cooked in large amounts of water which is subsequently discarded. In contrast, the use of cast-iron cookware can add to daily iron intake.

Finally, an individual's iron status alters iron absorption. Iron-deficient individuals are more efficient in absorbing iron than nondeficient individuals (Finch and Cook 1984; Hallberg 1984; Burton and Foster 1988; Fairbanks and Beutler 1988; Guthrie 1989).

Iron Deficiency

Iron deficiency is the most common nutritional deficiency in the world. Worldwide, it is estimated to affect hundreds of millions of individuals. In North America, iron deficiency most frequently occurs in children 1 to 3 years of age, in adolescent males, and in females during their childbearing years. Data collected by the U.S. Department of Agriculture reveal that 3% to 12% of 11- to 14-year-old boys and 2.5% to 14% of females over the age of 11 have impaired iron status (Finch and Cook 1984; Guthrie 1989).

Iron deficiency is the outcome of one or more factors: inadequate diet, impaired absorption, blood loss, or frequent pregnancies in rapid succession. Because the body is very efficient in conserving iron supplies, an iron-poor diet is rarely the primary cause of deficiency in adults. The two most common causes of the deficiency in adults in the United States are excessive blood loss due to gastrointestinal tumors or ulcers, and increased menstrual bleeding.

In contrast to adults, infants frequently develop iron deficiency as a result of inadequate dietary intake. The need for iron in relation to body size and food intake is greater during infancy than at any other time of life. Neither breast milk nor cow's milk can meet the infant's requirement of 6 to 15 mg of iron a day. If the mother consumes an adequate diet during pregnancy, the infant will have sufficient iron stores for the first three months of life. If the mother's iron intake is not adequate, however, the infant may become iron-deficient, particularly if fed only milk after 4 to 6 months of age. Iron deficiency can also develop in children during periods of rapid growth when intake fails to meet needs. Moderate iron-deficiency anemia has been documented in approximately 25% of infants and young children hospitalized in the United States. Finally, a number of conditions, such as intestinal parasites, geophagia (clay eating), and decreased intestinal absorption of iron, can exacerbate the symptoms of iron deficiency (Burton and Foster 1988; Fairbanks and Beutler 1988).

In iron deficiency, a gradual and well-defined sequence of events occurs, eventually leading to iron-deficiency anemia. The first stage is depletion of iron stores and is evidenced by a decrease in the concentration of serum ferritin. During the second stage, there is a reduction in transport iron and an increase in iron absorption. In the final stage, anemia develops when the supply of transport iron decreases sufficiently to limit the concentration of hemoglobin. Severe iron-deficiency anemia is characterized by hypochromia and microcytosis of the red blood cells. Red blood cells become small and pale and have a reduced hemoglobin content and oxygen-carrying capacity. These changes reflect unfavorably on most body functions (Finch and Cook 1984; Dallman 1986).

Clinically, the symptoms of iron-deficiency anemia include weakness, fatigue, difficulty breathing during exercise, headache, and palpitations.

Gastrointestinal complaints including nausea, constipation or diarrhea, abnormal appetite, and epigastric distress are also common. The skin and mucous membranes are pale in proportion to the reduction in circulating hemoglobin. Nails may become pale, thin, brittle, longitudinally ridged, and then concave or spoon-shaped. Coldness and paresthesia of the hands and feet are also common.

IRON DEFICIENCY AND BEHAVIOR

Descriptions of the behavioral correlates of iron-deficiency anemia in both adults and children frequently include irritability, shortened attention span, pica, and fatigue. A number of studies have also indicated that productivity of individuals engaged in hard physical labor is reduced in the presence of iron deficiency (Edgerton et al. 1982; Finch and Cook 1984; Fairbanks and Beutler 1988).

During the last decade, more detailed information about the behavioral effects of iron deficiency has come from research on infants and young children. Studies in infants have used the Bailey Scales of Infant Development which measure developmental abilities during the first 24 months of life. Iron-deficient infants generally score lower on the Bailey Scale than nondeficient infants. For example, Lozoff and colleagues (1982a, 1982b, 1982c) working in Guatemala reported that developmental test scores of anemic infants aged 6 to 24 months were significantly lower than those of nonanemic control infants. Moreover, anemic infants were less active, persistent, reactive, and responsive, and more tense and fearful, than nonanemic infants. Six to eight days of oral iron therapy did not reverse the behavioral deficits of the anemic infants. Thus, the deficits of the anemic group cannot be unequivocally attributed to a lack of iron. However, no significant differences were found between the deficient and nondeficient infants in birth histories, socioeconomic level, or general nutritional condition that might otherwise explain the lower developmental test scores of the anemic babies.

In a subsequent study, Walter, Kovalskys, and Stekel (1983) found that 15 days of oral iron therapy for 15-month-old infants with iron-deficient anemia did lead to significant improvement in cooperativeness and attention span and better performance on developmental tests. The differences in the effectiveness of iron therapy between this study and that of Lozoff and colleagues suggest that more than 6 to 8 days of iron replacement may be necessary to reverse the detrimental consequences of anemia.

Further evidence of the deleterious effects of iron deficiency on behavior comes from studies conducted by Pollitt and co-workers in Cambridge, Massachusetts, of mildly iron-deficient 3- to 6-year-old children (Pollitt et al. 1982; Pollitt, Leibel, and Greenfield 1983). Iron-deficient and nondeficient children were given the Stanford-Binet Intelligence Scale, as well as a behavioral test battery designed to study attention, learning, and memory. IQ scores did not differ as a function of iron status. However, deficient children took more trials to learn discrimination tasks and made more errors on simple memory tasks than nondeficient children. After 12 weeks of oral iron therapy, differences between the two groups were no longer observed. Pollitt and colleagues hypothesized that although iron deficiency does not affect innate intelligence, it can interfere with a child's ability to pay attention to relevant stimuli and thus potentially impair both learning and memory.

In further work in Guatemala, Pollitt (1987) found that iron-deficient 3- to 6-year-olds performed less well on discrimination tasks than nondeficient children. Iron-replacement therapy did not lead to a significant improvement in the children's performance, however, suggesting that they may have been suffering from other nutritional or health-related problems.

Three recent studies indicate that iron deficiency may also alter educational achievement and efficiency in problem solving in school-age children (Pollitt et al. 1985; Pollitt and Metallinos-Katsaras 1990). In a study in Central Java, iron-deficient children had significantly lower achievement scores on tests of math, biology, social sciences, and language than did nondeficient children. Anemic children treated with iron for five months showed significantly greater improvements in achievement tests scores than anemic children given a placebo. A second study in Egypt using a discrimination task confirmed the adverse effects of iron deficiency on cognitive behavior. Iron-deficient children performed more slowly and made more errors on a discrimination task than their nondeficient counterparts. Iron replacement therapy again led to significant improvements in performance (Pollitt et al. 1985).

A final study conducted in Thailand assessed the effects of 16 weeks of iron supplementation on IQ and educational achievement in 9- to 11-year-old children. Pollitt and colleagues found that iron-replete children achieved significantly higher scores on IQ tests and tests of language abilities than iron-deficient children (Pollitt and Metallinos-Katsaras 1990).

Research on the relationship between iron status and behavior leads to the following conclusions: iron deficiency is associated with less than optimal behavior in infants and children; and iron-replacement therapy in preschool and school-aged children with iron deficiency anemia leads to improvement in educational achievements (Pollitt and Metallinos-Katsaras 1990).

IRON AND THE CENTRAL NERVOUS SYSTEM

Research employing experimental animals has demonstrated that iron deficiency can alter the functioning of the central nervous system. Iron is a cofactor for the enzymes tyrosine hydroxylase and tryptophan hydroxylase, which are essential for the synthesis of the neurotransmitters dopamine, norepinephrine, and serotonin. Iron deficiency may thus modify production of these neurotransmitters. Further, iron is involved in several steps in the degradation of these transmitters.

Although iron deficiency may influence the synthesis and breakdown of neurotransmitters, its most profound effect is on the binding of these substances to postsynaptic receptor sites. In studies with rats, evidence has accumulated that iron deficiency is associated with a decrease in both dopamine and serotonin receptor binding sites. These abnormalities in binding are corrected by feeding animals an iron-rich diet. It has been suggested that some of the behavioral alterations observed in iron deficiency may be manifestations of changes in neurotransmitter receptor binding (Tucker and Sandstead 1982; Youdim et al. 1982; Dallman 1986).

It seems clear that iron deficiency is associated with deficits in brain functioning and cognitive behavior. This conclusion represents a major public health concern, not only in underdeveloped countries but also in the United States, where the prevalence of iron deficiency and anemia is approximately 4% among young children (Pollitt 1987).

ZINC

Zinc is essential for all living organisms. In humans, zinc is a component of a large number of enzymes that catalyze vital metabolic reactions. Because it facilitates the synthesis of DNA and RNA and thus participates in protein metabolism, zinc is also essential for human development. Zinc is particularly important in protein metabolism in tissues that undergo rapid turnover such as the gastrointestinal tract, taste buds, and skin. The mineral also helps promote the release of vitamin A from its storage site in the liver, fosters wound healing, and enhances the actions of a number of hormones (Robinson and Lawler 1982; Sandstead and Evans 1984; Burton and Foster 1988).

Requirements and Dietary Sources

The total amount of zinc in the human body is 2 to 3 g, with three-fourths of this amount concentrated in the skeleton. High concentrations of zinc are also found in the eyes, skin, and male reproductive system (Robinson and Lawler 1982; Guthrie 1989).

The recommended dietary allowance for zinc is 5 mg a day for infants, 10 mg a day for children from the ages of 1 to 11 years, 12 to 15 mg a day for adolescents and adults, and 15 to 19 mg a day for pregnant and lactating women (Table 4-1). Foods that help to meet these requirements include seafood, liver, red meat, and nuts (Table 4-3). Legumes and whole-grain products can also contribute significant amounts of zinc to the diet.

TABLE 4-3. Zinc Content of Selected Foods (per serving)

Food	Serving	Zinc (mg)
Oysters	4 oz	8.2
Roast beef	3 oz	5.3
Ground beef	3 oz	3.8
Pork	3 oz	3.2
Chicken	3 oz	2.5
Beans	8 oz dried (cooked)	1.8
Lima beans	4 oz	1.7
Peanut butter	2 T	1.0
Tuna fish	3 oz	0.9
Whole milk	8 oz	0.9
Cheddar cheese	1 oz	0.9
Green peas	4 oz	0.7
Corn, canned	4 oz	0.4
Green beans	4 oz	0.2
Banana	1 medium	0.2
Apple	1 medium	0.1

However, these foods also contain compounds such as fiber, phytates, and oxalates which interfere with intestinal absorption of zinc. Fruits and vegetables are low in zinc. The relatively minimal amounts of zinc in plant foods make zinc deficiency a serious concern for individuals eating a strictly vegetarian diet (Freeland-Graves et al. 1980; Moser-Veillon 1990).

Zinc Deficiency

EXPERIMENTAL ANIMALS

The essential nature of zinc for growth and development in animals has been recognized for over 50 years. In adult animals, zinc deficiency is characterized by depressed gonadal function, skin lesions, impaired wound healing, and suppressed immune responses. In rats, a zinc-deficient diet rapidly leads to anorexia characterized by large fluctuations in daily food intake and weight loss (Chesters and Quarterman 1970; Wallwork, Fosmire, and Sandstead 1981).

Teratogenic Effects. Teratogenesis is the term for abnormal fetal development resulting from toxic agents or the lack of critical nutrients. In 1966, Hurley and Swenerton discovered that maternal zinc deficiency had profound teratogenic effects in rats (Hurley and Swenerton 1966). In rats and other mammals, zinc deficiency during gestation or lactation adversely affects growth, physical development, and the subsequent behavior of the offspring. Pups of rats made zinc-deficient for even short periods of time during pregnancy frequently develop major congenital malformations involving the skeleton, heart, eyes, gastrointestinal tract, and lungs.

Development of the central nervous system is particularly impaired by zinc deficiency. In rats, severe prenatal zinc deficiency is associated with neural tube defects, hydrocephaly, exencephaly, and anencephaly (Keen and Hurley 1987; Record 1987). Zinc deficiency during the last trimester of gestation or during the early postnatal period is associated with significant reductions in brain weight and brain levels of DNA, RNA, and protein. Postnatal zinc deficiency may also impair the growth and biochemical maturation of the hippocampus and cerebellum. In general, zinc deficiency during the prenatal or early postnatal periods appears to delay CNS development by seriously impairing the process of mitosis (Sandstead, Gillespie, and Brady 1972; McKenzie, Fosmire, and Sandstead 1975; Dvergsten et al. 1983; Dreosti 1984).

Zinc deficiency during prenatal or early postnatal development also alters later behavior. Adult rats and monkeys with such histories generally are less active, more susceptible to stress and ulcer formation, and more aggressive than their normal counterparts. Moreover, higher brain functions, including both short-term and long-term memory, are adversely affected. It has been hypothesized that the deficits observed in long-term memory may be related to the impairments in hippocampal maturation resulting from early zinc deficiency (Halas, Heinrich, and Sandstead 1979; Halas 1983; Strobel and Sandstead 1984).

HUMANS

Zinc deficiency in humans is relatively prevalent throughout the world. Symptoms of severe zinc deficiency were first documented in the early 1960s in Iran and Egypt. Subsequently, this deficiency has been reported as a significant health problem in Turkey, Portugal, Morocco, and Yugoslavia. In the United States, mild to moderate zinc deficiency has been associated with strict vegetarian diets, alcoholism, liver and renal disease, parenteral nutrition, pregnancy and lactation, and old age (Prasad 1985; Burton and Foster 1988). In humans, as in experimental animals, an adequate supply of dietary zinc is particularly important during periods of rapid growth and development.

Acrodermatitis Enteropathica (AE). This rare genetic disorder is inherited as an autosomal recessive characteristic and leads to functional zinc deficiency. The fundamental defect is an inability to absorb zinc from the gastrointestinal tract due to binding (chelation) of the metal by an oligopeptide. In normal infants, this peptide is destroyed by an enzyme secreted in the intestinal lining. Infants with AE fail to produce this enzyme, so zinc is bound to the oligopeptide, preventing absorption and leading to a functional deficiency. Because the oligopeptide is not produced in the digestion of human milk, AE is not observed before weaning from breast milk (Prasad 1988; Walling, Householder, and Walling 1989).

When weaned from breast milk, a previously healthy infant with AE develops severe gastrointestinal problems including diarrhea and malabsorption which can lead to malnutrition. Clinically, AE is also characterized by skin and bowel lesions, an increased susceptibility to infections, growth retardation, and hypogonadism (Prasad 1988).

Alterations in mood and behavior are a common feature of AE. Children with the disease are generally lethargic and irritable, and rarely smile or display an interest in their environment. They may also fail to exhibit normal behavioral development and suffer from emotional disorders, tremors, and cerebellar ataxia (Prasad 1988; Walling, Householder, and Walling 1989).

If undiagnosed and untreated, AE is often fatal, with death resulting from infection and/or malnutrition. Zinc supplementation rapidly reverses the symptoms of acrodermatitis enteropathica.

Nutritional Zinc Deficiency. Severe zinc deficiency was first described by Prasad and colleagues in a group of young Egyptian and Iranian men suffering from growth retardation and hypogonadism (Prasad, Halsted, and Nadimi 1961; Prasad 1988). Many of these men looked like young adolescent boys although they were actually in their early twenties. In addition to growth retardation and delayed sexual maturation, they displayed anemia, dermatitis, impaired liver function, anorexia, and neurosensory and behavioral abnormalities. The majority came from the lowest socioeconomic strata of their villages and lived on diets consisting mainly of unleavened wheat bread and vegetables. Meat and dairy products were rarely available. In Iran, geophagia, which can impair zinc absorption, and in Egypt, parasitic infections, which can result in abnormal zinc losses from the body, were common among the young men. The diagnosis of zinc deficiency was confirmed by measurements of plasma, red blood cells, and hair concentrations of the mineral. The effects of zinc supplementation on these young men's symptoms was striking. After several months of supplementation, many of the men had grown several inches, gained substantial weight, displayed accelerated sexual maturation, and demonstrated improvements in anemia, liver functioning, and dermatological symptoms (Prasad 1985, 1988).

Behaviorally, nutritional zinc deficiency is characterized by irritability, emotional disorders, tremors, and occasional cerebellar ataxia with problems of balance and fine motor control. Neurosensory complications including abnormal adaptation to darkness and other visual problems may accompany severe deficiency.

Abnormalities in taste and smell are also common in zinc-deficient patients. A decreased sense of taste (hypogeusia) and smell (hyposmia) have been observed in individuals suffering from low dietary intake of zinc, liver disease, malabsorption syndrome, and chronic uremia. For example, patients with chronic renal failure frequently display a decreased ability to detect salty, sweet, bitter, and sour tastes. Supplementing the diet of these patients with zinc improves their ability to detect all but sour tastes. At present, the mechanisms by which zinc affects taste and smell have not been clearly defined; however, the data suggest that taste and smell receptors may be altered. In zinc-deficient patients, reversible alterations in the architecture of the taste buds have been demonstrated using both light and electron microscopy (Henkin et al. 1982; Prasad 1985).

Potential Teratogenic Effects. A direct relationship between zinc deficiency and abnormal development of the CNS has not been established in humans. Nevertheless, current evidence suggests that the human fetus is no less vulnerable to the teratogenic effects of zinc depletion than the offspring of other species (Dreosti 1984). Support for this hypothesis comes from observations that in regions where zinc deficiency is prevalent, there is a high incidence of anencephaly and other developmental CNS defects. Additional evidence of the teratogenic potential of zinc deficiency comes from studies that examined the outcome of pregnancies in women with acrodermatitis enteropathica prior to the recognition of the therapeutic value of zinc. In three women with AE, seven pregnancies resulted in one spontaneous abortion, and two infants were born with major congenital defects similar to the CNS and skeletal anomalies seen in the offspring of zinc-deficient rats. This percentage of abnormal births (43%) greatly exceeds that found in normal populations (<4%). Finally, studies in Sweden investigating the relationship between maternal zinc levels and pregnancy outcomes have demonstrated that women with low serum zinc levels are significantly more likely to have abnormal deliveries and infants with congenital malformations than women with higher zinc levels (Apgar 1985; Keen and Hurley 1987).

It recently has been recognized that the North American diet may not provide optimal amounts of zinc. Recent analyses of typical diets in the United States reveal that the average zinc content is slightly below the RDA at 9.0 mg a day for women and 14.3 mg a day for men. Marginal zinc deficiency may be associated with hypoguesia, delayed wound healing, and growth failure, all of which are common in a significant proportion of the population. Moreover, as maternal zinc deficiency has been associated with low birth weight infants and is a suggested cause of abnormalities in CNS development, marginal zinc deficiency during pregnancy should be considered a serious problem (Burton and Foster 1988; Guthrie 1989; Moser-Veillon 1990).

IODINE

Iodine is an indispensable component of the thyroid hormones triiodothyronine (T_3) and tetraiodothyronine (T_4 or thyroxine), which regulate the rate of oxidation within the cells and thereby influence physiological and mental development, the functioning of nervous and muscle tissue, and energy metabolism. Iodine is particularly important during fetal development and is critical for normal maturation of the central nervous system (Robinson and Lawler 1982: Burton and Foster 1988; Stanbury 1988).

Requirements and Dietary Sources

Approximately three-quarters of the 15 to 25 mg of iodine in the body is concentrated in the thyroid gland with the remainder found in the salivary and mammary glands, gastric mucosa, and kidneys. The recommended dietary allowances for iodine are 40 to 50 ug/day for infants, 70 to 120 ug/day for children up to 10 years of age, and 150 ug/day for adolescents and adults. The RDAs for pregnant and lactating women are 175 and 200 ug, respectively (see Table 4-1).

The iodine content of both plant and animal foods depends primarily on the iodine content of the soil and therefore is highly variable. Soils from areas near ocean waters, which have a high concentration of iodine, typically contain large amounts of iodine. In contrast, mountainous parts of the world, including the Andes, Alps, Pyrenees, and Himalayas, have soils from which most of the iodine has been removed by the natural forces of glaciation, weathering, and erosion. Thus, plants or animals raised on iodine-rich soils near the seacoast have more iodine than those raised on iodine-poor soils commonly found in mountainous and inland regions.

Saltwater fish, shellfish, and seaweed are important sources of iodine. These foods are not frequently consumed in large quantities, however, and are unavailable or expensive in areas where the iodine content of the soil is low.

For most people in the United States, iodized salt represents the major source of dietary iodine. In this country, iodized salt contains 0.01% potassium iodine or 76 ug of iodine per g. Assuming that the average adult uses 6 to 6.5 g of salt a day, daily iodine intake from salt is 450 to 500 ug or approximately three times the RDA (Robinson and Lawler 1982; Burton and Foster 1988; Guthrie 1989).

Metabolism and Physiology

Iodine is consumed in foods as either inorganic iodine or part of an organic compound from which it must be freed for use by the body. Inorganic iodine and iodine freed from organic compounds are reduced to iodide and rapidly absorbed from the small intestine. The effectiveness of iodide absorption partly depends on the level of circulating thyroid hormones, with low levels enhancing absorption. The majority of iodide in the circulation is taken up by the thyroid gland and used in the production of thyroid hormones. The remainder is taken up by the kidney and excreted in the urine.

Iodide taken up or "trapped" by the thyroid gland is oxidized to iodine and then combined with the amino acid tyrosine to be stored as part of thyroglobulin, a glycoprotein. When blood levels of thyroid hormones become low, nerve cells in the hypothalamus secrete thyrotropin-releasing hormone (TRH), which travels via the hypophyseal portal blood system to the pituitary gland where it stimulates the release of thyroid-stimulating hormone (TSH). TSH then travels to the thyroid gland and activates an enzyme that breaks down thyroglobulin into compounds containing either one or two molecules of iodine. These molecules are combined to form the thyroid hormones T_3, with three molecules of iodine, or T_4, with four molecules. The hormones then travel to each cell in the body to regulate cellular respiration (Figure 4-1).

Iodine Deficiency

EXPERIMENTAL ANIMALS

Iodine deficiency has profound effects on the development of the central nervous system in mammalian species. Sheep have been used extensively for studies of the developmental consequences of iodine deficiency be-

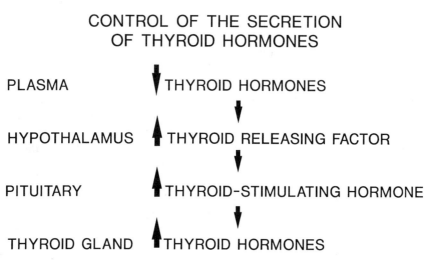

CONTROL OF THE SECRETION
OF THYROID HORMONES

PLASMA   THYROID HORMONES

HYPOTHALAMUS   THYROID RELEASING FACTOR

PITUITARY   THYROID-STIMULATING HORMONE

THYROID GLAND   THYROID HORMONES

Figure 4-1. Regulation of thyroid hormone secretion. When plasma levels of the thyroid hormones T_3 and T_4 decrease, the hypothalamus increases production of thyrotropin-releasing hormone which travels in the hypophyseal portal blood system to the pituitary and stimulates production of thyroid-stimulating hormone (TSH). TSH is transported to the thyroid gland where it stimulates T_3 and T_4 formation.

cause they are convenient models for the study of maternal–fetal relationships. Severe iodine deficiency in ewes produces goiter, low plasma T_4 and T_3 levels, and elevated TSH levels. When deficient ewes are mated, they experience a significantly higher rate of spontaneous abortions and stillbirths than nondeficient animals. Further, the deficiency severely affects the development of the remaining fetuses, which display goiter, reduced levels of thyroid hormones, decreased growth rates, delayed bone maturation, and anomalies in heart and lung development. Brain development also is severely altered by iodine deficiency. Lowered brain weights and levels of DNA are noted by day 70 of gestation. As the fetuses mature, morphological abnormalities in the cerebral hemispheres and cerebellum and retarded myelination of neurons in the cerebral hemispheres and brain stem are observed (Hetzel and Mano 1989).

Alterations in brain development similar to those found in sheep have been detected in rats born to iodine-deficient dams. Additionally, fetal iodine deficiency in rats decreases blood flow to the cerebral cortex, reduces the number of cortical neurons, leads to a decline in dendritic branching, and decreases synaptic connections among cells of the CNS. Behaviorally, rats suffering from fetal iodine deficiency display problems of coordination and impairments in learning to perform tasks (Hetzel and Mano 1989).

HUMANS

Iodine deficiency in the United States and other western countries has virtually been eliminated by the use of iodized salt and the availability of food from a variety of geographical areas. However, iodine deficiency continues to be a major public health problem in parts of the world characterized by iodine-poor soil and primitive food transportation systems. It has been estimated that as many as 800 million people live in iodine-deficient environments and are at risk for iodine deficiency. The consequences are obvious in mountainous areas in the Himalayas, Andes, and China, as well as in frequently flooded inland regions of India and Bangladesh (Hetzel and Dunn 1989; Hetzel and Mano 1989).

In adults, the absence of sufficient dietary iodine leads to the depletion of thyroid iodine stores and thereby limits the production of thyroid hormones. A decrease in plasma T_3 and T_4 levels triggers the secretion of TSH, which causes the cells of the thyroid gland to increase in both size and number. The enlarged thyroid gland is more efficient at trapping circulating iodide, which may partly compensate for the lack of dietary iodine. This enlargement of the thyroid gland is called goiter and is prevalent in parts of the world where iodine intake is below 50 ug/day. As many as 200 million people in the world may suffer from goiter (Stanbury 1977; Hetzel and Dunn 1989).

While iodine deficiency plays the primary role in the development of goiter, certain foods contain substances called goiterogens that interfere with the production of the thyroid hormones. Many of these foods (e.g., cassava, maize, bamboo shoots, millet, and sweet potatoes) are dietary staples in areas of the world where iodine deficiency is prevalent, and thus contribute to goiter formation (Stanbury 1977; Hetzel and Dunn 1989).

In addition to leading to goiter, iodine deficiency is associated with a variety of symptoms indicative of insufficient thyroid hormone synthesis. Individuals with severely depressed levels of the hormones typically display cold intolerance, weight gain, decreased basal metabolic rate, enlargement of the tongue, brittle hair and nails, constipation, and reduced cardiac functioning (Smith 1989).

Behavioral symptoms include slowed reflexes, problems with coordination, slurred speech, fatigue, apathy, depression, and impairments in memory. It has been suggested that iodine deficiency may contribute to the high degree of apathy and decreased initiative observed in some communities in northern India (Hetzel and Dunn 1989; Smith 1989).

Fetal Development. Severe endemic goiter is almost always accompanied by certain distinctive characteristics. Individuals displaying this set of characteristics are called "cretins." They are clearly recognized as being different from the remainder of the population by their short stature, mental deficiency, and problems of coordination and gait, and they frequently are deaf-mute. Endemic cretinism, which occurs when iodine intake is below 25 ug/day, remains prevalent in many parts of the world; for example, in areas of India, Indonesia, and China, up to 10% of the population may suffer from the disorder (Stanbury 1977; Hetzel and Dunn 1989).

Two subtypes of cretinism have been distinguished: neurological and myxedematous. Individuals with neurological cretinism, which is more common, typically are deaf-mute and display problems of movement and gait, as well as spastic neurological signs. In comparison, individuals with myxedematous cretinism tend to be shorter in stature and not to be deaf or mute, and display the symptoms of hypothyroidism. The two subtypes of cretinism tend to predominate in different geographical areas, but they are not mutually exclusive. Mixed forms of cretinism with both neurological and myxedematous features do occur (Stanbury 1977; Hetzel and Dunn 1989).

The administration of iodine does little to reverse the symptoms of established cretinism. When iodine prophylaxis is introduced into a community, however, new cases of endemic cretinism are rarely observed. These observations provide strong evidence that iodine deficiency during fetal development is the principal cause of endemic cretinism. It has been hypothesized that iodine deficiency during the early fetal period results in the neurological form of cretinism, and iodine deficiency during late fetal and postnatal periods leads to myxedematous cretinism.

Iodine readily crosses the placenta. If the mother is deficient, however, the fetus will be denied iodine because the mother's need for the mineral takes precedence. During the nursing period, the maternal thyroid gland traps available plasma iodine and thereby limits the amount in breast milk. The lack of both prenatal and postnatal iodine can severely impair the production of the thyroid hormones that are essential for normal brain development (Stanbury 1977; Hetzel, Chavedej, and Potter 1988).

Examination of the brains of individuals with cretinism have revealed widespread atrophy of the cerebral cortex and subcortical areas of the brain stem (Hetzel, Chavedej, and Potter 1988).

In communities where cretinism is common, a substantial proportion of the population may have lesser degrees of retardation as a result of early iodine deficiency. These individuals are not so readily identifiable because they lack the physical characteristics or developmental impairments of cretinism. In support of this idea, Greene (1977) working in rural Ecuador found that in addition to the 5.7% of the adult population who were deaf-mute cretins, another 17.4% of the population displayed more moderate neurological deficits and behavioral limitations. Further, Stanbury and colleagues working in the same area of Ecuador found that children whose mothers had received iodized oil prior to or during pregnancy did substantially better on tests of intellectual functioning than age- and sex-matched children whose mothers did not receive iodine (Stanbury 1977). The results of these studies suggest that early iodine deficiency leads to a continuum of neurological and behavioral problems that extend all the way from severe classic cretinism to milder forms of mental retardation. Iodine may thus have a profound impact on the life of a community. The presence of a large subgroup of people who are mildly to moderately retarded in their physical skills and intellectual abilities could be devastating to the social and economic development of a village community (Stanbury 1977).

If given in time, before permanent changes occur in the thyroid gland, iodine replacement can reverse goiter formation and other symptoms of iodine deficiency and, if given to women prior to conception, can prevent the development of cretinism. Within the last decade, control programs have been initiated in many parts of the world. Iodized salt, administration of iodized oil, and the addition of iodine to the drinking water are all presently being employed. However, there continues to be a wide gap between knowledge of methods of eliminating the deficiency and the application of this knowledge in developing countries. Recent initiatives endorsed by the World Health Organization and the United Nations encourage the hope that substantial progress in the prevention of iodine deficiency will be made in the next decade (Stanbury 1988; Hetzel and Dunn 1989).

CONCLUSION

The intake of essential minerals is as crucial for normal brain development and functioning as the intake of sufficient protein, energy, and vitamins. In adults, mineral deficiencies can lead to a variety of alterations in behavior including irritability, reduced attention span, fatigue, memory impairments, and depression. These consequences can be rapidly reversed by providing sufficient quantities of the mineral in the diet. The deleterious effects of mineral deficiencies unfortunately are not reversible if the deficiency occurs during a critical stage of brain development. Maternal deficiencies of both zinc and iodine during fetal development can be teratogenic, and lead to permanent impairments in brain function and behavior.

Because mineral deficiencies are among the most common nutritional problems, serious consideration must be given to ways to combat these deficiencies. Better methods of food distribution, more accurate and frequent determinations of nutrient intake, and improved education in nutrition may help alleviate these problems.

REFERENCES

Apgar, J. 1985. Zinc and reproduction. *Annual Review of Nutrition* 5:43–68.

Avioli, L. V. 1988. Calcium and phosphorous. In *Modern Nutrition in Health and Disease,* 7th ed., ed. M. E. Shils and V. R. Young, pp. 142–158, Philadelphia: Lea & Febiger.

Burton, B. T. and W. R. Foster. 1988. *Human Nutrition.* New York: McGraw-Hill.

Chesters, J. K. and J. Quarterman. 1970. Effects of zinc deficiency on food intake and feeding patterns of rats. *British Journal of Nutrition* 24:1061–1069.

Dallman, P. R. 1986. Biochemical basis for the manifestations of iron deficiency. *Annual Review of Nutrition* 6:13–40.

Dreosti, I. E. 1984. Zinc in the central nervous system: The emerging interactions. In *The Neurobiology of Zinc: Physiochemistry, Anatomy and Techniques,* ed. C. J. Fredrickson, G. A. Howell, and E. J. Kasarskis, pp. 1–26. New York: Alan R. Liss.

Dvergsten, C. L., G. J. Fosmire, D. A. Ollerich, and H. H. Sandstead. 1983. Alterations in the postnatal development of the cerebellar cortex due to zinc deficiency. I: Impaired acquisition of granule cells. *Brain Research* 271:217–226.

Edgerton V. R., Y. Ohira, G. W. Gardner, and B. Senewiratne. 1982. Effects of iron-deficiency anemia on voluntary activities in rats and humans. In *Iron Defi-*

ciency: Brain Biochemistry and Behavior, ed. E. Pollitt and R. L. Liebel, pp. 141–160. New York: Raven Press.

Fairbanks, V. F. and E. Beutler. 1988. Iron. In *Modern Nutrition in Health and Disease*, 7th ed., ed. M. E. Shils and V. R. Young, pp. 193–226. Philadelphia: Lea & Febiger.

Finch, C. A. and J. D. Cook. 1984. Iron deficiency. *American Journal of Clinical Nutrition* 39:471–477.

Food and Nutrition Board, Commission on Life Sciences, National Research Council, 1989. *Recommended Dietary Allowances*, 10th ed. Washington, D.C.: National Academy Press.

Freeland-Graves, J. H., M. L. Ebangit, and P. J. Hendrikson. 1980. Alterations in zinc absorption and salivary sediment zinc after a lacto-ovo-vegetarian diet. *American Journal of Clinical Nutrition* 33:1757–1766.

Greene, L. S. 1977. Hyperendemic goiter, cretinism, and social organization in highland Ecuador. In *Malnutrition, Behavior and Social Organization*, ed. L. S. Greene, pp. 55–94. New York: Academic Press.

Guthrie, H. A. 1989. *Introductory Nutrition*. Boston: Times Mirror/Mosby.

Halas, E. S. 1983. Behavioral changes accompanying zinc deficiency in animals. In *Neurobiology of the Trace Elements*, vol. 1, ed. I. E. Dreosti and R. M. Smith, pp. 213–243. Clifton, N.J.: Humana Press.

Halas, E. S., M. D. Heinrich, and H. H. Sandstead. 1979. Long-term memory deficits in adult rats due to postnatal malnutrition. *Physiology and Behavior* 22:991–997.

Hallberg, L. 1984. Iron. In *Present Knowledge in Nutrition*, ed. R. E. Olson et al., pp. 459–478. Washington, D.C.: Nutrition Foundation.

Henkin, R. I., R. L. Aamodt, R. P. Agarwal, and D. A. Foster. 1982. The role of zinc in taste and smell. *Current Topics in Nutrition and Disease* 6:161–188.

Hetzel, B. S., J. Chavedej, and B. J. Potter. 1988. The brain in iodine deficiency. *Neuropathology and Applied Neurobiology* 14:93–104.

Hetzel, B. S. and J. T. Dunn. 1989. The iodine-deficiency disorders: Their nature and prevention. *Annual Review of Nutrition* 9:21–38.

Hetzel, B. S. and M. T. Mano. 1989. A review of experimental studies of iodine deficiency during fetal development. *Journal of Nutrition* 119:145–151.

Hurley, L. S. and H. Swenerton. 1966. Congenital malformations resulting from zinc deficiency in rats. *Proceedings of the Society for Experimental Biology and Medicine* 123:692–697.

Keen, C. L. and L. S. Hurley. 1987. Effects of zinc deficiency on prenatal and postnatal development. *Neurotoxicology* 8:378–386.

Lozoff, B., G. Brittenham, F. E. Viteri, and J. J. Urrutia. 1982a. Behavioral abnormalities in infants with iron-deficiency anemia. In *Iron Deficiency: Brain*

Biochemistry and Behavior, ed. E. Pollitt and R. L. Leibel, pp. 183–194. New York: Raven Press.

Lozoff, B., G. Brittenham, F. E. Viteri, A. W. Wolf, and J. J. Urrutia. 1982b. The effects of short-term oral iron therapy on developmental deficits in iron-deficient anemic infants. *Journal of Pediatrics* 100:351–357.

Lozoff, B., G. Brittenham, F. E. Viteri, A. W. Wolf, and J. J. Urrutia. 1982c. Developmental deficits in iron-deficient infants: Effects of age and severity of iron lack. *Journal of Pediatrics* 101:948–951.

McKenzie, J. M., G. J. Fosmire, and H. H. Sandstead. 1975. Zinc deficiency during the latter third of pregnancy: Effects on fetal rat brain, liver and placenta. *Journal of Nutrition* 105:1466–1475.

Moser-Veillon, P. B. 1990. Zinc: consumption patterns and dietary recommendations. *Journal of the American Dietetic Association* 90:1089–1093.

Pollitt. E. 1987. Effects of iron deficiency on mental development: Methodological considerations and substantive findings. In *Nutritional Anthropology,* ed. F. E. Johnson, pp. 225–254. New York: Alan R. Liss.

Pollitt, E., R. L. Leibel, and D. B. Greenfield. 1983. Iron deficiency and cognitive test performance in preschool children. *Nutrition and Behavior* 1:137–146.

Pollitt, E. and E. Metallinos-Katsaras, 1990. Iron deficiency and behavior. Constructs, methods and validity of the findings. In *Nutrition and the Brain,* vol. 8, ed. R. J. Wurtman and J. J. Wurtman, pp. 101–146, New York: Raven Press.

Pollitt, E., A. G. Soemantes, F. Yunis, and N. S. Scrimshaw. 1985. Cognitive effects of iron-deficiency anaemia. *Lancet* 1:158.

Pollitt, E., F. Viteri, C. Saco-Pollitt, and R. L. Leibel. 1982. Behavioral effects of iron-deficiency anemia in children. In *Iron Deficiency: Brain Biochemistry and Behavior,* ed. E. Pollitt and R. L. Leibel, pp. 195–208. New York: Raven Press.

Prasad, A. S. 1985. Clinical manifestations of zinc deficiency. *Annual Review of Nutrition* 5:341–363.

Prasad, A. S. 1988. Clinical spectrum and diagnostic aspects of human zinc deficiency. In *Essential and Toxic Trace Elements in Human Health and Disease,* pp. 3–53, New York: Alan R. Liss.

Prasad, A. S., J. A. Halsted, and M. Nadimi. 1961. Syndrome of iron-deficiency anemia, hepatospenomegaly, hypogonadism, dwarfism and geophagia. *American Journal of Medicine* 31:532–546.

Randall, H. T. 1988. Water, electrolytes, and acid-base balance. In *Modern Nutrition in Health and Disease,* 7th ed., ed. M. E. Shils and Y. R. Young, pp. 108–141. Philadelphia: Lea & Febiger.

Record, I. R. 1987. Zinc deficiency and the developing embryo. *Neurotoxicology* 8:369–378.

Robinson, C. H. and M. R. Lawler. 1982. *Normal and Therapeutic Nutrition.* New York: Macmillian. Orlando, FL: Academic Press.

Sandstead, H. H. and G. W. Evans. 1984. Zinc. In *Present Knowledge in Nutrition*, ed. R. E. Olson et al., pp. 479–505. Washington, D.C.: Nutrition Foundation.

Sandstead, H. H., D. D. Gillespie, and R. N. Brady. 1972. Zinc deficiency: Effect on brain of the suckling rat. *Pediatric Research* 6:119–125.

Smith, M. A. 1989. Thyroid disorders. In *Pharmacotherapy: A Pathophysiologic Approach*, ed. J. T. DiPiro et al., pp. 791–804. New York: Elsevier.

Stanbury, J. B. 1977. The role of the thyroid in the development of the human nervous system. In *Malnutrition, Behavior, and Social Organization*, ed. L. S. Greene, pp. 39–54. New York: Academic Press.

Stanbury, J. B. 1988. Iodine. In *Modern Nutrition in Health and Disease*, 7th ed., ed. M. E. Shils and V. R. Young, pp. 227–237. Philadelphia: Lea & Febiger.

Strobel, D. A. and H. H. Sandstead. 1984. Social and learning changes following prenatal or postnatal zinc deprivation in rhesus monkeys. In *The Neurobiology of Zinc*, ed. I. E. Dreosti and R. M. Smith, pp. 121–138. New York: Alan R. Liss.

Tucker, D. M. and H. H. Sandstead. 1982. Body iron stores and cortical arousal. In *Iron Deficiency: Brain Biochemistry and Behavior*, ed. E. Pollitt and R. L. Leibel, pp. 161–181. New York: Raven Press.

Walling, A., M. Householder, and A. Walling. 1989. Acrodermatitis enteropathica. *American Family Physician* 39:151–154.

Wallwork, J. C., G. J. Fosmire, and H. H. Sandstead. 1981. Effect of zinc deficiency on appetite and plasma amino acid concentrations in the rat. *British Journal of Nutrition* 45:127–136.

Walter, R., J. Kovalskys, and A. Stekel. 1983. Effect of mild iron deficiency on infant mental development scores. *Journal of Pediatrics* 102:519–522.

Youdim, M. B. H., S. Yehuda, D. Ben-Shachar, and R. Ashkenazi. 1982. Behavioral and brain biochemical changes in iron-deficient rats: The involvement of iron in dopamine receptor function. In *Iron Deficiency: Brain Biochemistry and Behavior*, ed. E. Pollitt and R. L. Leibel, pp. 39–56. New York: Raven Press.

5

Too Much of a Good Thing? Excess Intake of Vitamins and Minerals

MEGAVITAMIN THERAPY

The past 30 years have witnessed a striking escalation in the average American's concern with nutrition and health. One of the most obvious signs of this concern is the zeal with which 50 to 60 million Americans each day dutifully swallow pills containing lavish allotments of vitamins and minerals. Believing that vitamin and mineral supplements will prevent a variety of diseases from the common cold to arthritis and cancer, delay the aging process, alleviate feelings of fatigue, and generally improve psychological well-being, these individuals are stimulating the development of a multibillion dollar business. Sales of vitamins, either as single nutrients or multinutrient supplements, now average over 2 billion dollars a year.

As we saw in the preceding chapters, vitamins and minerals play an important role in nutrition. Deficiencies of these micronutrients have both physiological and psychological consequences which are ameliorated when the nutrient is made available. The knowledge that small amounts of vitamins and minerals are helpful in treating deficiency conditions has led to the assumption that larger amounts of these nutrients must also have beneficial effects. This assumption has been formalized by practitioners promoting megavitamin therapy for the treatment of a variety of ills, but most prominently psychological disorders.

Megavitamin therapy is defined as the use of massive doses of vitamins (typically 10 to 1,000 times the recommended dietary allowance) and large amounts of minerals in the treatment of disease. The term was first used in the early 1950s to describe the treatment of schizophrenia with large doses of niacin (vitamin B_3) (e.g., 3 to 30 g a day). The popularity of megavitamin therapy increased dramatically in 1968 when Nobel prize winner Linus Pauling proposed that large concentrations of vitamins are critical for optimal mental functioning. Observing that mental imbalances develop in humans as a result of nutritional deficiencies, Pauling hypothesized that some forms of mental illness might be due to vitamin deficiencies occurring on diets generally considered adequate. He further proposed that as a result of biochemical individuality, people differ with respect to the amounts of critical nutrients that reach the central nervous system. Thus, some individuals could suffer from a localized avitaminosis and possibly develop "cerebral pellagra" without any other manifestations of the disease. Pauling then advanced the idea that these conditions could be cured by increasing vitamin intake to elevate levels of the needed vitamins within the central nervous system. Pauling coined the term orthomolecular psychiatry for this form of treatment (Pauling 1968). The terms orthomolecular psychiatry and megavitamin therapy are now used interchangably for the treatment of behavioral disorders with large amounts of vitamins and minerals.

Since 1968, orthomolecular psychiatry has been promoted as a panacea for a host of behavioral problems including schizophrenia, mental retardation, attention deficit disorder, autism, and drug addiction. Advocates of this therapy have joined together to form their own medical society and to publish the *Journal of Orthomolecular Psychiatry*.

Ethical Issues

Over the past 20 years, a schism has developed between megavitamin therapists and more traditional medical practitioners and scientists. Proponents of megavitamin therapy have frequently based their claims of success on individual case studies and nonsystematic manipulations of vitamin doses and treatment procedures. Although early proponents of megavitamin therapy employed double-blind controlled procedures, subsequent investigators have disgarded these procedures on the basis of ethical considerations. Megavitamin therapists have argued that it is unethical to withhold treatment from one group of subjects, as is required in a double-blind placebo experiment (see Chapter 1), when one knows that the treatment is effective. Because megavitamin therapists believe that individuals may differ widely in their vitamin requirements, they also feel that one cannot simply employ a single dose level for all patients.

In contrast, more traditional researchers have eschewed individual case reports and have maintained that strict experimental methods must be used if valid conclusions are to be made. These researchers have supported the use of double-blind measurements, appropriate placebos, valid and reliable measures of behavior, and proper statistical analysis of data (Lipton, Mailman, and Nemeroff 1979). As will be seen in the following sections, little evidence of the efficacy of megavitamin therapy in the treatment of behavioral disorders has been found when these types of experimental procedures have been employed.

The result of this division has been a relative decline of interest in research on the role of vitamins and minerals in the treatment of behavioral problems. Megavitamin therapists have refused to conduct double-blind studies for ethical reasons, while their more traditional counterparts have rejected further experimentation on the basis that the case against megavitamin therapy has been proven. This is an unfortunate situation: even though the impressive claims of megavitamin therapists have not been upheld when more scientific testing methods have been employed, it may be too early to totally dismiss the megavitamin researchers. It is possible that certain subgroups of clinical populations may be amenable to treatment by means of dietary manipulation. Without further research, however, this possibility cannot be addressed.

TREATMENT OF SCHIZOPHRENIA

One of the most controversial questions concerning megavitamin therapy is its effectiveness in the treatment of schizophrenia. The original rationale for the use of megadoses of vitamins, particularly niacin, for the treatment of schizophrenia was based on pharmacological rather than nutritional considerations. It was hypothesized that schizophrenia is the result of abnormal metabolism of neurotransmitters in the central nervous system. More specifically, schizophrenia was attributed to the formation of aberrant methylated derivatives of the neurotransmitter epinephrine. These derivatives were believed to be hallucinogenic agents. It was further proposed that abnormal methylation could be reduced or eliminated if a significant competitor for the free methyl groups could be introduced. Niacin is a potent methyl acceptor, and so it was suggested that large amounts of niacin could block the formation of abnormal derivatives of epinephrine.

Two Canadian psychologists, Abram Hoffer and Humphrey Osmond, were the first to explore the use of niacin in the treatment of schizophrenia. In 1952, they began administering niacin to schizophrenic patients, with reportedly good results. One of their most striking successes was a 17-year-old boy who was excited and overactive, and suffered frequent hallucinations. Electroconvulsive shock and insulin-coma treatments had been effective to some degree but were terminated when the boy developed facial palsy. The boy's condition then rapidly deteriorated. Osmond and Hoffer began administering 5 g of niacin and 5 g of vitamin C a day. Improvement was dramatic: the patient was better the next day, almost normal ten days later, and able to leave the hospital permanently within two months (Hoffer et al. 1957).

Intrigued by this success, Hoffer and co-workers initiated a more scientific assessment of the efficacy of large doses of niacin. They performed several double-blind experiments (Hoffer et al. 1957; Hoffer 1962). In their first study, schizophrenic patients were randomly assigned to one of three groups: 3 g a day of nicotinic acid, 3 g a day of nicotinamide, or a placebo. Other treatments, including electroconvulsive therapy and sedation, were used as needed. After 30 days of treatment, the vitamin groups showed slightly greater improvement in symptom intensity than the placebo group. More convincing evidence was provided by observations during the next four years: the vitamin groups showed significantly greater improvement in adjustment and fewer relapses than the placebo group. In a subsequent study, Hoffer found that patients given nicotinamide displayed greater improvement during hospitalization than patients given a placebo. In this group of patients, the relapse rate did not differ as a function of vitamin therapy (Hoffer et al. 1957).

Hoffer and colleagues (Hoffer et al. 1957) originally proposed that the effectiveness of niacin in the treatment of schizophrenia was primarily due to its role as a methyl acceptor and the consequent reduction in the formation of endogenous hallucinogenic compounds. With time and the publication of Pauling's 1968 paper, however, these investigators have subsequently concluded that schizophrenia is the direct result of niacin deficiency (Hoffer 1970). Treatment with niacin is thus believed to be beneficial because it cures niacin deficiency.

The results of some subsequent studies have demonstrated positive effects with niacin in the treatment of schizophrenia (e.g., Denson 1962), but this finding has not been universal (e.g., Ashby, Collings, and Bassett 1960; Greenbaum 1970; Ban 1981). The most comprehensive evaluation of using niacin to treat schizophrenia was undertaken in a series of studies sponsored by the Canadian Mental Health Association (Ban 1981). The first study in this series compared the effectiveness of nicotinic acid, nicotinamide, and a placebo in 30 newly hospitalized schizophrenic patients. Results of this study indicated that the overall therapeutic efficacy of nicotinic acid or nicotinamide as the sole medication was not superior to that of an inactive placebo. The mean length of first hospitalization was 90 days in the placebo group, 135 days in the nicotinic acid group, and 162 days in the nicotinamide group (Ban 1981). A second study tested the effectiveness of nicotinic acid as an adjuvant medication in newly hospitalized schizophrenic patients treated with standard antipsychotic medications. The results again did not demonstrate a positive role for the use of large doses of vitamins in the treatment of schizophrenia. Patients given nicotinic acid in doses up to 3 g a day actually had longer hospital stays and required larger doses of antipsychotic drugs than patients in the placebo group. Subsequent studies by the Canadian group examined the effectiveness of using niacin in the treatment of chronic schizophrenics, and niacin in combination with pyridoxine or vitamin C in treating chronic hospitalized patients. In each case, megavitamin therapy proved ineffective.

Thus, the original studies of Hoffer and colleagues indicated that megavitamin therapy could have beneficial effects on schizophrenia, but later research has not supported this finding. A number of factors may contribute to these inconsistent results. First, schizophrenia is not a unitary disorder. The symptoms of schizophrenia vary to a sufficient degree that the disease has been divided into several subtypes. Paranoid schizophrenia is characterized by delusions of grandeur, persecution, or control. Disorganized schizophrenia represents a total break with reality. Individuals with this form of the disease are generally incoherent and display grossly disorganized behavior and flat or inappropriate affect. Catatonic schizophrenics may exhibit silence and rigidity, or more rarely wild excitement and hyperactivity.

Not all individuals with schizophrenia can be diagnosed as having a particular subtype of the disease. Many display different symptoms at different times, and many have no distinct pattern of symptoms other than thought disturbances. For this reason, it appears that a more important distinction among individuals with schizophrenia may be the rate of symptom onset. If an episode of the disease develops rapidly, with symptoms including hallucinations and delusions, it is diagnosed as acute schizophrenia. Acute schizophrenics respond well to antipsychotic medications, tend to get better relatively rapidly, and may not suffer from further episodes of the disease. In comparison, symptoms of chronic schizophrenia initially are not severe, but gradually worsen until the individual needs hospitalization. The prognosis for this form of the disease is poor, with periodic relapses throughout life.

Unfortunately, the majority of studies examining the effects of megadoses of vitamins in treating schizophrenia have not differentiated among the various forms of the disease. It is possible that vitamin therapy is more effective for one subtype of the disease than another. Indeed, megavitamin therapists have claimed that vitamin supplements are more effective with acute rather than chronic schizophrenics, although this claim has not been well documented. Thus, the effects of megavitamin therapy must be assessed for different subgroups of schizophrenics, before any firm conclusions can be drawn about the value of the treatment.

A second factor that makes it difficult to compare studies evaluating the use of megavitamins for the treatment of schizophrenia is variance of dosages of vitamins, as well as the combinations of vitamins used. Third, in many experiments, other treatments, including antipsychotic medication and electroconvulsive shock therapy, have been used in conjunction with megadoses of vitamins. Thus, it is impossible to separate out the effects of megavitamin therapy from those of other treatment modalities.

Finally, in the years since megavitamin therapy for schizophrenia was first proposed, substantial evidence has accumulated that suggests the biochemical abnormality associated with the acute form of the disease lies not in the formation of aberrant methylated derivatives of norepinephrine, or cerebral niacin deficiency, but rather in increased activity of the neurotransmitter dopamine. Support for the dopamine theory of schizophrenia comes from a variety of sources. First, it is well established that the drugs successful in treating acute schizophrenia act by blocking dopamine receptors, particularly in the mesolimbic system of the brain. Indeed, the correlation between the therapeutic effectiveness of a drug and its ability to block the action of dopamine on its postsynaptic receptors is extremely high. A second argument for the dopamine hypothesis is that drugs, like amphetamines, which increase activity at dopamine receptors, can produce symptoms of schizophrenia in normal individuals and worsen symptoms of the disease in schizophrenics. Additionally, some autopsy studies have found abnormally high concentrations of dopamine in the brains of schizophrenics. While "positive" symptoms of schizophrenia such as hallucinations, delusions, and thought disorders are believed to be due to abnormalities in the functioning of dopaminergic neurons, it recently has been suggested that the "negative" symptoms—including social withdrawal, flattened emotional response, and poverty of thought and speech—generally associated with chronic forms of the disease are the result of the loss of brain tissue (Graham 1990).

In conclusion, we can make no definitive statements about the value of megavitamins for the treatment of schizophrenia. Although megavitamin therapy certainly is not a cure for the disease, it is possible that such treatment may palliate symptoms for some small number of schizophrenics. The only way in which the efficacy of megavitamin therapy can truly be evaluated however, is by the use of appropriately designed double-blind experiments. Unfortunately, both orthomolecular psychiatrists and more traditional medical researchers currently seem unwilling to pursue this line of research.

DOWN'S SYNDROME AND OTHER FORMS OF MENTAL RETARDATION

Down's syndrome is a chromosomal abnormality that results from improper cell division during fetal development. The majority of individuals with Down's sydrome have an extra or third copy of chromosome 21 (trisomy 21) because the normally paired chromosomes do not separate appropriately during egg or sperm development. Distinctive physical appearance and mental retardation are typical sequelae of this chromosomal abnormality. Intelligence quotients (IQs) of children with Down's syndrome range from extremely low to a high of 80. On the average, IQs are from 40 to 50. Anomalies of the central nervous system, including reduction in weight of the brain stem, pons, medulla, and cerebellum; delayed myelination; and abnormal formation of dendritic spines in the cerebral cortex are frequently associated with Down's syndrome (Spreen et al. 1984).

The frequency of Down's syndrome is approximately 2 per 1,000 births for mothers in all age groups. However, as a woman becomes older the probability of chromosomal abnormalities increases, and after the age of thirty, the likelihood of having a child with Down's syndrome doubles for each successive five-year period.

A variety of medical treatments, including dimethyl sulfoxide, fetal cell therapy, glutamic acid, pituitary extracts, and 5-hydroxytryptophan have been promoted for Down's syndrome. Unfortunately, none of these treatments has stood up to the challenges posed by carefully conducted research. For example, dimethyl sulfoxide, fetal cell therapy, and 5-hydroxytryptophan have all been proven ineffective in studies that used appropriate control groups, blinded investigators, and standardized assessment measures (Pruess, Fewell, and Bennett 1989).

The idea that large doses of vitamins and minerals might be useful in the treatment of Down's syndrome came from reports demonstrating specific nutrient deficiencies (e.g., vitamin A, vitamin B_6, vitamin C, and zinc) in Down's syndrome children. These nutritional deficiencies have not been consistently observed, however, and low levels of nutrients in the blood of Down's syndrome patients have not been associated with any specific clinical symptoms (Barlow, Sylvester, and Dickerson 1981; Matin et al. 1981; Bennett et al. 1983; Justice et al. 1988; Pruess, Fewell, and Bennett 1989).

Dietary treatment of Down's syndrome was initiated over 50 years ago. In 1940, Dr. Henry Turkel began treating Down's syndrome patients with tablets containing a combination of 48 substances including vitamins, minerals, amino acids, enzymes, and hormones. Turkel claimed that this treatment improved intellectual functioning as well as the physical attributes of children with Down's syndrome (Turkel 1975). Turkel's claim suffers because it is based solely on his own observations of these children. It is impossible to determine if it was the treatment or some other aspect, for example, the increased attention that the children received, the experimenter's or parents' expectations, or normal developmental changes, that accounted for Turkel's results.

More recently, a study by Harrell and colleagues (1981) renewed medical and public interest in the potential benefits of megavitamin therapy for Down's syndrome. This study had an advantage over Turkel's work in that it used more scientifically sound methods. Harrell and her associates designed their study to test the hypothesis that mental retardation is in part a genetrophic disease, that is, a disease caused by genetically determined insufficiencies that may be prevented or at least ameliorated by augmenting the supply of one or more nutrients. To test this hypothesis, 22 mentally retarded children ranging in age from 5 to 15 years were examined. Five of the children were classified as having Down's syndrome, and the remainder were unclassified. The children were divided into two groups matched on the basis of IQ scores. For four months, 10 children received a nutritional supplement containing large amounts of 11 vitamins and 8 minerals, while the remaining 12 children received a placebo. Unfortunately, only 16 subjects, 5 receiving the nutritional supplement and 11 receiving the placebo, completed the first phase of the experiment. During a second four-month period, all of the remaining subjects were given the nutritional supplement. IQ scores of the 5 children who received the nutritional supplement during the first phase of the study increased an average of 5.0 points, and those of the children who received the placebo increased less than 1 point. At the end of the second phase, 3 of the 5 children who had received supplements throughout the experiment displayed further improvements in IQ scores. In the 10 subjects who received the supplement only during the final four months of the study, IQ increased an average of 10 points. Nutritional supplements were particularly effective in younger children and children with Down's syndrome. IQ scores of children with Down's syndrome increased from 10 to 25 points, and the children displayed improved eyesight as well as positive changes in physical appearance (Harrell et al. 1981).

The results of the study by Harrell and associates led to the hopeful conclusion that vitamin and mineral supplements could play a beneficial role in the treatment of Down's syndrome and other types of mental retardation. There are several problems with this study, however, that make such a conclusion tentative at best. For example, although the subjects in the two groups were matched on the basis of IQ, they were not matched on a number of other variables including age, sex, and parental education, all of which have been related to variations in intelligence test performance in children suffering from mental retardation. Moreover, of the 22 children initially enrolled, only 16 completed the study. The dropout rate for subjects was considerably higher in the group receiving the nutritional supplement (50%) than in the group receiving the placebo (8%). In addition, during the second phase of the experiment, the researchers who were testing the children were not blind to the experimental condition, but rather knew that all subjects were receiving the nutritional supplement.

Because of the important implications of the Harrell et al. (1981) study, a number of researchers have attempted to replicate this work while correcting some of its procedural shortcomings. These studies have specifically concentrated on the effects of nutritional supplements on intellectual abilities in children with Down's syndrome. For example, in a double-blind study, Weathers (1983) gave 24 Down's syndrome children from 6 to 17 years of age and living at home the same nutritional supplement used by Harrell and associates. After four months, the children's IQs, vision, and performance on a test of visual motor integration were compared to those of 23 children who had received a placebo. The two groups were matched on the basis of age, sex, initial IQ, early stimulation experiences, and prior nutritional supplementation. In contrast to the results of Harrell et al. (1981), vitamin and mineral supplements did not lead to improvements in

Down's syndrome symptomology. No significant differences in IQ, vision, or visual–motor integration skills were observed between the two groups; neither did evaluations of photographs indicate positive changes in appearance of the children given the nutritional supplements. Finally, on the basis of claims that nutritional therapy is most effective with younger children (Harrell et al. 1981; Rimland 1983), Weathers examined her results to determine whether children 6 to 9 years of age made greater improvements than subjects in older age groups. This was not the case.

Subsequent double-blind controlled studies using a variety of measures of intelligence and behavior have failed to find any differences between children given vitamin and mineral supplements and those given placebos. Further, no differences in nutritional status, appearance, health, vision, or hearing have been observed as a function of dietary manipulations (Bennett et al. 1983; Smith et al. 1984; Justice et al. 1988). Thus, the results of studies conducted since 1981 have not confirmed the conclusion of Harrell and co-workers (1981) that large doses of vitamins and minerals are an effective therapy for Down's syndrome.

It is interesting to note, however, that at the end of several studies (Weathers 1983; Smith et al. 1984), most parents of children in both the control and experimental groups decided to continue dietary treatment, in spite of the failure of the study to demonstrate their efficacy. Such a response may reveal persistent optimism, or an adherence to a "definition of the situation"; if one believes that nutritional supplements will bring beneficial results, then beneficial results will occur.

In all of the previously described studies on the effects of megavitamin therapy in Down's syndrome, the children were living at home; however, even in institutions where the diet was less varied than in a home setting, nutritional supplements did not produce positive outcomes (Coburn et al. 1983; Ellis and Tomporowski 1983; Ellman et al. 1984; Chanowitz et al. 1985). Ellis and Tomporowski (1983), for example, using the same nutritional supplements as Harrell et al. (1981), found no improvements in IQ or adaptive behavior in institutionalized mentally retarded adults after seven months of dietary treatment. Similar negative results were reported by Coburn and colleagues (1983) who studied the effects of supplements containing only the recommended dietary allowance of the various vitamins and minerals, as well as megadoses of these micronutrients.

Taken together, the results of investigations of the effects of megavitamin therapy on intellectual performance in mentally retarded individuals do not support the hypothesis that increases in nutrients improve mental functioning. None of these investigations reported negative side effects from megavitamin therapy; however, it has become increasingly apparent that large doses of certain vitamins such as A, D, and B_6 can have toxic consequences. Therefore, megavitamin therapy for mental retardation cannot be considered a benign treatment.

In conclusion, the lack of positive results and the potential toxicity of megavitamin therapy make the use of vitamin and mineral supplements in the treatment of mental retardation extremely questionable.

EFFECTS OF VITAMIN AND MINERAL SUPPLEMENTS ON INTELLIGENCE IN NORMAL CHILDREN

Results of a recent study conducted in Wales by Benton and Roberts (1988) suggest that a vitamin and mineral supplement can improve children's performance on tests of intellectual abilities. On the basis of dietary records taken over three days, these investigators hypothesized that some basically healthy children may be suffering from marginal nutritional deficiencies (e.g., vitamin D, folic acid, calcium, iodine, and iron). They further proposed that nutrient supplements could correct these deficits. To test their hypothesis, three groups of 30 children, matched according to gender, school performance, and home background, were tested. One group received no treatment, and the other two groups took either a vitamin and mineral supplement or a placebo, administered double-blind; that is, no parent, teacher, or child knew which group was taking the supplement or placebo. Children in the supplemented group, but not in the placebo group or in the group given no treatment, demonstrated a significant increase in nonverbal intelligence measured preceding and following the eight-month test period. No differences in verbal intelligence were observed.

Benton and Roberts (1988) suggested that nonverbal tasks may be more susceptible to nutrient manipulations because they do not require general information or vocabulary, but rather represent a more biological measure of intelligence than verbal ability. The growth of nonverbal intelligence parallels other physical dimensions such as brain weight and lung capacity, and peaks in the late teens or early twenties. In comparison, verbal intelligence relies more on the individual's cultural, educational, and environmental experiences, and peaks much later in life. An increase in verbal intelligence might be expected only after the potential offered by a better nourished brain had been exploited by a stimulating environment.

One implication of this study is that marginal dietary deficiencies could hamper neural functioning in children. If this provocative implication is confirmed by replication of Benton and Roberts' (1988) research, then the underlying mechanisms must be established.

TREATMENT OF AUTISM

Infantile autism is a devastating disorder that begins before 30 months of age and affects 3 to 4 out of every 10,000 children. The term autism refers to a lack of responsivity, or social indifference. The disorder may be manifested by impairments in language development; interest or fascination with unusual objects, such as water, fans, or other rotating objects; catastrophic responses to change; and insistence on sameness. The infant or child with autism fails to develop social relations with other individuals, including the parents. When autistic children are dealing with others, the lack of eye contact is unmistakable. Compulsive behaviors, including head banging, rocking, and stereotyped movements, are also typical. Feeding difficulties are common in infancy, and older children are often preoccupied with one particular food (Spreen et al. 1984).

In a study examining the effects of an experimental vitamin regimen (vitamin C, vitamin B_6, niacinamide, and pantothenic acid) among 200 autistic children, Rimland (1974) noted that vitamin B_6 produced positive changes in behavior. To more completely analyze this phenomenon, Rimland, Calloway, and Dreyfuss (1978) investigated the behavioral consequences of removing vitamin B_6 from the normal vitamin and mineral supplements of 16 autistic children ranging in age from 4 to 19 years. Each child's behavior was rated by parents and teachers. Removal of B_6 from the diet led to a significant deterioration in behavior; in contrast, behavior improved when the vitamin was returned.

Although the results of the Rimland et al. (1978) study imply that vitamin B_6 supplements may be useful in the treatment of autism, there are a number of problems with this experiment which indicate that caution must be exercised in accepting its conclusions. First, the dose of B_6 varied widely among the children, as did the amount of time the children were maintained without the vitamin. Second, all of the children received a variety of other agents including vitamins, minerals, and drugs, as well as megadoses of vitamin C and niacin. In addition, the subjects in this study were widely spaced geographically (Florida to California) and contacted primarily by telephone or mail, leaving open the possibility that parents and teachers failed to understand the requirements of the study. Indeed, in some cases parents apparently provided the wrong supplement to their child. Finally, narrative reports and an individually developed target symptom checklist, rather than a standardized measurement scale, were used to evaluate behavior. Thus, behavioral assessment must be considered subjective at best.

In conclusion, until more definitive work is conducted, the use of megavitamin therapy for autism must viewed with skepticism.

ATTENTION DEFICIT HYPERACTIVITY DISORDER

Attention deficit hyperactivity disorder (ADHD) is the scientific name for what was has been called hyperactivity or hyperkinesis. ADHD is characterized by impulsive behavior, developmentally inappropriate inattention, significantly increased levels of motor activity, failure to follow through on tasks, and difficulties with organizing and completing work. It is estimated that as many as 3% of preadolescent children may suffer from ADHD, with the disorder 6 to 9 times more frequent in boys than in girls (American Psychiatric Association 1987). A variety of factors, including food additives, sugar, family dysfunction, and perinatal difficulties, have been offered as causes for ADHD (see chapters 7, 8, and 9). However, at present the cause or causes of ADHD remain unknown (Stimmel 1989; Zametkin 1989).

Medical treatment for children with ADHD has relied primarily on administration of stimulant drugs, such as amphetamines and methylphenidate (Ritalin). These drugs tend to increase levels of activity in adults, but have the paradoxical effect of reducing hyperactive behavior and increasing vigilance, persistence, impulse control, and goal-directed behavior in children with ADHD. It has been hypothesized that amphetamines and methylphenidate "normalize" the hyperkinetic child by improving the child's ability to pay attention to relevant stimuli, rather than by sedating the child. Unfortunately, these drugs have a number of side effects. One of the most disturbing is a reduction in appetite which can lead to a suppression of growth. Stimulant drugs also lead to insomnia in some children. Finally, because the exact mechanisms by which stimulant drugs act and the long-term effects of daily stimulant use in children aged 6 to 16 remain unknown, these drugs should not be prescribed indiscriminately to control the behavior of children. An accurate diagnosis of ADHD by an experienced physician, rather than the anecdotal reports of parents or teachers, must be used as a rationale for prescribing them.

It has been suggested that megavitamin therapy may be a useful adjunct in the treatment of ADHD (Cott 1972; Coleman et al. 1979; Brenner 1982). In 1972, using doses of niacin, ascorbic acid, and pyridoxine from 100 to 300 times the recommended dietary allowance, Cott reported that megavitamin therapy decreased hyperactivity and improved both concentration and attention span, and subsequently learning capacity, in children with ADHD. Unfortunately, Cott's report was based on anecdotal evidence rather than on a well-controlled study. Better evidence of the possible helpful effects of vitamin therapy in ADHD comes from a study by Coleman and colleagues (1979), who used double-blind techniques to compare the effects of pyridoxine (B_6) administration to those of methylphenidate in six hyperactive children between the ages of 8 and 13. The results indicated that pyridoxine might be as effective as methylphenidate in the treatment of children with ADHD. Both parents and teachers rated children as somewhat less hyperactive when pyridoxine was administered than when methylphenidate was given. The children were most active during a placebo period when neither the vitamin nor drug was given. Although the results of this study are provocative, they must be viewed as only a beginning.

Brenner (1982) also reported positive effects of pyridoxine in controlling symptoms of ADHD in some children. However, he found that in others the vitamin either had no effect or actually increased hyperactive behavior. Other children improved following pharmacological doses of thiamin, niacin, or a combination of B-complex vitamins with minerals. From his observations, Brenner (1982) concluded that while there are multiple causes for ADHD, in a significant number of cases the disorder is the result of vitamin deficiencies.

Although megavitamin treatment of ADHD appears to have led to positive outcomes, this result has not been universal (Arnold et al. 1978; Haslam, Dalby, and Rademaker 1984). To assess Cott's (1972) original claim for vitamin treatment of ADHD, Arnold and colleagues (1978), using a double-blind procedure with 31 hyperactive children, examined the effects of the megavitamin regimen advocated by Cott. No differences in behavior were observed as a function of the megavitamin regimen. In a more recent double-blind study (see chapter 1), Haslam, Dalby, and Rademaker (1984) also reported that Cott's megavitamin regimen was ineffective in the management of ADHD. In this study, both teachers' ratings of conduct problems and parents' ratings of hyperactivity were higher when children were receiving vitamins than when they were receiving a placebo. Additionally, several children withdrew from the study while receiving vitamin supplements because of gastrointestinal complaints, suggesting the potential toxicity of megadoses of these vitamins.

In conclusion, vitamin therapy may be useful for a small proportion of children with ADHD, but it is not a panacea. Further, the possible serious side effects of megadoses of vitamins make this form of treatment for ADHD questionable.

VITAMIN B$_6$ (PYRIDOXINE) IN THE TREATMENT OF PREMENSTRUAL SYNDROME

Premenstrual syndrome (PMS) has been defined as a cyclical condition occurring in the second half of the menstrual cycle that is relieved within 24 to 48 hours of the onset of menstruation. The most common symptoms are fluid retention, breast swelling and pain, headaches, and mood changes including increased irritability and tension alternating with depression. Less frequent symptoms involve lethargy, food cravings, loss of concentration, reduction in coordination, backache, and skin problems (Brush 1988).

It has been hypothesized that vitamin B$_6$ might help to ameliorate many of the psychological symptoms of PMS. This hypothesis is based, in part, on the fact that pyridoxal phosphate serves as an essential cofactor in the synthesis of the neurotransmitters serotonin, norepinephrine, and dopamine. Low levels of B$_6$ thus could lead to a decrease in the production of these neurotransmitters. Reductions in serotonin or norepinephrine are associated with depression and alterations in eating behavior.

The effectiveness of B_6 in the treatment of PMS remains controversial. A number of studies have demonstrated partial improvement in symptoms as a result of the administration of high doses of B_6 ranging from 40 to 500 mg daily, or from 25 to 300 times the recommended dietary allowance (Bassler 1988; Brush 1988). For example, Brush (1988) reported that doses of 150 to 200 mg/day could benefit women suffering from PMS. Using a very informal rating scale, Brush found that symptoms of PMS were either eliminated or decreased in 60% to 70% of women taking the vitamin. Unfortunately, it is difficult to specifically evaluate the effects of B_6 on PMS from this report as all of the women, as well as their physicians, knew that vitamin supplements were being given. A more critical test of the efficacy of B_6 in the treatment of PMS would be a double-blind experiment comparing the effects of the vitamin with that of a placebo. In addition, although Brush reported only minor side effects with B_6, including nausea, indigestion, dizziness, and tingling feelings in the hands and feet, recent research has indicated that large doses of the vitamin may lead to sensory neuropathy.

Because no prescription is required and popular promotion of the use of B_6 for PMS is widespread, many women are taking the vitamin on their own initiative, without proper medical supervision. It must be kept in mind that women often do not respond to B_6. Considering this possible lack of responsiveness in conjunction with the potential toxicity of the vitamin, unsupervised self-medication with B_6 cannot be recommended.

VITAMIN AND MINERAL TOXICITY

Fat-Soluble Vitamins

The potential toxic effects of large doses of the fat-soluble vitamins A, D, E, and K have been recognized for some time. Fat-soluble vitamins are not efficiently excreted from the body; large amounts can be stored and accumulate to toxic levels. As the doses of fat-soluble vitamins recommended by megavitamin therapists frequently range from 10 to 100 times the recommended dietary allowance, it is important to review the potential adverse effects of these large doses. Table 5-1 summarizes the recommended adult intake, estimated toxic dose for adults, and symptoms of toxicity for both fat- and water-soluble vitamins.

VITAMIN A

The signs and symptoms of hypervitaminosis A, the most common form of vitamin toxicity, vary considerably depending on the age of the individual, the amount of the vitamin consumed, and the duration of excess intake.

TABLE 5-1. Potential Toxic Effects of Vitamins

Vitamin	RDA[a]	Potential Toxic Dose[b]	Toxic Effects
Vitamin A	800–1000 ug	15,000–100,000 ug	Headache, vertigo, fatigue, nausea, hair loss, dermatitis, reabsorption of bone, anorexia, cerebral edema, teratogenesis
Vitamin D	10 ug	125 ug	Nausea, polyuria, kidney failure, hypercalcemia of bone, cardiovascular changes
Vitamin E	8–10 mg	300–600 mg	Nausea, diarrhea, muscle weakness, headaches, visual problems
Thiamine	1.1–1.5 mg	Unknown	Headache, insomnia, hypotension, weakness
Niacin	15–20 mg	1000–10,000 mg	Flushing, hypotension, gastrointestinal problems, hepatotoxicity
Pyridoxine	1.5–2.0 mg	200 mg	Peripheral neuropathy, ataxia, sensory impairments
Vitamin C	60 mg	2000–4000 mg	Gastrointestinal problems, increased risk of kidney stones

[a] Recommended dietary allowance for adults.
[b] Minimal toxic dose.

For adults, the toxic oral dose of Vitamin A is estimated to range from 25,000 to 50,000 iu per day. Adverse effects may occur in children with doses as low as 1500 iu/kg body weight per day. The U.S. Food and Drug Administration has been concerned about the effects of vitamin A toxicity, but has been unable to impose limits on the amount of the vitamin included in nonprescription multivitamin tablets. The availability of low-cost, high-potency vitamin A preparations is an ever-present risk because of the tendency of some people to oversupplement their diet (McLaren 1982; Arroyave 1988; Hegarty 1988; Guthrie 1989; Hathcock et al. 1990).

There have been reports of Arctic explorers developing acute symptoms of vitamin A toxicity after consuming several hundred thousand micrograms of the vitamin, which is found in the liver of seals and polar bears. Headache, vertigo, blurred vision, vomiting, and peeling of the skin are the usual consequences. Chronic toxicity in adults is characterized by headaches, drowsiness, nausea, loss of hair, dry and itchy skin, diarrhea, rapid reabsorption of bone, and amenorrhea (failure to menstruate) in women. Slow recovery without reported aftereffects occurs following withdrawal of the vitamin.

In addition to the symptoms exhibited by adults, infants and young children given large doses of vitamin A for extended periods of time display anorexia, enlargement of the liver and spleen, double vision, and symptoms suggestive of a brain tumor including hyperirritability, hydrocephalus, and increased intracranial pressure. When excessive vitamin A administration stops, these symptoms slowly disappear (McLaren 1982; Arroyave 1988; Guthrie 1989; Hathcock et al. 1990).

Excess vitamin A intake during pregnancy presents a particular problem. Vitamin A and other retinoids are teratogenic in a variety of species and have been associated with malformations of the kidney and nervous system in newborn human infants. Isotretinoin, or 13-cis-retinoic acid (Accutane), a derivative of vitamin A, was first marketed in the United States in September 1982 for the treatment of severe cystic acne. Since that time, a number of reports of teratogenesis resulting from maternal use of the drug have been published (e.g., Rosa 1983; Braun et al. 1984; Fernhoff and Lammer 1984; Lott et al. 1984). Characteristic features of isotretinoin toxicity include cardiovascular deficits; small, malformed ears; and abnormal facial development including a high forehead and hypoplastic nasal bridge. The central nervous system may be particularly sensitive to the teratogenic effects of isotretinoin. Infants whose mothers took the drug during pregnancy display abnormal reflexes and obvious psychomotor retardation. Longitudinal studies have revealed severe mental retardation as these children develop. Computed cranial tomography (CT scan) and post-mortem examinations of the brains of infants exposed to isotretinoin during fetal development have uncovered alterations in the form of the cerebral ventricles; hydrocephalus; a small, abnormally developed cerebellum; malformations of the hippocampus; and anomalies of the brain stem.

The teratogenic effects of vitamin A in animals and the clinical studies of fetal isotretinoin toxicity strongly suggest that large doses of vitamin A during the first trimester of pregnancy may be associated with craniofacial malformations and severe abnormalities in the development of the central nervous system. For this reason, extreme care should be used in prescribing isotretinoin and related drugs, and in promoting the use of vitamin supplements with high levels of vitamin A, to women of childbearing age.

VITAMIN D

Most cases of hypervitaminosis D have occurred due to large and prolonged therapeutic doses used to treat vitamin D deficiency states. Doses five to ten times the recommended daily allowance may prove toxic in sensitive individuals. In adults, excess vitamin D can lead to nausea, polyuria, kidney failure, cardiovascular changes, and hypercalcemia of bone and soft tissues. The withdrawal of all sources of the vitamin alleviates these symptoms.

Infants may be particularly sensitive to vitamin D. Typical symptoms of vitamin D toxicity in the infant include anorexia, irritability, weakness, constipation, vomiting, failure to thrive, and increased levels of serum calcium. Prolonged hypercalcemia can lead to calcification of renal tissue and subsequent kidney failure. The level of vitamin D intake that brings on hypercalcemia ranges from a low of 10 ug/day in very sensitive infants to 100 ug/day in children given the vitamin for periods of four months or more. Since a relatively low level of vitamin D can produce toxicity in infants and children, dietary supplements are not recommended for children drinking more than two glasses of milk per day (McLaren 1982; Arroyave 1988; Guthrie 1989).

VITAMIN E

Although many people take vitamin E in amounts of 100 times or more than the recommended dietary allowance, the vitamin does not appear to cause the toxicity problems associated with vitamins A and D. However, recent anecdotal reports suggest that gastrointestinal distress including nausea and diarrhea, muscle weakness, headaches, visual problems, and decreased wound healing may occur when daily intakes of vitamin E reach levels of 300 to 600 mg. Additionally, there may be problems with blood clotting if vitamin D status is marginal (Arroyave 1988; Guthrie 1989).

VITAMIN K

Large doses of vitamin K are not recommended in any type of megavitamin treatment, and it is rarely available for over the counter sale; thus, vitamin K toxicity is not considered a problem.

Water-Soluble Vitamins

In contrast to the fat-soluble vitamins, water-soluble vitamins are generally excreted rapidly in the urine when consumed in large doses. For this reason, it has been assumed that large doses of water-soluble vitamins are safe and harmless. However, recent work has indicated that excess amounts of some of these vitamins, including niacin, vitamin C, and vitamin B_6, can have toxic effects. There are five discrete mechanisms by which high doses of water-soluble vitamins may produce toxic effects in humans (Alhadeff, Gualitieri, and Lipton 1984):

- Vitamins or their metabolites may have direct toxic effects.
- Megadoses of water-soluble vitamins may lead to dependency states, and withdrawal symptoms may develop if they are abruptly discontinued.
- Vitamins may mask the symptoms or signs of a concurrent disease.

- Vitamins may interact with drugs or with other vitamins.
- The use of megadoses of water-soluble vitamins may be associated with concurrent intake of high doses of fat-soluble vitamins.

THIAMIN (VITAMIN B₁)

The potential of thiamin toxicity is low, but adverse side effects from large doses have been reported. Symptoms of thiamin toxicity include headache, irritability, insomnia, rapid pulse, hypotension, tremors, and weakness (Aldaheff, Gualitieri, and Lipton 1984; Blair 1986).

NIACIN (VITAMIN B₃)

Although niacin is not extremely toxic, in the massive doses used in megavitamin therapy, the vitamin is not devoid of deleterious consequences. A variety of side effects including flushing of the face, heartburn, nausea, vomiting, diarrhea, dermatological problems, tachycardia, and low blood pressure have been associated with excessive intake of niacin or niacinamide.

Nicotinic acid (but not niacinamide) leads to the release of the vasodilator histamine. As a result, flushing of the face is a common side effect of nicotinic acid. Because niacin can release histamine, care should be exercised in the use of the vitamin by individuals suffering from peptic ulcers and asthma. Large doses of niacin may also lead to hepatotoxicity and associated jaundice. Finally, there is some evidence that daily doses of 3 g of niacin or more can increase cardiac arrhythmias, as well as result in hyperglycemia, ketonuria, and glucosuria, particularly in diabetic individuals (Lipton, Mailman, and Nemeroff 1979; Alhadeff, Gualitieri, and Lipton 1984; Arroyave 1988).

PYRIDOXINE (VITAMIN B₆)

Megadoses of pyridoxine have been recommended for the treatment of a wide range of psychological disturbances including schizophrenia, depression, ADHD, autism, and premenstrual syndrome. Unfortunately, recent evidence indicates that large doses are toxic to the peripheral nervous system. In 1983, Schaumburg and colleagues reported seven cases of sensory neuropathy after a minimum dose of 2 g per day of pyridoxine for four months. This reaction occurred more rapidly with higher doses (5 g) of the vitamin. The symptoms consisted of unsteady gait and numb feet, followed by numbness and clumsiness of the hands. Additionally, a loss of vibratory sensations and diminished or absent tendon reflexes were observed. Studies of nerve conduction indicated dysfunction of the distal portions of sensory peripheral nerves, and nerve biopsies in two patients demonstrated widespread nonspecific axonal degeneration. Neurological disabilities slowly improved when the patients stopped taking the vitamin (Schaumburg et al. 1983).

Subsequent studies have substantiated and extended Schaumburg et al.'s (1983) observations (e.g., Parry and Bredsen 1985; Albin et al. 1987). For example, Parry and Bredsen (1985) found that doses as small as 200 mg a day could lead to sensory neuropathy. They also reported an inverse relationship between dose, duration of administration, and the appearance of sensory neuropathy, and evidence of central nervous system damage resulting from prolonged administration of higher doses of pyridoxine.

Taken together, these studies clearly demonstrate the toxic effects of excess amounts of pyridoxine. Preparations of the vitamin are available over the counter in tablet sizes of up to 1,000 mg. It is thus quite possible for individuals to consume potentially toxic doses. The public should be informed of the conceivable dangers of large doses of pyridoxine and use these vitamin supplements only with extreme caution.

VITAMIN C

Vitamin C in high doses has been recommended for the treatment of the common cold, anxiety, cancer, schizophrenia, heavy metal intoxication, and heroin addiction. On an acute basis, however, large doses of vitamin C can lead to diarrhea and abdominal cramps. Prolonged use of high doses of the vitamin can elevate urinary oxalate excretion and thereby increase the risk of kidney stones (Alhadeff, Gualitieri, and Lipton, 1984; Blair 1986). It has also been reported that high levels of vitamin C intake may interfere with the absorption of vitamin B_{12}.

CONCLUSION

At this time, there is little evidence supporting the efficacy of megavitamin therapy in the treatment of behavioral disorders. To the contrary, megavitamin therapy may prove not only ineffective, but actually deleterious. It has been assumed by many that because they are "natural" components of the diet, vitamins are safe to consume in excess. However, large amounts of both fat- and water-soluble vitamins act primarily as pharmacological agents, with potentially toxic consequences. In addition to having potentially harmful physical effects, taking megadoses of vitamins may result in a sense of false security and prevent people from seeking appropriate medical care. Thus, it can be concluded that megavitamin therapy is unwarranted in the majority of situations in which it is currently recommended in the popular literature.

REFERENCES

Albin, R. L., J. W. Albers, H. S. Greenberg, J. B. Townsend, R. B. Lynn, J. M. Burke, and A. G. Alessi. 1987. Acute sensory neuropathy-neuronopathy from pyridoxine overdose. *Neurology* 37:1729–1732.

Alhadeff, L., C. T. Gualitieri, and M. Lipton. 1984. Toxic effects of water-soluble vitamins. *Nutrition Reviews* 42:33–40.

American Psychiatric Association. 1987. *Diagnostic and Statistical Manual of Mental Disorders,* 3rd ed., rev. Washington, D.C.: American Psychiatric Association.

Arnold, L. E., J. Christopher, R. D. Huestis, and D. J. Smeltzer. 1978. Megavitamins for minimal brain dysfunction. *Journal of the American Medical Association* 240:2642–2643.

Arroyave, G. 1988. Risks and abuses of megadoses of vitamins. *Food and Nutrition Bulletin* 10:21–25.

Ashby, W. R., G. H. Collings, and M. Bassett. 1960. The effects of nicotinamide and placebo on the chronic schizophrenic. *Journal of Mental Science* 106:1555–1559.

Ban, T. A. 1981. Megavitamin therapy in schizophrenia. In *Nutrition and Behavior,* ed. S. A. Miller, pp. 247–253. Philadelphia: Franklin Institute.

Barlow, P. J., P. E. Sylvester, and J. W. T. Dickerson. 1981. Hair trace metal levels in Down's syndrome patients. *Journal of Mental Deficiency Research* 25:161–168.

Bassler, K. H. 1988. Megavitamin therapy with pyridoxine. *International Journal of Vitamin and Nutrition Research* 58:105–118.

Bennett, F. C., S. McClelland, E. A. Kriegsmann, L. B. Andrus, and C. J. Sells. 1983. Vitamin and mineral supplementation in Down's syndrome. *Pediatrics* 72:707–713.

Benton, D. and G. Roberts. 1988. Effect of vitamin and mineral supplementation on intelligence of a sample of schoolchildren. *Lancet* 1:140–143.

Blair, K. A. 1986. Vitamin supplementation and megadoses. *Nurse Practitioner* 11:19–36.

Braun, J. T., R. A. Franciosi, A. R. Mastri, R. M. Drake, and B. L. O'Neil. 1984. Isotretinoin dysomorphic syndrome. *Lancet* 1:506–507.

Brenner, A. 1982. The effects of megadoses of selected B-complex vitamins on children with hyperkinesis: Controlled studies with long-term follow-up. *Journal of Learning Disabilities* 15:258–264.

Brush M. G. 1988. Vitamin B_6 treatment of premenstrual syndrome. In *Clinical and Physiological Applications of Vitamin B_6,* ed. J. E. Leklem and R. D. Reynolds, pp. 363–379. New York: Alan R. Liss.

Chanowitz, J., G. Ellman, C. Silverstein, G. Zingarelli, and E. Ganger. 1985.

Thyroid and vitamin-mineral supplements fail to improve IQs of mentally retarded adults. *American Journal of Mental Deficiency* 90:217–219.

Coburn, S. P., W. E. Schaltenbrand, J. D. Mahuren, R. J. Clausman, and D. Townsend. 1983. Effect of megavitamin treatment on mental performance and plasma vitamin B_6 concentrations in mentally retarded young adults. *American Journal of Clinical Nutrition* 38:352–355.

Coleman, M., G. Steinberg, J. Tippett, H. N. Bagavan, D. B. Coursin, M. Gross, C. Lewis, and L. DeVeau. 1979. A preliminary study of the effect of pyridoxine administration in a subgroup of hyperkinetic children: A double-blind crossover comparison with methylphenidate. *Biological Psychiatry* 14:741–751.

Cott, A. 1972. Megavitamins: The orthomolecular approach to behavioral disorders and learning disabilities. *Academic Therapy* 7:245–258.

Denson, R. 1962. Nicotinamide in the treatment of schizophrenia. *Diseases of the Nervous System* 23:167–172.

Ellis, N. R. and P. D. Tomporowski. 1983. Vitamin/mineral supplements and intelligence of institutionalized mentally retarded adults. *American Journal of Mental Deficiency* 88:211–214.

Ellman, G., C. Silverstein, G. Zingarelli, E. Schafer, and L. Silverstein. 1984. Vitamin-mineral supplement fails to improve IQs of mentally retarded young adults. *American Journal of Mental Deficiency* 88:688–691.

Fernhoff, P. M. and E. J. Lammer. 1984. Craniofacial features of isoretinoin embryopathy. *Journal of Pediatrics* 105:595–597.

Graham, R. B. 1990. *Physiological Psychology*. Belmont, CA: Wadsworth.

Greenbaum, C. H. C. 1970. An evaluation of niacinamide in the treatment of childhood schizophrenia. *American Journal of Psychiatry* 127:129–132.

Guthrie, H. A. 1989. *Introductory Nutrition*. St. Louis, MO: Times Mirror/Mosby.

Harrell, R. F., R. H. Capp, D. R. Davis, J. Peerless, and L. R. Ravitz. 1981. Can nutritional supplements help mentally retarded children? An exploratory study. *Proceedings of the National Academy of Sciences* 78:574–578.

Haslam, R. H. A., J. T. Dalby, and A. W. Rademaker. 1984. Effects of megavitamin therapy on children with attention deficit disorders. *Pediatrics* 74:103–111.

Hathcock, J. N., D. G. Hatton, M. Y. Jenkins, J. T. McDonald, P. R. Sundaresan, and W. L. Wilkening. 1990. Evaluation of vitamin A toxicity. *American Journal of Clinical Nutrition* 52:183–202.

Hegarty, V. 1988. *Decisions in Nutrition*. St. Louis, MO: Times Mirror/Mosby.

Hoffer, A. 1962. *Niacin Therapy in Psychiatry*. Springfield, IL: Charles C. Thomas.

Hoffer, A. 1970. Pellegra and schizophrenia. *Psychosomatics* 11:522–525.

Hoffer, A., H. Osmond, M. J. Callbeck, and I. Kahan. 1957. Treatment of schizophrenia with nicotinic acid and nicotinamide. *Journal of Clinical and Experimental Psychopathology* 18:131–158.

Justice, P. M., S. Kamath, P. W. Langenberg, H. H. Sandstead, D. B. Milne, and G. F. Smith. 1988. Micronutrients status of children with Down's syndrome: A comparative study of the effect of megadoses of vitamins with minerals or placebo. *Nutrition Research* 8:1251–1258.

Lipton, M. A., R. B. Mailman, and C. B. Nemeroff. 1979. Vitamins, megavitamin therapy, and the nervous system. In *Nutrition and the Brain*, vol. 3, ed. R. J. Wurtman and J. J. Wurtman, pp. 183–264. New York: Raven Press.

Lott, I. T., M. Bocian, H. W. Pribram, and M. Leitner. 1984. Fetal hydrocephalus and ear abnormalities associated with maternal use of isoretinoin. *Journal of Pediatrics* 105:597–600.

Matin, M., P. Sylvester, D. Edwards, and J. Dickerson. 1981. Vitamin and zinc status in Down's syndrome. *Journal of Mental Deficiency Research* 25:121–126.

McLaren, D. S. 1982. Excessive nutrient intakes. In *Adverse Effects of Foods*, ed. E. F. P. Jelliffe and D. B. Jelliffe, pp. 367–387. New York: Plenum.

Parry, G. J. and D. E. Bredsen. 1985. Sensory neuropathy with low-dose pyridoxine. *Neurology* 35:1466–1468.

Pauling, L. 1968. Orthomolecular psychiatry. *Science* 160:265–271.

Pruess, J. B., R. B. Fewell, and F. C. Bennett. 1989. Vitamin therapy and children with Down's sydrome: A review of the research. *Exceptional Children* 55:336–341.

Rimland, B. 1974. An orthomolecular study of psychotic children. *Journal of Orthomolecular Psychiatry* 3:371–377.

Rimland, B. 1983. Vitamin/mineral supplementation for mental retardation (letter to the editor). *Lancet* 2:744–745.

Rimland, B., E. Calloway, and P. Dreyfus. 1978. The effect of high doses of vitaman B$_6$ on autistic children: A double-blind crossover study. *American Journal of Psychiatry* 135:472–475.

Rosa, F. W. 1983. Teratogenicity of isoretinoin. *Lancet* 2:513.

Schaumburg, H., J. Kaplan, A. Windebank, N. Vick, S. Rasmus, D. Pleasure, and M. J. Brown. 1983. Sensory neuropathy from pyridoxine abuse. *New England Journal of Medicine* 309:445–448.

Smith, G. F., D. Spiker, C. P. Peterson, D. Cicchetti, and P. Justine. 1984. Use of megadoses of vitamins and minerals in Down's syndrome. *Journal of Pediatrics* 105:228–234.

Spreen, O., D. Tupper, A. Risser, H. Tuokko, and D. Edgell. 1984. *Human Developmental Neuropsychology*. New York: Oxford University Press.

Stimmel, G. L. 1989. Disorders of infancy and children. In *Pharmacotherapy A Pathophysiologic Approach*, ed. J. T. Piro, R. L. Talbert, P. E. Hayes, G. C. Yee, and L. M. Posey, pp. 671–677, New York: Elsevier.

Turkel, H. 1975. Medical amelioration of Down's syndrome incorporating the orthomolecular approach. *Journal of Orthomolecular Psychiatry* 4:102–115.

Weathers, C. 1983. Effects of nutritional supplementation on IQ and certain other variables associated with Down's syndrome. *American Journal of Mental Deficiency* 88:214–217.

Zametkin, A. J. 1989. The neurobiology of attention-deficit hyperactivity disorder: a synopsis. *Psychiatric Annals* 19:584–586.

6

Heavy Metals, Nutrition, and Behavior

In Chapter 4, we examined the essential role of trace elements in the normal functioning of the nervous system. There are, however, a number of trace elements, most often heavy metals, for which no biological function has been established. Included among these heavy metals are lead, mercury, arsenic, antimony, cadmium, and aluminum. Heavy metals enter our food supply from cookware and other food containers, vehicular wastes such as auto exhaust, industrial processes and wastes, and agricultural products such as fertilizers and pesticides. When ingested in sufficient quantities, many of these heavy metals can be extremely toxic.

Metals are toxic in varied ways. Most often, metals act indirectly through destruction of tissues and processes important in organs such as the kidney and liver. Some metals are suspected of being carcinogenic or teratogenic. Toxicity of heavy metals is influenced by numerous factors including the level and duration of ingestion, age, species, sex, nutritional adequacy of the diet, physical condition, and the capacity of different tissues to store the metals.

It has been well established that several of the heavy metals are potent neurotoxins and can have detrimental effects on behavior. This chapter concentrates on four of these metals, lead, mercury, aluminum, and cadmium. The adverse consequences of lead and mercury on neurological functioning and behavior in humans are well documented. Although most of the data on the neurological and behavioral effects of aluminum and cadmium have come from research with experimental animals, there is certainly reason to believe that these metals have detrimental consequences in our own species.

LEAD

Lead has many industrial and domestic applications and is ubiquitous in our environment. For many years, lead was widely used as a pigment in house paints. Although the use of lead-based paints is now severely restricted, the paint continues to be found in many older dwellings. Exposure to lead can result from ingestion of peeling paint or from inhalation of dust containing paint residues. Additionally, lead is present in some foods and beverages (e.g., contamination from cans, improperly glazed ceramics), in drinking water (e.g., leaching of lead in piping from soft water), and in air (contaminated by automobile exhaust and by lead smelter fumes).

The toxic qualities of lead have been recognized since antiquity. Lead poisoning, which is sometimes called "plumbism" from the Latin word for lead, was first described by the Greek poet-physician Niacander over 2,000 years ago. Throughout history, no other metal has stirred up as much controversy and policy discussion as lead. Initial interest in the clinical consequences of lead toxicity centered on the effects of high levels of the metal resulting from industrial exposure. More recently, however, data demonstrating adverse effects of lead in children at doses previously believed to be harmless have shifted attention to the neurotoxic and behavioral consequences of low-level lead exposure (Chisholm 1971; Smith 1985; Needleman 1987, 1989; Ernhart et al. 1989; Ruff and Bijur 1989).

Absorption, Distribution, and Excretion

Lead readily enters the body via the gastrointestinal tract and lungs, and most individuals have a measurable body burden of lead. Under usual conditions of dietary exposure (0.2–2.0 mg lead/day), adults absorb approximately 5 to 10% of ingested lead through the gastrointestinal tract. A variety of factors, however, influence lead absorption. For example, fasting increases absorption, with fasted subjects typically absorbing from 15 to 20% of ingested lead. Moreover lead competes with other divalent ions, such as calcium and zinc, for absorption. Diets deficient in these micronutrients increase both lead absorption and its toxicological potential. The influence of calcium seems to be mediated at the level of the gastrointestinal tract, since calcium-deficient diets affect the toxicity of ingested but not injected lead. Studies with experimental animals have demonstrated that lead absorption varies directly as a function of the fat content of the diet. Age also modifies lead absorption, with children absorbing more of the metal than adults. It has been estimated that children from 3 months to 8 years of age may absorb as much as 50% of ingested lead (Petit and Alfano 1983; Skerfving 1988).

Lead absorbed from the gastrointestinal system is distributed by the blood to other tissues. Lead is retained in three body compartments. In the first compartment, the blood, the metal is bound to erythrocytes and has a half-life of 25 to 30 days. In the second compartment, the soft tissues (kidney and liver), it has a half-life of several months. With time, lead is redistributed and deposited in the third compartment, bone and other calcified tissues. Approximately 90% to 95% of the body's burden of lead is concentrated in bone, where the half-life of the metal may be as long as 30 to 40 years.

In humans, lead excretion is accomplished primarily by the urinary system with concentrations of lead in the urine directly proportional to that in plasma. Lead is also excreted in feces, and in sweat and breast milk, and deposited in hair and nails (Klaassen 1980; Petit and Alfano 1983).

After establishment of a steady state early in life, the daily intake of lead approximates output, and concentrations in soft tissue vary little across time under normal conditions. Since the rate of lead that can be excreted from the body is limited, however, even a small increase in daily intake can produce an increase in the body's burden of lead. The average daily intake of lead is approximately 0.3 mg, and a positive lead balance starts at an intake of 0.6 mg. Because lead is slowly deposited in bone, this latter amount will not normally produce overt toxicity over a lifetime. When lead intake is great, however, deposition in bone is too slow to protect the soft tissues. The time it takes to accumulate toxic amounts of lead shortens disproportionately as the amount ingested rises. Thus, a daily intake of 2.5 mg of lead would require nearly four years for a toxic amount of lead to accumulate in the soft tissues of the body, but daily intake of 3.5 mg would produce toxic levels within a few months (Klaassen 1980).

One difficulty in assessing the toxic effects of lead is knowing how to determine the body's burden of lead. Most early research evaluating the effects of lead relied on concentrations of the metal in blood. Unfortunately, blood lead levels can only provide a measure of relatively recent exposure to the metal (several months). Thus, blood lead levels are not appropriate for determining the consequences of lead exposure in early life on later behavior. To overcome this difficulty, recent studies have begun to use measures that provide more accurate estimates of previous lead exposure, such as lead concentrations in teeth (e.g., Needleman et al. 1979).

The blood-brain barrier initially inhibits massive entry of lead into the brain. With time and the accumulation of the metal in the body, however, it does cross the blood-brain barrier, with concentrations in the brain being proportional to those in the blood. Because the blood-brain barrier is more permeable in the young organism, the passage of lead into the central nervous system is significantly greater in young animals than in older ones. For example, the amount of lead accumulated in the brain is three times higher in 10-day old monkeys than in adult monkeys, after the same amount of lead exposure. Once it enters the brain, lead is not evenly distributed. The greatest accumulations are found in the hippocampus, cerebellum, hypothalamus, striatum, cortex, and midbrain (Petit and Alfano 1983).

Clinical Consequences of Lead Poisoning

ADULTS

In adults, lead poisoning most often occurs in the workplace. The prevalence of occupational lead exposure in a wide variety of industries has been well established, and it is estimated that approximately 1.5% of all American workers are exposed to significant amounts of the metal. A substantial proportion of these workers may experience symptoms of lead toxicity. The lead-poisoned adult typically presents with pallor, abdominal pain, constipation, vomiting, anemia, and frequently the presence of a blue "lead line" on the gums.

A variety of other symptoms indicative of damage to the central nervous system have been well documented. Indications of lead poisoning include

Abdominal pain

Gastrointestinal problems, such as nausea, diarrhea, or constipation

Peripheral neuropathy

Muscle weakness, particularly in the arms and legs

Fatigue

Headache

Anorexia and weight loss

Anemia

Hyperirritability

Sleep disturbances

Depression, hostility, and general dysphoria

Additionally, psychological and neuropsychological tests have revealed deficits in long-term memory, concentration, verbal ability, visual–spatial abstraction, and psychomotor performance.

Symptoms of peripheral neuropathy are also common in the lead-poisoned adult. Peripheral neuropathy is generally manifested by muscle weakness and disturbances in the motor system, with unilateral or unequal bilateral paralysis of the extensor muscle groups in the hands and feet. The muscles affected appear to be those that are used most frequently. Wrist drop and weakness of the small muscles of the hands are considered classic symptoms of lead toxicity. Occasionally, changes in sensory systems, such as paresthesia or patches of analgesia or anesthesia, are associated with exposure to lead (McConnell 1983; Petit and Alfano 1983).

INFANTS AND CHILDREN

In the United States, childhood lead poisoning is almost exclusively seen in children of preschool age who live in substandard housing and are exposed to lead-based paints, or dust and soil in which lead from paint or gasoline has settled. Children living in such environments frequently display symptoms of pica, which is the ingestion of nonfood items including paint chips and other lead-contaminated items. Children can also be exposed to lead in contaminated drinking water, such as from lead pipes or leached lead solder. Although the use of lead solder in food containers has decreased dramatically in recent years, and lead in food has thus declined, sufficient amounts remain in the food supply to measurably add to the total lead levels of many children in this country (Anonymous 1988). Of the total amount of lead to which a 2-year old child is exposed, approximately 45% comes from food, 45% from dust and the intake of nonfood items, 9% from water, and 1% from air (Miller 1989).

The characteristics of acute lead poisoning in infants and children are somewhat different from those seen in adults. More specifically, in adults symptoms of peripheral nerve damage predominate over those of CNS damage, whereas in children the exact opposite is found. Some of the consequences of lead poisoning in children include

Decreased appetite

Abdominal pain and vomiting

Clumsiness

Fatigue progressing to intermittant drowsiness and stupor

Unwillingness to play

Irritability

Ataxia

Speech problems

Impairments on psychometric tests

Encephalopathy

Seizures

Coma

The onset of lead poisoning can be insidious. For the first four to six weeks of exposure there may be no symptoms at all. Minor complaints including fatigue, headache, decreased appetite, irritability, abdominal pain, and vomiting then begin to appear. However, as these are all rather nonspecific symptoms which could be the result of a variety of childhood diseases, lead poisoning may not be suspected at this point. As exposure to the metal continues, fatigue may progress to intermittent drowsiness and stupor, vomiting may become persistent and forceful, and speech problems and difficulties with balance and walking may develop. In the most severe stages of lead poisoning, seizures, coma, and death can occur (Chisholm 1971; Klaassen 1980; McConnell 1983; Petit and Alfano 1983).

Even the symptoms of severe lead encephalopathy are relatively non-specific, resembling those of brain abscesses and tumors, or of viral or bacterial infections of the brain. Therefore, diagnosis depends first on a high level of suspicion. To make a positive diagnosis it is necessary to determine body levels of lead. Once a diagnosis is made, treatment should be immediately initiated. Typical treatment for lead poisoning uses chelating agents (from the Greek "chele," meaning claw) which firmly bind to metal atoms, sequestering them and making them highly soluble. These agents remove lead from tissues, for excretion through the kidney and liver. With chelating agents, high levels of lead in the body can be rapidly reduced to levels approaching normal, and many of the symptoms of severe lead toxicity reversed (Chisholm 1971; Klaassen 1980).

Until 1943, it was believed that children who recovered from episodes of clinical lead poisoning did not suffer any lasting consequences. In 1943, however, Byers and Lord discovered that children who experienced lead poisoning early in life later developed a variety of behavioral and neurological problems. These children performed poorly in school, had difficulties in performing spatial tasks, and displayed a number of behavioral difficulties including hyperactivity, short attention span, and impulsivity. Subsequent research has demonstrated that behavioral problems, mental retardation, and permanent brain damage are frequent sequelae of early exposure to high lead levels.

Neurotoxicological Consequences of Lead Poisoning

A variety of anatomical alterations in both the central and peripheral nervous systems are associated with lead poisoning. Because the development of lead encephalopathy is more common in children than adults, the majority of research on the effects of lead on the CNS has concentrated on the developing organism. Reduced brain size or weight is frequently observed in experimental animals exposed to lead during development. Although damage occurs throughout the brain, it most frequently is observed in the cerebral cortex, cerebellum, and hippocampus.

Lead primarily appears to affect the blood vessels serving the brain. In both experimental animals and humans exposed to high levels of lead, capillaries within the brain are frequently either dilated or narrowed, and often necrosed and thrombotic. Changes in neurons and glial cells may be secondary consequences of the effects of lead on these small-caliber blood vessels.

Studies in experimental animals exposed to lead during development have revealed abnormalities in neuronal maturation, retardation in myelination, and alterations in glial cell structure. Decreases in dendritic arborization, particularly in the Purkinje cells of the cerebellum and cells of the hippocampal dentate gyrus, and reductions in the development of the axonal system of the hippocampus have also been observed in lead-poisoned animals.

The effects of lead on a number of neurotransmitter systems have also been assessed. Lead inhibits neuronal release of the neurotransmitter acetylcholine and produces a marked decrease in its turnover, particularly in cells in the hippocampus, resulting in a substantial reduction in cholinergic functioning. Research examining the effects of lead on other neurotransmitter systems has been less conclusive. However, there is some suggestive evidence of an increase in presynaptic catecholaminergic function in lead-exposed animals (McConnell 1983; Petit and Alfano 1983).

The peripheral nervous system is also affected by lead. In humans, it can produce axonal degeneration in cells in both the spinal cord and the peripheral nerves. Additionally, although not observed in humans, segmental demyelination of peripheral nerves has been reported in a number of species including rats, guinea pigs, and cats. It has been suggested that both axonal degeneration and demyelination may be secondary to damage to the vascular system serving the peripheral nervous system. Finally, neurophysiological examinations have revealed reductions in motor nerve conduction velocity and electromyographic abnormalities in human patients (Petit and Alfano 1983; Skerfving 1988).

Low-Level Lead Exposure and Behavior in Children

The gradual disappearance of lead-based paints, and the removal of lead from gasoline which in the United States has resulted in a 99% decrease in the amount of alkyl lead introduced into the atmosphere, has been accompanied by a steady reduction in the number of cases of severe lead poisoning in children. However, recent studies have suggested that levels of lead previously thought to be safe may cause deficits in neuropsychological development and behavior (Needleman 1989; Davis et al. 1990).

Initial evidence was provided in a study by Needleman and colleagues examining the effects of relatively low levels of lead exposure on academic achievement, performance on standardized intelligence tests, motor coordination, attention level, and a number of behavioral tasks, of 6- and 7-year-old children (Needleman et al. 1979; Needleman 1982). Determinations of exposure were made on the basis of dentine lead levels. First- and second-grade children whose teeth contained 24 or more parts per million (ppm) lead were classified as having high lead levels, and those whose teeth contained 6 or less ppm as having low lead levels. Children who had birth weights below 2,500 g or a history of head injury, or who had been diagnosed as having a prior episode of lead poisoning, were excluded from the study. Children with high dentine lead levels scored significantly lower on intelligence tests; displayed more impairments in tests of attention, verbal performance, and auditory processing; and received more negative teacher ratings than children with low lead levels.

In a follow-up study published 11 years later, Needleman and co-workers reexamined IQs, neurobehavioral functioning, and school performance in a portion of the individuals who had initially been studied as primary school children (Needleman et al. 1990). Continued impaired neurobehavioral functioning was directly related to dentine lead levels at the ages of 6 and 7. Young adults who had demonstrated high dentine lead levels as children displayed a significantly higher risk of dropping out of school and of having a reading disability than those who had lower dentine levels as children. Higher lead levels in childhood also were associated with lower vocabulary and verbal-reasoning scores, poor hand–eye coordination, longer reaction times, lower class standing, and increased absenteeism in high school.

From the results of these studies, Needleman and associates concluded that exposure to lead, even at levels that do not produce overt symptoms of poisoning, has detrimental effects on neurobehavioral and intellectual functioning that can persist until at least early adulthood. These conclusions have been supported by the results of a number of other experiments (e.g., Yule et al. 1981; Maracek et al. 1983; Lansdown et al. 1986; Dietrich et al. 1987; Fulton et al. 1987; Bergomi et al. 1989; Winneke et al. 1989; Davis et al. 1990). As a result, the accepted threshold for lead-engendered neurotoxicity in children has declined steadily. In 1988, the Agency for Toxic Substances and Disease Registry, in consultation with the Environmental Protection Agency, concluded that the threshold of lead in the blood for neurobehavioral toxicity was 0.5 to 0.7 umol per liter (10 to 15 ug per deciliter). Using this criterion, it has been estimated that 3 to 4 million American children have blood lead levels sufficient to cause detrimental neurobehavioral consequences (Anonymous 1988).

While a positive relation between low-level lead exposure and deficits in neuropsychological development has been frequently reported, its exact nature remains controversial. It has been argued that body lead levels in children act primarily as a marker for lower socioeconomic status, decreased social stimulation, and poorer quality of the caretaking environment, and that when these factors are adequately controlled, adverse behavioral effects cannot be attributed to lead with any certainty (Smith 1985; Ernhart et al. 1987, 1989; Ruff and Bijur 1989). It also has been suggested that the reported effects of low levels of lead could be confounded by the presence of other environmental toxins, or by concurrent nutritional deficiencies (Ruff and Bijur 1989). For example, children living near lead smelters are exposed to airborne cadmium as well as lead. There is suggestive evidence that cadmium, like lead, can alter neurobehavioral functioning and is associated with low birth weight, which can alter behavioral development. Thus, it is possible that the effects of cadmium on the nervous system account for some of the decrements in performance observed in studies of lead toxicity. Concurrent nutritional deficiencies could also confound studies of lead toxicity; as an illustration, children with elevated blood lead levels are more likely to have low iron stores than children with lower lead levels (Yip, Norris, and Anderson 1981). Just as low to moderate exposure to lead, iron deficiency has been associated with decrements in intellectual performance (see Chapter 4). It is therefore conceivable that the link between lead and behavior could be accounted for by a causal relationship between iron deficiency and behavior (Ruff and Bijur 1989).

Although a variety of factors may interact with the effects of lead on behavior, we cannot ignore the potential link between lead and behavioral disruptions. Rather, more research is needed to determine if and how low levels of lead influence the nervous system and behavior, and how lead interacts with other variables to alter neurobiological functioning in young children.

Given the known toxicity of high levels of lead and the potentially detrimental consequences of exposure to lower levels, serious consideration must continue to be given to reducing lead in our environment. Exposure to lead paint in old housing and lead from other sources deposited in dust and soil remains a significant problem. Unfortunately, most of the present methods of removing and disposing of lead from homes and other sites are relatively crude and can be dangerous to workers. New methods for de-leading the approximately 2 million homes with deteriorating paint and inhabited by young children are urgently needed (Anonymous 1988; Needleman 1989).

MERCURY

Mercury, an element found in rocks, soil, water, and air, has been mined for thousands of years. Throughout history, the metal has served a wide variety of industrial uses. Additionally, for hundreds of years, compounds containing the element formed a significant part of the physician's medical arsenal. Mercury was incorporated into ointments for skin diseases, cathartics, diuretics, germicides, and even teething powders. Before the discovery of antibiotics, although not effective, mercury was the treatment of choice for syphilis.

While mercury is an extremely useful compound, its toxic potential has been recognized for centuries. Almost 2,000 years ago Pliny the Elder recognized mercury as an occupational hazard for Spanish miners. As a result of the toxicity of the metal, only criminals and slaves were employed in the dreaded Almaden mercury mines in Spain. Mercury poisoning was one of the earliest occupational diseases to be identified, and inspired the first industrial hygiene laws on record. Technological advances during the last hundred years have been accompanied by a large increase in the emission of mercury into the environment, such as through the discharge of industrial wastes into rivers, lakes, and oceans (Amin-Zaki 1982; Weiss 1983; Clarkson 1988; Choi 1989).

Discussion of mercury poisoning is complicated by the fact that the various forms of the element have their own distinctive toxic properties. Inorganic mercury exists in three oxidation states: elemental, mercurous, and mercuric mercury. In its organic forms, mercury is covalently linked to at least one carbon atom. There are a wide variety of organic compounds, but from the toxicological standpoint, the short-chain alkyl compounds present the most serious concerns. These compounds are metabolically stable and can easily cross most diffusion barriers in the body including the blood-brain barrier and placenta (Aschner and Aschner 1990). As we shall see, these compounds are potent neurotoxins and can produce irreversible damage in both the adult and developing brain.

Inorganic Toxicity

Elemental mercury is liquid at room temperature. Mercury can be ingested orally without ill effects, but its vapor represents a serious industrial hazard. Liquid metallic mercury can seep into cracks in surfaces such as floors, from which it can invisibly volatilize. Home exposure can result from misuse or accidental spillage. By spreading the metal into cracks and crevices, attempted cleanup with a household vacuum cleaner can magnify the contamination of the home. Once inhaled, mercury vapor is dissolved in the blood and rapidly carried to the brain where it is oxidized to mercuric mercury (Hg^{++}). Because this form of the metal does not readily cross the blood-brain barrier, mercury is retained within the brain (Weiss 1983; Clarkson 1988; Aschner and Aschner 1990).

During the 18th and 19th centuries, the most frequently noted symptom of inorganic mercury poisoning in adults was tremor. This tremor, called "hatter's shakes" in the 1800s because so many workers in the felt hat industry suffered from it, developed first in the facial muscles and then progressed to the fingers and hands. As exposure continued, tremors attacked the tongue, speech became slurred, and the victim began to walk with a jerky, ataxic gait. Cognitive changes such as memory loss also have been associated with mercury toxicity (Weiss 1983; Clarkson 1988). Awareness of mercury toxicity has led to substantial efforts to decrease occupational exposure and to a subsequent reduction in reports of severe tremor. However, subtle changes in nervous system functioning, including insomnia, fatigue, irritability, and loss of appetite, continue to occur as a result of occupational exposure to mercury.

The extensive use of mercurous chloride in teething powders and other medications earlier in this century was identified in 1948 as the cause of the relatively common childhood disease acrodynia, or "pink disease" (Warkany and Hubbard 1948, 1951). The disease was characterized by a bright pink color of the hands, feet, and face; excessive salivation and perspiration; rashes; and marked nervous system disturbances including severe pain in the arms and legs, irritability, insomnia, photophobia, and colicky crying. The removal of mercury from teething powders and other medications has led to the virtual elimination of pink disease (Weiss 1983; Clarkson 1988). Inorganic mercury poisoning in children is now almost nonexistent.

Organic Toxicity and Minamata Disease

Organic methylmercury compounds were first synthesized in 1865. Shortly afterward, it was recognized that these compounds were potent central nervous system poisons. However, the discovery that compounds containing methylmercury could be used to protect grains from fungal growth overrode concerns about potential toxicity. From the 1940s until the early 1970s, methylmercury fungicides were used in extensively in North America and Europe, as well as in developing countries. In the early 1970s, however, reports from developing countries of serious outbreaks of methylmercury poisoning among farmers and their families led to the termination of the use of these fungicides (Bakir et al. 1973; Clarkson, Amin-Zaki, and Al-Tikriti 1976; Amin-Zaki 1982).

While the toxicity of methylmercury has long been recognized, our knowledge of the truly devastating consequences of exposure to this chemical can be dated to the 1950s when an outbreak of methylmercury poisoning was documented in Minamata, a fishing village on the coast of the Japanese island of Kyushu. Minamata was the home of the Chisso chemical plant which in 1932 began production of acetaldehyde, a chemical used in making plastics, drugs, and perfumes that requires the use of mercury as a catalyst. During the early 1950s, the company escalated production, which resulted in an increase in the discharge of mercury into Minamata bay. Methylmercury was produced by the methylation of inorganic mercury compounds by methanogenic bacteria present in the aquatic sediment and then was taken up by fish living in the bay (Smith and Smith 1975; Harada 1982).

The first clues that exposure to methylmercury might be causing problems in Minamata were noted in 1950. Catches of fish decreased, shellfish died, and poisoned fish floated to the surface of the bay. In 1953, large numbers of water birds displayed difficulties in flying, and cats in fishing villages began to exhibit symptoms of abnormal behavior and to die suddenly. Minamata disease, as methylmercury poisoning has come to be known, was identified in humans in 1956. The condition, initially called the "strange disease," was first documented in a 5-year-old girl suffering symptoms of severe brain damage: she could not walk, her speech was incoherent, and she was delirious. Within several days, her younger sister was brought to the hospital suffering from similar symptoms. As the year progressed, the number of patients with symptoms of the "strange disease" steadily increased. At first, unable to connect the symptoms to any single source, doctors offered a number of diagnoses including encephalitis, alcoholism, cerebral palsy, and infantile paralysis. In 1959, however, an environmental survey revealed extraordinarily high levels of methylmercury in Minamata bay. This finding, coupled with experiments demonstrating that exposure to methylmercury in cats produced symptoms similar to those of the "strange disease," led to the conclusion that the cause of the disease was mercury poisoning (Smith and Smith 1975; Harada 1982).

The consumption of fish from Minamata bay represented the primary source of methylmercury exposure. Fish and shellfish in the bay took up methylmercury and then were consumed by local fishermen and their families. The amount of fish consumed, the length of time during which intake occurred, and the methylmercury concentrations in the fish were all directly associated with the health consequences of mercury exposure. It has been estimated that if a person ate 100 g per day of fish containing 500 ug/kg of methylmercury, he or she would have a daily intake of 50 ug of methylmercury, substantially greater than the maximum allowable intake of 30 ug recommended by the Food and Agricultural Organization/World Health Organization (FAO/WHO) Expert Committee on Food Additives (Inskip and Piotrowski 1985). Intake of fish in Japan has been calculated to be from 80 to 90 g per day, and it has been established that the fishermen and their families in the Minamata region consumed two to four times more fish than the average Japanese household (Harada 1982). Whereas mercury concentrations in most marine and freshwater fish are less than 100 to 200 ug/kg wet weight, the two major fish species in Minamata bay were found to contain from 2,600 to 6,600 ug/kg (Choi 1989). Thus, it is obvious that consumption of fish from Minamata bay could have led to toxic levels of methylmercury.

During the 1960s and 1970s, several other serious outbreaks of methylmercury poisoning occurred. The most catastrophic took place in Iraq during the fall and winter of 1971–1972. Throughout the country, more than 6,500 individuals were admitted to hospitals with methylmercury poisoning, and over 450 individuals died from the toxic effects of the metal. The outbreak was caused by the consumption of homemade bread made from wheat treated with a methylmercury fungicide. The wheat, which was shipped to Iraq from Mexico, was intended only for planting purposes and was delivered throughout the country. The sacks of grain carried a warning label; however, the label was written in Spanish, a language obviously unfamiliar to Iraqi farmers. The grain also was dyed red, a customary procedure to indicate treatment with methylmercury. Unfortunately, the dye was easily removed by washing, but the methylmercury fungicide was not. To test for toxicity, some farmers fed the washed grain to their animals. Seeing no deleterious effects after several days of feeding, the farmers assumed that the grain was safe and could be made into bread. However, symptoms of methylmercury poisoning typically take several weeks or months to appear. Thus, the farmers' assumptions were proven false. Individuals of all ages and both sexes consumed the contaminated bread and were exposed to methylmercury (Clarkson, Amin-Zaki, and Al-Tikriti 1976).

CONSEQUENCES IN ADULTS

The central nervous system is the primary target of methylmercury poisoning. Most symptoms of the disease are clearly associated with damage to the central nervous system:

Sensory disturbances

Paresthesia

Numbness in fingers and toes

Constriction of the visual field

Hearing impairment

Pain in limbs

Motor disturbances

Weakness, unsteadiness of legs, falling

Ataxic gait

Tremors

Adiadochokinesia (inability to perform rapid alternating movements)

Dysarthria (thick, slurred speech)

Other

Mental disturbances (e.g., forgetfulness, irritability)

Headaches

Increased salivation

Symptoms appear only after a relatively long latency period of a few weeks to several months. Typically, there are no warning signals. Symptoms generally begin with numbness of the extremities and difficulties in hand movements and in grasping things. As the disease progresses, more serious problems develop including loss of coordination, ataxic gait, dysarthria, muscle weakness, and tremor. If exposure to methylmercury continues, these problems gradually increase in severity, leading finally to general paralysis, deformity, difficulty in swallowing, convulsions, and death. In moderate to severe cases of methylmercury poisoning, visual disturbances and hearing impairments are also present. One of the classic characteristics of Minamata disease is constriction of the visual field. Individuals with the disease gradually loose peripheral vision, which leads to other problems such as impaired night vision. The ability to track visual targets may also be impaired. Finally, alterations in behavior including irritability and memory loss are frequently associated with Minamata disease.

In adults, especially in those less severely affected, some gradual improvement may be seen in muscle weakness, ataxia, and dysarthria when methylmercury intake is stopped. Visual changes improve only slightly, however, and most patients have permanent damage to their sight. Individuals suffering from the most severe cases of methylmercury poisoning do not improve with time, and are left physically and mentally incapacitated. The fact that the damage produced by methylmercury can be irreversible indicates that attempts at treatment must be initiated as soon as possible. Treatment involves removal of methylmercury from the body using various chelating agents. As treatment is not as effective in patients demonstrating the extreme consequences of Minamata disease, in most cases asymptomatic individuals having high blood levels of methylmercury are treated first.

Autopsies of patients with Minamata disease have revealed symptoms associated with selective damage to specific regions of the central nervous system (Figure 6-1). For example, coordination problems have been directly related to degeneration of granule cells in the cerebellum. Deficits in the visual system result primarily from damage to the calcarine fissure of the visual cortex, the region that receives information from the peripheral portions of the visual field, and sensory and motor problems are consequences of damage to the motor and sensory cortex (precentral and postcentral gyri). Although damage to the central nervous system in Minamata disease is irreversible, some functional recovery may appear in individuals as alternative nerve pathways adapt to the damage.

Peripheral nerve damage, most notably destruction and demyelination in sensory nerve fibers in the extremities, has also been observed in Minamata disease (Smith and Smith 1975; Clarkson, Amin-Zaki, and Al-Tikriti 1976; Harada 1982; Weiss 1983; Clarkson 1988; Burbacher, Rodier, and Weiss, 1990).

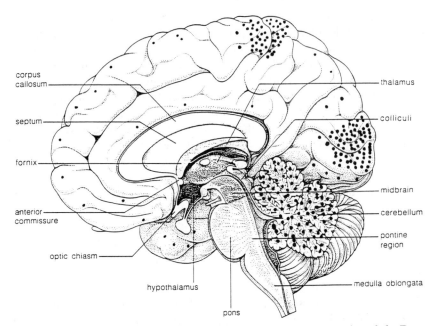

Figure 6-1. Areas of the brain damaged in Minamata disease in the adult. Damage is greatest in the cerebellum, visual cortex located above the cerebellum, and sensory and motor cortex located at the top of the brain.

CONGENITAL (FETAL) MINAMATA DISEASE

Beginning in the late 1950s, many cases of congenital idiocy accompanied by a variety of neurological symptoms were noted in the area of Minamata. Although it was suspected that these children might be suffering from methylmercury poisoning, they were diagnosed as having cerebral palsy since none of them had eaten contaminated fish. There were, however, no abnormal factors associated with the mother's pregnancy or delivery that might have caused cerebral palsy. The only common factor found among these children was that their mothers had eaten large amounts of fish during pregnancy. Subsequent investigations revealed that a large proportion of the affected children had a family member with Minamata disease. In addition, the mercury content in the hair of these children, who had been born from 1955 to 1958, was still high in 1961. Finally, autopsies of the brains of two of the children revealed damage indicative of methylmercury poisoning. Taking these observations together, it was concluded that methylmercury had passed through the placenta, causing congenital (fetal) Minamata disease (Smith and Smith 1975).

In the Iraqi outbreak of methylmercury poisoning, a number of infants of mothers who had consumed contaminated bread during lactation displayed clinical symptoms of congenital Minamata disease; however, the symptoms were milder than those observed in Minamata. These findings suggest that exposure to methylmercury via nursing may have less serious consequences than prenatal exposure.

Transplacental transfer of methylmercury takes place rapidly. Methylmercury concentrations in cord blood are approximately 20% higher than in maternal blood, probably because fetal hemoglobin binds more readily with the toxin than does adult hemoglobin. Moreover, methylmercury readily enters the fetal brain, leading to higher concentrations than in the maternal brain. Methylmercury is also secreted in breast milk. Continued ingestion of milk containing methylmercury will slow down the rate of decline of body mercury in infants prenatally exposed to the toxin. Suckling infants can accumulate high blood levels of methylmercury if their mothers have been heavily exposed (Amin-Zaki 1982).

The developing nervous system is particularly sensitive to methylmercury poisoning. The clinical characteristics of congenital Minamata disease include a number of obvious signs of central nervous system damage. In Minamata, prenatally exposed infants displayed symptoms of extensive brain damage, including:

Mental retardation

Developmental delays

Cerebellar abnormalities

Dysarthria

Ataxia

Deformities of limbs

Primitive reflexes

Extrapyramidal hyperkinesis

Strabismus

Nystagmus

Decreased visual acuity

Hypersalivation

Growth impairments

Convulsive seizures

Although the children in Iraq who were exposed to methylmercury in breast milk were not as severely affected as the children from Minamata, they did demonstrate delayed motor and language development, as well as abnormal neurological signs which became more obvious as they grew older.

Autopsies have revealed that the pattern of brain damage in congenital Minamata disease is different from the adult pattern. In general, destruction of the brain in congenital Minamata disease is not as specific as in the adult form of the disease. The brains of children with congenital Minamata disease are significantly smaller than those of normal children (Figure 6-2). Brain weight may be reduced from one-third to one-half that of age-matched controls. Thinning of the corpus callosum, hypoplasia of the white matter of the cerebrum and cerebellum, and underdevelopment of the basal ganglia have also been observed. On a microscopic level, the cerebral cortex displays a disorganization of cortical architecture due to a decrease in the number of nerve cells. Additionally, neurons are abnormally oriented in many areas of the cortex. Recent work has demonstrated that the teratogenic actions of methylmercury in the central nervous system are primarily the result of disruption of early biochemical mechanisms that control cellular replication, differentiation, and migration. This disruption leads to aberrant patterns of neuronal architecture, synaptic development, and synaptic physiology (Slotkin and Bartolome 1987; Choi 1989).

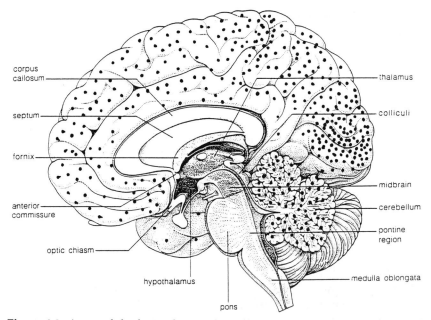

Figure 6-2. Areas of the brain damaged in congenital Minamata disease. Brain damage is more diffuse when methylmercury exposure occurs during fetal development than when it occurs in adults.

The Continuing Problem of Methylmercury Toxicity

Although measures have been taken to reduce methylmercury contamination of our waters and the chemical is no longer used as a fungicide, methylmercury toxicity cannot be relegated to history. Methylmercury is extremely persistent: it has been estimated that it may remain in the sediments of rivers and lakes for as long as 70 years. As methylmercury passes up the food chain, it also bioconcentrates, because most organisms retain rather than excrete the majority of the methylmercury they ingest (Pim 1981).

Relatively high levels of mercury in fish and fish products continue to be reported. The concentrations of methylmercury in fish depend upon a variety of factors, including the species of fish, age of the fish, and the location where the fish was caught. In general, predatory fish at the top of the aquatic food chain, for example, ocean species such as shark, tuna, and swordfish, and freshwater species such as pike, have the highest concentrations of mercury. Mercury levels also increase with the age of the fish. In freshwater species, local contamination by mercury and acidification of bodies of water by acid rain and the impoundment of water for large hydroelectric plants have led to higher concentrations of methylmercury. Thus, although in most fish mercury concentrations are less than 100 to 200 ug/kg, pike from contaminated waters in Canada have been found to have levels as high as 9,000 to 22,000 ug/kg.

In view of changing dietary preferences for fish over red meat as a source of protein, the possibility of methylmercury poisoning through consumption of contaminated fish is a serious concern. Recent studies have suggested that long-term daily intake of as little as 85 g of tuna by pregnant women could have deleterious effects on their offspring. As a result of the many industrial and commercial uses of mercury, problems of disposing contaminated wastes, increasing levels of the metal in food as a consequence of acid rain, and lack of a simple method for detecting low levels of exposure, it is probable that the risk of methylmercury poisoning will not rapidly disappear (Clarkson 1988; Choi 1989; Aschner and Aschner 1990).

ALUMINUM

Aluminum is the third most common element and most abundant metal, and constitutes approximately 8% of the earth's crust. Aluminum is usually found in combination with oxygen as alumina (Al_2O_3) and is also present in approximately 300 different minerals. Because of its abundance, humans are naturally exposed to high amounts of the metal. The amount of aluminum in plants and animals varies directly with the quantity of the metal present in the environment. The effects of the metal are particularly prominent in areas of the world where high levels are found in or can be leached out of the soil by acid rain. In addition to the aluminum found in the natural environment, we are exposed to it in the form of cosmetics, antacids, beverage containers, and drinking water (aluminum sulfate is used for water purification).

For hundred of years aluminum was thought to be safe. However, two relatively recent developments have led to the conclusion that it is a potent neurotoxin. First, it was discovered that aluminum is associated with dialysis dementia, and second, research has suggested that the metal might be related to senile dementia, or Alzheimer's disease (Petit 1983; Boegman and Bates 1984).

Absorption and Distribution

Aluminum is absorbed across the gastrointestinal tract and, like other metals, can compete with various elements for absorption from the gut. For example, aluminum competes with fluoride for absorption. Thus, increasing fluoride in the diet reduces both aluminum absorption and its neurotoxic potential. It has also been reported that nutritional deficiencies of calcium and magnesium in the presence of excess aluminum can lead to increased absorption of the metal from the gut and deposition of aluminum in the CNS (Yase 1980). Once aluminum has been absorbed from the gut, it enters the general circulation and is distributed to a variety of tissues including bone, liver, and muscle. In addition, aluminum can readily cross the blood-brain barrier to enter the CNS. Although aluminum accumulates throughout the brain, higher concentrations are found in gray matter than in white matter (Petit 1983; Boegman and Bates 1984; Yokel 1989).

Neurotoxicity of Aluminum

High levels of aluminum are clearly toxic to the CNS. In some experimental animals, including cats, dogs, and rabbits, administration of aluminum is associated with a progressive encephalopathy characterized by degeneration of cerebral nerve cells, brain stem demyelination, and severe neurofibrillary degeneration. The terms "neurofibrillary degeneration" or "neurofibrillary tangle" refer to the accumulation of tangles of neurofibers within the neuron. Neurons contain three types of fibrous elements: neurotubules, neurofilaments, and microfilaments. In normal neurons, neurotubules and neurofilaments are long, straight, threadlike fibers running through and parallel to the long axis of dendrites and axons. These fibers provide a cytoskeletal net that aids in the growth and development of cell processes. Neurotubules are also important for the transport of substances, such as enzymes and neurotransmitter precursors, within the axonal and dendritic systems. Disruption of these fibers alters transport of essential material to cellular processes, and thus may be associated with alterations in neurotransmitter functioning and the dendritic structure of the neuron (Petit 1983; Boegman and Bates 1984).

Although neurofibrillary tangles develop in response to elevated aluminum levels in some species, this is not universally the case. Brain aluminum concentrations 6 to 10 times that required to produce encephalopathy in cats and rabbits fail to produce any chronic neurofibrillary degeneration in the rat. Similarly, administration of large single doses of aluminum in monkeys produces no neurofibrillary degeneration. Neurofibrillary tangles have not been observed in vivo in human patients undergoing dialysis despite very high tissue levels of aluminum (Petit 1983; Boegman and Bates 1984).

Recent work has shown that aluminum also modifies the functioning of the blood-brain barrier, which regulates the exchange of material between the peripheral circulation and the CNS. Aluminum binds to the endothelial cells that make up the blood-brain barrier and is deposited around the blood vessels in patients with dementia. It has been hypothesized that the binding of aluminum to the blood-brain barrier alters the regulation of the entry rate of normally nontoxic, behaviorally active substances (e.g., hormones, peptides, or drugs) into the CNS. In addition, the alteration in membrane functioning of the blood-brain barrier could promote the uptake of toxic compounds into the CNS and account for some of the neurotoxic qualities of aluminum (Banks and Kastin 1989).

The behavioral effects of aluminum have only recently been investigated. Studies in experimental animals suggest that aluminum leads to deficits in motor coordination, learning, and memory. In normal elderly humans, high serum concentrations of aluminum have been associated with impaired visuomotor coordination and problems with long-term memory (Bowdler et al. 1979; Yokel 1989).

ALUMINUM AND DIALYSIS DEMENTIA

A possible relationship between aluminum and dialysis encephalopathy was first hypothesized in 1976 by Alfrey, LeGendre, and Kaehny. Dialysis encephalopathy, or dialysis dementia, is a neurological syndrome that has been observed in some patients requiring long-term renal dialysis. It is characterized by language disturbances, personality changes that include paranoia and confusion, impaired mathematical ability, cognitive decline, and delirium. As the disease progresses, loss of muscle coordination, marked motor abnormalities, seizures, and finally death may occur. The exact cause of dialysis dementia remains unknown; however, the evidence strongly implicates aluminum. Striking elevations in aluminum levels in muscle, bone, and brain gray matter have been reported in dialysis patients. Neurological symptoms begin to appear when the tissue content of aluminum reaches or exceeds 10 to 20 times that found in normal brains.

The increase in the body burden of aluminum in dialysis dementia has been associated with high levels of the metal in the water used to make up the dialysate. When deionized water is substituted for untreated tap water, a reduction in the symptoms of dementia has been observed (Alfrey, LeGendre, and Kaehny 1976; McDermott et al. 1978; Petit 1983; Markesbery and Ehmann 1988).

Despite high levels of aluminum in the brains of patients with dialysis dementia, autopsies have not revealed any specific neuropathological changes such as neurofibrillary tangles. Without obvious changes in the brain, one of the major unanswered questions is the cause of the observed cognitive and behavioral alterations. It has been hypothesized that although aluminum levels are markedly elevated in dialysis dementia, the metal may not have a directly toxic effect, but function to displace another essential trace element necessary for normal neuronal functioning. More research on other trace elements is clearly needed to test this hypothesis (Petit 1983; Markesbery and Ehmann 1988).

DOES ALUMINUM PLAY A ROLE IN ALZHEIMER'S DISEASE?

Increased levels of aluminum have also been implicated in Alzheimer's disease (AD). Clinically, AD is characterized by the progressive deterioration of cognitive functions. Initial symptoms of the disease include deficits in short-term memory and problems of orientation with respect to time and place. As AD progresses, patients demonstrate deficits in problem-solving skills, conceptual abilities, insight, language skills, long-term memory, and motor performance. Personality changes including irritability, lability of mood and affect, anxiety, and depression are also common. In the terminal stages, patients may be unable to function autonomously and require total nursing care (Ereshefsky, Rospond, and Jann 1989).

It has been estimated that AD affects from 2% to 6% of the population over the age of 65 and is the fourth or fifth leading cause of death in this country. The diagnosis of AD is obtained by excluding other specific diseases and is confirmed only at autopsy by the presence of specific types of damage within the CNS. Pathologically, there is a reduction in brain weight and generalized cortical atrophy. Microscopically, there is evidence of neuronal loss and gliosis, dendritic abnormalities, and the formation of neurofibrillary tangles and neuritic plaques (clusters of degenerating nerve terminals). Alterations in levels of neurotransmitters including reductions in acetylcholine, norepinephrine, and serotonin have also been reported (Markesbery and Ehmann 1988; Ereshefsky, Rospond, and Jann 1989).

The etiology and specific pathophysiology of AD remain unknown. However, the neurofibrillary tangles of AD are similar to those observed in animals exposed to high levels of aluminum. In support of the possibility of aluminum involvement, elevations in brain aluminum levels have been reported in patients with AD (Crapper, Krishman, and Quittkat 1976), with concentrations of aluminum greatest in cortical sites where neurofibrillary tangles were most dense.

Although the preceding data suggest a role for aluminum in AD, other findings indicate that it is certainly not the primary cause of the disease. For example, elevated levels of aluminum have not been consistently found in the brains of patients with AD, and there are data to suggest that aluminum accumulation might be a normal consequence of aging, rather than being specific to AD. Moreover, careful examination of the neurofibrillary tangles found in AD have revealed that they are not the same as those seen in aluminum-exposed animals. The neurotangles found in AD are paired filaments twisted in a double helix, and those found in aluminum-exposed animals are composed of single untwisted filaments. In addition, as previously discussed, the elevated aluminum content found in the brains of patients with dialysis dementia is not associated with the development of neurofibrillary tangles (Petit 1983; Markesbery and Ehmann 1988).

In conclusion, the role of aluminum in AD remains controversial. One question which remains unanswered is whether the aluminum deposition observed in neurofibrillary tangles and neuritic plaques is a primary or secondary phenomenon. It has been hypothesized that an unknown primary pathogenic event in AD alters the brain's aluminum metabolism so that the metal gains access to brain tissue compartments from which it is normally excluded (Crapper, McLachlan, and DeBoni 1980). Aluminum might therefore be a secondary factor contributing to the pathogenesis of AD. However, this hypothesis remains to be tested.

CADMIUM

In nature, cadmium is usually found in association with zinc, and is obtained as a byproduct in the extraction processes for zinc and other metals. Cadmium is used in electroplating, batteries, pigments for paints, and stabilizers for plastics, and as an alloy with copper for coating telephone cables, trolley wires, and welding electrodes. The metal also is a common contaminant of phosphate fertilizers and sewage sludge. Cadmium reaches the environment from mines, smelters, the electroplating industry, and power plants burning fossil fuels. Emissions of the metal into the air eventually settle on the ground where the metal is transferred to plants, and thus to humans.

Cadmium is taken up from the soil through the roots of plants and then is conveyed to other parts of the plant. The amount of cadmium absorbed by plants is influenced by a variety of factors, including the pH of the soil; the level of other minerals, such as calcium, in the soil; and the use of phosphate fertilizers. In general, the levels of cadmium in cereals, vegetables, and fruits grown in uncontaminated soils is small. In contaminated areas, however, where for example sewage sludge has been applied to the soil, substantial levels of cadmium can accumulate in cereal grains such as rice and wheat, and in quick-growing leafy vegetables such as spinach. As a result of consuming grains and vegetables containing cadmium, animals used for human food almost always contain some of the metal. In animals, the highest levels of cadmium are found in the kidneys and liver. Fish tend to contain relatively low levels of cadmium; however, shellfish including oysters, lobsters, and crabs, especially those growing in industrially contaminated water, can contain very high levels (Lindsay and Sherlock 1982; Whanger 1982; Avridson 1983).

Absorption and Distribution

Cadmium enters the body primarily by way of the gastrointestinal tract and respiratory system. Gastrointestinal absorption of the metal is very low, ranging from 4% to 6% in humans. Diets low in protein, calcium, or iron can increase cadmium absorption and exacerbate the toxic effects of the metal. Cadmium absorbed from the intestine is transported by the blood to other organs, particularly the kidney and liver, where approximately 50% of the metal is deposited. Excretion of cadmium from the body occurs via the urine and feces, and is very low in normal humans, with the biological half-life of the metal ranging from 10 to 30 years for the total body. Cadmium accumulates with age; for example, little of the metal is present at birth, but relatively high levels are present in the kidneys of adults (Whanger 1982; Avridson 1983).

It is estimated that daily intake of cadmium from food in this country is approximately 50 ug and that intake of 250 to 350 ug per day could produce toxic effects. At current levels of intake, therefore, cadmium toxicity is not a significant health problem. However, a number of factors, including nutritional status, can affect toxicity. Individuals who consume food or water prepared or stored in galvanized containers, and those who are exposed to the element in industrial occupations, may be particularly susceptible to cadmium poisoning (Lindsay and Sherlock 1982; Whanger 1982).

Cadmium is a chronic toxin that accumulates in the body, especially in the kidneys. The metal thus may not manifest its deleterious consequences for many years. Long-term exposure to cadmium is toxic to a variety of organ systems including the lungs, bone, and liver, as well as the kidneys. Research with humans and experimental animals also indicates that the metal may serve as a neurotoxin. In humans, chronic exposure to cadmium dust can lead to loss of the sense of smell (anosmia) which can be reversed if exposure to the metal dust is discontinued.

Neurotoxic Potential of Cadmium

In experimental animals, cadmium has been found to have deleterious effects on both the peripheral and central nervous systems. Rats given cadmium chloride in their drinking water for extended periods of time develop symptoms of peripheral neuropathy including weakness in the hind legs, muscle atrophy, and degeneration of myelin. Other work has revealed that acute administration of large doses of cadmium can produce hemorrhagic lesions in sensory ganglia in a number of species including rats, guinea pigs, hamsters, and mice. Cadmium-induced hemorrhagic lesions in ganglia are associated with damage to nerve cells which appears to be secondary to vascular destruction. Cadmium may also inhibit the transmission of chemical signals at the neuromuscular junction. This effect is believed to be the result of inhibition of calcium functioning at the presynaptic nerve terminal which leads to a reduction in the release of the neurotransmitter acetylcholine from the nerve endings (Avridson 1983).

In general, the blood-brain barrier limits entry of cadmium into the CNS. However, the metal may readily enter the CNS in areas where the blood-brain barrier is lacking, such as the choroid plexus and pituitary. Administration of cadmium produces hemorrhagic lesions within the brains of both rats and rabbits. However, the distribution of these lesions differs between the species, with more pronounced damage to the cerebellum in rabbits than in rats. These lesions are accompanied by degenerative alterations in adjacent nerve and glial cells (Avridson 1983).

The developing organism appears to be particularly sensitive to the toxic effects of cadmium. Indeed, it has been established that the metal is a teratogen. Malformations resulting from cadmium administration to pregnant animals include defects of the face and upper jaw, rib fusions, and limb defects. Cadmium also affects the developing nervous system and leads to neural tube defects (e.g., hydrocephaly and exencephaly). Prenatal exposure to cadmium may also modify later behavior; for example, mice display alterations in reflex responses, hypoactivity, impairments in coordination, and decrements in learning (Pierro 1983).

In general, there has been little research conducted on the neurotoxic and teratogenic effects of cadmium in humans. However, in view of the numerous reports of its neurotoxic effects in experimental animals, and increased industrial production of cadmium, more intensive research is warranted.

CONCLUSION

It is clear that contamination of our food and water supply by heavy metals can have detrimental effects on brain development and functioning, and consequently, behavior. Lead pollution poses the biggest threat to public health and has received the most attention in both the scientific and lay communities. The damaging effects to the human nervous system from mercury, aluminum, and possibly cadmium however, should not be disregarded. More research on the neurotoxicological consequences of these metals is certainly in order. In addition, both government and industry should initiate comprehensive programs to help alleviate environmental exposure to these potent neurotoxins.

REFERENCES

Alfrey, A. C., LeGendre, G. R., and Kaehny, W. D. 1976. The dialysis encephalopathy syndrome: Possible aluminum intoxication. *New England Journal of Medicine* 294:184–188.

Amin-Zaki, L. 1982. Mercury in food. In *Adverse Effects of Foods,* ed. E. F. P. Jelliffe and D. B. Jelliffe, pp. 149–159. New York: Plenum.

Anonymous. 1988. Childhood lead poisoning: Report to the United States Congress by the agency for toxic substances and disease registry. *Journal of the American Medical Association* 260:1523–1533.

Aschner, M. and J. L. Aschner. 1990. Mercury neurotoxicity: Mechanisms of blood-brain barrier transport. *Neuroscience and Biobehavioral Reviews* 14: 169–176.

Avridson, B. 1983. Cadmium toxicity and neural cell damage. In *Neurobiology of the Trace Elements: Neurotoxicology and Neuropharmacology,* vol. 2, ed. I. E. Dreosti and R. M. Smith, pp. 51–78. Clifton, NJ: Humana Press.

Bakir, F., Damluji, S. F., Amin-Zaki, L., Murtadha, M., Khalidi, A., Al-Rawi, N. J., Tikriti, S., Dahir, H. I., Clarkson, T. W., Smith, J. C., and Doherty, R. A. 1973. Methylmercury poisoning in Iraq. *Science* 181:230–241.

Banks, W. A. and Kastin, A. J. 1989. Aluminum-induced neurotoxicity: Alterations in membrane function at the blood-brain barrier. *Neuroscience and Biobehavioral Reviews* 13:47–53.

Bergomi, M., Borella, P., Fantuzzi, G., Vivoli, G., Sturloni, N., Cavazzuti, G., Tampieri, A., and Tartoni, P. L. 1989. Relationship between lead exposure indicators and neuropsychological performance in children. *Developmental Medicine and Child Neurology* 31:181–190.

Boegman, R. J. and Bates, L. A. 1984. Neurotoxicity of aluminum. *Canadian Journal of Physiology and Pharmacology* 62:1010–1014.

Bowdler, N. C., Beasley, D. S., Fritze, C., Goulette, A. M., Hatton, J. D., Hession, J., Ostman, D. L., Rugg, D. J., and Schmittdiel, C. J. 1979. Behavioral effects of aluminum ingestion on animal and human subjects. *Pharmacology Biochemistry and Behavior* 10:505–512.

Burbacher, T. M., P. M. Rodier, and B. Weiss. 1990. Methylmercury developmental neurotoxicity: a comparison of effects in humans and animals. *Neurotoxicology and Teratology* 12:191–202.

Byers, R. K. and Lord, E. E. 1943. Late effects of lead poisoning on mental development. *American Journal of Diseases of Children* 66:471–494.

Chisholm, J. J. 1971. Lead poisoning. *Scientific American* 224:15–23.

Choi, B. H. 1989. The effects of methylmercury on the developing brain. *Progress in Neurobiology* 32:447–470.

Clarkson, T. W. 1988. Mercury toxicity. In *Essential and Toxic Trace Elements in Human Health and Disease,* ed. A. S. Prasad, pp. 631–643. New York: Alan R. Liss.

Clarkson, T. W., Amin-Zaki, L., and Al-Tikriti, S. K. 1976. An outbreak of methylmercury poisoning due to consumption of contaminated grain. *Federation Proceedings* 35:2395–2399.

Crapper, D. R., Krishman, S. S., and Quittkat, S. 1976. Aluminum, neurofibrillary degeneration and Alzheimer's disease. *Brain* 99:67–80.

Crapper-McLachlan, D. R., and DeBoni, U. 1980. Aluminum in human brain disease: An overview. *Neurotoxicology* 1:3–16.

Davis, J. M., D. A. Otto, D. E. Weil, and L. D. Grant. 1990. The comparative developmental neurotoxicity of lead in humans and animals. *Neurotoxicology and Teratology* 12:215–229.

Dietrich, K. N., Krafft, K. M., Bornschein, R. L., Hammond, P. B., Berger, O., Succop, P. A., and Bier, M. 1987. Low-level fetal lead exposure effects on neurobehavioral development in early infancy. *Pediatrics* 80:721–730.

Ereshefsky, L., Rospond, R., and Jann, M. 1989. Organic brain syndromes, Alzheimer type. In *Pharmacotherapy: A Pathophysiological Approach,* ed. J. T. DiPiro et al., pp. 678–696. New York: Elsevier.

Ernhart, C. B., Morrow-Tlucak, M., Marler, M. R., and Wolf, A. W. 1987. Low-level lead exposure in the prenatal and early preschool periods: Early preschool development. *Neurotoxicology and Teratology* 9:259–270.

Ernhart, C. B., Morrow-Tlucak, M., Wolf, A. W., Super, D., and Drotar, D. 1989. Low-level lead exposure in the prenatal and early preschool periods: Intelligence prior to school entry. *Neurotoxicology and Teratology* 11:161–170.

Fulton, M., Raab, G., Thomson, G., Laxen, D., Hunter, R., and Hepburn, W. 1987. Influence of blood lead on the ability and attainment of children in Edinburgh. *Lancet* 1:1221–1226.

Harada, M. 1982. Minamata disease: Organic mercury poisoning caused by ingestion of contaminated fish. In *Adverse Effects of Foods,* ed. E. F. P. Jelliffe and D. B. Jelliffe, pp. 135–148. New York: Plenum.

Inskip, M. J. and Piotrowski, J. T. 1985. Review of the health effects of methylmercury. *Journal of Applied Toxicology* 5:113–123.

Klaassen, C. D. 1980. Heavy metals and heavy-metal antagonists. In *The Pharmacological Basis of Therapeutics,* ed, A. G. Gilman, L. S. Goodman, and A. Gilman, pp. 1615–1637. New York: Macmillan.

Lansdown, R., Yule, W., Urbanowitz, M. A., and Hunter. J. 1986. The relationship between blood-lead concentrations, intelligence, attainment and behavior in a school population: The second London study. *International Archives of Occupational and Environmental Health* 57:225–235.

Lindsay, D. G. and Sherlock, J. C. 1982. Environmental contaminants. In *Adverse Effects of Foods,* ed. E. F. P. Jelliffe and D. B. Jelliffe, pp. 85–110. New York: Plenum.

Maracek, J., Shapiro, I. M., Katz, S. H., and Hediger, M. L. 1983. Low-level lead exposure in childhood influences neuropsychological performance. *Archives of Environmental Health* 38:355–359.

Markesbery, W. R. and Ehmann, W. D. 1988. Trace elements in dementing disorders. In *Nutritional Modulation of Neural Function,* ed. J. E. Morley, M. B. Sterman, and J. H. Walsh, pp. 179–190. New York: Academic Press.

McConnell, P. 1983. Neurotoxic effects of lead. In *Neurobiology of the Trace Elements: Neurotoxicology and Neuropharmacology,* vol. 2, ed. I. E. Dreosti and R. M. Smith, pp. 141–166. Clifton, NJ: Humana Press.

McDermott, J. R., Smith, A. I., Ward, M. K., Parkinson, I. S., and Kerr, D. N. S. 1978. Brain aluminum concentration in dialysis encephalopathy. *Lancet* 1:901–903.

Miller, R. W. 1989. The metal in our mettle. *FDA Consumer,* pp. 24–27.

Needleman, H. L. 1982. The neurobehavioral consequences of low lead exposure in childhood. *Neurobehavioral Toxicology and Teratology* 4:729–732.

Needleman, H. L. 1987. Low-level lead exposure in the fetus and young child. *Neurotoxicology* 8:389–394.

Needleman, H. L. 1989. The persistent threat of lead: A singular opportunity. *American Journal of Public Health* 79:643–645.

Needleman, H. L., Gunnoe, C., Leviton, A., Reed, R., Peresie, H., Maher, C., and Barrett, P. 1979. Deficits in psychologic and classroom performance of children with elevated dentine lead levels. *New England Journal of Medicine* 300:689–695.

Needleman, H. L., Schell, A., Bellinger, D., Leviton, A., and Allred, E. N. 1990. The long-term effects of exposure to low doses of lead in childhood: An 11-year follow-up report. *New England Journal of Medicine* 322:83–88.

Petit, T. L. 1983. Aluminum neurobehavioral toxicology. In *Neurobiology of the Trace Elements: Neurotoxicology and Neuropharmacology,* vol. 2, ed. I. E. Dreosti and R. M. Smith, pp. 237–274. Clifton, NJ: Humana Press.

Petit, T. L. and Alfano, D. P. 1983. Neurobiological and behavioral effects of lead. In *Neurobiology of the Trace Elements: Neurotoxicology and Neuropharma-*

cology, vol. 2, ed. I. E. Dreosti and R. M. Smith, pp. 97–139. Clifton, NJ: Humana Press.

Pierro, L. J. 1983. Cadmium and teratogenesis of the central nervous system. In *Neurobiology of the Trace Elements: Neurotoxicology and Neuropharmacology,* vol. 2, ed. I. E. Dreosti and R. M. Smith, pp. 79–96. Clifton, NJ: Humana Press.

Pim, L. R. 1981. *The Invisible Additives: Environmental Contaminants in our Food,* Toronto, Canada: Doubleday.

Ruff, H. A. and Bijur, P. E. 1989. The effects of low to moderate lead levels on neurobehavioral functioning in children: Toward a conceptual model. *Journal of Developmental Behavioral Pediatrics* 10:103–109.

Skerfving, S. 1988. Toxicology of inorganic lead. In *Essential and Toxic Trace Elements in Human Health and Disease,* ed. A. S. Prasad, pp. 611–630. New York: Alan R. Liss.

Slotkin, T. A. and Bartolome, J. 1987. Biochemical mechanisms of developmental neurotoxicity of methylmercury. *Neurotoxicology* 8:65–84.

Smith, M. 1985. Recent work on low-level lead exposure and its impact on behavior, intelligence, and learning: A review. *Journal of the American Academy of Child Psychiatry* 24:24–32.

Smith, W. E. and Smith, A. M. 1975. *Minamata.* New York: Holt, Rinehart and Winston.

Warkany, J. and Hubbard, D. M. 1948. Mercury in the urine of children with acrodynia. *Lancet* 1:829–830.

Warkany, J. and Hubbard, D. M. 1951. Adverse mercurial reactions in the form of acrodynia and related conditions. *American Journal of Diseases of Children* 81: 335–373.

Weiss, B. 1983. Behavioral toxicology of heavy metals. In *Neurobiology of the Trace Elements: Neurotoxicology and Neuropharmacology,* vol. 2, ed. I. E. Dreosti and R. M. Smith, pp. 1–50. Clifton, NJ: Humana Press.

Whanger, P. D. 1982. Factors affecting the metabolism of nonessential metals in foods. In *Nutritional Toxicology,* vol. 1, ed. J. N. Hathcock, pp. 163–208. New York: Academic Press.

Winneke, G., Brockhaus, A., Collet, W., and Kramer, U. 1989. Modulation of lead-induced performance deficit in children by varying signal rate in a serial choice reaction task. *Neurotoxicology and Teratology* 11:587–592.

Yase, Y. 1980. The role of aluminum in CNS degeneration with the interaction of calcium. *Neurotoxicology* 1:101–109.

Yip, R., Norris, R. N., and Anderson, A. S. 1981. Iron status of children with elevated blood lead concentrations. *Journal of Pediatrics* 98:922–924.

Yokel, R. A. 1989. Aluminum produces age-related behavioral toxicity in the rabbit. *Neurotoxicology and Teratology* 11:237–242.

Yule, W., Lansdown, R., Millar, I. B., and Urbanowitz, M. A. 1981. The relationships between blood lead concentrations, intelligence and attainment in a school population: A pilot study. *Developmental Medicine and Child Neurology* 23:567–576.

7

Food Additives: Are There Behavioral Risks?

Food additives are substances deliberately added to food for such purposes as extending shelf life, protecting nutritional value, enhancing flavor, and improving color. It is estimated that from 2,500 to 3,000 agents are presently being used as food additives.

Although food additives are useful, they are not always essential to the manufacture of food products. Indeed, over the past 30 years, as a result of studies demonstrating the potential toxicity of some food additives, the use of some of these substances has been increasingly questioned. For example, research has indicated that a number of additives, such as the artificial sweetener cyclamate, and sodium nitrite, which provides the red color to frankfurters, sausages, and hams, may be carcinogenic. Moreover, it has been claimed that food additives may have adverse behavioral effects.

This chapter evaluates the claims that food additives can negatively influence behavior. Before beginning this evaluation, however, we will examine the history of food additives in this country, safety testing of new food additives, and the exact uses of these substances in our food supply.

GOVERNMENT REGULATIONS AND FOOD ADDITIVES

The use of food additives is not new; spices, minerals, flavors, preservatives, and ripening agents have been added to foods for thousands of years. However, it is only during the last 200 years that food additives have become a cause for social concern. From ancient times to the beginning of the nineteenth century, the addition of chemicals to foods was a minor component of food production. Since food was procured personally from friends or from local suppliers, transactions which required large measures of personal accountability, deceptive adulteration was not an issue. However, as Western societies moved from being agrarian to industrial during the 1800s, and both storage times and distribution channels lengthened, the temptation and opportunity for intentional adulteration of the food supply grew. During this period, chalk was added to watered-down milk to make it look whiter, lard was used to extend butter, copper salts were added to vegetables to make them look greener, arsenic and boric acid were sprinkled on meat and fish to slow spoilage, and lead oxide, lead chromate, mercuric sulfide, and copper arsenite were used to color candy.

In the United States, such practices were first attacked by Dr. Harvey W. Wiley, chief chemist in the U.S. Department of Agriculture, who initiated a crusade against food adulteration and related abuses in 1883. He began by analyzing food for adulterants and by assembling a group of healthy adult male volunteers, known as Wiley's "poison squad," who were fed various chemicals to assess their toxicity. Wiley's reports in the press and speeches to civic groups decried food adulteration and led to public outrage. This outrage was strengthened by the publication in 1906 of Upton Sinclair's novel *The Jungle,* which described the conditions of the meat-packing industry in Chicago. In his novel, Sinclair described sausage made of spoiled meat that was chemically treated to disguise the fact that it had begun to rot, and the handling of meat by tubercular workers. As a result of the public pressure generated by Wiley and Sinclair, the first Pure Food and Drug Law was signed by President Theodore Roosevelt in 1906 (Root and de Rochemont 1976; Levine, Labuza, and Morley 1985; Fennema 1987; David 1988).

The 1906 Pure Food and Drug Law prohibited the addition of any substances to food that rendered it injurious to consumers' health. This law improved the quality of the American food supply, but it was not a panacea. The primary problem was that the law left it to the federal government to prove that any added substances were harmful. This provision led to frequent conflicts between government and industry. In 1911, when Dr. Wiley began to conduct experiments to demonstrate that some of the preservatives, colors, and other additives used in canned foods were dangerous to health, food processors denounced him for "socialist interference" and attempted to get rid of him by claiming that one of the members of his department was receiving a larger salary than legally mandated. Although Wiley was exonerated, he resigned in disillusionment from government service in 1912 (Root and de Rochemont 1976).

The inadequacies in the 1906 law became more evident with the rapid advances and increasing complexities in food technology, industry, and distribution that took place in the ensuing 30 years. As a result of these changes and consumer pressure during the 1930s, the Food, Drug and Cosmetic Act was passed into law in 1938. The objectives of this law were "safe, effective drugs and cosmetics; pure, wholesome foods; and honest labeling and packaging." In the intervening decades, this act has been amended a number of times. One of the most important legal changes occurred in 1958, when the Food Additives Amendment was enacted by

Congress. This amendment was designed to regulate both intentional and incidental additives, and relieved the government of having to prove a substance was unsafe by placing the burden of proof on the food industry. In 1960, a similar amendment concerning color additives was passed. This amendment dictates that before use, any synthetic color must be proven safe, and that each batch of color produced must be tested and certified as chemically pure (Federal Food, Drug, and Cosmetic Act 1986).

The 1958 Food Additive Amendment requires that all substances intended to be added to food receive prior approval from the Food and Drug Administration (FDA). Approval is based on scientific data provided by the manufacturer. These data must demonstrate the usefulness of the substance and the absence of deleterious consequences when the substance is used in foods in the amounts and manner proposed.

The 1958 amendment, however, specifically exempted several hundred substances that had historically been added to foods and were presumed to have very low toxicity. In the early 1960s, a listing of these substances was published under the title, "Substances Generally Recognized as Safe" (Select Committee on GRAS Substances 1982). These exempted food additives became known as GRAS substances. In 1969, the FDA began a comprehensive reevaluation of their safety. As a result of this reevaluation, the GRAS list was divided into five categories. Class I substances, which include the majority of all GRAS products, have been declared safe for use at current and future anticipated levels under good manufacturing practices. Class 2 substances are safe for use at current levels, but more research has been deemed necessary to determine if increased consumption would constitute a dietary hazard. Sucrose, vitamins A and D, and iron are in this group. Class 3 substances are currently allowed in foods, but additional research is required to determine their safety. This class includes caffeine and the preservatives butylated hydroxyanisole and butylated hydroxytoluene. Class 4 substances require caution in their use, or their addition to foods should be prohibited. Included are salt and four modified starches. Finally, Class 5 is comprised of substances for which there are insufficient data to evaluate their safety (Irving 1982; Winter 1989).

Another important component of the 1958 Food Additives Amendment is the Delaney clause which states that an additive is prohibited if, at any level of feeding whatsoever, it induces cancer in experimental animals. This clause has been invoked a number of times in the past 30 years, most notably when the artificial sweetener saccharin was reported to cause bladder cancer in rats. On the basis of the Delaney clause, in 1977 the FDA issued a ban on saccharin. This action, clearly in line with a law designed to ensure public health, provoked such a public outcry that Congress overrode the FDA's ban (see chapter 10).

TESTING OF NEW FOOD ADDITIVES

As mentioned previously, before a substance can be marketed as a food additive, the manufacturer must provide the FDA with appropriate material stating the intended use and safety of the additive. Included in this information must be

- The name and chemical composition of the additive.
- The conditions of the proposed use of the additive, and samples of its proposed labeling.
- Data on the physical or other effects that the additive is intended to produce, and the quantity of the additive required to produce such effects.
- A description of the methods for determining the quantity of the additive in or on food.
- Reports of studies made with respect to the safety of the additive including the methods and controls used in conducting these studies.

The last condition, concerning toxicological evaluation, is the most critical and most often the factor responsible for rejection or delays in the approval of a new additive (Senti 1988).

The safety of food additives is generally assessed in animal feeding studies, which is necessary because of the obvious constraints on using humans as test subjects. Animal studies are effective for evaluating the acute toxicity of food additives, but less so for evaluating their sublethal and carcinogenic effects which may only arise from long periods of use. Additional problems with animal studies as predictors for human safety are that

- Differences in the kinetics of absorption, distribution, or excretion of the food additive may exist between the test species and man.
- Some toxic consequences that occur in humans, such as headache, depression, and anxiety, cannot be evaluated in animals.
- Some toxic effects that occur at a very low frequency in animals may be missed with the usual toxicity studies of 25 to 30 animals per group, even if several species are used.
- Interactions among dietary components increase the difficulty of extrapolating from animal data to humans (Dwyer 1982; Fennema 1987).

Three general types of studies are typically required to assess the safety of new food additives.

1. Acute oral toxicity tests in a minimum of two species, one of which should be a nonrodent. These tests are used to determine the LD_{50}

(the dose of the additive at which 50% of the animals will die) as well as to assess premortal signs of toxicity.

2. Short-term oral toxicity studies, a minimum of 90 days in rodents and 6 months in nonrodents, using several different doses of the additive. These tests measure the effects of the additive on growth, physical appearance, behavior, and liver and renal functioning, in addition to hemocytological changes. The short-term tests also may be extended to provide reproductive and teratogenic data in rodents. At the termination of these tests, autopsies of the animals are conducted, including weighing of all major organs and examinations for histopathological changes.

3. Long-term oral toxicity tests lasting a minimum of two years. The observations are similar to those made in the short-term tests, but one of the main purposes of these tests is to determine if the proposed additive is carcinogenic (Senti 1988).

In the regulation of new food additives, the FDA uses a "safety factor" to limit human dietary intake to the maximum allowable daily intake (ADI). The ADI is typically determined by dividing the highest dietary dose level found to cause no detrimental effects in toxicological studies in animals by 100 (Rulis 1987).

Given the requirements set forth by the federal government, it should be obvious that the cost, in both time and money, of introducing a new additive is high. Testing alone may take 4 to 10 years and cost from $500,000 to $10 million (Levine, Labuza, and Morley 1985).

CLASSIFICATION OF FOOD ADDITIVES

Food additives are frequently classified according to their intended use in foods. Preservatives, antioxidants, sequestrants, and nutritional supplements are added to foods to improve shelf life or nutritional value. Preservatives, which prevent or inhibit spoilage due to bacteria, yeasts, or molds, are essential under modern conditions of food storage, packaging, and distribution. Commonly used preservatives include both natural substances, such as salt (to cure meat) and sugar (in jams and jellies), and synthetic products, such as sodium nitrate (added to cured meats to prevent the growth of *Clostridium botulinum*) and benzoic acid (added to carbonated beverages to prevent microbial spoilage). The addition of sorbic acid to beverages and calcium propionate to bread can prevent the growth of spoilage molds.

Antioxidants prevent rancidity and other oxidative changes in foods, and are thus important for extending the shelf life of vegetable and animal fats. Among the more common antioxidants are butylated hydroxyanisole, butylated hydroxytoluene, and ascorbic acid.

Sequestrants are used to bind or chelate trace metals that may induce or accelerate changes in flavor, color, or turbidity of a food product. Included in this category are ethylenediamine tetracetic acid (EDTA), citric acid, calcium acetate, sodium phosphate, and tartaric acid.

Vitamins and minerals are added to many foods to restore nutritional value that is lost in processing. For example, B vitamins are added to bread and cereals, and vitamin C to fruit drinks. Moreover, some foods are supplemented with micronutrients in which, because of their relatively low availability in the food supply, the consumer might otherwise become deficient (e.g., vitamin D in milk, iron in infant formulas, and iodine in table salt).

Emulsifiers, stabilizers, anticaking agents, humectants, and texturizing agents are used to alter the physical properties of foods. Emulsifiers such as lecithin and propylene glycol facilitate the dispersion of oils in water and are essential for the production of salad dressings, margarine, cheese spreads, frozen desserts, and confectionery products. Stabilizers and thickeners, such as pectin, gelatin, and synthetic gums, enhance the texture of foods such as processed cheese, puddings, soups, and candy, and prevent the formation of ice crystals in ice cream and frozen desserts. Anticaking agents including aluminum calcium silicate and magnesium silicate are used to prevent lumping and permit free flow in foods such as salt, baking powder, and confectioner's sugar, and humectants are added to bakery products to prevent the loss of moisture. Texturizing agents maintain the crispness or firmness of pickled and canned vegetables.

Acids, alkalis, buffers, and neutralizing agents are added to many processed foods in which the degree of acidity or alkalinity is important. Manufacturers of soft drinks, baked goods, processed cheese, and chocolate employ these additives extensively.

Sensory additives make food more appealing and include both flavoring agents and food colors. Flavoring agents comprise the largest category of food additives: estimates of the number of flavors available range from 1,100 to 1,400. These agents include spices, herbs, essential oils, sugar, and a large number of chemical substances isolated from both natural and synthetic sources. They are used not only to provide taste properties to food, but also to mask objectionable qualities and to adjust for natural variations in the flavor intensity of foods. Related to flavoring agents are substances known as flavor enhancers, such as monosodium glutamate, which augment the natural taste of a food.

Both natural and synthetic products are used as food colors. Natural pigments, such as those derived from saffron, grapes, carrots, and paprika, are used to color a variety of foods, but synthetic dyes are generally preferred for their greater stability, superior intensity of color, and uniformity. Although small in number, synthetic colors have probably received the most attention with respect to their value to our food supply and their potential toxic effects (Berdick 1982; Yetiv 1986; Senti 1988).

FOOD ADDITIVES AND BEHAVIOR

The preceding section clearly demonstrates that food additives have a variety of positive benefits. Additives make foods from around the world available throughout the year. Thus, they help to provide a varied food supply and reduce the possibility of nutritional deficiencies. They can also lower the cost of food, which is particularly important for people with low incomes. While food additives have many benefits, however, they also have negative aspects. It has been argued that many food additives, particularly flavorings and colors, offer little if any practical value. Food additives such as sugar have promoted the development of "junk foods" that are high in flavor and calories, but low in nutrients. More seriously, some food additives have been associated with the development of cancer (e.g., saccharin, cyclamate, and nitrites) and can cause problems for people with inherited physiological disorders. For example, aspartame may be harmful to individuals with phenylketonuria (see chapter 10).

One of the most common negative claims about food additives is that they can provoke or exacerbate a variety of behavioral problems including depression, dizziness, blurred vision, insomnia, nervousness, migraines, and hyperactivity. Of these complaints, scientists, educators, and parents over the past two decades have become particularly concerned about the role of additives in hyperactive behavior in children or, as the condition is officially categorized by the American Psychiatric Association, attention deficit hyperactivity disorder (ADHD) (Weiss 1983).

ADHD is characterized by developmentally inappropriate inattention, impulsive behavior, significantly elevated levels of motor activity, emotional lability, and learning problems. At home, attentional difficulties may be manifested by a failure to follow through on tasks and the inability to stick to activities, including play, for appropriate periods of time. In school, the child with ADHD is inattentive and impulsive, and has difficulty organizing and completing work. In approximately half of the cases, the onset of ADHD is before the age of 4. As many as 3% of preadolescent children may suffer from ADHD, with the disorder six to nine times more common in boys than in girls (American Psychiatric Association 1987).

In the early 1970s, Dr. Benjamin Feingold, a pediatrician and allergist, called attention to the increasing use of food additives in the American diet and hypothesized that these additives might play a causal role in childhood hyperactivity (Feingold 1973, 1975). To test his hypothesis, Feingold began treating hyperactive children with a diet free of food additives. In addition, as some individuals who have an allergic reaction to yellow food dye also react to acetylsalicylic acid (aspirin), he advocated the removal of food containing natural salicylates (e.g., almonds, apples, all berries, apricots, cucumbers, oranges, raisins, tomatoes, and green peppers) from the diet of hyperactive children. On the basis of his clinical work, Feingold claimed that a diet free of food additives and natural salicylates led to dramatic improvements in hyperactive behavior, with 50% to 70% of children placed on the diet displaying complete remission. Feingold insisted that to obtain success, adherence to the diet was mandatory (any lapse could lead to a return of symptoms), successful treatment required that the entire family be on the diet, and an individual sensitive to food additives must avoid them for life. Feingold's ideas were widely publicized and rapidly gained acceptance among the lay public (Lipton, Nemeroff, and Mailman 1979; Conners 1984).

The potential importance of Feingold's claims did not go unnoticed in the scientific community. Indeed, a number of studies assessing Feingold's hypothesis were almost immediately initiated. Open clinical trials, in which parents or physicians placed children on additive-free diets, have supported Feingold's claims, but carefully controlled double-blind studies have not yielded such positive results (e.g., Conners et al. 1976; Harley et al. 1978; Goyette, Conners, and Petti 1978; Weiss et al. 1980; Kaplan et al. 1989).

The first controlled study examining Feingold's hypothesis was published by Conners and colleagues in 1976. This study examined the effects of the Feingold diet on parent and teacher ratings of behavior of 15 children from the ages of 6 to 12 who had been diagnosed as having ADHD. After a four-week baseline period, approximately half of the children were placed on the Feingold diet, and the remaining children were given a control diet that required the same amount of time in shopping, preparation, and monitoring. After four weeks, the dietary conditions were switched. Prior to the start of the experiment, parents were told that their child would try both diets, that either might produce improvement, and that it was necessary to follow both diets for comparison. Both parents and teachers reported fewer hyperactive symptoms on the Feingold diet as compared to the pretreatment baseline. In addition, teachers noted a significant reduction of symptoms on the Feingold diet as compared to the control diet; however, the parents did not make this same observation.

The results of the study by Conners and colleagues suggest that a diet free of natural salicylates and artificial flavors and colors can reduce the symptoms of childhood hyperactivity. However, there are several factors that make this suggestion tentative. First, a marked order effect was observed: significant differences between the two dietary regimens were found when the experimental diet was presented after, but not when it preceded, the control diet. Such an effect could be due to the fact that the observers had a clearer basis on which to judge improvement after the control diet failed to produce any noticeable changes. Second, the difference between teacher and parent ratings of behavior on the Feingold diet indicates that the positive effects of an additive-free diet may be limited to structured environments, such as those found in the classroom, and may not carry over to an unstructured home situation. Finally, careful inspection of individual ratings of children in the study reveals that only four or five of the children were seen as improved by both parents and teachers. These results led the authors to conclude that there may be a small subgroup of hyperkinetic children who are actually sensitive to food additives (Conners et al. 1976).

The results of subsequent studies have provided some support for the idea that a small proportion of hyperactive children may react adversely to food additives. For example, using a dietary replacement paradigm, Harley and colleagues (1978) compared the effects of Feingold's diet to an additive-containing diet. Food for the families in this study was furnished by the experimenters, and neither the researchers nor the family knew which diet was being consumed at a particular time; dietary conditions were alternated so that all families were exposed to both diets. No significant improvements in behavior were noted by teachers or objective raters in the 36 school-age hyperactive boys in the study. Some parents did report improvement on the Feingold diet, but only when the additive-free diet was given after the control diet. When 10 preschool children were tested under the same conditions, all of their mothers and most of their fathers rated the children as more improved on the Feingold diet than on the control diet. Harley and colleagues concluded, "While we feel confident that the cause–effect relationship asserted by Feingold is seriously overstated with respect to school-age children, we are not in a position to refute his claims regarding the possible causative effect played by artificial food colors on preschool children" (p. 827).

One problem with dietary replacement studies is that the experimental and control diets generally differ not only with respect to the presence of food additives, but also in nutritional value (e.g., carbohydrate content; vitamin and mineral levels). Thus, it is difficult to determine if the differences observed in behavior between an additive-free and control diet are the result of additives per se, or other dietary factors. A second problem with dietary replacement studies is that they are very expensive to conduct. To help overcome these problems, a number of researchers have evaluated the effects of food additives on hyperactive behavior using a dietary challenge paradigm (see chapter 1). In these studies, children reported by their parents to respond positively to the Feingold diet have been blindly "challenged" with food additives. Although some challenge studies have demonstrated that food additives lead to increased hyperactivity in a small percentage of children (Conners 1980; Swanson and Kinsbourne 1980; Rowe 1988), others have found that additives have no detrimental effects (Conners 1980; Weiss et al. 1980; Mattes and Gittelman 1981). Several factors may account for the discrepancies among dietary challenge studies. For example, the types and amounts of food additives used in these studies have varied substantially. It has been argued that the level of food additives in some experiments was too low to produce adverse behavioral effects; however, it should be noted that results of studies using larger doses have been both positive and negative. In addition, age may alter sensitivity to food additives. In general, preschool-age children have been found to be more sensitive to food additives than older children (Harley et al. 1978; Conners 1980; Weiss et al. 1980; Kaplan et al. 1989).

From the preceding data several inferences can be drawn about the effects of food additives on hyperactive behavior. First, Feingold's claims and those from other open trials have been overstated, and at best, only a small percentage of hyperactive children may be adversely affected by food additives. Second, preschool-age children may be more sensitive to food additives than older children. Third, there may be a dose–response curve for food additives just as there is for any toxic substance, but this has yet to be demonstrated.

In conclusion, the research data on food additives and behavior are such as to preclude any major legislative or administrative action to remove food additives or severely limit their use. Additional research, however, seems warranted. Several recommendations for future research strategies have been made by the National Institutes of Health Consensus Development Panel (1983). First, the panel recommended the development of standardized instruments for the assessment of cognitive, attentional, and behavioral changes in hyperactive children receiving different types of therapy. Second, the panel advocated additional dietary research providing precise definitions of the dietary agent being tested, and considerations of synergistic effects of simultaneous exposure to additional dietary or other agents. With respect to dietary conditions, the panel also advised checks on the adequacy of blinding techniques and repetitive evaluations. Finally, research with experimental animals examining the biological activity of food additives was encouraged.

MONOSODIUM GLUTAMATE

Monosodium glutamate (MSG) is a flavor enhancer that is both added to and occurs naturally in foods (Table 7-1). Nearly 100 years ago, it was discovered that MSG was the ingredient responsible for the flavoring-enhancing properties of sea tangle, a seaweed traditionally used in Japanese cooking. In the early 1900s, shortly after its isolation and identification, commercial production of MSG was initiated. Because of its favorable effects on the flavor of a wide variety of foods, including meats,

TABLE 7-1. Natural Glutamate and Added Levels of MSG to Selected Foods

Approx. Free Glutamate Levels mg/100 g food		Approx. Level of Addition of MSG (mg/100 g food)[a]	
Roquefort cheese	1280	Milk products	460
Parmesan cheese	1200	Nuts, nut products	390
Milk	640	Gelatine, puddings, fillings	240
Tomato juice	260	Soups	240
Red grapes	184	Processed vegetable juice	200
Broccoli	176	Egg products	200
Tomato	140	Processed fruits and juices	150
Potato	102	Poultry products	120
Strawberries	44	Baked goods, baking mixes	70
Orange juice	19		

[a] MSG expressed as glutamic acid.
Source: Adapted from Garattini 1979.

poultry, seafood, and some soups and vegetables, commercial usage of MSG has increased dramatically over the past 80 years. World production of MSG is estimated to exceed 300,000 tons per year. Due to its extensive and long-standing use as a food additive, MSG was placed on the GRAS list of substances published in the early 1960s (Cagen 1977; Weiss 1983).

MSG is the sodium salt of glutamic acid (glutamate), an amino acid found in a wide variety of natural foods. After ingestion MSG is converted to glutamic acid within the gastrointestinal tract. Recent evidence suggests that glutamate is the principal excitatory neurotransmitter within the central nervous system. In large amounts, exogenous glutamate may also be a potent neurotoxin, particularly in developing organisms.

Neurotoxic Effects in Experimental Animals

Initial evidence of the neurotoxic consequences of MSG was provided by experiments demonstrating that administration of large amounts of MSG produced retinal damage in newborn mice (Lucas and Newhouse 1957). Further support for the neurotoxic potential of MSG was furnished in 1969 by Olney, who reported that a single subcutaneous injection of MSG resulted in selective lesions of the arcuate nucleus and median eminence of the hypothalami of infant mice (Olney 1969). This finding stimulated a large number of studies aimed at examining the physiological consequences of the lesions and evaluating their extent with respect to such variables as the animal's age and species, and route of administration. Results of these studies revealed that parenteral administration of MSG to both neonatal mice and rats results in a syndrome characterized by damage to the hypothalamus, arrested skeletal growth, obesity, infertility, abnormalities of the endocrine system, and increased irritability (e.g., Burde, Schanker, and Kayes 1971; Bunyan, Murrell, and Shah 1976; Pizzi and Barnhart

1976; Nikoletseas 1977; Kanarek et al. 1979; Kanarek and Marks-Kaufman 1981).

One of the most obvious outcomes of MSG administration in rodents is the development of obesity. Mice treated with MSG as neonates demonstrate an increase in both body weight and accumulation of body fat. They also generally weigh less than untreated controls, but are considered obese because they have significantly more body fat than untreated animals. Although animals treated with MSG are fatter, they actually consume less food than controls (e.g., Olney 1969; Pizzi and Barnhart 1976; Nikoletseas 1977; Kanarek et al. 1979; Kanarek and Marks-Kaufman 1981).

Endocrinologic abnormalities are also a frequent concomitant of neonatal MSG administration. Decreases in pituitary, testicular, and ovarian weights have been observed in mice, rats, and hamsters receiving subcutaneous doses of MSG. Decreases in growth hormone, luteinizing hormone, follicle-stimulating hormone, and prolactin levels have been associated with these changes in the endocrine system (Garattini 1979).

In all of the preceding studies, MSG was given parenterally (e.g., subcutaneous or intraperitoneal injections). Although interesting from a toxicological point of view, these studies provide little information about the effects of high doses of MSG in food products. Several studies have indicated a clear-cut difference between the toxicity of MSG given parenterally and when taken in the diet. Specifically, it has been found that the neurotoxic, endocrinologic, and behavioral effects of parenteral MSG are completely lacking when the compound is fed to experimental animals. The lack of toxicity can be explained by the fact that the compound encounters two powerful barriers, intestinal and hepatic, which are not present when it is given parenterally. Most of the ingested glutamic acid is transaminated in the intestinal mucosa to form alanine, while the glutamic acid that escapes this mechanism and reaches the portal circulation is metabolized in the liver. Thus, plasma levels of glutamic acid are considerably lower when MSG is consumed than when it is given by other routes (Garattini 1979).

Despite the fact that MSG only appears to have neurotoxic effects when it is administered parenterally, baby food manufacturers voluntarily removed MSG from infant and toddler foods in the early 1970s.

Neurotoxic and Behavioral Effects in Humans: The Chinese Restaurant Syndrome

In April 1968, Dr. Robert Ho Man Kwok, in a letter to the *New England Journal of Medicine,* described a variety of symptoms that he and others experienced after eating in Chinese restaurants in the United States. The symptoms Dr. Kwok described were numbness at the back of the neck that gradually radiated down both arms and the back, general weakness, and palpitations. Kwok reported that these symptoms typically began 15 to 20 minutes after eating Chinese food and occurred particularly when northern Chinese food was served. He also stated that he had never experienced such symptoms when he lived in China, and that many of his Chinese friends also had similar reactions only when they ate in Chinese restaurants in the United States. Kwok suggested that the symptoms might be caused by some component of cooking wine, the high salt content of northern Chinese cuisine, or the MSG that was used (Kwok 1968). The set of symptoms Kwok described quickly became known as Chinese Restaurant syndrome (CRS).

Within weeks, Kwok's letter sparked lively controversy in the pages of the *New England Journal of Medicine*. Several detractors wrote letters literally calling Kwok's experiences a "crock." A number of individuals rallied to Kwok's defense, however, writing of similar symptoms after eating Chinese foods and other foods containing MSG, including matzoh ball soup and pork pies (Ambos et al. 1968; Schaumburg and Byck 1968).

Attempts to document CRS in the laboratory have proven elusive. Although anecdotes abound of headaches, numbness, flushing, chest pain, facial pressure and burning, dizziness, gastric discomfort, asthma, psychiatric reactions, and cardiac arrhythmia following ingestion of MSG, it has proven difficult to consistently provoke these symptoms under controlled conditions (Gore 1982; Kenney 1986; Zautcke, Schwartz, and Mueller 1986).

In 1969, Schaumburg and colleagues initiated research examining the role of MSG in Chinese Restaurant syndrome. Using single-blind methods in which the experimenter but not the subjects knew which substance was given, 36 subjects were challenged with oral and intravenous doses of MSG. All of the subjects experienced at least one of the symptoms originally described by Kwok; however, doses as high as 12 g were needed to produce these symptoms. The threshold dose of MSG for producing symptoms of CRS was found to be 3 to 4 g. Schaumburg and colleagues also reported that monosodium L-glutamate produced the symptoms of CRS, but that monosodium D-glutamate, monosodium L-aspartate, sodium chloride, and glycine did not (Schaumburg et al. 1969).

Although some subsequent studies have provided support for a causative role of MSG in the development of CRS (e.g., Kenney and Tidball 1972; Ghadimi and Kumar 1972), other work has not provided such evidence (e.g., Rosenblum, Bradley, and Coulston 1971; Gore and Salmon 1980; Kenney 1986). For example, Gore and Salmon (1980) tested 55 subjects with 6 g of MSG and did not find even one subject who demonstrated the classic symptoms of CRS. One interesting difference between the work of Gore and Salmon and studies that strongly suggest that MSG causes CRS is that subjects in the former study not only were unaware that they were receiving MSG, but also had never heard of CRS. Gore (1982) hypothesized that knowledge of CRS may have biased the results of previous studies. In support of this hypothesis, in an epidemiological study of CRS, Kerr and colleagues (1979) found that in their total population of 3,000 individuals who were questioned about reactions to foods, there was a very low incidence of classic CRS symptoms (1 to 2%), and the symptoms were associated with Chinese food in only 0.19% of the cases. When the results were analyzed by whether or not the subjects had heard of CRS, however, then 12% of those familiar with the syndrome complained of its symptoms.

The results of research examining the role of MSG in CRS can be summarized as follows. First, characteristic symptoms of CRS can be provoked in a limited number of individuals at high concentrations of MSG (3% of an aqueous solution). Second, symptoms following the administration of MSG are not consistent and can vary on a day-to-day basis. Indeed, the classic triad of symptoms (numbness, general weakness, and palpitations) described by Kwok (1968) are rarely reported together. Third, the experience of symptoms does not correlate with plasma levels of glutamate. Finally, the sensations of warmth or burning are not accompanied by any changes in skin temperature, and sensations of pressure or tightness are not associated with recordable activity of the underlying muscles (Kenney 1986; Zautcke, Schwartz, and Mueller 1986).

From the preceding results it can be concluded that some individuals have adverse reactions to MSG, but the proportion of the population negatively affected by this food additive is relatively small. In addition, the reaction to MSG, while uncomfortable, is a transitory, benign process with an excellent prognosis for immediate and rapid recovery. Individuals who experience adverse reactions can avoid MSG by not using it in cooking, carefully reading the labels of processed foods, and requesting that it not be added to restaurant foods.

SULFITES

Sulfites have been used for centuries to preserve foods and include potassium bisulfite, potassium metabisulfite, sodium bisulfite, sodium sulfite, and sulfur dioxide. These substances inhibit the enzymatic browning of fresh fruits and vegetables, control the nonenzymatic browning of dried fruits, and inhibit the growth of microorganisms in fermented foods such as beer and wine. Sulfites are found in jams, pickles, relishes, fruit drinks, and seafood. Until recently, sulfiting agents were commonly used to keep fruits and vegetables fresh in salad bars (Parker, Sussman, and Krondl 1988).

While the general population can consume large quantities of sulfites without adverse effects, 5% to 10% of individuals with asthma may have devastating reactions following the ingestion of these chemicals.

Symptoms of sulfite reaction range from flushing of the face, throat swelling, itching of the mouth and skin, and asthmatic attacks to anaphylactic shock and even death (Lessof 1987; Parker, Sussman, and Krondl 1988). Because of the severe reactions that can occur from sulfites, their use on raw fruits and vegetables has recently been banned in the United States and Canada. In addition, the FDA has required that the presence of sulfites in detectable amounts (10 parts per million) be indicated on the labels of all packaged goods.

CONCLUSION

Controversy over the value of food additives will certainly continue into the next century. Although vigilance is in order, the fact is that with respect to food safety, additives are placed under more scrutiny than any other food component. At present, the data indicate that additives have more beneficial than harmful consequences.

REFERENCES

Ambos, M., N. R. Leavitt, L. Marmorek, and S. B. Wolschina. 1968. Sin cib-syn: Accent on glutamate (letter). *New England Journal of Medicine* 279:105–106.

American Psychiatric Association. 1987. *Diagnostic and Statistical Manual of Mental Disorders,* 3rd ed. (rev.). Washington, DC: American Psychiatric Association.

Berdick, M. 1982. Safety of food colors. In *Nutritional Toxicology,* vol. 1, ed. J. N. Hathcock, pp. 383–434. New York: Academic Press.

Bunyan, J. E., A. Murrell, and P. P. Shah. 1976. The induction of obesity in rodents by means of monosodium glutamate. *British Journal of Nutrition* 35:25–39.

Burde, R. M., B. Schanker, and J. Kayes. 1971. Acute effects of oral and subcutaneous administration of monosodium glutamate on the arcuate nucleus of the hypothalamus in mice and rats. *Nature* 233:58–60.

Cagen, R. H. 1977. A framework for the mechanisms of actions of special taste substances: The example of monosodium glutamate. In *The Chemical Senses and Nutrition,* ed. M. R. Kare and O. Maller, pp. 343–360. New York: Academic Press.

Conners, C. K. 1980. *Food Additives and Hyperactive Children.* New York: Plenum.

Conners, C. K. 1984. Nutritional therapy in children. In *Nutrition and Behavior,* ed. J. Galler, pp. 159–192. New York: Plenum.

Conners, C. K., C. H. Goyette, D. A. Southwick, J. M. Lees, and P. A. Andrulonis. 1976. Food additives and hyperkinesis: A controlled double-blind experiment. *Pediatrics* 58:154–166.

David, T. J. 1988. Food additives. *Archives of Disease in Childhood* 63:582–583.

Dwyer, J. 1982. Commercial additives. In *Adverse Effects of Foods,* ed. E. F. P. Jelliffe and D. B. Jelliffe, pp. 163–194. New York: Plenum.

Federal Food, Drug, and Cosmetic Act, as Amended, and Related Laws. 1986. Washington D.C.: U.S. Government Printing Office.

Feingold, B. F. 1973. *Introduction to Clinical Allergy,* Springfield, IL: Charles C Thomas.

Feingold, B. F. 1975. Hyperkinesis and learning disabilities linked to artificial food flavors and colors. *American Journal of Nursing* 75:797–803.

Fennema, O. R. 1987. Food additives: An unending controversy. *American Journal of Clinical Nutrition* 46:201–203.

Garattini, S. 1979. Evaluation of the neurotoxic effects of glutamic acid. In *Nutrition and the Brain,* vol. 4, ed. R. J. Wurtman and J. J. Wurtman, pp. 79–124, New York: Raven Press.

Ghadimi, M. D. and S. Kumar. 1972. Current status of monosodium glutamate. *American Journal of Clinical Nutrition* 25:643–645.

Gore, M. 1982. The Chinese restaurant syndrome. In *Adverse Effects of Foods,* ed. E. F. P. Jelliffe and D. B. Jelliffe, pp. 211–223. New York: Plenum.

Gore, M. and P. R. Salmon. 1980. Chinese restaurant syndrome: Fact or fiction? *Lancet* 1:251–252.

Goyette, C. H., C. K. Conners, and T. A. Petti. 1978. Effects of artificial colors on hyperkinetic children: A double-blind challenge study. *Psychopharmacology Bulletin* 14:39–40.

Harley, J. P., R. S. Ray, L. Tomasi, P. L. Eichman, C. G. Matthews, R. Chun, C. S. Cleeland, and E. Traisman. 1978. Hyperkinesis and food additives: Testing the Feingold hypothesis. *Pediatrics* 61:818–828.

Irving, G. W. 1982. Determination of GRAS status of food ingredients. In *Nutritional Toxicology,* vol. 1, ed. J. H. Hathcock, pp. 435–450. New York: Academic Press.

Kanarek, R. B. and R. Marks-Kaufman. 1981. Increased carbohydrate consumption induced by neonatal administration of monosodium glutamate to rats. *Neurobehavioral Toxicology and Teratology* 3:343–350.

Kanarek, R. B., J. Meyers, R. G. Meade, and J. Mayer. 1979. Juvenile-onset obesity and deficits in caloric regulation by MSG-treated rats. *Pharmacology, Biochemistry and Behavior* 10:717–721.

Kaplan, R. J., J. McNicol, R. A. Conte, and H. K. Moghadm. 1989. Dietary replacement in preschool-aged hyperactive boys. *Pediatrics* 83:7–17.

Kenney, R. A. 1986. The Chinese restaurant syndrome: An anecdote revisited. *Chemical Toxicology* 24:351–354.

Kenney, R. A. and C. S. Tidball. 1972. Human susceptibility to oral monosodium L-glutamate. *American Journal of Clinical Nutrition* 25:140–146.

Kerr, G. R., M. Wu-Lee, M. El-Lozy, R. McGandy, and F. J. Stare. 1979. Prevalence of the Chinese restaurant syndrome. *Journal of the American Dietetic Association* 75:29–33.

Kwok, R. H. M. 1968. Chinese restaurant syndrome (letter). *New England Journal of Medicine* 278:225.

Lessof, M. H. 1987. Adverse reactions to food additives. *Journal of the Royal College of Physicians of London.* 21:237–240.

Levine, A. S., T. P. Labuza, and J. E. Morley. 1985. Food technology: A primer for physicians. *New England Journal of Medicine* 312:628–633.

Lipton, M. A., C. B. Nemeroff, and R. B. Mailman. 1979. Hyperkinesis and food additives. In *Nutrition and The Brain,* vol. 4, ed. R. J. Wurtman and J. J. Wurtman, pp. 1–27. New York: Raven Press.

Lucas, D. R. and J. P. Newhouse. 1957. The toxic effects of sodium L-glutamate on the inner layers of the retina. *American Medical Association Archives of Ophthalmology* 58:193–201.

Mattes, J. A. and R. Gittelman. 1981. Effects of artificial food colorings in children with hyperactive symptoms. *Archives of General Psychiatry* 38:714.

National Institutes of Health Consensus Development Panel. 1983. National Institutes of Health consensus development conference statement: Defined diets and childhood hyperactivity. *The American Journal of Clinical Nutrition* 37:161–165.

Nikoletseas, M. M. 1977. Obesity in exercising hypophagic rats treated with monosodium glutamate. *Physiology and Behavior* 19:767–773.

Olney, J. W. 1969. Brain lesions, obesity and other disturbances in mice treated with monosodium glutamate. *Science* 164:719–721.

Parker, S. L., G. L. Sussman, and M. Krondl. 1988. Dietary aspects of adverse reactions to foods in adults. *Canadian Medical Association Journal* 139:713–718.

Pizzi, W. J. and J. E. Barnhart. 1976. Effects of monosodium glutamate on somatic development, obesity and activity in the mouse. *Pharmacology, Biochemistry and Behavior* 51:551–557.

Root, R. and R. de Rochemont. 1976. *Eating in America: A History.* New York: Ecco Press.

Rosenblum, I., J. Bradley, and P. Coulston. 1971. Single- and double-blind studies with oral monosodium glutamate in man. *Toxicology and Applied Pharmacology* 18:367–373.

Rowe, K. S. 1988. Synthetic food colourings and 'hyperactivity': a double-blind crossover study. *Australian Paediatrics Journal* 24:143–147.

Rulis, A. M. 1987. Safety assurance margins for food additives currently in use. *Regulatory Toxicology and Pharmacology* 7:160–168.

Schaumburg, H. H. and R. Byck. 1968. Sin cib-syn: Accent on glutamate (letter). *New England Journal of Medicine* 279:105.

Schaumburg, H. H., R. Byck, R. Gerstl, and J. H. Mashman. 1969. Monosodium L-glutamate: Its pharmacology and role in the Chinese restaurant syndrome. *Science* 163:826–828.

Select Committee on GRAS Substances. 1982. Insights on Food Safety: An Evaluation. Springfield, VA.: National Technical Information Service, PB83-154146, U.S. Department of Commerce.

Senti, F. R. 1988. Food additives and contaminants. In: *Modern Nutrition in Health and Disease,* ed. M. E. Shils and V. R. Young, pp. 698–711, Philadelphia: Lea & Febiger.

Swanson, J. M. and Kinsbourne, M. 1980. Food dyes impair performance of hyperactive children on a laboratory learning test. *Science* 207:1485–1486.

Weiss, B. 1983. The behavioral toxicity of food additives. In *Nutrition Update,* vol. 1, ed. J. Weininger and G. M. Briggs, pp. 21–38. New York: Wiley.

Weiss, B., J. H. Williams, S. Margen, B. Abrams, B. Caan, L. J. Citron, C. Cox, J. McKibben, D. Ogar, and S. Schultz. 1980. Behavioral response to artificial food colors. *Science* 207:1487–1488.

Winter, R. 1989. *Consumer's Dictionary of Food Additives*. New York: Crown.

Yetiv, J. Z. 1986. *Popular Nutritional Practices: A Scientific Appraisal*. Toledo, OH: Popular Medicine Press.

Zautcke, J. L., J. A. Schwartz, and E. J. Mueller. 1986. Chinese restaurant syndrome: A review. *Annals of Emergency Medicine* 15:1210–1213.

8

Caffeine and the Methylxanthines

Caffeine is the world's most popular drug and is taken regularly in coffee, tea, cocoa, cola drinks, chocolate, and over-the-counter medicines.

Despite its popularity, the use of caffeine has not been without controversy. Following the introduction of coffee into England at the beginning of the seventeenth century, a group of women published a pamphlet in 1674 entitled "The Women's Petition Against Coffee, representing to public consideration the grand inconveniences occurring to their sex from the excessive use of the drying and enfeebling liquor." The women forcefully argued that the use of coffee by men resulted in severely diminished sexual excitability and potential sterility (Ray 1978).

Controversy followed the introduction of caffeine-containing beverages to the United States. Catharine Beecher, a popular critic of American life, wrote in 1856 that "alcohol and opium, tea and coffee, simply stimulate the brain and nervous system. . . . This stimulus is always followed by a reaction of debility, which is proportional to the degree of previous stimulation." She was particularly distressed by women's use of coffee and tea and further penned, "multitudes of wives and mothers become feeble, irritable, and miserable from the daily exhaustion caused by these narcotic stimulants. They feel the loss of their tea and coffee almost as much as the inebriate misses his daily libations" (Beecher 1856, cited in Whorton 1982).

Certainly, ideas about the evils of caffeine have been revised since the 1850s. During the last ten years, however, there has been a significant resurgence in concern about the detrimental effects of caffeine consumption. Studies conducted during the late 1970s implicated caffeine in a wide variety of health-related problems including cardiovascular disease, cancer, behavioral disorders, and birth defects. After reviewing the use, metabolism, and physiological effects of caffeine and related compounds, this chapter will examine the evidence for and against caffeine.

ORIGINS OF THE USE OF THE METHYLXANTHINES

Caffeine is a white, bitter, crystalline alkaloid, one of a family of compounds named xanthine stimulants, or methylxanthines. There are a large number of methylxanthines, but only three commonly occur in foods: caffeine, which is the main xanthine derative in coffee, theophylline, which is the major xanthine derivative in tea, and theobromine, which is the primary xanthine derivative in cocoa (Rall 1985).

Records of caffeine use date back at least 1,600 years. The popularity of caffeine-containing drinks stems from the ancient discovery that these beverages have stimulant effects which elevate mood, decrease fatigue, and increase the capacity for work. There are many colorful stories describing how caffeine and the other methylxanthines were discovered. One of the more popular stories of coffee's discovery is the tale of Kaldi, an Arabian goatherd. Kaldi's goats would occasionally wander away to the mountains, and after one such trip the goatherd noticed that the animals were behaving quite strangely. They bounced around the hillside like young kids and swiftly darted off upon seeing the goatherd. One day Kaldi followed the goats and ate some of the red berries he saw them nibbling. He found that he was extremely happy and had boundless energy. The story continues that a holy man watching this scene was instructed by a vision of Mohammed to boil the berries in water and to give this liquid to the brothers in his monastery to help them stay awake during their long hours of prayer (Ray 1978; Graham 1978; Rall 1985).

There are as many legends about the origin of tea as there are about coffee. According to one story, Daruma, the founder of Zen Buddhism, once fell asleep while mediating. When he awoke he was so mortified that he cut off his eyelids and threw them to the ground. Where they fell, a plant grew. From the leaves of this plant, *Camellia sinensis,* a beverage could be made that maintained wakefulness (Ray 1978).

The cacao tree, the source of the cacao bean and its by-product chocolate, originated in the new world. The Aztecs, who were as addicted to chocolate as we are to coffee, had a legend that Quetzalcoatl, the god of air, gave them a gift from Paradise, the chocolate or cacao tree. Remembering this legend, Linneaus named the tree *Theobroma cacao,* or "food of the gods" (Ray 1978).

SOURCES AND LEVELS OF INTAKE

Worldwide caffeine consumption is estimated at 70 mg per person per day, which is roughly the equivalent of one cup of coffee per day for every man, woman, and child on earth. In the United States, over 80% of the adult population consumes caffeine on a regular basis, contributing to a per capita consumption of 211 to 238 mg per day (Gilbert 1976, 1984; Graham 1978).

The most common source of caffeine is coffee. More than 75% of the caffeine consumed in the United States is in coffee. A 5-oz cup of coffee contains from 40 to 176 mg of caffeine. As shown in Table 8-1, caffeine

TABLE 8-1. Caffeine Content of Selected Beverages, Foods, and Drugs

Substance	Serving Size	Caffeine Content (mg/serving)
Percolated coffee	5-oz cup	64–124
Drip coffee	5-oz cup	56–176
Instant coffee	5-oz cup	40–108
Decaffeinated coffee	5-oz cup	2–5
Brewed tea	5-oz cup	8–91
Instant tea	5-oz cup	24–31
Cocoa	5-oz cup	2–7
Chocolate milk	8-oz glass	2–7
Cola beverage	12-oz glass	30–60
Milk chocolate candy	1-oz bar	1–15
Bittersweet chocolate	1-oz bar	25–35
Chocolate ice cream	2/3 cup	4–5
Anacin	1 tablet	32
Excedrin	1 tablet	65
Dristan	1 tablet	30
No-Doz	1 tablet	100

Source: Adapted from Barone and Roberts 1984; Clementz and Daily 1987; Leonard, Watson, and Mohs 1987.

content varies as a function of the species of coffee bean plant, type of processing (e.g., ground or instant), method of brewing (e.g., percolator or drip), amount of coffee used, and the length of brewing time (Graham 1978; Barone and Roberts 1984; Clementz and Dailey 1988).

The second most common source of caffeine is tea. Approximately 15% of the caffeine consumed in the United States comes from tea. By weight, tea contains more caffeine than coffee, but fewer grams of tea leaves are required to brew a cup of tea than grams of coffee beans are needed to make a cup of coffee. Thus, a cup of tea typically contains less caffeine than a comparable amount of coffee. A 5-oz cup of tea contains from 8 to 91 mg of caffeine depending on the species of tea, method of processing, and brewing time. A cup of tea also contains 1 mg of the methylxanthine theophylline.

Another source of caffeine is chocolate, which comes from the cacao tree of the Amazon rain forest. Although only a small percentage of the average adult's caffeine intake comes from chocolate, it can be a major source of caffeine for children. A 5-oz cup of hot chocolate has 4 mg of caffeine, and an 8-oz glass of chocolate milk has 5 mg. A cup of hot chocolate also contains approximately 250 mg of the methylxanthine theobromine.

Substantial amounts of caffeine are also consumed in cola beverages and other soft drinks. A 12-oz cola beverage contains 30 to 60 mg of caffeine.

Approximately half of the caffeine in a cola beverage comes from the kola nut base, and the remaining caffeine, the byproduct of the decaffeination of coffees and teas, is added by manufacturers to enhance flavor. (Gilbert, 1981).

Finally, caffeine is added to a large number of over-the-counter medications including headache remedies, cold preparations, decongestants, diuretics, and appetite suppressants (Clementz and Dailey 1988).

METABOLISM OF THE METHYLXANTHINES

The metabolism of the three methylxanthines is similar; however, most of the available information is about caffeine metabolism. In adults, more than 99% of ingested caffeine is rapidly absorbed from the gastrointestinal tract and distributed to all tissues in the body within 5 minutes. Peak blood levels of caffeine are reached 15 to 45 minutes after ingestion. Depending on a variety of factors, including age, gender, and activity level of the individual, the plasma half-life of caffeine varies from 3 to 7 hours. Caffeine is almost completely metabolized by the liver, where it is demethylated and converted to the metabolites 1-methyl uric acid and 1-methyl xanthine. These metabolites are excreted primarily by the kidneys, although traces may appear in the feces, saliva, semen, and breast milk. Of the total caffeine consumed, 3% to 6% is excreted unchanged by the kidney. Caffeine metabolism is slower in newborn infants, adults with liver disease, women using oral contraceptives, and women during the second half of pregnancy, and it is faster in smokers (Rall 1985; Leonard, Watson, and Mohs 1987) (Table 8-2).

TABLE 8-2. Metabolism of Caffeine

Condition	Plasma Half-Life[a] (hours)
Normal adult	3–7
Second half of pregnancy	6–14
Chronic oral contraceptive use	6–14
Premature infants	50
Patient with hepatic cirrhosis	60

[a] The half-life of a drug is the time required for the initial peak blood level to decrease by one-half.
Source: Adapted from Rall 1985.

PHYSIOLOGICAL EFFECTS

Caffeine, theophylline, and theobromine affect the cardiovascular, respiratory, gastrointestinal, renal, muscular, and nervous systems as follows:

Stimulate the central nervous system

Stimulate the cardiac muscle

Relax the smooth muscles

Stimulate gastric acid secretion

Act as a diuretic

Elevate plasma free fatty acids and glucose

The three methylxanthines have similar chemical structures (Figure 8-1) and effects on the body. However, their potency varies according to the physiological system under consideration, as seen in Table 8-3. For example, caffeine and theophylline are very strong central nervous system stimulants, and theobromine has minimal stimulatory effects. In comparison, theophylline has the greatest and caffeine the least effect on the cardiovascular system (Ray 1978; Rall 1985).

Cardiovascular System

The methylxanthines' actions on the cardiovascular system are complex and sometimes antagonistic. The effects depend to some degree on dose and route of administration, the individual's history of caffeine consumption, and other physiological and environmental factors. In general, the methylxanthines stimulate cardiovascular functioning and at high doses can lead to increases in blood pressure and heart rate. Cardiac arrhythmias can occur in individuals particularly sensitive to caffeine and in people who drink an excessive amount of caffeine-containing beverages (Rall 1985).

Smooth Muscle

The methylxanthines relax a variety of smooth muscles. Their most important action in this respect is their ability to relax the smooth muscles of the bronchi in the lungs. As a result of its potent action as a bronchodilator, theophylline is frequently used in the management of asthmatic patients. Theophylline compounds are given as prophylactic therapy for asthma and are used as adjuncts in the treatment of prolonged asthma attacks (Rall 1985).

CAFFEINE

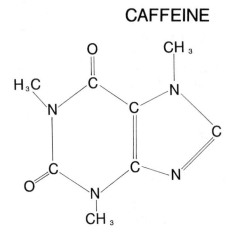

THEOBROMINE

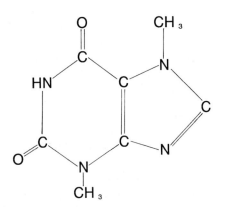

THEOPHYLLINE

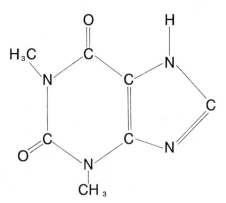

Figure 8-1. Chemical structure of the methylxanthines: caffeine, theophylline, and theobromine.

TABLE 8-3. Relative Potency of the Methylxanthines

	Caffeine	Theophylline	Theobromine
CNS stimulation	1[a]	2	3
Respiratory stimulation	1	2	3
Diuresis	3	1	2
Cardiac stimulation	3	1	2
Smooth muscle relaxation	3	1	2
Skeletal muscle relaxation	1	2	3

[a] 1 = the most potent.

Gastrointestinal System

Caffeine increases the secretion of both gastric acid and pepsin, the enzyme that initiates the breakdown of proteins in the stomach. Both coffee and decaffeinated coffee stimulate gastric acid and pepsin secretion more than caffeine alone, however, suggesting that another compound in coffee exerts a significant effect on the gastrointestinal system. The increase in gastrointestinal secretions that results from coffee consumption makes coffee potentially detrimental for individuals suffering from gastric ulcers (Rall 1985; Leonard, Watson, and Mohs 1987).

Renal System

Caffeine, theophylline, and theobromine all affect the renal system by their diuretic action on the kidneys, increasing urine volume and sodium excretion (Rall 1985; Leonard, Watson, and Mohs 1987).

NEUROPHYSIOLOGICAL AND BEHAVIORAL EFFECTS

All of the physiological effects of the methylxanthines are of importance, but it is the actions of these drugs on the central nervous system and on behavior that contribute most significantly to their use.

Actions on the Central Nervous System

Caffeine, theophylline, and theobromine all act as CNS stimulants, with caffeine having the most potent effects. These drugs directly activate the cerebral cortex. Following intake of as little as 150 mg of caffeine (about two cups of coffee), the cortex, which is involved in higher mental functioning, exhibits a pattern of electrical activity indicative of arousal. Higher doses of caffeine (500 mg, or four to five cups of coffee) stimulate the medulla, a region of the hindbrain that contains areas associated with the control of respiration, cardiovascular functioning, and muscular activity. By augmenting the sensitivity of these medullary centers to the stimulatory actions of carbon dioxide, caffeine increases respiration rates. This action makes caffeine useful for treating respiratory depression resulting from overdoses of drugs such as heroin and morphine.

At even higher doses (1,000 mg), insomnia and restlessness are common and may be accompanied by mild delirium. Sensory disturbances, including ringing in the ears and flashes of light, are common. Fatal poisoning with caffeine, although rare, can occur with acute doses of 5,000 to 10,000 mg. The symptoms of severe caffeine toxicity include seizures, convulsions, vomiting, tachycardia, ventricular arrhythmias, and death due to pulmonary edema, ventricular fibrillation, and cardiopulmonary arrest (Ray 1978; Rall 1985; Leonard, Watson, and Mohs 1987).

Behavioral Effects

In general, the behavioral consequences of caffeine are directly linked to its actions on the CNS. In individuals who regularly consume caffeine, 50 to 300 mg (one to three cups of coffee) typically result in increased alertness and decreased fatigue and can improve performance of gross motor skills. In regular caffeine users, doses as low as 32 mg can significantly improve visual reaction times and auditory alertness (Goldstein, Kaizer, and Warren 1965; Clubley et al. 1979; Lieberman et al. 1987; Roache and Griffiths 1987; Zwyghuizen-Doorenbos et al. 1990).

While caffeine can offset fatigue-induced decrements in some motor tasks and facilitate simple reaction time and vigilance tasks, it can also interfere with the performance of delicate motor movements. There is no convincing evidence that caffeine improves intellectual abilities, except perhaps when a normal performance level has been lowered by fatigue and boredom. In nonusers, caffeine typically leads to nervous feelings and thus can have disruptive effects on the performance of tasks (Dews 1982; Weiss and Laites 1962; Loke, Hinrichs, and Ghoneim 1985; Loke 1988).

Sleep is the function most sensitive to caffeine. Caffeine alters sleep patterns by delaying sleep onset, shortening sleep time, reducing the average depth of sleep, and worsening the subjective quality of sleep. Large individual differences, however, are observed in these effects. Caffeine's effects on the quantity and quality of sleep are influenced by a number of factors, including amount consumed and the individual's prior history of caffeine consumption (Goldstein, Warren, and Kaizer 1965).

Caffeine Intoxication

Large quantities of caffeine can cause headache and nervousness. When over 1,000 mg/day are consumed, behavior similar to anxiety neurosis has been reported. At this dose, flushing of the face, chilliness, irritability, and loss of appetite may be present (McKim 1986). This disorder has been labeled caffeinism or caffeine intoxication and is listed in DSM-IIIR (American Psychiatric Association 1987) as an organic mental disorder, or a disorder in which the cause—caffeine consumption—is known.

Diagnostic Criteria for Caffeine Intoxication

A. Recent consumption of caffeine, usually in excess of 250 mg.
B. At least five of the following signs:
Restlessness
Nervousness
Excitement
Insomnia
Flushed face
Diuresis
Gastrointestinal disturbance
Muscle twitching
Rambling flow of thought and speech
Tachycardia or cardiac arrhythmia
Periods of inexhaustibility
Psychomotor agitation
C. Not due to any physical or other mental disorder, such as an anxiety disorder. (American Psychiatric Association 1987, p. 139)

An individual must meet criteria A, B, and C for a diagnosis of caffeine intoxication to be established. The cure for this disorder is relatively simple: the elimination of caffeine from the diet. As detailed in the next section, however, the abrupt removal of caffeine can lead to severe withdrawal symptoms.

Caffeine and Anxiety

Case studies have revealed that symptoms of caffeine intoxication are sometimes indistinguishable from those of anxiety neurosis. The similarity between these two conditions has led to the hypothesis that there may be a direct association between caffeine intake and anxiety levels. In support of this hypothesis, significant correlations between caffeine consumption and anxiety levels have been found in both college students and psychiatric patients (Greden et al. 1978; Gilliland and Andress 1981; Boulenger and Uhde 1982; Loke 1988). In contrast to these findings, however, a study by the National Institutes of Health of over 3,800 normal individuals uncovered no associations between caffeine intake and anxiety (Eaton and McLeod 1984).

Although for the majority of the population caffeine consumption does not appear to be directly associated with anxiety, there may be subpopulations in which caffeine intake can prompt symptoms of anxiety. One such subpopulation may be individuals suffering from panic disorder. Panic disorder is characterized by episodes of recurrent anxiety or panic that occurs at unpredictable times (American Psychiatric Association 1987). People with panic disorder have been reported to consume less caffeine and to experience more anxiety and panic following caffeine consumption than controls (Boulenger et al. 1984; Clementz and Dailey 1988). These results suggest that limiting caffeine consumption should be recommended for individuals suffering from panic disorder.

Development of Tolerance of and Physical Dependence on Caffeine

In the field of pharmacology, tolerance refers to any situation in which repeated administration of the same dose of a drug results in gradually diminishing effects. Thus, the second or tenth dose of a drug does not have as great an effect as the first dose. Eventually the original dose of the drug will have minimal effects. Many drugs have multiple actions that result from their effects on different physiological systems. Tolerance may develop to some actions of a drug but not to others. For example, less tolerance develops to caffeine's effects on the CNS than to most of its other effects (Ray 1978). However, results of a recent study examining the effects of caffeine on alertness and sleep patterns indicate that tolerance to caffeine's effects on these behaviors may develop after as little as four days of exposure to the drug (Zwyghuizen-Doorenbos et al. 1990).

In a nonuser, caffeine typically leads to feelings of anxiety and nervousness; however, tolerance to these feelings develops within several weeks when an individual becomes a regular caffeine consumer.

Physical dependence is the condition in which discontinuing the use of a drug leads to a characteristic set of symptoms called withdrawal syndrome. Over the past decade, physical dependence on caffeine has been well documented. Headache is the most commonly reported symptom of caffeine withdrawal, followed by a constellation of other symptoms associated with fatigue and anxiety:

Headache

Mental depression

Fatigue

Listlessness

Sleepiness

Decreased alertness

Anxiety

Nervousness

Muscle tension

The severity of withdrawal symptoms varies from mild to extreme and appears to be directly related to the amount of caffeine regularly consumed. Caffeine withdrawal symptoms generally begin 12 to 24 hours after terminating intake, peak in 20 to 48 hours, and continue for 5 to 7 days (Griffiths, Bigelow, and Liebson 1986; Griffiths and Woodson 1988).

Modes of Action

A number of theories have been advanced to explain the CNS effects of caffeine and the other methylxanthines. One of the first theories was that the methylxanthines exert their effects by inhibiting the enzyme phosphodiesterase. This enzyme breaks down cyclic $3',5'$-adenosine monophosphate (cAMP), which has a variety of actions within the body such as acting as a "second messenger" to translate extracellular messages into intracellular responses (Rall 1985). Inhibition of phosphodiesterase by caffeine would reduce the catabolism of cAMP, leading to an increase in cAMP levels. This increase could stimulate activity within the CNS. One difficulty with this theory is that the behavioral effects of caffeine occur at doses many times lower than those required to inhibit phosphodiesterase activity (Fernstrom and Fernstrom 1984).

Experiments demonstrating that caffeine can block or antagonize the effects of some antianxiety agents in humans have led to the theory that caffeine may work by blocking the benzodiazepene receptor in the CNS. Antianxiety agents such as diazepam (Valium) and chlordiazepoxide (Librium) belong to a class of drugs called benzodiazepenes. It is believed that these compounds produce their antianxiety effects by acting at specific receptor sites in the brain. Further, it has been hypothesized that the brain produces its own antianxiety substances that function like benzodiazepene. By blocking benzodiazepene receptor sites, caffeine could inhibit the activity of the brain's natural antianxiety agents. This inhibition could help to explain the symptoms of anxiety produced by large doses of caffeine (Hirsh 1984; McKim 1986).

Recently, evidence has accumulated that strongly suggests adenosine mediates the behavioral actions of caffeine and the other methylxanthines. Adenosine is a constituent of adenosine triphosphate (ATP) and nucleic acids. Adenosine dilates blood vessels in both the brain and coronary circulation, inhibits the breakdown of fat, and decreases blood lipids. In the CNS, adenosine is an electrophysiological, biochemical, and behavioral depressant that typically decreases neuronal activity. These effects are the opposite of many of caffeine's commonly observed actions

TABLE 8-4. Contrasting Actions of Caffeine and Adenosine

Response	Caffeine	Adenosine
Blood pressure	Increase	Decrease
Urine output	Increase	Decrease
Intestinal peristalsis	Increase	Decrease
Bronchial tone	Decrease	Increase
Lipolysis	Increase	Decrease
Neurotransmitter release	Increase	Decrease
Neuronal firing	Increase	Decrease

(Table 8-4). Caffeine at doses comparable to that contained in a few cups of coffee occupies 50% of the adenosine receptors in the CNS. By blocking the receptor sites, caffeine may prevent adenosine from inhibiting neuronal firing, thereby allowing increased stimulation of neuronal activity and behavior (Hirsh 1984; Snyder 1984).

Alterations in the adenosine receptors also appear to play a role in the development of tolerance to and physical dependence on caffeine. Chronic caffeine intake leads to an increase in the number of adenosine receptor sites, and presumably to their sensitivity to adenosine. A new balance may be reached between endogenous adenosine and the presence of exogenous caffeine, leading to a reduction in some of the physiological and behavioral actions of the drug. If this balance is suddenly shifted by decreasing or abruptly stopping caffeine intake, then the excess adenosine receptors would no longer be blocked by caffeine, and the physiological responses to adenosine could become exaggerated. These exaggerated responses may contribute to caffeine withdrawal symptoms (Hirsh 1984; Griffiths and Woodson 1988).

THERAPEUTIC USES

The methylxanthines can be effective remedies for a number of clinical conditions including breathing problems in infants and attention deficit disorder in children.

Sleep Apnea

Caffeine and theophylline have been used successfully in the treatment of sleep apnea in premature infants. Respiratory abnormalities have been found in 25% of premature infants weighing under 2,500 g and 84% of infants weighing under 1,000 g, including periods during sleep when breathing may cease for 10 to 20 seconds (sleep apnea). Sleep apnea poses a threat of recurrent hypoxemia and neurological damage. Both caffeine and theophylline can reduce the incidence and duration of apnea in premature infants. Theophylline may also be effective in decreasing the incidence of apnea in full-term infants with respiratory abnormalities associated with sudden infant death syndrome (Rall 1985).

Attention Deficit Hyperactivity Disorder

Caffeine has been used as a treatment for attention deficit hyperactivity disorder (ADHD) in children. ADHD is a syndrome that begins early in life and is characterized by hyperactivity, distractibility, aggressiveness, and antisocial behavior (see chapter 7). Although the physiological mechanism is unknown, 60% to 70% of children with ADHD respond well to pharmacological stimulants such as amphetamines and methylphenidate. These stimulants can produce rapid changes in behavior including increased attention span, decreased hyperactivity, and reduced impulsivity.

The practice of maintaining young children on potent pharmacological agents for several years is not a desirable one. As caffeine is also a CNS stimulant, but apparently more benign than the other stimulants, it has been a suitable candidate for testing in the treatment of this disorder. In an initial study, children diagnosed with ADHD were given two cups of coffee a day in place of their stimulant medicine. No difference in behavior was noted between the periods when the children received a stimulant medication, methylphenidate, and when they received coffee. During both treatment periods, the children were significantly less hyperactive than when they received no drugs (Schnackenberg 1973). Unfortunately, both the subjects and their parents were aware of the experimental manipulations. Subsequent and better designed studies have demonstrated that caffeine can lead to some behavioral improvement in children with ADHD, but typically less than that produced by treatment with prescription drugs. Thus, the available data indicate that caffeine is only of limited value in the treatment of ADHD and not an effective substitute for more powerful stimulants (Huestis, Arnold, and Smeltzer 1975; Connors 1979; Rumsey and Rapoport 1983).

CAFFEINE AND DISEASE

Cardiovascular Disease

A number of studies have evaluated the effects of caffeine on cardiovascular disease. Early studies suggested that consumption of more than six cups of coffee a day was associated with an increased risk for myocardial infarction (Jick et al. 1973; Rosenberg et al. 1980); however, subsequent experiments have produced contradictory results. For example, a long-term study of 5,000 men and women in Framingham, Massachusetts, has found no evidence of a direct link between heart disease and caffeine intake (Dawber, Kannel, and Gordon 1974). Further, no associations between coffee intake and myocardial infarctions or risk of ischemic heart disease have been reported in studies from Georgia, Hawaii, and Sweden (Curatolo and Robertson 1983).

Epidemiological studies have suggested that excessive caffeine intake may be detrimental in individuals prone to cardiac arrhythmias. However, only limited clinical studies have addressed this suggestion (Curatolo and Robertson 1983).

Cancer

Epidemiological studies conducted during the 1970s and 1980s demonstrated a relationship between coffee drinking and urinary, pancreatic, and ovarian cancer (Grice 1984). For example, MacMahon et al. (1981), comparing coffee intake in 369 patients with pancreatic cancer and 644 control patients, found a strong connection between coffee intake and pancreatic cancer in both men and women. A nonsignificant inverse relationship, however, was found between tea intake and pancreatic cancer. These results suggest that caffeine per se may not be associated with an increased risk of pancreatic cancer. Moreover, subsequent studies have not confirmed a direct connection between caffeine intake and pancreatic cancer. Similar controversy exists for a relationship between caffeine consumption and other forms of cancer (Grice 1984).

A large number of studies with experimental animals have attempted to confirm or refute a link between caffeine intake and cancer. In the majority of these studies, rats and other experimental animals were fed large doses of caffeine or coffee for extended periods of time. In none of these studies was caffeine found to be a carcinogen (Grice 1984).

The results of epidemiological and animal studies lead to the conclusion that at levels typically consumed, caffeine is not a carcinogenic agent.

Caffeine and Pregnancy

A great deal of publicity has been generated about the potentially harmful effects on the fetus of caffeine intake during pregnancy. Caffeine readily cross the placenta and accumulates in the fetus. Concern about the use of caffeine in pregnancy was sparked by studies demonstrating that caffeine could act as a teratogen in laboratory animals. In these studies, giving caffeine to pregnant animals resulted in abnormal organ development in a low to moderate percentage of the offspring. The most commonly observed abnormalities were facial and limb defects. However, high doses of caffeine were needed to produce these effects, particularly when it was incorporated into the animal's food or water. In general, even with these high doses, only a low proportion of the offspring were affected. Lower doses of caffeine given to pregnant animals had negligible effects on fetal development. Thus, the overall data from animal studies imply that caffeine intake in moderate amounts poses little hazard to the developing mammalian embryo (Wilson and Scott 1984).

To further assess the teratogenic potential of caffeine, a number of epidemiological studies have examined the relationship between caffeine consumption during pregnancy and the risk of preterm deliveries, low birth weights, and congenital malformations. Two studies done in the Boston area, one at Harvard and the other at Boston University, indicate that moderate consumption of caffeine by pregnant women does not adversely affect their offspring. In the Harvard study, more than 12,000 women were interviewed shortly after their deliveries about a wide variety of factors including the number of cups of coffee and tea they had consumed each day during the first trimester of pregnancy. The first trimester of pregnancy is the period when organ development is occurring most rapidly. Infants of these women were assessed for low birth weight and for birth defects. Women who consumed four or more cups of coffee per day were no more likely to have a low birth weight infant or a child with malformations than were women who drank no coffee (Linn et al. 1982; Leviton 1988).

One problem with the Harvard study was that caffeine intake was only indirectly measured from estimates of coffee and tea consumption. Women who drink neither tea nor coffee may consume other beverages, such as cola drinks, or take over-the-counter medicines containing caffeine (Leviton 1988). This problem was eliminated in the Boston University study, which measured total maternal caffeine consumption during the first trimester of pregnancy. As in the Harvard study, no evidence of an increased risk of birth defects was found as a function of caffeine consumption (Rosenberg et al. 1982). The data from these studies and others suggest that moderate caffeine consumption during pregnancy does not increase the risk for low birth weight or congenital malformations (Leviton 1988).

Other Health-Related Conditions

Caffeine consumption has also been linked to benign lumps of the breast, or fibrocystic disease (Minton et al. 1979). Some women with cysts report that they experience prompt relief from the associated pain when they eliminate caffeine from their diet. However, experimental studies have found only a very modest relationship between methylxanthine consumption in the form of tea or coffee, and either benign fibrocystic disease of the breast or malignant breast tumors (Marshall, Graham, and Swanson 1982; Heyden and Muhlbaier 1984; Rohan, Cook, and McMichael 1989).

Elimination of caffeine-containing beverages from the diet has also been reported to ameliorate some of the symptoms of premenstrual syndrome (PMS). To examine the role of caffeine in PMS, Rossignol (1985) questioned 295 college sophomores about the presence and severity of PMS, their consumption of caffeine-containing beverages, and their use of over-the-counter drugs containing caffeine. The prevalence of PMS, and in particular moderate to severe symptoms, increased with greater consumption of caffeine-containing beverages. It is interesting that for this population cola beverages represented the major source of caffeine consumption. Other interpretations of these results are possible, for example, that consumption of large amounts of any liquid, not only caffeine-containing beverages, may be related to PMS. However, the data do suggest a role for caffeine in PMS.

CONCLUSION

Caffeine is a food component with pronounced effects on the brain and behavior. Caffeine acts as a CNS stimulant and as such activates behavior, relieves fatigue, and can aid in the performance of simple psychomotor tasks. These stimulant actions help to account for the worldwide popularity of caffeine-containing beverages and foods.

Although caffeine recently has been accused of contributing to a variety of health-related problems, in moderate amounts it does not appear to have detrimental effects on health. At higher doses, however, caffeine consumption may lead to insomnia, restlessness, nervousness, and other symptoms. Further, it is possible to develop physical dependence on caffeine. Cessation of caffeine intake leads to a well documented withdrawal syndrome characterized by headaches and fatigue. Finally, caffeine may exacerbate symptoms in individuals with a predisposition for cardiac arrhythmias, panic disorder, fibrocystic breast disease, and premenstrual syndrome.

More research is certainly needed to resolve the health risk controversy surrounding caffeine. For example, it is important to discover how other habits (e.g., smoking, alcohol consumption, and exercise) interact with caffeine. Until this research is conducted, it can be concluded that individuals who consume moderate amounts of caffeine and other methylxanthines should not be concerned for their health with regard to methylxanthine consumption if they maintain other life style habits in moderation.

REFERENCES

American Psychiatric Association. 1987. *Diagnostic and Statistical Manual of Mental Disorders, Third Edition Revised.* Washington, D.C.: American Psychiatric Association.

Barone, J. J. and H. Roberts. 1984. Human consumption of caffeine. In *Caffeine,* ed. P. B. Dews, pp. 59–76. New York: Springer Verlag.

Boulenger, J. P. and T. W. Uhde. 1982. Caffeine consumption and anxiety: Preliminary results of a survey comparing patients with anxiety disorders and normal controls. *Psychopharmacology Bulletin* 18:53–57.

Boulenger, J. P., T. W. Uhde, E. A. Wolff, III, and R. M. Post. 1984. Increased sensitivity to caffeine in patients with panic disorder. *Archives of General Psychiatry* 41:1067–1071.

Clementz, G. L. and J. W. Dailey. 1988. Psychotropic effects of caffeine. *American Family Physician* 37(5):167–172.

Clubley, M., C. E. Bye, T. A. Henson, A. W. Peck, and C. J. Riddington. 1979. Effects of caffeine and cyclizine alone and in combination on human performance, subjective effects and EEG activity. *British Journal of Clinical Pharmacology* 7:157–163.

Conners, C. K. 1979. The acute effects of caffeine on evoked response, vigilance, and activity level in hyperkinetic children. *Journal of Abnormal Child Psychology* 7:145–151.

Curatolo, P. W. and D. Robertson. 1983. The health consequences of caffeine. *Annals of Internal Medicine* 98:641–653.

Dawber, T. R., W. B. Kannel, and T. Gordon. 1974. Coffee and cardiovascular disease: Observations from the Framingham study. *New England Journal of Medicine* 291:871–874.

Dews, P. B. 1982. Caffeine. *Annual Review of Nutrition* 2:323–341.

Eaton, W. W. and J. McLeod. 1984. Consumption of coffee or tea and symptoms of anxiety. *American Journal of Public Health* 74:66–68.

Fernstrom, J. D. and M. H. Fernstrom. 1984. Effects of caffeine on monoamine neurotransmitters in the central and peripheral nervous system. In *Caffeine,* ed. P. B. Dews, pp. 107–118. New York: Springer Verlag.

Gilbert, R. M. 1976. Caffeine as a drug of abuse. In *Research Advances in Alcohol and Drug Problems,* ed. R. J. Gibbins, Y. Israel, H. Kalant, R. E. Popham, W. Schmidt, and R. G. Smart, pp. 49–176. New York: Wiley.

Gilbert, R. M. 1981. Caffeine: Overview and anthology. In *Nutrition and Behavior,* ed. S. A. Miller, pp. 145–166. Philadelphia: Franklin Institute.

Gilbert, R. M. 1984. Caffeine consumption. In *Methylxanthine Beverages and Foods: Chemistry, Consumption, and Health Effects,* ed. G. A. Spiller, pp. 185–213. New York: Alan R. Liss.

Gilliland, K. and D. Andress. 1981. Ad lib caffeine consumption, symptoms of caffeinism and academic performance. *American Journal of Psychiatry* 138:512–514.

Goldstein, A., S. Kaizer, and R. Warren. 1965. Psychotropic effects of caffeine in man: II. Alertness, psychomotor coordination and mood. *Journal of Pharmacology and Experimental Therapeutics* 150:146–151.

Goldstein, A., R. Warren, and S. Kaizer. 1965. Psychotropic effects of caffeine in man: I. Individual differences in sensitivity to caffeine-induced wakefulness. *Journal of Pharmacology and Experimental Therapeutics* 149:156–159.

Graham, D. M. 1978. Caffeine: Its identity, dietary sources, intake and biological effects. *Nutrition Reviews* 36(4):97–102.

Greden, J. F., P. Fontaine, M. Lubetsky, and K. Chamberlin. 1978. Anxiety and depression associated with caffeinism among psychiatric inpatients. *American Journal of Psychiatry* 135:963–966.

Grice, H. C. 1984. The carcinogenic potential of caffeine. In *Caffeine,* ed. P. B. Dews, pp. 201–220. New York: Springer Verlag.

Griffiths, R. R., G. E. Bigelow, and I. A. Liebson. 1986. Human coffee drinking: Reinforcing and physical dependence-producing effects of caffeine. *Journal of Pharmacology and Experimental Therapeutics* 239:416–425.

Griffiths, R. R. and P. P. Woodson. 1988. Caffeine physical dependence: A review of human and laboratory animal studies. *Psychopharmacology* 94:437–451.

Heyden, S. and L. H. Muhlbaier. 1984. Prospective study of "fibrocystic breast disease" and caffeine consumption. *Surgery* 96:479–484.

Hirsh, K. 1984. Central nervous system pharmacology of the dietary methylxanthines. In *Methlyxanthine Beverages and Foods: Chemistry, Consumption and Health Effects,* ed. G. A. Spiller. pp. 235–301. New York: Alan R. Liss.

Huestis, R. D., L. E. Arnold, and D. J. Smeltzer. 1975. Caffeine versus methylphenidate and d-amphetamine in minimal brain dysfunction: A double-blind comparison. *American Journal of Psychiatry* 132:868–870.

Jick, H., O. S. Miettinen, R. K. Neff, S. Shapiro, O. P. Heinonen, and D. Slone. 1973. Coffee and myocardial infarction. *New England Journal of Medicine* 289:63–67.

Leonard, T. K., R. R. Watson, and M. E. Mohs. 1987. The effects of caffeine on various body systems: A review. *Journal of the American Dietetic Association* 87:1048–1053.

Leviton, A. 1988. Caffeine consumption and the risks of reproductive hazards. *Journal of Reproductive Medicine* 33:175–178.

Lieberman, H. R., R. J. Wurtman, G. G. Emde, C. Roberts, and I. L. G. Coviella. 1987. The effects of low doses of caffeine on human performance and mood. *Psychopharmacology* 92:308–312.

Linn, S., S. C. Schoenbaum, R. R. Monson, B. Rosner, P. G. Stubblefield, and K. J. Ryan. 1982. No association between coffee consumption and adverse outcomes of pregnancy. *New England Journal of Medicine* 306:141–145.

Loke, W. H. 1988. Effects of caffeine on mood and memory. *Physiology and Behavior* 44:367–372.

Loke, W. H., J. V. Hinrichs, and M. M. Ghoneim. 1985. Caffeine and diazepam: Separate and combined effects on mood, memory, and psychomotor performance. *Psychopharmacology* 87:344–350.

MacMahon, B., S. Yen, D. Trichopoulos, K. Warren, and G. Nardi. 1981. Coffee and cancer of the pancreas. *New England Journal of Medicine* 304:630–633.

Marshall, J., S. Graham, and M. Swanson. 1982. Caffeine consumption and benign breast disease: A case-control comparison. *American Journal of Public Health* 72:610–612.

McKim, W. A. 1986. *Drugs and Behavior.* Englewood Cliffs, NJ: Prentice-Hall.

Minton, J. P., M. K. Foecking, D. J. T. Webster, and R. H. Matthews. 1979. Caffeine, cyclic nucleotides, and breast disease. *Surgery* 86:105–109.

Rall, T. W. 1985. Central nervous system stimulants: The methlyxanthines. In *The Pharmacological Basis of Therapeutics,* ed. A. G. Gilman, L. S. Goodman, T. W. Rall, and F. Murad, pp. 589–603. New York: Macmillan.

Ray, O. 1978. *Drugs, Society and Human Behavior.* Saint Louis, MO: C. V. Mosby.

Roache, J. D. and R. R. Griffiths. 1987. Interactions of diazepam and caffeine: Behavioral and subjective dose effects in humans. *Pharmacology, Biochemistry and Behavior* 26:801–812.

Rohan, T. E., M. G. Cook, and A. J. McMichael. 1989. Methylxanthines and benign proliferative epithelial disorders of the breast in women. *International Journal of Epidemiology* 18:626–633.

Rosenberg, L., A. A. Mitchell, S. Shapiro, and D. Slone. 1982. Selected birth defects relating to caffeine-containing beverages. *Journal of the American Medical Association* 247:1429–1432.

Rosenberg, L., D. Slone, S. Shapiro, D. Kaufman, P. Stolley, and O. Miettinen. 1980. Coffee drinking and myocardial infarction in young women. *American Journal of Epidemiology* 111:675–681.

Rossignol, A. M. 1985. Caffeine-containing beverages and premenstrual syndrome in young women. *American Journal of Public Health* 75:1335–1337.

Rumsey, J. M. and J. L. Rapoport. 1983. Assessing behavioral and cognitive effects of diet in pediatric populations. In *Nutrition and the Brain,* vol. 6, ed. R. J. Wurtman and J. J. Wurtman, pp. 101–161. New York: Raven Press.

Schnackenberg, R. C. 1973. Caffeine as a substitute for schedule II stimulants in hyperkinetic children. *American Journal of Psychiatry* 130:796–798.

Snyder. S. H. 1984. Adenosine as a mediator of the behavioral effects of xanthines. In *Caffeine,* ed. P. B. Dews, pp. 129–141. New York: Springer Verlag.

Weiss, B. and V. G. Laties. 1962. Enhancement of human performance by caffeine and the amphetamines. *Pharmacology Reviews* 14:1–36.

Wilson, J. G. and W. J. Scott. 1984. The teratogenic potential of caffeine in laboratory animals. In *Caffeine,* ed. P. B. Dews, pp. 165–187. New York: Springer Verlag.

Whorton, J. C. 1982. *Crusaders for Fitness.* Princeton, NJ: Princeton University Press.

Zwyghuizen-Doorenbos, A., T. A. Roehrs, L. Lipschutz, V. Timms, and T. Roth. 1990. Effects of caffeine on alertness. *Psychopharmacology* 100:36–39.

9

Sugar and Behavior

Of the many components in our diets, none has been condemned as frequently and as vehemently as sugar. Studies reviewed by the federal government indicate that after salt and sodium, sugar is the food ingredient people most consistently want to avoid and the one they look for most often on a food label's list of ingredients (Lecos 1980, 1988). In recent years, the use of sugars in the diet has become an extremely controversial issue involving scientists, dietitians, physicians, government officials, and private citizens. Sugar has been blamed, although in some cases wrongly, for a myriad of ills including obesity, diabetes, dental disease, and behavioral disorders. Modern attitudes toward sugar have led some to conclude that our society suffers from "saccrophobia" or the fear or sugar (Fischler 1987).

The public strongly believes that sugar has negative effects on behavior. This belief has been fostered by popular reports blaming sugar for a multiplicity of adverse behavioral outcomes including hyperactivity, depression, mental confusion, memory loss, irritability, schizophrenia, drug and alcohol addiction, and antisocial behavior (Dufty 1975; Ketcham and Mueller 1983; Schoenthalar 1983a).

One of the most celebrated examples of society's negative views of sugar comes from the case of San Francisco city supervisor Dan White, who shot and killed the city's mayor and another city supervisor. White's lawyers argued that their client had acted irrationally and suffered from "diminished mental capacity" as a result of his overconsumption of sugar-containing "junk" foods. On the basis of this argument, which has become known as the "Twinkie defense," White was convicted of manslaughter rather than first degree murder.

How valid are our fears about sugar? To answer this question, it is important to review the scientific evidence. This chapter pays particular attention to recent research addressing the role of sugar in hyperactive behavior, sugar's association with hypoglycemia, and the proposed relation between sugar and antisocial behavior.

SUGAR: WHAT IS IT?

Before examining sugar's effects on behavior, it is necessary to define the term sugar. While many different types of sugars are found in our foods, most people use the word sugar to describe the simple carbohydrate sucrose. Sucrose is commercially produced from sugar cane and sugar beets, and is the sugar that we find on our tables and typically use in cooking. Additionally, it is found in maple syrup, molasses, and in small quantities in a variety of fruits and vegetables.

Chemically, sucrose is a disaccharide composed of the two monosaccharides fructose and glucose. As only monosaccharides are absorbed across the small intestine, sucrose is broken down into its monosaccharide components in the digestive tract. After absorption from the gastrointestinal tract, monosaccharides are carried in the blood to the liver and other tissues. As fructose is rapidly metabolized to glucose in the intestinal mucosa and liver, any discussion of carbohydrate metabolism is essentially a discussion of glucose metabolism (Robinson and Lawler 1982). Glucose is the metabolic fuel for most cells in the body and is the principal fuel for the cells in the central nervous system. The importance of glucose to energy metabolism requires that blood glucose levels be maintained within relatively narrow limits. The regulation of blood glucose is controlled by a number of hormones, including insulin, glucagon, thyroid hormone, and adrenocorticotropic hormone. These hormones act to alter glucose absorption, regulate the conversion of glucose to glycogen (the storage form of carbohydrate in the body), control the synthesis of fat from glucose, and eliminate glucose in the urine when the renal threshold is exceeded.

Of all of the organs and tissues in the body, the central nervous system (CNS) is most dependent upon the minute-by-minute supply of glucose from the blood. Glucose is indispensable for maintaining the functional integrity of nervous tissue. The importance of glucose to the CNS is evidenced by the rapid development of hypoglycemic shock when blood glucose levels are lowered. As an example, administration of large doses of insulin, which decreases availability of glucose to the CNS by stimulating peripheral utilization of the sugar, can lead to hypoglycemic shock characterized by seizures, coma, and possibly irreversible brain damage. The importance of glucose to the CNS has obvious implications for the effects of sugar on behavior.

SUGAR CONSUMPTION

During the last century, consumption of sucrose in the United States has increased dramatically (Robinson and Lawler 1982; Drewnowski 1988). Estimates are that at the turn of the century, the typical American ate

35 lbs of sucrose a year. By 1972, we were eating over 100 lbs of sucrose per person (Lecos 1985). In the last 18 years, annual sucrose consumption has decreased, with per capita consumption at approximately 65 lbs in 1986. However, during the same period, total intake of sweeteners has increased. This increase is due to the use of corn sweeteners, which are produced by the enzymatic breakdown of cornstarch. In the United States, yearly intake of corn sweeteners now averages over 50 lbs per person (Lecos 1985; Hegarty 1988). Corn sweeteners are similar in taste to sucrose but are substantially less expensive to produce. They are now found as the predominant sweeteners in a variety of foods including soft drinks, canned items, jellies and jams, and salad dressings. Thus, total intake of sweeteners has continued to rise, reaching 125 lbs per person in 1985 (Lecos 1985; Franz and Maryniuk 1987; Drewnowski 1988) (Figure 9-1).

There are many obvious sources of sucrose and other sweeteners in our diet, such as the sugar we add to our coffee and tea, and that found in candy, cake, and cookies. However, less apparent sources of sugar also contribute to our intake. Commercial food processors use sucrose and

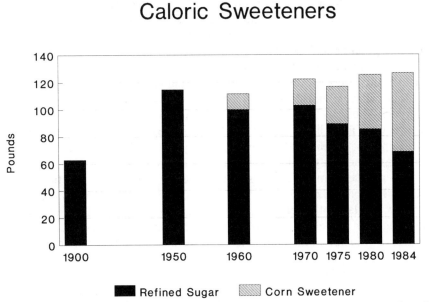

Figure 9-1. Yearly per capita intake of caloric sweeteners. Although intake of refined sugar has decreased substantially since 1950, total intake of caloric sweeteners has increased as a result of the use of corn sweeteners.

corn sweeteners for a variety of reasons, including to add bulk, prevent spoilage, and help browning in foods ranging from breakfast cereals to peanut butter, meat products, and even some medications (including children's vitamins). Totalling intake from all of these sources, sugar represents about 20% of the average American's overall caloric intake. However, in certain groups of individuals such as preadolescents, whose consumption of sugar-containing beverages is high, intake may be considerably greater (Morgan and Zabik 1981; Dahlqvist 1984; Alfin-Slater and PiSunyer 1987; Folsom et al. 1987; Franz and Maryniuk 1987; Drewnowski 1988).

One of the obvious reasons for our consumption of sweeteners is their pleasant taste. Most animals, including humans, display strong preferences for sweet-tasting substances. Ancient cave drawings tell us of prehistoric man's taste for honey, figs, and dates. The beekeeping practices of the Egyptians are depicted in paintings from tombs dating as early as 2600 B.C. (Darby, Ghalioungui, and Grivetti 1977).

There is substantial evidence that our preferences for sweets are innate, rather than learned (Beauchamp and Cowart 1987; Ramirez 1990). Investigations of newborn infants' taste responses have consistently demonstrated that sweet foods are highly acceptable. Concentrated sucrose solutions placed on the tongue of newborns elicit facial expressions resembling smiles (Steiner 1973). Additionally, infants consume significantly more sweet-tasting formulas than nutritionally similar nonsweet formulas (Fomon et al. 1983). While there is evidence that sweet preferences decrease with age, sweet-tasting foods remain highly palatable throughout life (Beauchamp and Cowart, 1987).

Our preference for sweet tastes may have evolved as a selective advantage. Fruits, berries, and other sweet-tasting plant foods are likely to be high in calories, and those with bitter or sour tastes are more often poisonous. Thus, by developing a preference for sweet tastes, primitive people were more likely to consume safer, more nutritious foods. Since the development of refined sugar and the ready availability of prepared foods, this preference may no longer serve such a beneficial role.

The phrase "empty calories" is frequently used in conjunction with sugar. This phrase refers to the fact that sucrose and related sugars provide energy, but lack other essential nutrients. However, there is no evidence that sugar on grapefruit, in coffee or tea, or eaten in a snack can cancel the nutritive value of an adequate diet. It is only when sucrose calories interfere with or replace a normal diet that sugar becomes an inadequate food item deserving the designation "empty calories."

Sucrose intake has been proposed to be a causative factor in a variety of illnesses including obesity, heart disease, and diabetes (Yudkin 1964, 1972). With reference to obesity, for example, it has been suggested that calories from sucrose are more fattening than those from other foods. In reality, calories from sucrose are no more fattening than the same number of calories from protein or fat (Danowski and Sunder 1981). Further, available evidence indicates that high sucrose consumption is not a primary causative factor in cardiovascular disease, diabetes, or impaired glucose tolerance (Franz and Maryniuk 1987).

There is a strong link between sucrose intake and dental caries. Sugar can provide the energy necessary for bacterial growth in the mouth, which leads to the gradual accumulation of plaque, a sticky carbohydrate–bacterial matrix. Additionally, acids formed by the bacteria while digesting the sugar substrate gradually erode the tooth enamel and bring about decay. Although sugar intake contributes to dental problems, other factors such as the texture of food and length of time it remains on the teeth, the pH of the saliva, other nutrients, and the general health of the individual also play a role in dental problems.

SUGAR AND HYPERACTIVITY

One pervasive idea about sugar is that it can cause hyperactivity and attention deficits in children. This idea has been accepted by both educational professionals and parents. For example, in a recent survey in the Louisville, Kentucky, area, over 90% of the teachers interviewed reported that they believed that the consumption of sugar-containing foods adversely affected classroom behavior and academic performance (McLoughlin and Nall 1988). Among parents, medically unsupervised dietary intervention, particularly reducing intake of sugar-containing foods, is a strategy frequently implemented to help a child with supposed sugar reactivity. Sugar's negative image is not restricted to parents and teachers. In a survey in the state of Washington, 45% of the primary care physicians who responded recommended a low-sugar diet for hyperactive children (Bennett and Sherman 1983).

All children experience periods of increased activity; however, when psychologists and other professionals use the term "hyperactivity" they are referring to a specific type of behavioral problem. Hyperactivity, or attention deficit hyperactivity disorder (ADHD) as the condition is officially recognized by the American Psychiatric Association, is characterized by developmentally inappropriate inattention, impulsive behavior, and significantly increased levels of gross motor activity:

Diagnostic Criteria for Attention Deficit Hyperactivity Disorder

A. A disturbance of at least six months during which at least eight of the following are present:
   (1) often fidgets with hands or feet or squirms in seat (in adolescents, may be limited to subjective feelings of restlessness)
   (2) has difficulty remaining seated when required to do so

(3) is easily distracted by extraneous stimuli

(4) has difficulty awaiting turn in games or group situations

(5) often blurts out answers to questions before they have been completed

(6) has difficulty following through on instructions from others (not due to oppositional behavior or failure of comprehension), e.g., fails to finish chores

(7) has difficulty sustaining attention in tasks or play activities

(8) often shifts from one uncompleted activity to another

(9) has difficulty playing quietly

(10) often talks excessively

(11) often interrupts or intrudes on others, e.g., butts into other children's games

(12) often does not seem to listen to what is being said to him or her

(13) often loses things necessary for tasks or activities at school or at home (e.g., toys, pencils, books, assignments)

(14) often engages in physically dangerous activities without considering possible consequences (not for the purpose of thrill-seeking), e.g., runs into street without looking

B. Onset before the age of seven

C. Does not meet the criteria for a Pervasive Developmental Disorder. (From American Psychiatric Association 1987, p. 52–53.)

It has been estimated that as many as 3% of preadolescent children may suffer from ADHD, with the disorder six to nine times more common in boys than in girls (American Psychiatric Association 1987).

At home, attentional difficulties are manifested by a failure to follow through on tasks and the inability to stick to activities, including play, for appropriate periods of time. In the classroom, the child shows inattention and impulsivity, and has difficulties staying with tasks and organizing and completing work. Group situations can be particularly difficult for children with ADHD. Many parents may describe their children as hyperactive, but only a professional can provide an accurate diagnosis of the disorder.

Once an accurate diagnosis of ADHD is reached, the job of nutritionists and psychologists is to discover if sugar consumption contributes to the symptoms of the disorder. Well controlled experimental studies are important to this discovery process.

Correlational Studies

Correlational studies provide suggestive evidence about the association of sugar intake and ADHD. In these studies, children's habitual intake of sugar-containing foods has been related to behavioral measures of ADHD. In one of the first experiments examining the role of sugar in hyperactive behavior, Prinz and colleagues (1980) obtained seven-day dietary records for hyperactive and normal 4- to 7-year-old children. Trained observers, who were unaware of the nature of the experiment, then rated the children during play for a variety of behaviors including destructive-aggressive acts (attempts to damage, strike, kick, or throw objects in the room), restlessness (repetitive arm, leg, hand, or head movements), and overall movement. Hyperactive and normal children consumed equivalent amounts of sugar-containing foods. However, for the hyperactive children, the amount of sugar products consumed, the ratio of sugar to nutritional foods (foods and beverages that are neither sugar products nor refined carbohydrates), and the carbohydrate : protein ratio all were positively correlated with destructive-aggressive and restless behaviors. In contrast, sugar intake was not correlated with destructive-aggressive behavior in the normal group, but was correlated with total body movement. While these results were carefully interpreted by Prinz and colleagues as only suggestive evidence of a role for sugar intake in hyperactive behavior, the data were rapidly translated in the popular media as confirming a causal relationship between sugar consumption and hyperactivity. Although the majority of studies conducted on sugar and hyperactive behavior in the past decade have not confirmed the work of Prinz, the original interpretation of this work continues to be part of the folklore about diet and behavior.

Subsequent correlational studies of sugar intake and hyperactivity have not supported Prinz's and colleagues' data. Wolraich and co-workers (1985), for example, investigating the association between sugar intake and performance on 37 behavioral and cognitive variables in hyperactive and normal boys, found that sugar intake was not reliably related to destructive-aggressive behavior. Sugar intake of the hyperactive boys was positively correlated with (1) ankle movement, (2) movement around the room, (3) more attention shifts, and (4) less time spent on a task.

One problem with these correlational studies is that they were based on a retrospective assessment of the children's food intake, and thus only provided information on what the children had been eating several weeks prior to behavioral measurements. Sugar's effects on behavior may be more immediate. Most parents and teachers report that sugar adversely alters behavior within a half-hour to one hour after consumption.

A second problem with these studies is that it is impossible to determine cause–effect relationships. Although sugar intake may increase activity, it is just as plausible that children who are more active choose to consume more sugar-containing foods than their less active counterparts. Also, parents may use sweet snacks to placate a more active or disruptive child. Moreover, it is possible that a third variable, such as socioeconomic status, has a causal effect on sucrose and hyperactive behavior and thereby makes it appear as though these two primary variables are related.

Dietary Challenge Studies

To determine causality, experimental studies that systematically manipulate sugar intake and observe its effect on behavior are required. The most commonly used procedure to accomplish this goal is the dietary challenge. This method attempts to approximate real-life situations commonly reported by parents to demonstrate the adverse effects of refined sugar on their children's behavior including hyperactivity, aggression, irritability, and decreased attention span. In challenge studies, children's behavior is rated for several hours after they have consumed a sugar-containing food or beverage, or a placebo containing an artificial sweetener. To prevent expectations from influencing the results, double-blind procedures should be used. The dietary challenges are packaged and presented in such a manner that neither the children nor the experimenters can detect which substance is being presented. Additionally, a crossover procedure should be employed, in which the children are given the sugar-containing item on one day and the placebo on another, with the order of presentation varying among subjects.

In one of the first studies using the dietary challenge technique, sugar reactivity was examined in 50 5- to 17-year-old children whose mothers reported that they responded negatively to sugar (Gross 1984). The children were observed by their mothers for several hours after the children had drunk a glass of lemonade sweetened with either 75 g of sucrose (equivalent to the amount of sugar in two 12-oz cans of soda) or saccharin. The mothers did not know if their children had received the sucrose- or saccharin-sweetened lemonade. Three tests of each lemonade were done. Not one of the 50 children showed a negative response to sucrose. This study suffers from a number of weaknesses, including no control over the order of presentation of the drinks or any measure of when and how much of the lemonade was actually consumed. However, it has the strengths of being conducted in a natural setting and using mothers, who are most often the source of claims about the adverse effects of sugar, as raters.

In a better controlled double-blind crossover study, Behar and colleagues (1984) investigated the effects of sucrose on behavior in 6- to 14-year-old boys whose parents believed that they had experienced adverse behavioral reactions to sugar. After an overnight fast, the boys were given a lemon-flavored beverage containing either glucose, sucrose, or saccharin. Motor activity, spontaneous behavior, and performance of psychological tests were assessed for five hours after the boys drank the beverages. The only significant finding in this study was that the boys were *less* active three hours after consuming the sugar-containing beverages than after consuming the saccharin placebo.

Similar negative findings were reported by Wolraich and colleagues (1985) who conducted two carefully controlled challenge studies assessing the effects of sucrose ingestion on the behavior and learning abilities of 7- and 12-year-old boys. In both studies, the boys were admitted to a clinical research center, where they were given a sucrose-free diet for three successive days. On day 1, baseline measures of behavior and cognitive performance were taken. On days 2 and 3, the boys drank a fruit-flavored drink containing either sucrose or aspartame of equivalent sweetness. In the first study, the drink was given after lunch and in the second, in the morning after an overnight fast. Sugar intake did not affect behavior or performance on a number of cognitive tasks designed to measure attention, memory, and learning abilities.

One problem with the preceding studies is that they were conducted in a laboratory environment. This rather unnatural environment may mask sugar's effects on behavior. To circumvent this problem, Milich and Pelham (1986) incorporated the dietary challenge design into a treatment program for hyperactive boys. The boys fasted overnight and at 8 A.M. drank Kool-Aid sweetened with either sucrose or aspartame. They were then evaluated for positive behaviors (e.g., following rules, sharing, saying something nice) and negative behaviors (e.g., noncompliance, teasing, name-calling) during a recreational period, and for academic performance in the classroom. Sugar intake had no adverse effects on behavior or academic performance.

Similar results were obtained by Kaplan et al. (1986), who examined the behavioral effects of breakfast meals in which dietary protein, fat, and carbohydrates were controlled while sucrose and total calories were varied. The children received 12 high-sucrose breakfasts and 12 low-sucrose breakfasts (containing aspartame) in this randomly designed crossover study. Although the children consumed significantly more sugar when given the high-sucrose breakfasts, no significant differences in behavior as a function of diet were noted by teachers who were unaware of the dietary control conditions.

A study by Ferguson and colleagues (1986) has the advantage over previous work of examining the behavioral effects of several doses of sugar and an aspartame placebo. Children from 5 to 13 years of age who were reported by their parents to have adverse behavioral responses to sugar were fed a low-sucrose diet for several weeks. The children's performance on a task requiring sustained attention and on a series of tests examining learning, memory, and problem-solving abilities was assessed after they had drunk beverages containing varying amounts of sucrose or aspartame. Once again, sucrose had no deleterious effects on any of the measured variables.

As correlational studies (Prinz 1980) suggested that younger children might be more susceptible to the adverse effects of sucrose, Kruesi and colleagues (1987) initiated a dietary challenge study in preschool-age boys with alleged reactivity to sugar. After the children had consumed beverages containing either sucrose, glucose, saccharin, or aspartame, general activity and destructive-aggressive behaviors were rated in a laboratory situation and by their mothers during an ordinary day at home. Again, no significant differences were observed in behavior as a function of sugar intake. Similar negative results have recently been reported by Rosen and co-workers (1988) who assessed the effects of sugar on the behavior of preschool boys and girls.

Taken together, the results of dietary challenge studies do not support the idea that sugar plays a major role in childhood hyperactivity. In studies using normal and hyperactive children of varying ages and in a range of experimental situations, sugar intake had no adverse effects on behavior. Although the experimental evidence is weak, parents and teachers continue to supply anecdotal reports of the deleterious consequences of sugar intake. How do we reconcile these discrepancies?

Several factors could contribute to the differing views of scientists and of parents and teachers. One limitation of previous dietary challenge studies is that in most, only a single dose of sucrose was used. The amount of sucrose used in these studies may have been too small, relative to the children's normal daily intake. Larger amounts of sucrose may have produced negative behavioral reactions. Along similar lines, challenge studies can be criticized because they do not allow for the assessment of chronic sugar consumption, which may produce behavioral effects not detectable in single-challenge tests. To help solve these problems, precise dietary histories and dose-response determinations of sucrose effects on behavior are required.

Another difficulty with dietary challenge studies is the choice of an appropriate placebo. In most studies, researchers have focused on disguising the placebo so that it was indistinguishable from the sugared drink or food. Beverages or foods containing either aspartame or saccharin have accordingly been used. While this procedure successfully blinds the subjects to the nature of the food or beverage being consumed, it does not control for the fact that the challenge drink or food not only contains sugar but also provides substantial calories, and the placebo offers limited or no calories. This variable presents the possibility that any changes in behavior could be attributed to the caloric load rather than to the sugar.

An additional problem faced by researchers using the dietary challenge approach is determining what behaviors to study. Hyperactive children exhibit a variety of behavioral problems; however, there are no logical guidelines about which specific behaviors should be negatively affected by sugar intake, other than those subjectively reported by parents. The effects of sugar on behavior may be subtle and even differ from child to child. It may be that the research conducted thus far has failed to pinpoint the appropriate behaviors.

Time parameters may also be important in determining sugar's effect on behavior. Most experiments have limited behavioral observations to only one interval after sugar ingestion and may have missed the critical period for sugar's effects on behavior.

Finally, the results of challenge studies may be accurate, but parents and teachers may be misperceiving a relation between sugar and behavior. Hyperactive children have difficulty in altering their behavior to changing environmental demands. Thus, in school these children frequently have trouble changing their behavior from the relatively unstructured nature of a snack or party period to the more structured demands of the class. Because many of the foods children consume during unstructured periods have a high sugar content, it may be that the association teachers report between sugar and behavioral problems really represents the children's difficulty in getting back to classwork following an exciting or unstructured activity. Similarly, parents often note behavioral deterioration after their child has consumed a sugar-containing food in a party situation. Hyperactive children are known to have more difficulty in groups, and the effects parents observe may be more a function of the situation than the consumption of high-sugar foods. Lastly, if parents believe that sugar has negative consequences, they may be more sensitive to their child's behavior after the child has consumed food containing sugar.

SUGAR, HYPOGLYCEMIA, AND BEHAVIOR

Sugar has been condemned as the cause of a large number of psychological problems, including but certainly not limited to anxiety, manic depression, schizophrenia, and alcohol and drug addiction (Ketcham and Mueller 1983; Phelps and Nourse 1986). One "physiological" explanation that has been proposed for sugar's adverse effects is hypoglycemia or "low blood sugar." Unfortunately, the term "hypoglycemia" has frequently been misused. Many doctors as well as patients are confused about the diagnosis, symptoms, and treatment of this condition. Additionally, a large amount of misleading information has found its way into the popular media and led to the self-diagnosis of hypoglycemia by many patients (Yager and Young 1974; Nelson 1985). Given the large amount of misinformation about hypoglycemia, it is worthwhile to review the scientific evidence for the existence of this disorder.

Clinically, hypoglycemia is defined by (1) low circulating blood glucose levels (50 mg/dl or less); (2) symptoms including sweating, tremulousness, palpitations, anxiety, headaches, weakness, and hunger; and (3) amelioration of symptoms when plasma glucose levels are restored to normal levels with the ingestion of food (Nelson 1985; McFarland, Baker, and Ferguson 1987). Hypoglycemia can occur in diabetic patients following the administration of insulin or oral hypoglycemic agents that stimulate the release of insulin from the beta cells of the pancreas. Other drugs, such as antibiotics, anti-inflammatory agents, and antidepressants; insulin-secreting tumors; and renal disease also can lead to hypoglycemia.

As previously noted, it has been hypothesized that sugar consumption is a causal factor in hypoglycemia. The rationale for this hypothesis begins with the assumption that simple sugars are more rapidly digested and absorbed than complex carbohydrates and therefore cause a greater increase in blood glucose values. This rapid rise in blood glucose stimulates insulin secretion, which has the counterregulatory effect of reducing blood glucose levels. This counterregulatory effect has been called reactive or functional hypoglycemia.

There are several problems, however, with the idea that sugar intake can cause reactive hypoglycemia. First, recent studies have shown that a simple distinction cannot be made between sugars and more complex carbohydrates with respect to blood glucose and insulin responses (Crapo 1985). In some cases, foods high in sugar actually lead to smaller increases in blood glucose levels than foods containing complex carbohydrates. For example, ice cream results in a more modest rise in blood glucose values than potatoes, wholemeal bread, or brown rice (Crapo 1985). Thus, the assumption that sugar-containing foods uniformly lead to wide swings in blood glucose values must be viewed with caution.

Another related problem is that low blood glucose levels are not consistently associated with clinical symptoms of hypoglycemia. Low blood glucose levels can occur without any symptoms of the disease. Some patients with inoperable insulin-producing tumors may adapt to blood glucose levels as low as 20 to 30 mg/dl without adverse effects. In contrast, symptoms of functional hypoglycemia are frequently reported in the absence of low blood glucose levels (Cahill and Soeldner 1974; McFarland, Baker, and Ferguson 1987).

This last point leads to the question of how functional hypoglycemia is diagnosed. In many cases, a diagnosis is made on the basis of symptoms without appropriate laboratory evidence. To confirm the diagnosis of hypoglycemia, a relationship must exist between low blood glucose levels and the symptoms of the disease. Until recently, a five-hour oral glucose tolerance test was used to assess functional hypoglycemia. Since the administration of a single large dose of glucose is not a naturally occurring event, physicians now recommend measurement of blood glucose levels following normal mixed meals. In either case, for a valid diagnosis of hypoglycemia, clinical symptoms must be associated with glucose levels below 50 mg/dl. In fact, patients whose glucose levels fall to this level following a glucose load or mixed meal are relatively rare. Additionally, a majority of individuals whose glucose levels fall below 50 mg/dl do not experience symptoms of hypoglycemia. These results have led investigators to conclude that true functional hypoglycemia is much less prevalent than reported in the popular media (Yager and Young 1974; Nelson 1985; McFarland, Baker, and Ferguson 1987).

Given the relative rarity of functional hypoglycemia, why has the disease become so popular? For individuals with psychological complaints, a diagnosis of hypoglycemia may have certain advantages. First, the diagnosis is socially acceptable. Rather than endure a "psychological" or otherwise stigmatizing condition, the patient can suffer from a respectable metabolic illness. Second, hypoglycemia gives patients a way of actively and easily dealing with their complaints. By following certain dietary prescriptions, patients believe they can effectively eliminate their emotional symptoms. In many cases, the act of attributing psychological problems to hypoglycemia and altering one's diet in response to this condition may provide some relief. Finally, a diagnosis of hypoglycemia may be preferable to facing the possibility that a more serious underlying condition exists (Yager and Young 1974).

In conclusion, contrary to popular belief, functional hypoglycemia resulting from excess sugar intake is a relatively rare condition. Most individuals who report adverse effects following sugar consumption have normal blood glucose profiles. However, it is important that these patients' complaints are not dismissed. Their symptoms may represent other serious physical or psychological conditions that require attention.

SUGAR AND ANTISOCIAL BEHAVIOR

During the last decade, theories relating diet to antisocial behavior or criminality have received increasing attention. Once relegated to articles and books directed at food faddists, such theories are now discussed at meetings of criminologists and found in books and articles aimed at personnel in the correctional and criminal justice systems. On the basis of these theories, correctional facilities in several states have revised their dietary policies to help control antisocial behavior. A variety of dietary factors, including food allergies or vitamin and mineral deficiencies, have been proposed as contributing to criminality. Recent work has even asserted that sugar consumption is directly related to antisocial behavior (Gray 1986).

Interest in the relation between sugar and antisocial behavior was originally sparked by correlational studies suggesting that hypoglycemia is common in criminals and delinquents displaying habitually violent behavior (Virkkunen 1986). It was proposed that intake of sugar and other refined carbohydrates could aggravate a hypoglycemic condition. Unfortunately, these early studies failed to use an oral glucose tolerance test (OGTT) to make the diagnosis of hypoglycemia, or they did not use standard criteria for evaluating the results of the OGTT. Additionally, no observations of behavioral symptoms were made during the OGTT. Thus, one cannot conclude that low blood glucose levels are associated with violent behavior (Gray 1986).

In subsequent studies examining the relation between hypoglycemia and violent behavior, OGTTs were performed with violent offenders and control subjects. Individuals diagnosed as suffering from either Intermittent Explosive Disorder or Antisocial Personality Disorder (American Psychiatric Association 1987) had lower serum glucose nadirs than controls. It was hypothesized that enhanced insulin secretion resulting from glucose intake was responsible for violent behavior (Virkkunen 1986).

Although individuals with a history of violent behavior had a greater tendency for hypoglycemia than controls, this finding cannot be viewed as unequivocal evidence of an association between hypoglycemia and antisocial behavior. No attempt was made in these studies to correlate low blood glucose levels with the symptoms of hypoglycemia (e.g., tremors, weakness, sweating, and hunger). Moreover, no evidence was presented to demonstrate that violent behavior actually occurred when insulin secretion was enhanced or low blood sugar levels were experienced. Recent work also has indicated that the OGTT may not be a good indicator of the changes in blood glucose levels that follow a normal meal. Thus, the finding that individuals with a history of violent behavior have lower glucose levels during an OGTT does not imply that they have lower glucose levels after normal meals. Finally, all of the violent offenders examined by Virkkunen (1986) had a history of alcohol abuse which clearly could influence their behavior.

In a series of studies employing a dietary replacement strategy, Schoenthaler has investigated the effects of reducing sugar consumption on antisocial behavior in inmates in juvenile detention facilities (Schoenthaler 1982, 1983a, 1983b, 1983c, 1985). A similar experimental approach was used in all studies. At a specific point in time, the institution modified its food policy in an effort to reduce sugar intake. Typical changes in the diet included substituting honey for table sugar; molasses for white sugar in cooking; fruit juices for Kool-Aid; unsweetened cereals for presweetened ones; and fresh fruit, peanuts, coconut, popcorn, and cheese for high-sugar desserts. The dependent measure in all of these studies was the number of disciplinary actions recorded by staff members before and during the change in food policy. On the basis of these studies, Schoenthaler has claimed that antisocial behavior in juvenile offenders can be decreased by 21% to 54% when sugar intake is reduced. As this claim has important policy implications, it warrants careful scrutiny.

The first problem posed by Schoenthaler's work is the identification of the independent variable, which was reported to be sugar intake. However, one does not have to be a nutritionist to appreciate that many of Schoenthaler's dietary manipulations are of dubious value in limiting sugar intake, because they merely replaced one sugar for another (e.g., honey for sucrose). Furthermore, no measurements of actual sugar intake were made in any of these studies. Thus, it is impossible to determine if the dietary changes actually led to a reduction in sugar consumption. Intake data are essential to establish if dietary manipulations had any effect and if the independent variable was operative (Hirsch 1987). Even if sugar intake was reduced, the diets consumed during the two periods would have varied in nutrient composition, making it impossible to attribute behavioral change to reduced sugar intake.

A second problem with these studies is that appropriate behavioral techniques were not used. None of the studies used standard double-blind procedures. Both subjects and institutional officials were aware of the dietary changes. The subjects' awareness of the changes, and also simply knowing they were in a study, could have led them to alter their behavior. As the observers were aware of the nature of the study, their expectations also may have influenced their observations.

The nature of the dependent variable also poses a problem. Official records of disciplinary actions were used to assess changes in antisocial behavior. In many institutions, the staff has the discretion whether or not to record an incident, and variation over time in the proportion of incidents reported may lead to erroneous results (Gray 1986). Also, in some of these studies, the dietary changes were made later in the subjects' incarceration (Schoenthaler 1983a). One might speculate that the number of disciplinary actions would decrease as the juveniles learned either the rules or how not to get caught.

In some of these studies, concern also must be expressed for the changing nature of the subject population. Some of the juveniles were included in both the control and treatment conditions, while others participated in one condition but not the other. Finally, questions have been raised with respect to the statistical methods that were used in these studies (Gray 1986).

Taken together, the studies by Schoenthaler provide little convincing evidence for the claim that sugar intake contributes to antisocial behavior. The flawed experimental design and inappropriate statistical analysis leave open the question of whether nonspecific factors were responsible for the effects attributed to diet.

The relationship of diet to antisocial behavior has important social implications and certainly warrants further study. However, future studies must have a better experimental design and incorporate several necessary features. First, the nature of the dietary change must be specified and actual food intake must be determined. Second, better definition of the dependent variable is required: What behaviors will be observed, and how and by whom will they be measured? Third, if possible, double-blind procedures should be employed, perhaps by introducing a few substitute foods for standard menu items (e.g., beverages and desserts containing artificial sweeteners for those containing sugar). The experimental and standard diets should be presented to the same group of individuals. Finally, proper statistical procedures are necessary (Gray 1986).

CONCLUSION

The original question posed in this chapter was how valid our fears are about sugar. Experimental evidence indicates that there is less to be concerned about than might be believed from popular portrayals of sugar. Sugar does not appear to be a major causative factor in hyperactivity, psychological disorders, or criminal behavior. It is certainly acceptable to occasionally indulge one's sweet tooth. However, this does not mean that sugar intake should not be watched. If sugar intake reaches levels that replace intake of essential nutrients, problems of malnutrition may result. The recommendation of the American Dietetic Association to maintain sugar intake at 10% to 15% of total caloric intake suggests a fair compromise (Franz and Maryniuk 1987).

REFERENCES

Alfin-Slater, R. and F. X. PiSunyer. 1987. Sugar and sugar substitutes. *Postgraduate Medicine* 82:47–56.

American Psychiatric Association. 1987. *Diagnostic and Statistical Manual of Mental Disorders, Third Edition Revised*. Washington, D.C.: American Psychiatric Association.

Beauchamp, G. K. and B. J. Cowart. 1987. Development of sweet taste, in *Sweetness*, edited by J. Dobbing, pp. 127–140. New York: Springer-Verlag.

Behar, D., J. L. Rapoport, A. A. Adams, C. J. Berg, and M. Cornblath. 1984. Sugar challenge testing with children considered behaviorally "sugar reactive." *Nutrition and Behavior* 1:277–288.

Bennett, F. C. and R. Sherman. 1983. Management of childhood "hyperactivity" by primary-care physicians. *Journal of Developmental and Behavioral Pediatrics* 4:88–93.

Cahill, G. F. and J. S. Soeldner. 1974. A non-editorial on non-hypoglycemia. *New England Journal of Medicine* 291:905–906.

Crapo, P. A. 1985. Simple versus complex carbohydrate in the diabetic diet. *Annual Review of Nutrition* 5:95–114.

Dahlqvist, A. 1984. Carbohydrates, in *Present Knowledge in Nutrition*, ed R. E. Olson et al., pp. 116–130. Washington, D.C.: Nutrition Foundation.

Danowski, T. S. and J. H. Sunder. 1981. Sugar and disease, in *Controversies in Nutrition*, ed. L. Ellenbogen, pp. 85–104. New York: Churchill Livingston.

Darby, W. J., P. Ghalioungui, and L. Grivetti. 1977. *Food: The Gift of Osiris.* New York: Academic Press.

Drewnowski, A. 1988. Sweet foods and sweeteners in the U.S. diet, in *Diet and Obesity,* ed. G. A. Bray et al., pp. 153–161. Basel: S. Karger.

Dufty, W. 1975. *Sugar Blues,* New York: Warner Books.

Ferguson, H. B., Stoddart, C., and Simeon, J. G. 1986. Double-blind challenge studies of behavioral and cognitive effects of sucrose-aspartame ingestion in normal children. *Nutrition Reviews* 44 (Suppl.):144–150.

Fischler, C. 1987. Attitudes towards sugar and sweetness in historical and social perspective, in *Sweetness,* ed. J. Dobbing, pp. 83–98, New York: Springer-Verlag.

Folsom, A. R., Jacobs, D. R., Luepker, R. B., Kushi, L. H., Guillum, R. F., Elmer, P. J., and Blackburn, H. 1987. Nutrient intake in a metropolitan area, 1973–74 vs 1980–82: The Minnesota heart survey. *American Journal of Clinical Nutrition* 45:1533–1540.

Fomon, S. J., Ziegler, E. K., Nelson, S. E., and Edwards, B. B. 1983. Sweetness of diet and food consumption by infants. *Proceedings of the Society for Experimental Biology and Medicine,* 173:190–193.

Franz, M. J. and Maryniuk, M. D. 1987. Position of the American Dietetic Association: Appropriate use of nutritive and non-nutritive sweeteners. *Journal of the American Dietetic Association* 87:1689–1693.

Gray, G. E. 1986. Diet, crime and delinquency: A critique. *Nutrition Reviews* 44 (Suppl.):89–93.

Gross, M. 1984. Effects of sucrose on hyperkinetic children. *Pediatrics* 74:876–878.

Hegarty, V. 1988. *Decisions in Nutrition.* St. Louis: Times Mirror/Mosby College Publishing.

Hirsch, E. 1987. Sweetness and performance, in *Sweetness,* ed. J. Dobbing, pp. 205–224. New York: Springer-Verlag.

Kaplan, H. K., F. S. Wamboldt, and M. Barnhart. 1986. Behavioral effects of dietary sucrose in disturbed children. *American Journal of Psychiatry* 143:944–945.

Ketcham, K. and L. A. Mueller. 1983. *Eating Right to Live Sober.* New York: Signet.

Kruesi, M. J. P., Rapoport, J. L., Cummings, M., Berg, C. J., Ismond, D. R., Flament, M., Yarrow, M., and Zahr-Waxler, C. 1987. Effects of sugar and aspartame on aggression and activity in children. *American Journal of Psychiatry* 144:1487–1490.

Lecos, C. W. 1980. Food labels and the sugar recognition factor. *FDA Consumer* April:3–5.

Lecos, C. W. 1985. Sugar, how sweet it is—and isn't. *FDA Consumer* February:21–23.

Lecos, C. W. 1988. We're getting the message about diet-disease links. *FDA Consumer* May:6–9.

McFarland, K. F., Baker, C., and Ferguson, S. D. 1987. Demystifying hypoglycemia. *Postgraduate Medicine* 82:54–65.

McLoughlin, J. A. and M. Nall. 1988. Teacher opinion of the role of food allergy on school behavior and achievement. *Annals of Allergy* 61:89–91.

Milich, R. and W. E. Pelham. 1986. Effects of sugar ingestion on the classroom and playgroup behavior of attention-deficit–disordered boys. *Journal of Consulting and Clinical Psychology* 54:714–718.

Morgan, K. J. and M. E. Zabik. 1981. Amount and food sources of total sugar intake by children ages 5 to 12 years. *American Journal of Clinical Nutrition* 34:404–413.

Nelson, R. L. 1985. Hypoglycemia: Fact or fiction? *Mayo Clinic Proceedings* 60:844–850.

Phelps, J. K. and Nourse, A. E. 1986. *The Hidden Addicition and How to Get Free.* Boston: Little, Brown.

Prinz, R. J., Roberts, W. A., and Hantman, E. 1980. Dietary correlates of hyperactive behavior in children. *Journal of Consulting and Clinical Psychology* 48:760–769.

Ramirez, I. 1990. Why do sugars taste good? *Neuroscience and Biobehavioral Reviews* 14:125–134.

Robinson, C. H. and Lawler, M. R. 1982. *Normal and Therapeutic Nutrition.* New York: Macmillan.

Rosen, L. E., M. E. Bender, S. Sorrel, S. R. Booth, M. L. McGrath, and R. S. Drabman. 1988. Effects of sugar (sucrose) on children's behavior. *Journal of Consulting and Clinical Psychology* 56:583–589.

Schoenthaler, S. J. 1982. The effect of sugar on the treatment and control of antisocial behavior: A double-blind study of an incarcerated juvenile population. *International Journal of Biosocial Research* 3:1–9.

Schoenthaler, S. J. 1983a. Diet and delinquency: A multi-state replication. *International Journal of Biosocial Research* 5:70–78.

Schoenthaler, S. J. 1983b. Diet and crime: An empirical examination of the value of nutrition in the control and treatment of incarcerated juvenile offenders. *International Journal of Biosocial Research* 4:25–39.

Schoenthaler, S. J. 1983c. The Los Angeles probation department diet-behavior program: An empirical analysis of six institutional settings. *International Journal of Biosocial Research* 5:88–98.

Schoenthaler, S. J. 1985. Nutritional policies and institutional antisocial behavior. *Nutrition Today* 20:16–25.

Steiner, J. E. 1973. The gustofacial response: Observations of normal and anencephalic newborn infants, in *Fourth Symposium on Oral Sensation and Perception: Development in the Fetus and Infant,* ed. J. F. Bosma, pp. 254–278. Washington, D.C.: U.S. Government Printing Office.

Wolraich, M., Milich, R., Stumbo, P., and Schultz, F. 1985. Effects of sucrose ingestion on the behavior of hyperactive boys. *Journal of Pediatrics* 106:675–682.

Yager, J. and Young, R. T. 1974. Non-hypoglycemia is an epidemic condition. *New England Journal of Medicine* 291:907–908.

Yudkin, J. 1964. Dietary fat and dietary sugar in relation to ischemic heart disease and diabetes. *Lancet* 2:4–6.

Yudkin, J. 1972. *Sweet and Dangerous.* New York: Bantam Books.

Virkkunen, M. 1986. Reactive hypoglycemic tendency among habitually violent offenders. *Nutrition Reviews* 44 (Suppl.):94–103.

10

Artificial Sweeteners: Do They Live Up to Expectations?

Over the past decade, the taste of the American public for both gourmet fare and fast foods has increased exponentially. It is impossible to find a major metropolitan area, and difficult to find a smaller city, without a fancy food store or gourmet deli. Our desire for convenient fast foods is clearly evidenced by the rise of fast food chains throughout the country. During this same period, however, there has also been a striking increase in public concern about excess caloric intake and its possible consequences: obesity, heart disease, and diabetes. It has been proposed that low-calorie or artificial sweeteners may help to satisfy our twin cravings for palatable, convenient foods and slimness (Lecos 1985).

Low-calorie sweeteners have become a way of life for many Americans. A recent national survey indicated that more than half of the adults in the United States regularly consume foods and beverages containing low-calorie sweeteners. A growing number of food products including soft drinks, instant coffee and tea, cereals, pudding and pie fillings, gelatin desserts, chewing gum, ice cream, and candy contain low-calorie sweeteners. When questioned, consumers most frequently state that they use these products to control or reduce weight, or to improve health (Calorie Control Council 1988).

Although it is predicted that the use of artificial sweeteners will continue to increase, their use is not without controversy. A number of scientists have expressed concern about the possible effects of these compounds on brain functioning and behavior. Recent studies also have called into question the value of artificial sweeteners in reducing caloric intake and controlling body weight.

Throughout the last hundred years a variety of compounds have been promoted as the perfect low-calorie sweetener; that is, having the taste of sugar, but without any detrimental consequences. Unfortunately, artificial sweeteners such as saccharin can leave a bitter aftertaste in the mouth, and a number of artificial sweeteners may have harmful side effects. For example, both saccharin and cyclamate have been reported to lead to cancer in experimental animals.

This chapter presents a brief history of the use of low-calorie sweeteners, focusing especially on aspartame which is the primary low-calorie sweetener produced and marketed today in this country. The final section of this chapter examines the usefulness of artificial sweeteners for reducing caloric intake and body weight.

HISTORY AND USE OF ARTIFICIAL SWEETENERS

Saccharin

Artificial sweeteners first attracted public interest in 1879 when saccharin, a coal tar derivative, was accidentally synthesized by Constantin Fahlberg, a chemist at Johns Hopkins University. Although originally intended for use as an antiseptic, saccharin's sweet taste, and value as an artificial sweetener, was soon recognized. By the turn of the century, saccharin, which is approximately 300 times sweeter than sucrose, had become a substitute for sugar in a variety of canned vegetables and beverages. In 1911, however, President Theodore Roosevelt charged a board of scientists with determining if saccharin could render a food injurious to health or adversely affect the quality of the food item. The board ruled that the amounts of saccharin consumed in the normal diet did not have detrimental effects on health. However, it also concluded that foods containing the sweetener should be considered adulterated and be plainly labeled to indicate that their intended use was for individuals who should limit sugar intake (Vander 1981; Miller and Frattali 1989).

Saccharin was used in moderation during the first three decades of the century. Its popularity surged during the 1940s as a result of sugar shortages and rationing during and after World War II. In 1976, approximately 3 million kilograms of saccharin were used in the United States, and the total value of foods and beverages containing saccharin had reached an estimated $2 billion. In 1977, however, experiments indicated that large amounts of saccharin could produce bladder tumors in rodents. On the basis of the Federal Food, Drug, and Cosmetic Act's Delaney Clause, which specifies that no substance can be added to the food supply if it has been shown to cause cancer in experimental animals, the Food and Drug Administration (FDA) promptly proposed a ban on saccharin. Public outcry over the ban was immediate, with Congress receiving over 100,000 letters opposing it. A number of prestigious medical groups, including the American Diabetic Association, the American Dental Association, and the American Cancer Society, added their voices, stating that saccharin's benefits to diabetic individuals and others needing to reduce sucrose intake far outweighed its potential risks. As a result, Congress passed the 1977 Saccharin Study and Labeling Act, which imposed a two-year moratorium on the ban of saccharin. The act also directed the FDA to further investigate the cancer-causing potential of saccharin and mandated that warning labels be used on all saccharin-containing products. The moratorium on saccharin has been extended several times (Vander 1981; Lecos 1985; Miller and Frattali 1989).

Cylcamate

Cyclamate was discovered in 1937 when a scientist at the University of Illinois inadvertently placed a cigarette on a pile of crystal powder. When the scientist began to smoke the cigarette, he found that the powder, a derivative of cyclohexylsulfamic acid, had a pleasant sweet taste. Cyclamate, which is approximately 30 times sweeter than sucrose, was introduced into foods and beverages in the United States in the early 1950s, and with saccharin dominated the artificial sweetener market through the late 1960s. In 1969, however, experiments suggested that cyclamate in the diet could induce bladder cancer in rats and mice. These findings led the FDA to impose a total ban on cyclamate in September 1970 (Lecos 1985).

Recently, the National Research Council reviewed the evidence on cyclamate's safety and concluded that the data did not indicate that cyclamates alone cause cancer, or that potentially hazardous metabolites of cyclamate are formed in humans. The review board also recommended that further studies be conducted to determine if (1) the risk of cancer is increased in heavy or long-term users of cyclamate, (2) there is a promotional or co-carcinogenic effect of cyclamate when it is used with saccharin or other substances, (3) DNA damage and gene mutation can result from cyclamate use, and (4) there is a relation between cyclamate use and testicular atrophy (National Research Council 1985).

Although in this country the ban on cyclamate continues, it presently is marketed in 40 countries, including Canada where it is used as a table-top sweetener and in drugs (Lecos 1985).

Aspartame

Within the last ten years, other low-calorie sweeteners have been eclipsed by the development and marketing of aspartame. Like saccharin and cyclamate, aspartame was discovered serendipitously. In the process of synthesizing peptide molecules for assaying potential drugs to treat ulcers, chemists at G. D. Searle & Company discovered that the methyl ester of the dipeptide containing the naturally occurring amino acids aspartate and phenylalanine (L-aspartyl L-phenylalanine methyl ester; see Figure 10-1) had a exceptionally sweet taste. Subsequent tests showed that aspartame is 180 to 200 times sweeter than sucrose and does not possess the bitter aftertaste frequently associated with other artificial sweeteners. Aspartame cannot be used in cooking or baking, however, because prolonged

ASPARTAME

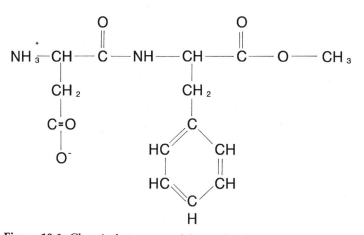

Figure 10-1. Chemical structure of the artificial sweetener aspartame.

heat results in the breakdown of the compound, with a consequent loss of sweetness (Mazur 1984).

The potential of aspartame as a low-calorie sweetener was immediately recognized by researchers at Searle, who conducted extensive experimental and clinical studies to assess the compound's safety. In 1973, Searle petitioned the FDA for approval to market aspartame (Federal Register 1981). After reviewing the data, in July 1974, the FDA approved the use of aspartame in foods such as breakfast cereals, dry beverage mixes, gelatins, puddings, and table-top sweeteners. However, as permitted by federal law, two scientists formally objected to this approval and requested that the FDA further evaluate the safety of aspartame. These scientists questioned the safety of both the aspartate and phenylalanine components of aspartame and expressed concern about the neurotoxic potential of the product in young children. To allow for the evaluation of these questions, the FDA revoked its approval of aspartame and established a Public Board of Inquiry (PBOI) to review data on the safety of the artificial sweetener. The PBOI held its hearings in early 1980 and concluded in a report to the FDA that the evidence did not support the charges that aspartame intake posed an increased risk of brain damage in children. On the basis of this report, the FDA approved the use of aspartame in dry foods in July 1981 and in carbonated beverages in July 1983 (Federal Register 1981; Lecos 1985; Stegink 1987).

Upon its approval for use in beverages, aspartame sales advanced from $74 million in 1982 to $336 million in 1983 (Lecos 1985). Aspartame sales have grown over the intervening years and are expected to continue to increase in the 1990s.

INTAKE AND PATTERNS OF CONSUMPTION

To assess the metabolic and physiological effects of aspartame, accurate estimates of intake are needed. These estimates can be determined by examining the aspartame content of foods and their patterns of consumption. To appreciate intake data, it is useful to know the aspartame content of several common foods: a 12-oz aspartame-sweetened carbonated soft drink has 150 to 200 mg; an 8-oz noncarbonated beverage contains 140 mg; one packet of Equal, which is equivalent to the sweetness of two teaspoons of sugar, contains 35 mg; and a 4-oz serving of an artificially sweetened gelatin dessert, 80 mg. Using this type of information, the Market Research Corporation of America tabulated the dietary records of 4,000 households over a two-week period and calculated mean daily aspartame intake at 11.1 mg/kg body weight, with the 99th percentile of daily intake at 34 mg/kg body weight (Federal Register 1981). The 99th percentile is a statistical measure that indicates 99 out of 100 individuals consume 34 mg/kg or less aspartame per day. For a 58 kg (128 lb) person, 34 mg/kg aspartame is equivalent to consuming 10 cans of an aspartame-sweetened soft drink or 57 packets of Equal.

METABOLISM AND METABOLIC CONSEQUENCES

When consumed, aspartame is metabolized in one of two ways. First, it can be hydrolyzed by proteolytic and hydrolytic enzymes in the intestinal lumen to aspartate, phenylalanine, and methanol. These compounds are then absorbed from the lumen and reach the portal blood in a manner similar to that of amino acids and methanol originating from intake of dietary protein and carbohydrates. Alternatively, aspartame may be de-esterified in the intestinal lumen to produce aspartyl-phenylalanine and methanol. The aspartyl-phenylalanine is directly absorbed into gut mucosal cells by peptide transport mechanisms and subsequently hydrolyzed into aspartate and phenylalanine. Objections to the use of aspartame as a food additive have been based on concerns that the sweetener could raise plasma concentrations of aspartate and phenylalanine to potentially harmful levels. In addition, apprehension has been voiced about the toxic effects of the methanol component of aspartame metabolism (Stegink, Filer, and Baker 1988).

ASPARTATE

Aspartate is an amino acid that can act as an excitatory neurotransmitter in the central nervous system (Cooper, Bloom, and Roth 1986). When the FDA first approved aspartame in 1974, objections were raised about the neurotoxic potential of aspartate (Olney 1976a, 1976b). These objections were based on findings that at high doses, aspartate increased plasma aspartate levels, which resulted in the destruction of nerve cells in the hypothalamus of neonatal rats and mice. Similar brain damage was observed following the administration of glutamic acid, another amino acid that serves as an excitatory neurotransmitter (Olney 1976a, 1976b; Reynolds, Butler, and Lemkey-Johnston 1976). Glutamic acid is a component of another commonly used food additive, monosodium glutamate (see chapter 7). Based on these findings, the question was posed whether the consumption of aspartame, alone or in conjunction with glutamate (as MSG), would increase plasma aspartate or glutamate levels sufficiently to produce brain damage in young children (Federal Register 1981).

A variety of experiments have appraised the effects of aspartame intake on plasma aspartate levels. In experimental animals, plasma levels of aspartate well over 20 times normal (> 110 umole/dl) are necessary to produce brain damage. In human subjects, administration of 50 mg/kg body weight, or 1.5 times the 99th percentile of projected intake of aspartame, does not produce a significant increase in plasma aspartate levels. Further, when subjects are given larger single doses of aspartame (100, 150, or 200 mg/kg body weight), plasma aspartate levels only increase three- to four-fold:

Plasma Aspartate Levels (umole/dl)

Aspartame Dose	Baseline	Mean Peak
10 mg/kg	0.16 ± 0.05	0.43 ± 0.23
150	0.27 ± 0.10	1.00 ± 0.40
200	0.22 ± 0.08	0.76 ± 0.57

These levels are less than those observed following normal consumption of protein-containing foods, and many times lower than those leading to brain damage in infant rodents (Stegink 1987).

One problem with the preceding studies is that the subjects were administered a single dose of aspartame. The average consumer, however, may consume aspartame-containing foods and beverages several times a day. To replicate this cumulative pattern of intake, Stegink, Filer, and Baker (1988) gave human subjects three successive 12-oz servings of a beverage containing 10 mg/kg aspartame at two-hour intervals. Plasma aspartate levels did not increase following repeated intake of the aspartame-sweetened beverage.

To assess the safety of long-term use of large doses of aspartame, Leon and colleagues (1989) gave healthy male and female subjects 25 mg/kg aspartame in capsule form, three times daily for 24 weeks. Total daily aspartame intake equaled 75 mg/kg, or 1.5 times the FDA's current acceptable daily intake of 50 mg/kg. Plasma aspartate levels in these subjects did not change as a function of continued intake of aspartame and were not significantly different from those of subjects given a placebo.

As mentioned previously, one concern expressed by the critics of aspartame was that the neurotoxicity of the compound might be enhanced if it were consumed with foods that contained MSG. To address this concern, Stegink, Filer, and Baker (1987) examined the effects of a meal containing both aspartame and MSG on plasma amino acid levels. The results of this study did not support the idea that a marked increase in plasma glutamate and aspartate concentrations would result when these two food additives were simultaneously consumed.

Based on the results of the preceding studies, it can be concluded that normal intake of aspartame does not result in toxic levels of plasma aspartate.

PHENYLALANINE

During the initial evaluation of aspartame, its phenylalanine content also came under scrutiny. This amino acid plays an important role in the genetic disorder phenylketonuria (PKU). In individuals with PKU, the enzyme phenylalanine hydroxylase, which normally converts phenylalanine to tyrosine, does not function properly. As a result, phenylalanine accumulates in many parts of the body where it can impede development. The central nervous system is particularly sensitive to the toxic effects of phenylalanine. In an untreated infant, the accumulation of phenylalanine can lead to severe mental retardation, decreased attention span, and lack of responsiveness to the environment. As they grow, these children suffer from seizures, spasticity, hyperactive reflexes, and tremor and can display abnormal patterns of electrical brain activity (Spreen et al. 1984).

To treat individuals with PKU, foods containing phenylalanine are eliminated from the diet. With this type of dietary regimen, the majority of the problems associated with PKU can be avoided. It was previously believed that treatment could be stopped when individuals with PKU reached 5 to 6 years of age and brain development had been completed. As a result of studies demonstrating reductions in IQ among children who discontinued treatment during early childhood, however, it is now recommended that treatment be continued at least through adolescence (Levy and Waisbren 1987).

Recently, both adolescents with PKU, but no longer on a phenylalanine-restricted diet, and their parents have expressed concern about inadvertent ingestion of aspartame-sweetened beverages, particularly at social gatherings. These concerns are heightened by recent suggestions that ingestion of carbohydrates with aspartame-sweetened beverages may increase phenylalanine transport into the brain, thus increasing the potential for harm. To address these concerns, the effects of ingesting an unsweetened and an aspartame-sweetened beverage (containing 200 mg of aspartame, the amount found in a 12-oz diet beverage) with or without 60 g of carbohydrate were assessed in adolescents with PKU and in control subjects. As expected, plasma phenylalanine levels of subjects with PKU were significantly greater than in controls; however, intake of 200 mg of aspartame ingested with or without carbohydrate did not increase plasma phenylalanine levels in either PKU or normal subjects.

Although the data suggest that normal levels of aspartame intake do not have adverse effects, this should not be interpreted to mean that individuals with PKU can be permitted unlimited access to aspartame-containing products. The magnitude of the effect of aspartame on plasma phenylalanine levels depends on the total dietary intake of the amino acid. Although aspartame-sweetened products would likely provide a relatively minor amount of the total phenylalanine intake of individuals not following a phenylalanine-restricted diet, they could be a major source of dietary phenylalanine in individuals on a restricted diet. Subjects with PKU should consume their phenylalanine allotment from nutrient-dense sources such as breads, cereals, vegetables, and fruits, and avoid intake of aspartame-containing products as a regular practice throughout life (Wolf-Novak et al. 1990).

To alert individuals with PKU to the presence of aspartame in a product, the FDA requires a package label stating ''Phenylketonurics: Contains Phenylalanine'' for all foods and beverages containing the sweetener.

The estimated frequency of PKU is one per 18,000 births. PKU has an autosomal recessive mode of genetic transmission; that is, to develop overt symptoms of PKU, an individual must receive a recessive gene from each parent. Individuals homozygous for PKU are identified at birth by a simple screening test. Individuals with one recessive gene for PKU are 300 times more numerous than those actually affected by the disease. Thus, approximately one in 60 people in the United States are heterozygote, or carry one gene for PKU (Spreen et al. 1984). Most of these people are unaware that they carry a gene for PKU. Fasting plasma phenylalanine levels are not markedly elevated in these individuals, and phenylalanine hydroxylase activity appears sufficient for normal functioning (Filer and Stegink 1989). The ability to metabolize phenylalanine into tyrosine, however, is diminished by half in individuals carrying the recessive gene.

A question raised by the marketing of aspartame was whether metabolism of the sweetener could increase plasma phenylalanine to levels that would be toxic to individuals heterozygous for PKU. Plasma phenylalanine concentration usually ranges from 6 to 12 umole/dl (Franz 1986; Filer and Stegink 1989). For nonphenylketonuric adults, children, and infants, the toxic threshold is 100 umole/dl, and for pregnant women it is 50 umole/dl, due to a 1 : 2 ratio gradient maintained by the placenta. That is, 50 umole in a pregnant woman creates plasma levels of 100 umole in the fetus (Franz 1986).

For nonphenylketonuric individuals, a dose of aspartame equivalent to the 99th percentile of daily intake (34 mg/kg) increases plasma phenylalanine levels from a fasting level of 6 umole/dl to 11 umole/dl, a value well within the normal range. A dose of 200 mg/kg aspartame raises plasma phenylalanine levels to 50 umole/dl, the toxic level for pregnant women. However, this dose is equivalent to daily intake of 600 packets of Equal™, or 24 liters of aspartame-sweetened beverages. In individuals heterozygous for PKU, 34 mg/kg aspartame increases plasma phenylalanine levels to 16 umole/dl, and 100 mg/kg elevates phenylalanine levels to 42 umole/dl (Filer and Stegink 1989). Thus, high levels of aspartame intake are required to produce toxic concentrations of phenylalanine.

It is important to remember, however, that the consumption of aspartame-sweetened foods and beverages frequently occurs in conjunction with intake of other phenylalanine-containing foods. At present we do not know the possible cumulative effects of these patterns of food intake on plasma phenylalanine levels. Although toxic levels of phenylalanine are required to produce mental retardation and related behavioral problems, recent data suggest a direct relationship between plasma phenylalanine levels and brain function in humans. That is, as phenylalanine concentrations increase above normal there may be a greater risk of developing intellectual and behavioral deficits. These data suggest that caution must be exercised in drawing conclusions about the safety of aspartame, particularly for individuals heterozygous for PKU (Pardridge 1986).

METHANOL

Methyl alcohol (methanol) is a natural constituent of the diet and an intermediary in cellular metabolism. By weight, aspartame is 10% methanol. Thus, one liter of an aspartame-sweetened beverage that contains 500 mg of aspartame would yield 50 mg of methanol (Pardridge 1986). This level is similar to the quantities of methanol found in canned fruit and vegetable juices. When metabolized, methanol is converted to formaldehyde and then to formate. Intake of large amounts of methanol elevates blood methanol and formate levels, and can produce a number of detrimental consequences including metabolic acidosis and blindness (Stegink 1987). Methanol levels rise directly as a function of aspartame intake. At a dose of 34 mg/kg aspartame, blood levels of methanol are minimal. Higher doses of 100 to 200 mg/kg aspartame are associated with blood methanol levels of 1.3 to 2.6 mg/dl, well below the toxic level of more than 1,000 mg/dl. No increases in plasma formic levels are observed with doses of aspartame as high as 200 mg/kg (Pardridge 1986; Filer and Stegink 1989).

BEHAVIORAL CONSEQUENCES

Following the marketing of aspartame as an ingredient in solid foods in 1981 and in carbonated beverages in 1983, the FDA received a number of consumer complaints related to the consumption of these products (Council on Scientific Affairs 1985). At the request of the FDA, the Centers for Disease Control investigated 517 of the complaints and found that the majority involved neurological or behavioral symptoms, followed by gastrointestinal, allergic, and menstrual ones.

Within the neurological and behavioral category the most commonly reported symptoms were headaches, insomnia, dizziness, fatigue, and mood alterations (anxiety, irritability, agitation, or depression). Symptoms were reported to occur after intake of all major types of aspartame-containing products, with table-top sweetener implicated in 38% and soft drinks in 26% of the complaints (Bradstock et al. 1986). Investigations demonstrated that most of the reported symptoms were mild and relatively common in the general population. In many instances, it appeared that aspartame intake did not cause a problem, but rather that there was a temporal coincidence between intake of the artificial sweetener and the symptom. However, a small percentage of complaints may have resulted from an as yet unidentified sensitivity in some individuals to aspartame in commonly consumed amounts (Bradstock et al. 1986).

Double-blind experiments can help to uncover an individual's sensitivity to aspartame and other food additives. Employing a double-blind procedure, Schiffman and associates (1987) examined the effects of aspartame (30 mg/kg body weight) and a placebo in 40 men and women who reported having headaches after eating aspartame-containing products. The results of this study did not support the idea that aspartame intake and headaches are causally related. Subjects had no more headaches after consuming aspartame than after consuming the placebo. Moreover, the frequency of other symptoms (e.g., dizziness, fatigue, nausea, and anxiety) did not differ between the aspartame and placebo conditions. Similar results were obtained by Leon and colleagues (1989), who found no significant differences in the number of headaches or other symptoms between subjects ingesting 200 mg/kg aspartame per day or a placebo for 24 weeks. Recent work has also demonstrated that intake of an single dose of aspartame equivalent to approximately two liters of aspartame-sweetened beverage does not cause significant changes in mood, cognition, reaction time or memory in healthy men and women (Lapierre et al. 1990).

Taken together, the preceding information indicates that aspartame is safe for most people. However, there are some individuals, for example those with PKU or with a particular sensitivity to the artificial sweetener, for whom aspartame intake could have deleterious consequences. For this reason, it is important that products be labeled with the milligrams of aspartame per serving so that consumers can make educated choices about their intake.

Newer Artificial Sweeteners

Acesulfame-K is a man-made, white odorless powder that is approximately 200 times sweeter than sucrose. Unlike aspartame, the sweetening power of acesulfame-K is not lost when the product is heated. Thus, an advantage of this product over aspartame is that it can be used in baked goods. Acesulfame-K is not metabolized and is excreted unchanged in the urine. Available data indicate that acesulfame-K does not produce cancer in experimental animals, even when large doses are administered for prolonged periods of time. Recently, acesulfame-K was approved by the FDA for use as a noncaloric table-top sweetener and as an ingredient in chewing gum, powdered beverage mixes, gelatins, and puddings (Anonymous 1988).

Thaumatin is a protein that occurs in the fruit of a West African plant. It is the sweetest substance presently known and is practically calorie-free on a per serving basis. Its safety and potential value as a commercial artificial sweetener are presently being explored.

ROLE IN THE CONTROL OF CALORIC INTAKE AND BODY WEIGHT

Obesity is one of the major health problems in today's society, with well over 30% of Americans substantially above their desirable weight (Bray 1987). The medical complications of obesity, which include hypertension, cardiovascular disease, and diabetes, as well as the social stigma placed on the obese, have provided impetus for the search for methods of weight control (Kanarek et al. 1984; see also chapter 13). In the last decade, there also has been a marked rise in the incidence of the eating disorders anorexia nervosa and bulimia (see chapter 14). Both of these conditions feature rigid, self-generated rules and rituals designed to restrict caloric intake that may lead to abnormally high consumption of foods containing artificial sweeteners.

Americans' concerns about caloric intake and body weight have led to an industry devoted to the development and marketing of foods that can satisfy the desire for pleasurable taste sensations and at the same time reduce caloric intake. Artificially sweetened foods certainly appear to fall into this category. However, the usefulness of these foods for weight control remains open to question.

In early research investigating the role of artificial sweeteners in weight control, Porikos and colleagues (Porikos, Booth, and Van Itallie 1977; Porikos, Hesser, and Van Itallie 1982; Van Itallie, Yang, and Porikos 1988) examined the effects of relatively long-term (one to two weeks) covert caloric dilution of the diet in normal and obese subjects. In these experiments, caloric intake decreased when aspartame-sweetened items were substituted for their sucrose-containing counterparts. Although the caloric content per gram of food was reduced by 25%, total caloric intake was reduced by only 15%. In addition, caloric intake increased as exposure to aspartame-sweetened foods lengthened. The results of these studies suggest that artificial sweeteners may be helpful to some degree to individuals wishing to reduce caloric intake. Because body weight was not determined in these studies, however, no conclusions about the role of artificial sweeteners in weight control can be reached.

Several recent studies suggest that artifically sweetened beverages may also be useful for weight control. In a study investigating the effects of drinking soda sweetened with aspartame or high-fructose corn syrup, for example, Tordoff and Alleva (1990) reported that over a three-week period daily energy intake and weight gain were greater when subjects drank 40 oz a day of the fructose-sweetened drink than when they consumed aspartame-sweetened soda.

In addition, there is evidence that the use of artificially sweetened foods may help obese individuals with the difficult problem of adjusting to a low-calorie diet (Kanders et al. 1988). Obese women consuming aspartame-containing foods in conjunction with a low-calorie diet lost more weight over a 12-week period (16.5 lb) than those consuming only the low-calorie diet (12.8 lbs). However, no differences in weight loss were observed in obese men as a function of the use of artificially sweetened products.

Although these findings imply that low-calorie foods may be helpful in controlling caloric intake, other data suggest that the use of artificially sweetened foods may have paradoxical effects on energy consumption. In a series of experiments, Blundell and co-workers investigated the effects of giving water, or beverages containing sugar, and a number of artificial sweeteners on feelings of hunger and satiety, food preferences, and energy intake (Blundell and Hill 1986; Blundell and Hill 1987; Blundell, Rogers, and Hill 1988; Rogers et al. 1988). As expected, as time passed after drinking water, nonobese young adults became hungrier and felt less full. Compared to water, beverages containing calories from glucose or sucrose reduced hunger and the desire to eat, and increased feelings of fullness. Relative to water, an aspartame-containing drink increased feelings of hunger and the desire to eat and reduced feelings of fullness. Similar effects on hunger and fullness were observed with the artificial sweeteners saccharin and acesulfame-K (Blundell and Hill 1987; Rogers et al. 1988). Further, on a list of 32 common foods, subjects checked fewer foods that they "would like to eat now" after the glucose or sucrose beverages, and more foods that they "would like to eat now" after the aspartame beverage than after water. Thus, it can be hypothesized that products containing artificial sweeteners may prompt people to eat more later than if they had not consumed the sweetened product. If such an increase in food intake followed each time an artificially sweetened food was consumed, over months a small but noticeable upward trend in body weight might result.

Studies examining the preceding hypothesis have not produced consistent results. Whereas some investigators have found that subjects report being hungrier and eat significantly more food after consuming artificially sweetened foods or beverages than after eating naturally sweetened items (Blundell, Rogers, and Hill 1988), other investigators have not observed increases in food intake following the consumption of articially sweetened fare (Rogers and Blundell 1989; Mattes 1990; Rogers, Pleming, and Blundell 1990; Rolls, Kim, and Fedoroff 1990).

Research on the regulation of food intake in humans has almost always used adults as experimental subjects. One exception is a recent study examining the effects of drinks sweetened with sucrose or aspartame on subsequent intake of pleasant tasting snack foods by 4- and 5-year-old children (Birch, McPhee, and Sullivan 1989). Relative to water, consumption of a sucrose-sweetened beverage reduced subsequent snack intake. In contrast to the adults studied by Blundell, Rogers, and Hill (1988), snack intake after drinking an aspartame-sweetened beverage was suppressed in the children. This effect was most pronounced 30 minutes after the children had consumed the artificially sweetened beverage. The foods most suppressed by both the caloric and noncaloric sweetened drinks were those least preferred by the children.

In a subsequent study, Anderson and co-workers (1989), working with 9- to 10-year-old children, reported that a preload of an aspartame-sweetened beverage did not affect hunger ratings or lunch-time food intake when compared with preloads of beverages containing either sucrose or sodium cyclamate.

From the available data it is evident that the value of artificially sweetened foods in controlling caloric intake and body weight is still to be determined. From the long-term studies that have been completed, one might counsel weight-conscious individuals that artificially sweetened foods can aid in managing caloric intake and help maintain compliance to low-calorie diets. However, short-term laboratory studies suggest that intake of artificially sweetened snacks can actually stimulate the desire for food. Several factors may help to explain these disparate findings. For example, normal weight and overweight individuals, or dieters and nondieters, may respond differently to artificially sweetened foods. The time of day, whether the artificially sweetened food is consumed as a snack or part of a meal, and if it is a beverage or solid food are all factors that may influence its effects on caloric management. More research is obviously needed before a final decision on the appropriate role for low-calorie sweeteners in the control of food intake and body weight can be made.

CONCLUSION

Moderation in the use of low-calorie sweeteners is prudent advice for people who choose to use them. There is no established need for these sweeteners, as it is possible to achieve nutritional adequacy and even caloric restriction without their use. However, they do offer the advantage of reducing the caloric content of a food without substantially altering its palatability. This advantage has made low-calorie sweeteners one of the most prevalent food additives in the American diet.

The popularity of low-calorie sweeteners is based, in part, on the belief that they provide a good method for controlling caloric intake and body weight. However, the scientific evidence implies that low-calorie sweeteners are not a panacea for weight control. Some research suggests that intake of low-calorie sweetened foods may actually increase subsequent food intake.

It is important that the public have accurate and complete information on which sweetener to use and how much is safe. Labeling products with the milligrams of sweetener per serving provides this information. Further, a greater variety of nonnutritive sweeteners would reduce the chances of consuming one agent in amounts that could be potentially harmful.

At the levels presently consumed in this country, low-calorie sweeteners do not appear to pose a health risk. However, as these sweeteners are being added to more and more foods, their safety should be periodically reassessed.

REFERENCES

Anderson, G. H., S. Saravis, R. Schacher, S. Zlotkin, and L. A. Leiter. 1989. Aspartame: Effect on lunch-time food intake, appetite and hedonic response in children. *Appetite* 13:93–103.

Anonymous. 1988. Acesulfame-K: A new artificial sweetener. *The Medical Letter* p. 116.

Birch, L. L., L. McPhee, and S. Sullivan. 1989. Children's food intake following drinks sweetened with sucrose or aspartame: Time course effects. *Physiology and Behavior* 45(2): 387–395.

Blundell, J. E. and A. J. Hill. 1986. Paradoxical effects of an intense sweetener (aspartame) on appetite. *Lancet* I:1092–1093.

Blundell, J. E. and A. J. Hill. 1987. Artificial sweeteners and the control of appetite: Implications for the eating disorders. In *The Future of Predictive Safety Evaluation*, vol. 2, ed. A. Worden, D. Parke, and J. Marks, pp. 263–282. Lancaster, England: MTP Press.

Blundell, J. E., P. J. Rogers, and A. J. Hill. 1988. Uncoupling sweetness and calories: Methodological aspects of laboratory studies on appetite control. *Appetite* 11(suppl.):54–61.

Bradstock, M. K., M. K. Serdula, J. S. Marks, R. J. Barnard, N. T. Crane, P. L. Remington, and F. L. Trowbridge. 1986. Evaluation of reactions to food additives: The aspartame experience. *American Journal of Clinical Nutrition* 43:464–469.

Bray, G. A. 1987. Overweight is risking fate. Definition, classification, prevalence, and risks. *Annals of the New York Academy of Sciences* 499:14–28.

Calorie Control Council. 1988. "A Review of Low-Calorie Sweetener Benefits." Atlanta, GA: Calorie Control Council.

Cooper, J. R, F. E. Bloom, and R. H. Roth. 1986. *The Biochemical Basis of Neuropharmacology.* New York: Oxford University Press.

Council on Scientific Affairs. 1985. Aspartame: Review of safety issues. *Journal of the American Medical Association* 254(3):400–402.

Federal Register. 1981. Aspartame: Commissioner's final decision. 46(142):38285–38299.

Filer, L. J. and L. D. Stegink. 1989. Aspartame metabolism in normal adults, phenylketonuric heterozygotes, and diabetic subjects. *Diabetes Care* 12(1):67–74.

Franz, M. 1986. Is it safe to consume aspartame during pregnancy? A review. *The Diabetes Educator* 12(2):145–148.

Kanarek, R. B., N. Orthen-Gambill, R. Marks-Kaufman, and J. Mayer. 1984. Obesity: Possible psychological and metabolic determinants. In *Nutrition and Behavior,* ed. Janina Galler, pp. 339–396. New York: Plenum.

Kanders, B. S., P. T. Lavin, M. B. Kowalchuk, I. Greenberg, and G. L. Blackburn. 1988. The effect of artificial sweeteners (aspartame) on weight loss, dietary compliance and quality of life. *Appetite* 11(Suppl.):73–84.

Lapierre, K. A., D. J. Greenblatt, J. E. Goddard, J. S. Harmatz and R. I. Shader. 1990. The Neuropsychiatric effects of aspartame in normal volunteers. *Journal of Clinical Pharmacology* 30:454–460.

Lecos, C. W. 1985. Sweetness minus calories = controversy. *FDA Consumer,* February: 18–23.

Leon, A. S., D. B. Hunninghake, C. Bell, D. K. Rassin, and T. R. Tephly. 1989. Safety of long-term large doses of aspartame. *Archives of Internal Medicine* 149:2318–2324.

Levy, H. L. and S. E. Waisbren. 1987. The PKU paradigm: The mixed results from early dietary treatment. In *Amino Acids in Health and Disease: New Perspectives,* ed. S. Kaufman, pp. 539–551. New York: Alan R. Liss.

Mattes, R. 1990. Effects of aspartame and sucrose on hunger and energy intake in humans. *Physiology and Behavior* 47:1037–1044.

Mazur, R. H. 1984. Discovery of aspartame. In *Asparatame,* ed. L. D. Stegink and L. J. Filer, pp. 3–7. New York: Marcel Dekker.

Miller, S. A. and V. P. Frattali 1989. Saccharin. *Diabetes Care* 12(1):75–80.

National Research Council. 1985. *Evaluation of Cyclamate for Carcinogenicity.* Washington, DC: National Academy Press.

Olney, J. W. 1976a. Brain damage and oral intake of certain amino acids. *Advances in Experimental Biology and Medicine* 69:497–507.

Olney, J. W. 1976b. L-glutamic and L-aspartic acids: A question of hazard? *Food and Cosmetic Toxicology* 13:595–596.

Pardridge, W. M. 1986. Potential effects of the dipeptide sweetener aspartame on the brain. In *Nutrition and the Brain,* vol. 7, ed. R. J. Wurtman and J. J. Wurtman, pp. 199–241. New York: Raven Press.

Porikos, K. P., G. Booth, and T. B. Van Itallie. 1977. Effect of covert nutritive dilution on the spontaneous food intake of obese individuals: A pilot study. *American Journal of Clinical Nutrition* 30:1638–1644.

Porikos, K. P., M. F. Hesser, and T. B. Van Itallie. 1982. Caloric regulation in normal weight men maintained on a palatable diet of conventional foods. *Physiology and Behavior* 29:293–300.

Reynolds, W. A., V. Butler, and N. Lemkey-Johnston. 1976. Hypothalamic morphology following ingestion of aspartame or MSG in the neonatal rodent and primate: A preliminary report. *Journal of Toxicology and Environmental Health* 2:471–480.

Rogers, P. J. and J. E. Blundell. 1989. Separating the actions of sweetness and calories: Effects of saccharin and carbohydrates on hunger and food intake in human subjects. *Physiology and Behavior* 45:1093–1099.

Rogers, P. J., J. Carlyle, A. J. Hill, and J. E. Blundell. 1988. Uncoupling sweet taste and calories: Comparison of the effects of glucose and three intense sweeteners on hunger and food intake. *Physiology and Behavior* 43(5):547–552.

Rogers, P. J., H. C. Pleming, and J. E. Blundell. 1990. Aspartame ingested without tasting inhibits hunger and food intake. *Physiology and Behavior* 47:1239–1243.

Rolls, B. J., S. Kim, and I. C. Fedoroff. 1990. Effects of drinks sweetened with sucrose or aspartame on hunger, thirst and food intake in men. *Physiology and Behavior* 48:19–26.

Schiffman, S. S., C. E. Buckley, III, H. A. Sampson, E. W. Massey, J. N. Baraniuk, J. V. Follett, and Z. S. Warwick. 1987. Aspartame and suceptibility to headache. *New England Journal of Medicine* 317(19):1181–1185.

Spreen, O., D. Tupper, A. Risser, H. Tuokko, and D. Edgell. 1984. *Human Developmental Neuropsychology.* New York: Oxford University Press.

Stefink, L. D. 1987. The aspartame story: A model for the clinical testing of a food additive. *American Journal of Clinical Nutrition* 46:204–215.

Steflink, L. D., L. J. Filer, and G. L. Baker. 1987. Plasma amino acid concentrations in normal adults ingesting aspartame and monosodium L-glutamate as part of a soup/beverage meal. *Metabolism* 36:1073–1079.

Stegink, L. D., L. J. Filer, and G. L. Baker. 1988. Repeated ingestion of aspartame-sweetened beverage: Effect on plasma amino acid concentrations in normal adults. *Metabolism* 37(3):246–251.

Tordoff, M. G. and A. M. Alleva. 1990. Effect of drinking soda sweetened with aspartame or high-fructose corn syrup on food intake and body weight. *American Journal of Clinical Nutrition* 51:963–968.

Vander, Arthur J. 1981. *Nutrition, Stress, and Toxic Chemicals.* Ann Arbor: University of Michigan Press.

Van Itallie, T. B., M.-U. Yang, and K. P. Porikos. 1988. Use of aspartame to test the body weight set point hypothesis. *Appetite* 11(Suppl.):68–72.

Wolf-Novak, L. C., L. D. Stegink, M. C. Brummel, T. J. Persoon, L. J. Flier, E. F. Bell, E. E. Ziegler, and W. L. Krause. 1990. Aspartame ingestion with and without carbohydrate in phenylketonuric and normal subjects: Effect on plasma concentrations of amino acids, glucose, and insulin. *Metabolism* 39:391–396.

11

Alcohol: Consequences on the Central Nervous System and Behavior

Alcohol is most frequently used and thought of as a drug, and therefore its relevance to the study of nutrition and behavior may seem curious. However, alcohol does have nutritional value and profoundly affects the intake, absorption, digestion, and metabolism of many essential nutrients. These alterations in nutrient intake can have significant effects on behavior. In addition, research conducted over the past 20 years has demonstrated that chronic alcohol consumption during pregnancy can act as a potent teratogen, permanently altering a child's CNS functioning and behavior.

In Western cultures, alcohol is the only drug with which self-induced intoxication is socially acceptable. In the United States, 95% of the adult population has voluntarily consumed alcohol, and approximately 70% are at least monthly users. It has been estimated that 8% of the adult population, or approximately 13 million people, suffer from alcoholism (McKim 1986). Chronic alcohol consumption has so many adverse consequences, that treatment of alcohol-related problems accounts for 12% of the U.S. health budget (Leccese 1991).

The following sections describe the metabolism of alcohol, its possible effects on nutritional status, the effects of alcohol on the CNS and behavior in adults, and finally the consequences of exposure to alcohol during the fetal period.

METABOLISM OF ALCOHOL

Ethanol is a small, water-soluble molecule that does not require digestion. It is rapidly absorbed by diffusion from the stomach and small intestine into the blood. Rate of absorption into the blood depends on the dose, concentration, and type of alcohol which is consumed. For example, diffusion of alcohol across the gastrointestinal tract increases with concentration, and therefore the alcohol from beverages with high alcohol content diffuses into the blood more rapidly than the same amount of alcohol mixed in a weaker concentration. The diffusion of alcohol is also facilitated by carbonation. Thus, alcohol in carbonated beverages (e.g., champagne, whiskey with soda) is more rapidly absorbed than that in noncarbonated drinks. Absorption can be delayed by food in the stomach and by drugs that decrease gastrointestinal mobility or blood flow.

Because alcohol is water soluble, it readily diffuses across cell membranes and is found in tissues in direct proportion to their water content. It easily crosses the blood-brain barrier and the placenta. The blood alcohol content of the drinker accurately reflects alcohol levels in the brain and fetus. In the fetus, alcohol is distributed to all tissues, with the liver, pancreas, kidney, lung, heart, and brain achieving the highest levels.

A small amount of alcohol is eliminated from the body unchanged, through breath, sweat, urine, and feces. However, most of the alcohol (90 to 95%) consumed is metabolized by oxidative enzymes in the liver. The critical enzyme is alcohol dehydrogenase, which converts alcohol to acetaldehyde. Acetaldehyde is then converted into acetyl-coenzyme A, which in turn is converted into carbon dioxide and water. Other enzyme systems, such as the microsomal ethanol oxidating system (MEOS), are also capable of metabolizing alcohol. The MEOS normally handles only 5% to 10% of the metabolism of alcohol; however, its activity increases proportionally with the level of alcohol in the blood (Abel 1984; McKim 1986).

Blood alcohol levels, which are expressed as mg of alcohol per 100 ml of blood, or as a percentage of blood, are used as a way of measuring the state of intoxication. In nonalcoholic individuals, blood alcohol levels above 25 mg per 100 ml of blood are associated with mild intoxication manifested by lack of coordination, altered mood, and impaired cognition. In most states, the blood alcohol levels legally defining intoxication range from 50 to 100 mg per 100 ml, or 0.05% to 0.10%. At this concentration of blood alcohol, signs of mental confusion and of vestibular and cerebellar dysfunction, nystagmus, diplopia, dysarthria, and ataxia, are common (Charness, Simon, and Greenberg 1989).

When men and women consume identical amounts of alcohol, blood alcohol will generally be higher in women. This is because women generally weigh less and have less body water in which alcohol can dissolve. Age also affects blood alcohol levels. Because the proportion of body water decreases with age, blood alcohol levels will be higher in older individuals than in younger ones after consumption of similar amounts of alcohol. Finally, reduced body weight and chronic malnutrition may be associated with higher blood alcohol levels.

INTERACTION OF ALCOHOL AND NUTRITION

Alcohol affects nutrition in numerous ways. Alcohol, which contains 7 kilocalories per gram, can displace calories from more nutritious foods, leading to deficiencies of essential nutrients. Although some alcoholic beverages such as beer and wine may contain small amounts of trace elements and some vitamins, they provide little nutritive value aside from their caloric content.

There is no single established dietary pattern for people who regularly consume alcohol. Social drinkers frequently meet the recommended daily allowances for essential nutrients even when consuming 10% to 15% of their daily calories from alcohol. A majority of moderate drinkers may add alcohol calories on top of a fairly consistent daily food intake. In contrast, the nutritional status of chronic alcoholics, who have a drinking pattern of several days of heavy alcohol consumption followed by a state of moderate to severe intoxication, is generally poor. The chronically alcoholic individual substitutes alcohol for much of his or her normal food intake, and therefore intakes of protein and essential micronutrients may be severely inadequate.

Alcohol consumption can also damage the gastrointestinal tract, resulting in impairments in digestion and absorption of nutrients. As a result of damage to the intestinal mucosa, for example, gastrointestinal absorption of the vitamins thiamin and B_{12} are frequently impaired in chronic alcoholics.

Habitual use of alcohol also alters the functioning of other important digestive organs, including the pancreas and liver. Alcohol-induced pancreatitis can lead to insufficiencies in pancreatic enzymes which may contribute to the malabsorption and steatorrhea commonly observed in alcoholics. In addition, pancreatitis may result in disturbances of fluid and electrolyte balance, and decrease nutrient intake. Liver damage, which is common in chronic alcoholics, alters the metabolism of many essential vitamins and minerals, including folic acid; pyridoxine; vitamins C, A, and D; and sodium, potassium, and magnesium.

Finally, money spent on alcohol reduces money available for food, which presents a particular problem for low-income families (Burton and Foster 1988; Shaw and Lieber 1988).

CONSEQUENCES OF ALCOHOL INTAKE IN ADULTS

Alcohol affects the CNS more markedly than any other system in the body. Although its exact mechanism of action is not well understood, it is clear that alcohol acts as a CNS depressant. Alcohol produces changes in the properties of the neural membranes, including alterations in ion permeability, cell metabolism, the conduction of electrical impulses down the axon, and the release of neurotransmitters. It is not known which, if any, of these changes are responsible for the behavioral consequences of alcohol. It has been hypothesized that some of alcohol's behavioral effects may not be due to alcohol itself, but are the result of the metabolism of the drug to acetaldehyde, which can alter the functioning of catecholamine neurotransmitters.

Acute Alcohol Intake. In general, the effects of alcohol on the CNS are directly proportional to the concentration of alcohol in the blood. Electrophysiological studies suggest that alcohol first exerts its depressant actions on those parts of the CNS involved in the most highly integrative functions. The brain stem reticular activating system, which plays a role in the maintenance of alertness, and certain areas of the cortex are particularly susceptible to alcohol. It has also been proposed that inhibitory synapses are depressed slightly earlier than excitatory ones. Thus, at low doses a state of disinhibition or mild euphoria may be induced by alcohol. At higher doses, when excitatory synapses are depressed, a progressive reduction in activity level predominates.

Behavioral responses to acute alcohol intoxication vary among individuals and depend to some degree on the individual's state of mind and the setting in which drinking occurs. In one situation alcohol may lead to relaxation and euphoria, and in another it may lead to withdrawal or aggressive behavior. State of mind and setting become progressively less important with increasing doses, since sedation predominates and activity decreases.

Alcohol, like other depressant drugs, acts as a sedative and induces sleep. The drug decreases the time it takes to go sleep, without affecting total sleep time. Alcohol can also alter the nature of sleep, decreasing the proportion of time spent in rapid eye movement (REM), the portion of sleep typically associated with dreaming. With relatively high doses of alcohol, REM sleep is depressed throughout the night, but after several nights of alcohol intake may return to normal. When alcohol intake stops, REM sleep rebounds above normal levels, leading to tossing and turning and unpleasant dreams. Alcoholics who stop drinking usually have a higher percentage of REM sleep and other disturbances in sleep patterns which may last for weeks or months.

Acute alcohol intake also decreases alertness, has a detrimental effect on vision, impairs performance on tests of reaction time and intellectual abilities, leads to disturbances in motor skills, and produces memory deficits. Alcohol amnesia or blackouts, after which the drinker is unable to remember anything about the events that occurred while he or she was intoxicated, are not uncommon among heavy drinkers (Richie 1980; McKim 1986; Charness, Simon, and Greenberg 1989).

Chronic Alcohol Intake. A number of neurological and mental disorders that have been associated with nutritional deficiencies, particularly of the B vitamins, are connected to chronic alcoholism. Peripheral nerve damage is initially characterized by paresthesia in the feet, and discomfort and fatigue in the muscles of the lower portions of the legs. These symptoms are usually followed by weakness in the toes and ankles, decreased fine movements, loss of vibratory sensations, and finally decreased sensation of pain and severe weakness of the hands and feet. Thiamin deficiency has been most strongly implicated in the etiology of alcoholic polyneuropathy. Deficiencies of other B vitamins, however, including, B_{12}, pyridoxine, nicotinic acid, and riboflavin, may also contribute to the symptoms of peripheral neuropathy.

Damage to the CNS is also common in chronic alcoholics. The first indications of CNS damage, which has been termed Wernicke's encephalopathy, are weakness of the eye muscles, gait disturbances, difficulties with short-term memory, and mental confusion. It has been well established that Wernicke's encephalopathy is a direct result of thiamin deficiency, which develops from a combination of poor diet and decreased intestinal absorption, decreased hepatic storage, and impaired use of the vitamin. Thiamin administration leads to improvements of ocular disturbances within hours to days, and to recovery from ataxia and confusion within days to weeks.

Continued use of alcohol can lead to Korsakoff's psychosis, a chronic mental disorder characterized by anterograde amnesia (inability to form new memories) and, to a lesser extent, retrograde amnesia (loss of past memories), disordered time sense, hallucinations, confabulation, and dementia. Autopsies of patients with Korsakoff's psychosis have revealed symmetrical brain lesions in the thalamus, hypothalamus, brain stem, midbrain, and cerebellum that are similar to lesions observed in experimental thiamin deficiency in animals. In addition to the similarity in damage to the CNS, a history of dietary deficiency in alcoholics with memory and learning deficits supports the idea that Korsakoff's psychosis is caused by thiamin deficiency. Unfortunately, because of the extensive CNS damage, Korsakoff's psychosis is only minimally responsive to thiamin administration (Shaw and Lieber 1988; Charness, Simon, and Greenberg 1989; see also chapter 3).

Although chronic alcoholism can produce brain damage in adults, alcohol exerts its most profound CNS effects during the fetal period. Recent work has established that alcohol abuse by pregnant women can result in significant physical and mental damage to their children. The effects of alcohol on fetal development are elaborated in the following section.

FETAL ALCOHOL SYNDROME

The detrimental consequences of alcohol consumption during pregnancy have been suspected since antiquity. The early Greeks prohibited drinking on the wedding night, fearing the birth of a damaged child, and the Greek philosopher Aristotle warned that women drunkards often gave birth to abnormal children.

The gin epidemic that occurred in England from 1720 to 1750 strengthened suspicions that alcohol could have deleterious effects on fetal development. The epidemic resulted from a large decrease in the price of the beverage, which occurred in 1720. Early in the eighteenth century, new sources of inexpensive food imports led to a decrease in the demand for domestic grain, resulting in lower prices and surplus commodities for farmers. England faced the prospect of an unfavorable trade balance. To help farmers sell their excess grain, Parliament promoted distilling and removed taxes on gin. Alcohol abuse became a major health problem, and the health of some infants was severely compromised. A report by the Royal College of Physicians described the offspring of alcoholic mothers as having a "starved, shriveled and imperfect look." To protect public health, including that of mothers and infants, Parliament reinstated the tax on alcoholic beverages in 1751 (Abel 1984).

At the turn of this century, alcohol abuse in the United States and other countries became an important social issue, and scientific studies on its association with birth defects were initiated. One of the first studies demonstrating the potentially deleterious outcome of maternal alcohol consumption was published in 1899 by Sullivan, who reported on higher mortality and morbidity among infants of female alcoholics, as compared with nonalcoholic relatives. Sullivan's work was not actively pursued by the medical community, however, and little was published on the teratogenic potential of alcohol during the next 70 years. (Sullivan 1899; Warner and Rosett 1975; Streissguth 1978; Sokol 1981; Abel 1984).

The modern era of interest in maternal alcohol consumption and fetal development dates from 1968, when Lemoine and colleagues in France published a study describing a distinct set of malformations in the offspring of female alcoholics (Lemoine et al. 1968). Since this paper was published only in French, little attention was paid to it at first in this country. Five years later, however, Ulleland's report of failure to thrive and developmental delays in the offspring of alcoholic mothers, and Jones and colleagues' characterization of a cluster of abnormal features in seven children born to chronic alcoholics, sharply focused attention on alcohol's teratogenic properties (Ulleland 1972; Jones et al. 1973).

The term fetal alcohol syndrome (FAS) was coined by Jones and colleagues in their 1973 publication to describe the constellation of abnormalities that they had observed. The classic features of FAS include pre- and postnatal growth retardation (with more severe retardation in length than in weight at birth), microcephaly, facial dysmorphic features, joint and limb anomalies, cardiac defects, and CNS abnormalities (Streissguth 1978; Nitowsky 1982; Abel 1984):

Characteristic Features of Fetal Alcohol Syndrome

Growth Retardation	
Prenatal	< 2 SD for height and weight
Postnatal	< 2 SD for height and weight
Microcephaly	Head circumference less than third percentile
Facial Characteristics	
Eyes	Short palpebral fissures, epicanthal folds, ptosis, strabismus, wide-set eyes
Ears	Posterior radiation
Nose	Short upturned; hypoplastic philtrum
Mouth	Thin upper lip, retrognathia, cleft lip or cleft palate
Skeletal	Aberrant palmar creases; limited joint movement
Cardiac	Atrial and ventricular septal defects, heart murmur, great vessel anomalies
Renogenital	Hydronephrosis, hypospadias, labial hypoplasia
Central Nervous System	Mild to moderate mental retardation, irritability, hyperactivity, delayed psychomotor development, learning disabilities

The Fetal Alcohol Study Group of the Research Society of Alcoholism has proposed that a diagnosis of FAS requires three specific types of symptoms: growth deficiency, facial anomalies, and central nervous system dysfunctions. If all three criteria cannot be met, the term "fetal alcohol effects" (FAE) is used for characteristics suspected of being related to prenatal alcohol exposure (Rosett 1980; Abel 1984)

One of the most significant features of FAS is that, with the exception of mental retardation, all of the characteristics of the syndrome can be easily identified and diagnosed in the newborn (Figure 11-1). The most common characteristics of FAS are prenatal growth deficiency and facial anomalies. Weight, height, and head circumference of children are typically two standard deviations below normal when corrected for gestational age. When other risk factors such as smoking and poor perinatal nutrition are present, growth retardation may be even more severe. Although postnatal catch-up growth may occur, most children with FAS continue to be smaller than average, particularly with respect to height and head circumference (Figure 11-2). Clarren and Smith have hypothesized that this persistent growth defect may be the result of a prenatal effect on cell proliferation, leading to diminished fetal cell number. (Clarren and Smith 1978; Streissguth 1978; Lee and Leichter 1982; Nitowsky 1982; Olsen, Rachootin, and Schiodt 1983; Little et al. 1990).

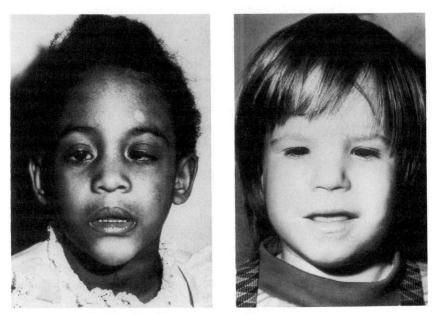

Figure 11-1. Two children displaying the classic facial dysmorphic features of fetal alcohol syndrome. From: Streissguth, A. P., Clarren, S. K., and Jones, K. L. 1985. Natural history of the fetal alcohol syndrome: A ten-year follow-up of eleven patients. *Lancet* 2:85–92.

BEHAVIORAL CONSEQUENCES

Of all of the characteristics of FAS, mental retardation resulting from CNS dysfunction is considered the most damaging and consistent consequence. It has been estimated that FAS is one of the three most frequent disorders (i.e., FAS, Down's syndrome, and spina bifida) in which mental retardation is a component. More important, perhaps, FAS is the only disorder that can be readily prevented by a change in behavior.

Children diagnosed with FAS display a broad range of intellectual functioning (scores on standardized IQ tests from 15 to 105), but most tend to suffer from mild to moderate mental retardation, with IQ scores from 50 to 65. The degree of retardation varies with the physical manifestations of FAS. Thus, children with more of the physical anomalies associated with FAS typically have lower IQs than those with fewer of the physical characteristics. The intellectual deficits suffered by FAS children are generally permanent and do not improve over time (Abel and Sokol 1986; Streissguth, Sampson, and Barr 1989).

Children with FAS display a multiplicity of other behavioral abnormalities consistent with CNS damage. Infants diagnosed with FAS are often

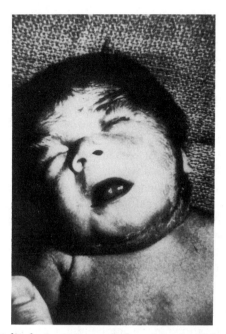

Figure 11-2. Infant displaying microcephaly and the facial dysmorphic features of fetal alcohol syndrome. From: Streissguth, A. P., Clarren, S. K., and Jones, K. L. 1985. Natural history of the fetal alcohol syndrome: A ten-year follow-up of eleven patients. *Lancet* 2:85–92.

tremulous, jittery, and irritable and display low levels of arousal, abnormal reflexes, hypertonia, and poor habituation to redundant stimuli. They have a weak sucking reflex which can lead to poor feeding, and a failure to grow normally during the postnatal period. Sleep abnormalities may also occur among infants exposed to high doses of alcohol during fetal development. As these infants get older they may have problems with fine motor coordination, language development, and visual memory.

In preschool and school-age children, prenatal exposure to alcohol has been associated with hyperactivity, decreased attentiveness, decrements in gross and fine motor performance, and problems of social compliance. Both IQ and behavioral problems appear to be directly related to the degree of alcohol exposure in utero (Streissguth, Sampson, and Barr 1989; Driscoll, Streissguth, and Riley 1990).

Adolescents and adults with FAS typically display poor concentration and attention, social withdrawal, impulsivity, periods of high levels of anxiety, and psychosocial maladjustment. It may be argued for adults that their maladaptive behaviors are a combination of the effects of prenatal alcohol exposure and environmental problems associated with parental alcoholism. However, it should be noted that the psychological problems of the adult with FAS are present even in individuals reared in foster or adoptive homes (Little and Streissguth 1981; Warren and Bast 1988; Streissguth, Sampson, and Barr 1989).

EFFECTS OF MATERNAL ALCOHOL INTAKE ON THE DEVELOPING NERVOUS SYSTEM

Most information on alcohol-induced damage to the CNS has been derived from studies with experimental animals and from autopsy studies of newborns of chronically alcoholic women. Microcephaly is the most commonly observed CNS abnormality.

Animal studies have revealed that prenatal exposure to alcohol is associated with a number of neuroanatomical aberrations in the hippocampus, including abnormal organization of neural fibers, fewer nerve cells, decreased dendritic size, and a reduction in the number of dendritic spines. These changes in the hippocampus, an area of the brain directly involved in learning and memory, may be associated with the behavioral problems noted in FAS.

Another part of the brain that may be particularly sensitive to alcohol is the cerebellum. Rats exposed to alcohol during the prenatal period demonstrate structural alterations in the cerebellum. Cerebellar hypoplasia also has been noted in autopsies of FAS children.

In addition to affecting the hippocampus and cerebellum, fetal alcohol exposure may inhibit dendritic branching in other areas of the brain. Underdevelopment of dendritic systems could lead to altered neuronal interconnectivity and changes in behavior (Abel 1984; Riley and Barron 1989).

HOW MUCH IS TOO MUCH?

One of the most frequently asked questions with respect to FAS is, "How much alcohol is necessary to produce the syndrome?" Unfortunately, the answer to this question is, very simply, that we don't know. What we do know is that there appears to be a direct relationship between the amount of alcohol consumed during pregnancy and FAS. That is, the more a mother drinks during pregnancy, the more likely she is to have a child with FAS. In addition, the severity of FAS symptoms increases directly as a function of alcohol consumption (Driscoll, Streissguth, and Riley 1990; Little et al. 1990).

Several problems are encountered when attempting to estimate the relationship between maternal alcohol consumption and the risk of FAS. First, reports of alcohol consumption during pregnancy may be inaccurate. Many mothers may underestimate their alcohol intake.

Second, insufficient information is presently available on patterns of alcohol intake during pregnancy. There may be critical periods during pregnancy when the fetus is particularly susceptible to the detrimental consequences of alcohol. Thus, it is important to know not only how much drinking occurred, but also when. Along similar lines, research with experimental animals suggests that consumption of large amounts of alcohol at one time (binge drinking) may detrimentally affect fetal development. At present, the effects of binge drinking on human development are unknown. There are also some indications that the longer a women has been a heavy drinker preceding her pregnancy, the more likely she is to have a child with FAS.

Third, a number of other variables, including nutritional status, multiple drug use, stressful life situations, and genetic factors, may interact with alcohol in the development of FAS. As yet, the precise role of these variables in FAS remains unknown (Kolata 1981; Abel 1984; Burd and Martsolf 1989; Ernhart et al. 1989).

The question of how much alcohol is safe during pregnancy thus continues to be unanswered. Many researchers argue that since no safe level of alcohol intake has been established, and there is no assurance that moderate drinking will not harm the fetus, women should abstain completely from drinking during pregnancy. However, some investigators have pointed out that many women drink occasionally during pregnancy with no evidence of harm to their offspring. These investigators also are concerned that the scientific establishment and government may be losing credibility by "crying wolf."

The decision whether to drink alcoholic beverages during pregnancy must obviously be made by each individual woman. Such decision making must take place in a context where women can be fully informed about the evidence concerning alcohol and pregnancy. Adopting the most conservative approach, the American Medical Association and the Surgeon General have recommended that pregnant women, or women attempting to conceive, should abstain from alcohol.

PREVALENCE OF FETAL ALCOHOL SYNDROME

It has been estimated that from 6 to 11 thousand children are born each year with major or minor physical birth defects resulting from prenatal alcohol exposure. Using data collected from a large number of studies conducted throughout the world, Abel and Sokol (1987) have estimated a worldwide incidence of 1.9 cases of FAS per 1,000 live births. A number of factors influence these rates. For the population most at risk, children of chronically alcoholic women, the incidence rate rises sharply, with estimates ranging from 25 to 59 per 1,000 live births. FAS occurs more frequently in the siblings of children with this syndrome. The risk for FAS has been reported to be 85 times greater in older siblings of FAS children (170 per 1,000 live births) and 350 times more frequent in younger siblings (771 per 1,000 live births) (Abel and Sokol 1987; Abel 1988).

It is not clear why some women give birth to children with FAS and others consuming equivalent amounts of alcohol do not. Many factors have been suggested that may alter the risk for FAS. For example, the reported higher prevalence of FAS in children born to women in lower socioeconomic classes suggests that variables related to social class, such as smoking, drug use, and poor nutrition, may increase the risk of FAS. Additional evidence that poor nutrition elevates the risk of FAS comes from observations that the mothers of FAS infants tend to be somewhat underweight and to gain less weight than recommended during pregnancy. Undernourished women may be at greater risk for having a child with FAS because they attain higher blood alcohol levels and metabolize alcohol more slowly than women who drink the same amount but weigh more due to appropriate nutrition.

Genetic factors may also contribute to differences in susceptibility to FAS. A number of studies have suggested that maternal levels of acetaldehyde, which itself can be a toxin, are important in determining if a child develops FAS. Recent work indicates that as a result of genetic factors, some individuals may achieve higher blood acetaldehyde levels than others. Thus, it might be predicted that the offspring of mothers who develop high levels of acetaldehyde after drinking are more susceptible to FAS (Abel 1984).

POTENTIAL MECHANISMS FOR THE TERATOGENIC EFFECTS OF ALCOHOL

Alcohol has many different types of effects on the body, and it is unlikely that all of these are mediated by the same mechanisms. For example, the growth-retarding effects of alcohol may be the result of different mechanisms from those that produce damage to the CNS.

Research on the possible teratogenic mechanisms involved in FAS has focused on direct alcohol toxicity, acetaldehyde toxicity, fetal hypoxia, nutritional deficits, and placental dysfunction. Both alcohol and its primary metabolite, acetaldehyde, are known tissue toxins that may directly interfere with fetal cellular growth and metabolism.

Indirect evidence indicates that fetal hypoxia may contribute to some of the adverse effects of maternal alcohol use. By reducing the amount of oxygen that cells receive during development, alcohol can lead to the structural and physiological abnormalities associated with FAS. One well-established consequence of long-term fetal hypoxia is growth retardation. Much of the support for the theory of alcohol-induced hypoxia comes from studies demonstrating that acute alcohol intake by pregnant women leads to fetal apnea. Studies with experimental animals have further revealed that maternal alcohol consumption reduces blood oxygen content in the fetus. Fetal hypoxia may also result from premature placental separation, amniotic fluid infections, anemia, and antepartum bleeding, all of which are more common in women who drink heavily during pregnancy than in abstainers. Finally, women who smoke and drink during pregnancy may be at particular risk for fetal hypoxia, since smoking is correlated with hypoxia due to increased carbon monoxide and carbon dioxide levels in the blood, decreased blood flow, and an inhibition of respiratory enzymes (Abel 1984).

Although undernutrition per se does not result in symptoms similar to FAS (see chapter 2), there is the possibility that alcohol-related nutritional deficiencies may contribute to the development of the syndrome. Chronic alcohol use can interfere with maternal nutrition at several levels. It is a source of energy that can displace normal nutrients and lead to reductions in intakes of protein, essential fats, vitamins, and minerals. Moreover, alcohol can hinder intestinal absorption of essential nutrients and alter nutrient metabolism, particularly in the liver. Finally, alcohol may cause nutritional losses such as elevated excretion of trace metals. Chronic alcohol intake may thus lead to poor maternal nutrition, preventing the fetus from obtaining adequate amounts of essential nutrients (Abel 1984; Fisher 1988).

One nutrient that has received particular attention with respect to FAS is zinc. This interest was stimulated by the observation that alcoholic women who delivered FAS babies had significantly lower plasma zinc levels than alcoholics whose infants were nonsymptomatic. Maternal zinc deficiency is known to be teratogenic, and there is a similarity between some of the malformations produced by zinc deficiency and those noted in FAS (see chapter 4). In addition, alcohol has an adverse effect on zinc nutrition and impairs placental transport of zinc. Finally, recent work in experimental animals has demonstrated that zinc deficiency can potentiate the teratogenic effects of alcohol (Keppen, Pysher, and Rennert 1985; Fisher 1988).

The intrauterine growth failure observed in FAS may result, in part, from alcohol's toxic effects on the placenta. The placenta serves at least three primary functions: it is a source of steroid hormones necessary for the maintenance of pregnancy, it produces polypeptide hormones which mobilize maternal nutrient stores, and it transfers maternal nutrients to the fetal circulation. Recent work indicates that alcohol impairs this last function. Specifically, alcohol may partially block the transport of essential amino acids from the mother to the fetus. The placenta itself may also oxidize ethanol, producing toxic amounts of acetaldehyde (Fisher 1988).

OTHER REPRODUCTIVE COMPLICATIONS OF MATERNAL ALCOHOL INTAKE

In addition to FAS, alcohol is associated with other complications of pregnancy. A higher incidence of spontaneous abortions, premature births, premature rupture of membranes, infections, abruptio placenta (premature detachment of the placenta), and congenital fetal abnormalities occur in women consuming substantial amounts of alcohol during pregnancy than in nondrinkers. For example, women who have one or more drinks a day have more spontaneous abortions, particularly during the second trimester of pregnancy, than women who abstained or were only occasional drinkers (Sokol 1981; Lele 1982; Mello, Mendelson, and Teoh 1989).

Finally, alcohol can impair reproductive functioning in men. Alcoholism is associated with testicular atrophy, low testosterone levels, impotence, and decreased sexual interest. Alcohol appears to inhibit testosterone synthesis, at least in part, by a direct toxic effect on the testes. Alcohol may also influence male reproductive functioning by altering the activity of the gonadotropic hormones produced in the pituitary gland.

The impact of paternal alcoholism on offspring is unknown. At present, there is no evidence of an increase in the incidence of anomalies among the children of male alcoholics. However, abnormalities in sperm morphology have been noted in male alcoholics. Although not all sperm are damaged, it is possible that a damaged sperm could fertilize an ovum and produce anomalies in the developing fetus (Abel 1984; Mendelson and Mello 1985).

CONSEQUENCES OF MATERNAL ALCOHOL INTAKE WHILE BREAST-FEEDING

After birth, an infant can be exposed to alcohol through the mother's milk, although the quantity of alcohol consumed would only be a fraction of the mother's intake. Studies with experimental animals suggest that the nursing infant can be affected by maternal alcohol intake; however, the effects of maternal alcohol consumption on the human infant are only beginning to be addressed. In a recent study, Little and colleagues (1989) reported that mental development measured by the Bayley Mental Development Index when children were a year old was not related to maternal drinking during breast-feeding. However, motor development measured by the Psychomotor Development Index was significantly lower in one-year-olds exposed to alcohol in breast milk. This relation was maintained even when the authors controlled for more than 100 potentially confounding variables, including alcohol exposure during gestation, other drug use during pregnancy and in the postpartum period, and nutrient intake. The authors concluded that neuroanatomical development may be adversely affected by exposure to alcohol in breast milk.

CONCLUSIONS

It is clear that there is much we need to learn about FAS. However, what may be most important to discover are the ways to prevent this major public health problem. One of the most promising prevention strategies appears to be professional education and intervention in the clinic or the physician's office. Early detection of women at risk of having a child with FAS may decrease its devastating consequences (Sokol and Abel 1988; Little et al. 1990).

CONCLUSION

The harmful consequences of excess alcohol intake cannot be over-stressed. In adults, chronic consumption of alcohol is associated with inadequate nutrition; damage to the gastrointestinal tract, pancreas, and liver; and profound alterations in CNS functioning and behavior. If consumed during pregnancy, alcohol can lead to devastating changes in the development of the CNS and produce long-term behavioral effects.

Although the adverse results of alcohol intake are well documented and recently have been emphasized in advertising campaigns and warnings on alcohol-containing beverages, alcohol intake remains a fact of life. Attempts to abolish alcohol from society, such as during the Prohibition era in the United States, have generally failed. It is imperative, therefore, that education about the effects of alcohol continue so that informed decisions can be made regarding the consumption of alcoholic beverages.

REFERENCES

Abel, E. L. 1984. *Fetal Alcohol Syndrome and Fetal Alcohol Effects*. New York: Plenum.

Abel, E. L. 1988. Fetal alcohol syndrome in families. *Neurotoxicology and Teratology* 10:1–2.

Abel, E. L. and R. J. Sokol. 1986. Fetal alcohol is now leading cause of mental retardation. *Lancet* II:1222.

Abel, E. L. and R. J. Sokol. 1987. Incidence of fetal alcohol syndrome and economic impact of FAS-related anomalies. *Drug and Alcohol Dependence* 19:51–70.

Burd, L. and J. T. Martsolf. 1989. Fetal alcohol syndrome: Diagnosis and syndromal variability. *Physiology and Behavior* 46:39–43.

Burton, T. B. and W. R. Foster. 1988. *Human Nutrition* New York: McGraw-Hill.

Charness, M. E., R. P. Simon, and D. A. Greenberg. 1989. Ethanol and the nervous system. *The New England Journal of Medicine* 321:442–453.

Clarren, S. K. and D. W. Smith. 1978. The fetal alcohol syndrome. *New England Journal of Medicine* 298:1063–1067.

Driscoll, C. D., A. P. Streissguth, and E. P. Riley. 1990. Prenatal alcohol exposure: comparability of effects in humans and animal models. *Neurotoxicology and Teratology* 12:231–237.

Ernhart, C. B., R. J. Sokol, J. W. Ager, M. Morrow-Tlucak, and S. Martier. 1989. Alcohol-related birth defects: Assessing the risk. *Annals of the New York Academy of Sciences* 562:159–172.

Fisher, S. E. 1988. Selective fetal malnutrition: The fetal alcohol syndrome. *Journal of the American College of Nutrition* 7:101–106.

Jones, K. L., D. W. Smith, C. N. Ulleland, and A. P. Streissguth. 1973. Pattern of malformations in offspring of chronic alcoholic mothers. *Lancet* 1:1267–1271.

Keppen, L. D., T. Pysher, and O. M. Rennert. 1985. Zinc deficiency acts as a co-teratogen with alcohol in fetal alcohol syndrome. *Pediatric Research* 19:944–947.

Kolata, G. B. 1981. Fetal alcohol advisory debated. *Science* 214:642–646.

Leccese, A. P. 1991. *Drugs and Society: Behavioral Medicines and Abusable Drugs.* Englewood Cliffs, NJ: Prentice-Hall.

Lee, M. and J. Leichter. 1982. Alcohol and the fetus. In *Adverse Effects of Foods,* ed. E. F. P. Jelliffe and D. B. Jelliffe, pp. 245–251. New York: Plenum.

Lele, A. S. 1982. Fetal alcohol syndrome: Other effects of alcohol on pregnancy. *New York State Medical Journal* July:1225–1127.

Lemione, P., H. Haronsseau, J. P. Borteryu, and J. C. Menuet. 1968. Les enfants de parents alcooliques. Anomalies observées. A propos de 127 cas. *Quest Medical* 25:476–482.

Little, B. B., L. M. Snell, C. R. Rosenfeld, L. C. Gilstrap III, and N. F. Gant. 1990. Failure to recognize fetal alcohol syndrome in newborn infants. *American Journal of Diseases of Children* 144:1142–1146.

Little, R. E., K. W. Anderson, C. H. Ervin, B. Worthington-Roberts, and S. K. Clarren. 1989. Maternal alcohol use during breast-feeding and infant mental and motor development at one year. *New England Journal of Medicine* 321:425–430.

Little, R. E. and A. P. Streissguth. 1981. Effects of alcohol on the fetus: Impact and prevention. *Canadian Medical Association Journal* 125:159–164.

McKim, W. A. 1986. *Drugs and Behavior: An Introduction to Behavioral Pharmacology.* Englewood Cliffs, NJ: Prentice-Hall.

Mello, N. K., J. H. Mendelson, and S. K. Teoh. 1989. Neuroendocrine consequences of alcohol abuse in women. *New York Academy of Sciences* 562:211–240.

Mendelson, J. H. and N. K. Mello. 1985. *Alcohol Use and Abuse in America.* Boston: Little, Brown.

Nitowsky, H. M. 1982. Fetal alcohol syndrome and alcohol-related birth defects. *New York State Journal of Medicine* July:1214–1217.

Olsen, J., P. Rachootin, and V. Schiodt. 1983. Alcohol use, conception time, and birth weight. *Journal of Epidemiology and Community Health* 37:63–65.

Richie, J. M. 1980. The aliphatic alcohols. In *The Pharmacological Basis of Therapeutics,* ed. A. G. Gilman, L. S. Goodman, and A. Gilman, pp. 376–390. New York: Macmillan.

Riley, E. P. and S. Barron. 1989. The behavioral and neuroanatomical effects of prenatal alcohol exposure in animals. *New York Academy of Sciences* 562:173–177.

Rosett, H. L. 1980. A clinical perspective of the fetal alcohol syndrome. *Alcoholism: Clinical and Experimental Research* 4:119–122.

Shaw, S. and C. S. Lieber. 1988. Nutrition and diet in alcoholism. In *Modern Nutrition in Health and Disease,* ed. M. E. Shils and V. R. Young, pp. 1423–1449. Philadelphia: Lea and Febiger.

Sokol, R. J. 1981. Alcohol and abnormal outcomes of pregnancy. *Canadian Medical Association Journal* 125:143–148.

Sokol, R. J. and E. L. Abel. 1988. Alcohol-related birth defects: Outlining current research opportunities. *Neurotoxicology and Teratology* 10:183–186.

Streissguth, A. P. 1978. Fetal alcohol syndrome: An epidemiological perspective. *American Journal of Epidemiology* 107:467–478.

Streissguth, A. P., Clarren, S. K., and Jones, K. L. 1985. Natural history of the fetal alcohol syndrome: A ten-year follow-up of eleven patients. *Lancet* 2:85–92.

Streissguth, A. P., P. D. Sampson, and H. M. Barr. 1989. Neurobehavioral dose-response effects of prenatal alcohol exposure in humans from infancy to adulthood. *Annals of the New York Academy of Sciences* 562:145–158.

Sullivan, W. C. 1899. A note on the influence of maternal inebriety on the offspring. *Journal of Mental Science* 45:489–503.

Ulleland, C. N. 1972. The offspring of alcoholic mothers. *Annals of the New York Academy of Sciences* 197:167–169.

Warner, R. H. and H. L. Rosett. 1975. The effects of drinking on offspring: An historical survey of the American and British literature. *Journal of Studies on Alcohol* 36:1395–1420.

Warren, K. R. and R. J. Bast. 1988. Alcohol-related birth defects: An update. *Public Health Reports* 103:638–642.

12

Diet, Neurotransmitters, and Behavior

In the preceding chapters, we have seen that nutritional variables play important roles in the functioning of the central nervous system and subsequent behavior. Deficiencies of essential nutrients can impair the function and development of the CNS, and result in profound behavioral disturbances. Brain functioning and behavior can also be adversely affected by contamination of food supplies with heavy metals (e.g., lead, mercury, and aluminum). In these situations, relatively long-term nutritional deficiencies or exposure to environmental toxins are necessary before alterations in brain functioning and behavior are observed.

Work conducted within the last 20 years has suggested that changes in short-term nutritional variables may also affect the brain and behavior. More specifically, it has been hypothesized that moment-to-moment changes in nutrient availability modify neurotransmitter synthesis and activity in the CNS. These modifications could have important consequences for behavior. For example, dietary-induced alterations in the activity of neurons containing the neurotransmitter serotonin, which is involved in the control of feeding behavior, could produce changes in food intake.

The idea that foods can alter neurotransmitter production, and thus act in some ways like psychoactive drugs, also has implications for the treatment of neurological and psychological disorders. Nutrients could act as therapeutic agents for these conditions. One example is the use of the amino acid tryptophan as a treatment for insomnia. Nutrients could also interact with drugs in ways that are either clinically beneficial or countertherapeutic. For instance, consumption of a high-protein diet reduces the brain influx, and thus the clinical benefits, of the drug L-dopa in patients with Parkinson's disease (Wurtman, R. J. 1987).

This chapter discusses the ways in which nutrients may alter neurotransmitter synthesis and activity, and then examines how these alterations may modify behavior.

PRECURSOR CONTROL OF NEUROTRANSMITTER SYNTHESIS

Approximately 30 to 40 substances are currently believed to act as neurotransmitters in the mammalian CNS. These compounds can be divided into three major chemical groups:

- Amino acids, for example, glycine, glutamine, and aspartate
- Peptides, including vasoactive intestinal polypeptide, endorphins, cholecystokinin, and thyrotropin-releasing hormone
- Monoamines, such as acetylcholine, dopamine, norepinephrine, and serotonin

Of these groups, the effects of nutritional variables on the synthesis and activity of the monoamines has been the most thoroughly investigated.

The monoamines are all low molecular weight, water-soluble amines that carry an ionic charge at physiologic pH. These neurotransmitters are synthesized in neurons from precursor molecules which must be obtained from the diet. Under appropriate conditions, increasing dietary intake of these precursors will stimulate neurotransmitter formation.

General Principles

Several conditions must be met before it can be concluded that the rates at which neurons synthesize a neurotransmitter are dependent upon the intake of a dietary precursor:

1. It must be demonstrated that the precursor cannot be synthesized in the brain and is obtained from the general circulation.

2. Plasma levels of the precursor normally fluctuate as a function of dietary intake.

3. The rate at which the precursor enters the brain varies directly with its concentration in plasma; there must not be an absolute blood-brain barrier for the precursor.

4. The enzyme that transforms the precursor to the neurotransmitter must be unsaturated, so that when presented with more of the precursor, it will immediately accelerate the synthesis of the neurotransmitter.

5. The enzyme that controls the synthesis of the neurotransmitter is not modified by feedback inhibition that could decrease its activity after the transmitter levels have been increased (Growden 1979).

Two neurotransmitters, acetylcholine and serotonin, appear to meet all of these criteria.

ACETYLCHOLINE

Dietary Control of Acetylcholine Synthesis

The neurotransmitter acetylcholine (Ach) is synthesized from choline and acetyl coenzyme A. Choline enters the brain via a transport system that allows it to cross the blood-brain barrier. Once in the brain, choline is taken up by the neuron, where in the presence of the enzyme choline acetyltransferase (CAT) the acetate ion is transferred from acetyl coenzyme A to the choline molecule, yielding one molecule of Ach and one of co-enzyme A (Figure 12-1).

The choline necessary for the production of Ach is derived from two sources: dietary choline, and choline synthesized in the liver. Choline is present as a constituent of the phospholipid lecithin (phosphatidyl choline) in a variety of foods including eggs, fish, liver, wheat germ, and peanuts. In addition, lecithin is often added to processed foods where it serves as an emulsifying agent and an antioxidant, and is available to the public as a dietary supplement sold in health food stores. The lecithin found in foods or in nutritional supplements is absorbed into the intestinal mucosa where it is rapidly hydrolyzed to free choline. Lecithin that is not hydrolyzed enters the bloodstream and is transported to the lymphatic circulation, where it is broken down more slowly to choline.

Intake of foods containing substantial amounts of choline or lecithin leads to elevations in plasma choline levels. Because choline can readily cross the blood-brain barrier, elevations in choline levels are translated into increased brain choline levels. Further, since the enzyme CAT is unsaturated when choline is within normal limits, increased neuronal levels of the precursor stimulate the synthesis of Ach. Diet-induced increases in neuronal Ach levels are associated with enhanced release of the neurotransmitter when cholinergic neurons are stimulated (Cohen and Wurtman 1976; Growden 1979; Fernstrom 1981; Wurtman, Hefti, and Melamed 1981; Wurtman, R. J. 1987; Wecker 1990).

Potential Clinical Applications of Diet-Induced Increases in Acetylcholine

It has been proposed that diet-induced increases in Ach may have beneficial effects in patients with neurological diseases associated with defi-

Choline acetyltransferase (CAT)

Acetyl CoA + Choline $\implies$ Acetylcholine + CoA

Figure 12-1. Synthesis of the neurotransmitter acetylcholine.

ciencies in the activity of cholinergic neurons, such as Huntington's disease, tardive dyskinesia, and Alzheimer's disease. Drugs that increase cholinergic transmission are typically used to treat these diseases, but their effectiveness is inconsistent. Moreover, the majority of these drugs have a short duration of action and produce unpleasant side effects, including vomiting, nausea, and mental dullness, which limit their effectiveness.

Administration of choline and lecithin lead to longer-term increases in Ach levels and result in fewer side effects than cholinergic drugs. Therefore, it is has been proposed that increasing the intake of these dietary components could provide a more efficacious and benign treatment for diseases associated with deficiencies in cholinergic neurotransmission. A large number of clinical experiments have assessed this possibility.

TARDIVE DYSKINESIA

Tardive dyskinesia (TD) is a neurological disorder that develops after prolonged treatment of three months or more with some antipsychotic medications (e.g., haloperidol and chlorpromazine). The disorder is characterized by hyperkinetic activity of the buccal-lingual-masticatory region, including jaw movements; protrusion of the tongue; smacking, puckering, and sucking lip movements; and difficulty swallowing. Choreoathetoid movements of the arms, hands, feet, and legs may also be present. TD is not an inevitable consequence of the use of antipsychotic medication, but develops in 10% to 20% of patients using these drugs for more than a year. Elderly patients and those with histories of extended exposure to high doses of antipsychotics, electroconvulsive therapy, organic brain syndrome, and alcohol or drug abuse have an increased risk of developing TD (Tarsy 1983; Batey 1989).

The exact cause of TD is unknown, but an imbalance in the relationship between dopaminergic and cholinergic neurons in the basal ganglia may be involved. This imbalance appears to favor dopamine transmission at the expense of Ach transmission. Research demonstrating that drugs that enhance Ach activity relieve the symptoms of TD, while drugs that reduce Ach activity exacerbate these symptoms, provides support for a role for decreased cholinergic activity in TD.

Administration of choline or lecithin has been associated with reductions in the number of abnormal movements of some patients with TD (Davis et al. 1976; Growden et al. 1977; Growden et al. 1978; Gelenberg, Doller-Wojcik, and Growden 1979; Jackson, Nuttall, and Perez-Cruet 1979). In a double-blind crossover study, Growden and colleagues (1977) found that choline administration increased plasma choline levels and suppressed involuntary facial movements in 9 of 20 patients with TD. No specific features were identified that distinguished patients who improved from those who did not. One problem with this study was that patients who ingested choline developed the aroma of rotten fish in their urine and sweat and on their breath, making a true double-blind study difficult, if not impossible. This odor is produced by the action of intestinal bacteria on choline. Because the odor does not occur after lecithin administration, subsequent studies have examined the effects of lecithin rather than choline on TD. The results of the majority of these studies indicate that lecithin is as effective as choline in suppressing TD. However, many patients develop abdominal cramps, nausea, and diarrhea when taking high doses of lecithin. Precursor therapy also does not consistently lead to improvements in the symptoms of TD (e.g. Branchey et al. 1979; Gelenberg et al. 1989). On the basis of the potential side effects, and of inconsistent results demonstrating the efficacy of choline and lecithin in the treatment of TD, it has been concluded that dietary treatment of TD is of limited clinical utility (Gelenberg et al. 1989).

HUNTINGTON'S CHOREA

Huntington's chorea (HC) is a chronic progressive neurological disorder with an autosomal dominant pattern of inheritance. Symptoms of the disorder generally begin when an individual is from 30 to 50 years of age. Characteristic symptoms include involuntary muscular contractions (chorea) that involve all of the skeletal muscles, resulting in restlessness, poor balance, and difficulty in walking. As the disorder progresses, signs of mental disturbances develop such as forgetfulness, inability to concentrate, confusion, personality changes, paranoia, and dementia. Autopsies of patients with HC have revealed a reduction in brain weight, particularly in the regions of the frontal and occipital lobes of the cortex, and the caudate nucleus in the basal ganglia.

Studies examining neurotransmitter functioning in HC provide evidence for a role for Ach in the disorder. Patients with HC have diminished levels of Ach; reductions in CAT, the enzyme that catalyzes the conversion of choline to Ach; and decreased numbers of postsynaptic Ach receptors. Further evidence that reductions in Ach contribute to the symptoms of HC comes from studies showing that drugs that increase Ach activity reduce the choreic movements characteristic of the disorder, and drugs that decrease Ach activity aggravate them.

It has been suggested that increasing Ach by administrating choline or lecithin could ameliorate some of the symptoms of HC. Several investigators have reported that choline treatment significantly improved balance, gait, and choreic movements in some patients with HC. However, this was not generally the case. Moreover, improvements were transient and did not persist for longer than two weeks, despite continued choline administration (Davis et al. 1976; Aquilonius and Eckernas 1977; Growden, Cohen, and Wurtman 1977; Growden 1979).

ALZHEIMER'S DISEASE

Alzheimer's disease (AD) is characterized by a slow, progressive deterioration of cognitive functions, which frequently leads to dementia within 5 to 10 years. The onset of AD is usually inconspicuous and often difficult to distinguish from many other psychological problems. Initially, an individual with AD may find it hard to concentrate and suffers from periods of short-term memory loss. As the disease progresses, memory loss becomes more severe and depression, apathy, anxiety, personality changes, and difficulties in completing simple tasks become common.

The cognitive deficits accompanying AD may be due, at least in part, to alterations in cholinergic activity in the CNS. Post-mortem examinations have revealed significant reductions in levels of CAT in the neocortex and hippocampus of AD patients. Indeed, a positive correlation between low CAT levels and profound dementia has been reported. Postsynaptic cholinergic muscarinic receptors appear to be normal in AD (Bartus et al. 1982), but recent work suggests that there may be selective degeneration of cholinergic nicotinic receptors in some brain regions, such as the nucleus basalis (Ereshefsky, Rospond, and Jann 1989).

Some investigators, assessing the effects of dietary treatment in AD patients, have reported improvements in cognitive functioning and social behavior following choline or lecithin administration. However, the majority have found little or no benefit from treatment with these dietary components (Growden 1979; Ereshefsky, Rospond, and Jann 1989).

It must be concluded that administration of choline and lecithin have limited benefits in the treatment of neurological diseases. There are several possible reasons for this conclusion. First, if there is extensive destruction of the presynaptic neurons that produce Ach, increases in plasma choline levels could not be translated into increased brain Ach levels. Second, if CAT levels are decreased, as is the case in HC and AD, transformation of brain choline to Ach would be reduced and thus prevent the effectiveness of precursor loading. Third, substantial reductions in the number of postsynaptic cholinergic receptors would limit the value of choline administration. Finally, the functioning of other neurotransmitters, such as dopamine and gamma-amino butyric acid, are altered in TD, HC, and AD. It is possible therefore that even if Ach synthesis and release were restored, other systems would still be defective, and thus neurological functioning continue to be abnormal (Growden 1979; Ereshefsky, Rospond, and Jann 1989).

SEROTONIN

Dietary Control of Serotonin Synthesis

The first step in the synthesis of the neurotransmitter serotonin (also called 5-hydroxytryptamine or 5-HT) is the uptake of the amino acid tryptophan from the blood into the brain. In the brain, tryptophan enters the neuron where it is converted to 5-hydroxytryptophan (5-HTP) in a reaction catalyzed by the enzyme tryptophan hydroxylase, and then 5-HTP is converted to serotonin in a reaction controlled by the enzyme 5-HTP decarboxylase. The rate-limiting step in the formation of 5-HT is the hydroxylation of tryptophan to 5-HTP. Because tryptophan hydroxylase is unsaturated at the concentrations of tryptophan normally found in the brain, brain tryptophan levels influence the rate of 5-HT synthesis (Figure 12-2).

Studies conducted with experimental animals at The Massachusetts Institute of Technology in the early 1970s demonstrated that brain tryptophan levels, and thus the synthesis of 5-HT, vary as a function of plasma tryptophan levels. Peripheral administration of tryptophan leads to rapid dose-related increases in brain tryptophan and 5-HT levels (Fernstrom and Wurtman 1971a).

Since increasing plasma tryptophan levels elevates brain tryptophan levels and accelerates 5-HT synthesis, the researchers at MIT predicted that similar results would occur following the consumption of a high-protein meal that naturally contained tryptophan. In contrast to their prediction, brain tryptophan and 5-HT levels were depressed, although plasma tryptophan levels were elevated, in fasted rats fed a high-protein

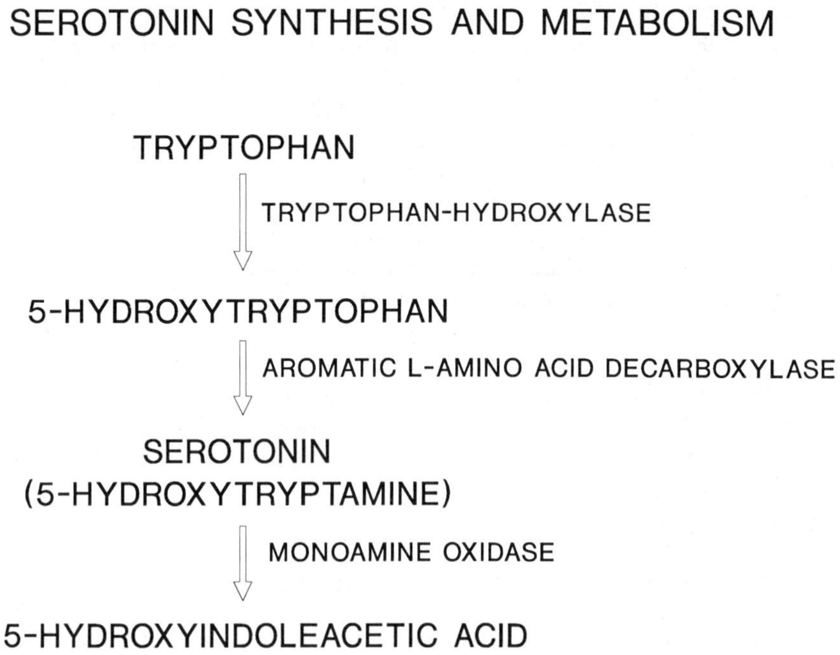

SEROTONIN SYNTHESIS AND METABOLISM

TRYPTOPHAN

TRYPTOPHAN-HYDROXYLASE

5-HYDROXYTRYPTOPHAN

AROMATIC L-AMINO ACID DECARBOXYLASE

SEROTONIN
(5-HYDROXYTRYPTAMINE)

MONOAMINE OXIDASE

5-HYDROXYINDOLEACETIC ACID

Figure 12-2. Synthesis of the neurotransmitter serotonin.

meal. This paradox arises because tryptophan is relatively scarce in protein, in comparison to the other large neutral amino acids (LNAAs: valine, tyrosine, leucine, isoleucine, and phenylalanine. Tryptophan and the other LNAAs share a common transport mechanism for crossing the blood-brain barrier. Thus, the other LNAAs compete with tryptophan for entry into the brain. Following a high-protein meal, plasma levels of the other LNAAs increase to a greater degree than plasma tryptophan levels. Thus, a high-protein meal gives the other LNAAs a competitive advantage for entry into the brain (Figure 12-3).

It was discovered in subsequent research that in contrast to high-protein meals, high-carbohydrate (protein-free) meals increased brain levels of tryptophan and 5-HT. As these high-carbohydrate meals contained no tryptophan, this finding again presented an intriguing paradox. It was soon recognized that brain tryptophan and 5-HT levels rose in fasted animals because carbohydrate intake stimulated insulin secretion. Insulin decreases plasma levels of the LNAAs by stimulating their uptake into muscle. The one exception is tryptophan, which remains in plasma. As a result of these insulin-induced changes, the plasma ratio of tryptophan to the other LNAAs is greatly increased, and more tryptophan enters the brain to be converted to 5-HT (Figure 12-4).

It is important to note that only a small amount of a high-quality protein such as casein in a meal (approximately 5% of its calories) can block the effects of carbohydrate on brain tryptophan levels (Yokogoshi and Wurtman 1986). In addition, the extent to which a high-carbohydrate meal raises brain tryptophan levels depends on whether other foods are present

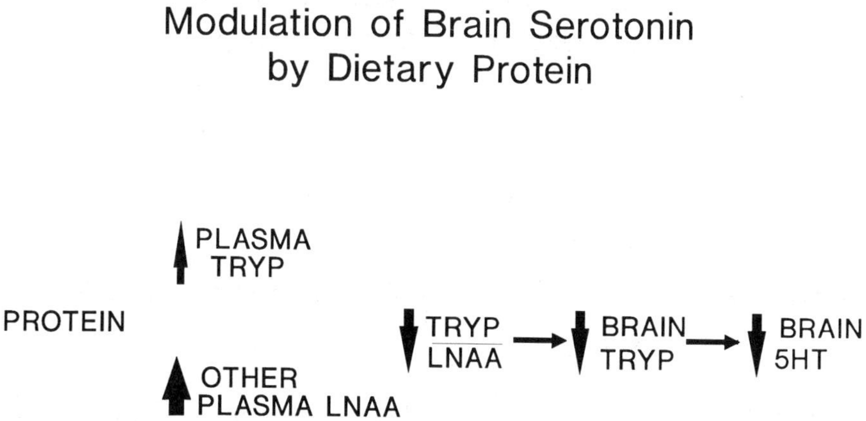

Modulation of Brain Serotonin by Dietary Protein

Figure 12-3. Intake of protein increases plasma levels of the large neutral amino acids (LNAAs) to a greater degree than levels of tryptophan (TRYP) thus decreasing the plasma ratio of TRYP to the other LNAAs. This leads to a decrease in TRYP entering the brain and a potential reduction in serotonin (5HT) synthesis.

in the stomach. For example, if sufficient protein remains in the stomach from a preceding meal, the effects of carbohydrate on brain tryptophan and 5-HT can be blunted.

These findings demonstrate that brain tryptophan and 5-HT are dependent on the ratio of plasma concentration of tryptophan to the sum of the concentration of the other LNAAs, rather than on absolute plasma tryptophan levels. Thus, if blood tryptophan levels rise but those of the other LNAAs do not, brain tryptophan and 5-HT will increase. However, if blood tryptophan remains constant but blood levels of the other LNAAs increase, brain tryptophan and 5-HT will decrease. Finally, if blood levels of both tryptophan and the LNAAs rise equivalently, no change in brain tryptophan and 5-HT will occur (Fernstrom and Wurtman 1971a and b; Fernstrom and Wurtman 1974; Fernstrom 1986; R. J. Wurtman 1987).

Behavioral Consequences of Diet-Induced Changes in Serotonin Synthesis

Serotonin plays a significant role in sleep and arousal, food intake, aggression, and sexual behavior. Serotonergic systems also appear to be important in the mediation of mood. Diet-induced alterations in serotonin could thus modulate these behaviors. There is evidence both supporting and refuting this proposition.

Modulation of Brain Serotonin by Dietary Carbohydrate

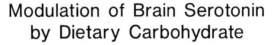

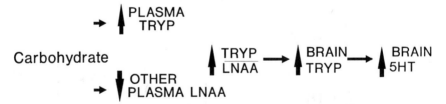

Figure 12-4. Intake of carbohydrate stimulates insulin secretion which decreases plasma levels of the large neutral amino acids (LNAAs) by stimulating their uptake into muscle. The one exception is tryptophan (TRYP) which remains in plasma. This leads to an increase in the plasma ratio of TRYP to the other LNAAs allowing more TRYP to enter the brain, and be converted to serotonin (5HT).

DIET, SEROTONIN, AND SLEEP

Research in experimental animals has established that 5-HT plays an important role in sleep. Manipulations that lower brain 5-HT levels produce insomnia, and those that increase 5-HT levels tend to be soporific. For example, destruction of the neurons of the raphe nuclei (an area of the hypothalamus), which are rich in 5-HT, depresses cerebral levels of 5-HT and significantly reduces sleep in cats (Jouvet 1968). Conversely, giving sufficient tryptophan to increase brain 5-HT by 10% to 20% decreases sleep latency in rats (Leathwood 1986).

Tryptophan also increases sleep in normal humans and has been recommended as a treatment for insomnia. Small doses reduce sleep latency, increase sleep duration, and decrease the frequency of wakenings during sleep in adult men and women (Wyatt et al. 1970; Hartman and Spinweber 1979; Hartman, Spinweber, and Ware 1983; Leathwood 1986). In addition, increasing the tryptophan content of infant formula can prolong sleep time in newborn infants (Yogman 1986).

Given the findings that a high-carbohydrate meal can elevate brain 5-HT, it has been predicted that carbohydrate intake should increase feelings of sleepiness. In support of this prediction, it has been reported that subjects who ate high-carbohydrate meals felt less alert than those who ate high-protein meals. Females characterized themselves as sleepier after consuming carbohydrate meals than after protein meals, and males described themselves as calmer. These effects occurred whether the mealtime was breakfast or lunch, and were not affected by the age of the subjects. These results suggest that mental alertness is lower following a carbohydrate rather than a protein meal perhaps as the result of increased cerebral 5-HT levels (Spring et al. 1986).

ROLE OF SEROTONIN IN FOOD INTAKE AND NUTRIENT SELECTION IN EXPERIMENTAL ANIMALS

There is substantial evidence that serotonergic neurons are important in the regulation of food intake. Treatments that increase the activity of serotonergic neurons consistently lead to reductions in food intake. Conversely, decreases in serotonergic activity have been associated with increases in food consumption (Blundell 1984; Samanin and Garattini 1990).

Serotonergic neurons appear to play a role in macronutrient intake, as well as in overall energy consumption. The evidence for this finding comes from studies examining changes in nutrient choice following experimental alterations in serotonergic systems. The majority of these experiments have assessed the effects of drugs that increase serotonergic activity (e.g., fenfluramine, fluoxetine, and tryptophan) on nutrient intake in rats given a choice of diets containing varying proportions of the macronutrients protein, fat, and carbohydrate. Initial experiments using this paradigm found that increases in 5-HT activity were accompanied by selective reductions in carbohydrate intake. Subsequent research, however, has indicated that a number of independent variables, including the age of the animals, diet composition, and feeding schedule, must be considered when assessing the effects of 5-HT on nutrient choice. When these variables are taken into account, elevations in 5-HT may lead to selective reductions in carbohydrate intake, but this is not a very robust phenomenon (Anderson 1979; Blundell 1984; Kanarek 1987).

It has been assumed that the effects of 5-HT on food intake and diet selection are mediated within the CNS. However, adjustments in food intake may also result from changes in peripheral serotonergic systems. The largest stores of 5-HT are not in the brain, but in the gastrointestinal tract. Modifying peripheral 5-HT, without changing brain levels, can affect feeding behavior. For example, peripheral administration of 5-HT that does not cross the blood-brain barrier inhibits total energy intake and selectively reduces fat intake (Pollack and Rowland 1981; Kanarek 1987). These results indicate that both central and peripheral serotonergic systems must be considered when evaluating the relationship of 5-HT and feeding behavior.

SEROTONIN, FOOD INTAKE, AND NUTRIENT SELECTION IN HUMANS

Extrapolating from research with experimental animals, it has been hypothesized that manipulations that increase serotonergic activity in the CNS should result in reductions in energy intake in our own species. Initial evidence in support of this hypothesis has come from experiments demonstrating that drugs that increase serotonergic activity in the CNS (e.g., fenfluramine) suppress energy intake in obese individuals. Detailed analysis of meal patterns has shown that these drugs control energy consumption by reducing meal size and decreasing the rate of food intake (Silverstone 1981; Nathan and Rolland 1987).

Recent experiments have suggested that in addition to reducing caloric intake, serotonergic drugs may alter nutrient choice. In these experiments, healthy subjects were given unlimited access to a vending machine that provided 8 to 10 different snack foods containing the same number of calories that were rich in either carbohydrate or protein. Snack intake was measured following administration of fenfluramine or a placebo. Relative to the placebo, fenfluramine selectively suppressed intake of the high-carbohydrate snacks (Wurtman and Wurtman 1984; Wurtman, J. J. 1987).

On the basis of the preceding work, it can be concluded that serotonergic neurons are essential in mediating carbohydrate intake, and manipulations that increase brain 5-HT levels may be particularly effective in treating obese individuals who report profound cravings for carbohydrates. Although these conclusions are intriguing, they must be viewed with some skepticism. In these studies, the majority of the high-carbohydrate snacks were higher in fat and generally more palatable than the high-protein snacks. It is thus possible that the primary action of fenfluramine is to reduce fat consumption and/or the intake of palatable foods. Another problem with these studies is that intake of high-protein snacks was negligible when subjects received the placebo. Therefore, it is impossible to determine whether fenfluramine could also reduce protein intake.

Another obvious way of increasing cerebral 5-HT levels is to administer its amino acid precursor, tryptophan. Studies employing this method have found that large doses of tryptophan reduce energy intake in normal-weight individuals. When food intake in these studies was examined for alterations in the selection of a particular nutrient, however, tryptophan had little or no effect. In general, tryptophan led to equivalent reductions in protein and carbohydrate intake (Silverstone and Goodall 1984: Hrboticky, Leiter, and Anderson 1985; Blundell and Hill 1987). The one exception was reported by Blundell and Hill (1987), who observed that when tryptophan was administered with a high-protein meal to normal-weight individuals, it selectively decreased the amount of carbohydrate subsequently consumed.

Thus, data from studies exploring the effects of fenfluramine and tryptophan on feeding behavior support the idea that increases in serotonergic activity are associated with reductions in energy intake in humans. However, they do not provide strong evidence for the proposal that increases in 5-HT lead to selective reductions in carbohydrate intake.

SEROTONIN, DIET, AND MOOD

Over the past 20 years, substantial evidence has accumulated implicating 5-HT in mood disorders. Individuals with these disorders suffer from pervasive and sustained alterations in emotions that, in the extreme, markedly affect their perception of the world. Among this group of mental disorders, major depressive illness, as defined by the American Psychiatric Association (1987), is most commonly encountered in clinical practice. Primary characteristics include a diminished interest or lack of pleasure in all, or almost all activity; sleep disturbances; fatigue or low energy levels; decreased ability to think or concentrate; feelings of worthlessness; disrupted eating patterns; and recurrent thoughts of death or suicide (American Psychiatric Association 1987).

The etiology of depressive illness cannot be explained by a single developmental, social, or biological theory. A variety of factors work together to precipitate the disorder. It does appear, however, that alterations in brain 5-HT contribute to the symptoms of depression in at least some patients. Drugs that decrease serotonergic activity (e.g., reserpine) may produce depressive symptoms, and drugs that increase serotonergic activity (e.g., tricyclic antidepressants or monoamine oxidase inhibitors) are useful in the treatment of depression. Several studies have also found that suicidal depression is related to decreased levels of 5-hydroxyindoleacetic acid (5-HIAA), the major metabolite of 5-HT. Post-mortem levels of 5-HT and 5-HIAA in brain and cerebrospinal fluid are generally reduced in patients who have committed suicide or who had a previous history of suicide attempts before succumbing to other causes. On the basis of these findings, it has been hypothesized that depression is caused, at least in part, by a deficiency of serotonergic activity within the CNS (Wells and Hayes 1989).

During the past 10 years, interest has grown in the potential relationship between some forms of depressive illness and appetitive behavior. One form of depressive illness that has been associated with alterations in feeding behavior is seasonal affective disorder (SAD), which appears in the late fall or early winter and lasts until the following spring. Sufferers complain of episodic bouts of depression, increased need for sleep, and difficulties in concentrating. In addition, many SAD patients report profound cravings for carbohydrate-rich foods. An association between depressive symptoms and a craving for carbohydrates has also been reported in women suffering from premenstrual syndrome and in obese individuals who snack extensively on carbohydrate-rich foods.

It has been suggested that the desire for carbohydrates exhibited by individuals with SAD, PMS, and carbohydrate-craving obesity (CCO) reflects the body's need to increase 5-HT levels. As previously described, intake of pure carbohydrates by experimental animals elevates cerebral 5-HT levels. It has been assumed that a similar process operates in humans, and that individuals suffering from SAD, PMS, or CCO consume excessive carbohydrates because doing so elevates cerebral 5-HT levels and thus leads to positive changes in mood. In support of this assumption, obese carbohydrate cravers reported feeling alert, vigorous, and less depressed after a pure carbohydrate meal. In contrast, obese subjects whose snack choices included protein as well as carbohydrates reported feeling sleepy and fatigued after consuming a pure carbohydrate meal. These differences in mood suggest that the preference or avoidance of carbohydrate snacks may be associated with changes in mood experienced after such snack consumption. Carbohydrate cravers presumably increase the synthesis and release of 5-HT by consuming carbohydrate-rich foods, which leads to an elevation in mood. By eating protein along with the carbohydrate, the noncarbohydrate cravers would prevent changes in serotonergic activity and thus avoid the resulting negative alterations in mood, such as sleepiness and fatigue (Wurtman, J. J. 1987; Wurtman and Wurtman 1989).

The idea that individuals consume foods to modulate mood is intriguing, but it also presents numerous problems. First, an objective definition of excessive carbohydrate intake is not available. The majority of studies addressing the role of carbohydrate consumption on mood have used subjects who defined themselves as carbohydrate cravers. Thus, the designation of carbohydrate craver has been based on the subject's own perception of his or her behavior, rather than on any objective criteria.

A second problem concerns the definition of a high-carbohydrate food. In many cases the foods that a subject defines as high in carbohydrates also contain a substantial amount of fat (e.g., ice cream, cake, and chocolate). Thus, subjects may be considered fat cravers as well as carbohydrate cravers. These foods are also highly palatable, and cravings for them may thus represent the desire for a pleasurable sensory experience rather than for a particular nutrient.

Foods that have been considered to be high in carbohydrates frequently contain some protein. This fact is significant, because it is known that in rats even 5% protein in a high-carbohydrate food can suppress the food's ability to raise brain tryptophan and 5-HT levels. If the same is true in humans, then the assumption that subjects crave these foods because they affect brain 5-HT levels must be seriously questioned (Fernstrom 1988).

Finally, recent physiological data indicate that dietary-induced alterations in the plasma ratio of tryptophan to the other LNAAs may have less effect on brain 5-HT levels and function than previously thought. There is now evidence that serotonergic neurons are equipped with powerful feedback mechanisms, which would limit the effects of alterations in neurotransmitter activity produced by dietary variables. For example, the injection of tryptophan leads to a reduction in the firing of serotonergic neurons, thus counteracting the increased release of serotonin that might otherwise occur. This feedback is probably produced by receptors for 5-HT located on the dendrites and cell body of the serotonergic neuron (Carlsson 1987; Garattini 1989).

Taken together, these problems must lead us to question the idea that the consumption of high-carbohydrate foods by individuals suffering from SAD, PMS, and CCO significantly alters brain 5-HT levels and thus modulates mood.

TRYPTOPHAN-ASSOCIATED EOSINOPHILIA-MYALGIA SYNDROME

Recent reports indicate a potentially serious danger in the use of tryptophan supplements. In the spring of 1989, descriptions of individuals suffering from a previously rare disorder termed eosinophilia-myalgia began appearing. The syndrome is characterized by a relatively sudden onset of symptoms including muscle pain, edema, dermatological problems such as alopecia and indurated skin, and pulmonary difficulties including dyspnea and mild hypoxemia. The disease is often severe, disabling, and chronic. One-third of the patients with the disease have thus far been hospitalized.

Epidemiological studies have revealed that almost all patients with the syndrome were consuming relatively large amounts of tryptophan for conditions such as insomnia, depression, and premenstrual syndrome.

The median dose ingested was 1.5 g per day, approximately two times the intake of the average American. Duration of intake ranged from a few weeks to several years.

The first step in treating this syndrome is clearly to stop taking tryptophan. Muscular symptoms can persist, however, and may even worsen after the use of tryptophan is discontinued. Therapy with corticosteroids has been found somewhat effective in relieving muscle pain and improving the cutaneous symptoms in some patients.

The exact cause of eosinophilia-myalgia is unclear. One possibility is that the tryptophan taken by individuals suffering from this disorder was contaminated during the manufacturing process. However, if a contaminant is responsible for this disorder it has yet to be identified, and the probability of contamination of tryptophan from different sources over a long period of time seems unlikely.

A second possibility is that the syndrome may be caused by an abnormal accumulation of metabolites of tryptophan. Patients who have adverse responses to the amino acid may have defects in tryptophan metabolism that lead to an increase in toxic metabolites when large amounts of the substance are consumed.

Finally, a number of patients who developed eosinophilia-myalgia were also taking antidepressant drugs. Because these drugs inhibit the uptake of serotonin, it is possible that concomitant use with tryptophan may result in the accumulation of tryptophan metabolites. Studies attempting to identify genetic and environmental cofactors that may increase the susceptibility to the disorder are currently being conducted.

To help to eliminate eosinophilia-myalgia, the Food and Drug Administration has banned the distribution and sale of tryptophan-containing dietary supplements (Medsger 1990; Clauw et al. 1990).

CONCLUSION

Research with experimental animals has demonstrated that dietary variables can influence neurotransmitter synthesis. The production and release of the neurotransmitters acetylcholine and serotonin can be stimulated by increasing intake of choline and tryptophan, respectively. Moreover, intake of a pure carbohydrate meal can augment serotonergic activity in the CNS. These findings have led to the hypothesis that the intake of particular nutrients can lead to relatively rapid alterations in behavior. While this hypothesis is intriguing, it remains to be proven. Research examining the role of dietary precursor therapy in humans with neurological and psychological disorders has produced equivocal results at best. Recent work has also indicated that intake of these dietary precursors can have serious side effects. More research is clearly needed before diet therapy can be recommended.

REFERENCES

American Psychiatric Association. 1987. *Diagnostic and Statistical Manual of Mental Disorders, Third Edition, Revised,* pp. 213–233. Washington, D.C., American Psychiatric Association.

Anderson, G. H. 1979. Control of protein and energy intake: Role of plasma amino acids and brain neurotransmitters. *Canadian Journal of Physiology and Pharmacology* 57:1043–1057.

Aquilonius, S. and Eckernas, S. 1977. Choline therapy in Huntington's chorea. *Neurology* 27:887–889.

Bartus, R. T., R. I. Dean, B. Beer, and A. S. Lippa. 1982. The cholinergic hypothesis of geriatric memory dysfunction. *Science* 217:408–417.

Batey, S. R. 1989. Schizophrenic disorders. In *Pharmacotherapy: A Pathophysiological Approach,* ed. J. T. DiPiro et al., pp. 714–728. New York: Elsevier.

Blundell, J. E. 1984. Serotonin and appetite. *Neuropharmacology* 23:1537–1551.

Blundell, J. E. and A. J. Hill. 1987. Influence of tryptophan on appetite and food selection in man. In *Amino Acids in Health and Disease: New Perspectives,* ed. S. Kaufman, pp. 403–419. New York: Alan R. Liss.

Branchey, M. H., L. B. Branchey, N. M. Bark, and M. A. Richardson. 1979. Lecithin in the treatment of tardive dyskinesia. *Communications in Psychopharmacology* 3:303–307.

Carlsson, A. 1987. Commentary. *Integrative Psychiatry* 5:238–239.

Clauw, D. J., D. J. Nashel, A. Umhau, and P. Katz. 1990. Tryptophan-associated eosinophilic connective-tissue disease. *Journal of the American Medical Association* 263:1502–1506.

Cohen, E. L. and R. J. Wurtman. 1976. Brain acetylcholine: Control by dietary choline. *Science* 191:561–562.

Davis, K. L., L. E. Hollister, J. D. Barchas, and P. A. Berger. 1976. *Life Sciences* 19:1507–1516.

Ereshefsky, L., R. Rospond, and M. Jann. 1989. Organic brain syndromes, Alzheimer type. In *Pharmacotherapy: A Pathophysiological Approach,* ed. J. T. DiPiro et al., pp. 678–696. New York: Elsevier.

Fernstrom, J. D. 1981. Effects of precursors on brain neurotransmitter synthesis and brain functions. *Diabetologia* 20:281–289.

Fernstrom, J. D. 1986. Acute and chronic effects of protein and carbohydrate ingestion on brain tryptophan levels and serotonin synthesis. *Nutrition Reviews* 44(Suppl.):25–36.

Fernstrom, J. D. 1988. Tryptophan, serotonin and carbohydrate appetite: Will the real carbohydrate craver please stand up? *Journal of Nutrition* 118:1417–1419.

Fernstrom, J. D. and R. J. Wurtman. 1971a. Brain serotonin content: Physiological dependence on plasma tryptophan levels. *Science* 173:149–152.

Fernstrom, J. D. and R. J. Wurtman. 1971b. Brain serotonin content: Increase following ingestion of carbohydrate diet. *Science* 174:1023–1025.

Fernstrom, J. D. and R. J. Wurtman. 1974. Nutrition and the brain. *Scientific American* 230:84–91.

Garattini, S. 1989. Further comments. *Integrative Psychiatry* 6:235–238.

Gelenberg, A. J., J. C. Doller-Wojcik, and J. H. Growden. 1979. Choline and lecithin in the treatment of tardive dyskinesia: Preliminary results from a pilot study. *American Journal of Psychiatry* 136:772–776.

Gelenberg, A. J., J. Wojcik, W. E. Falk, B. Bellinghausen, and A. B. Joseph. 1989. CDP-choline for the treatment of tardive dyskinesia: A small negative series. *Comprehensive Psychiatry* 30:1–4.

Growden, J. H. 1979. Neurotransmitter precursors in the diet: Their use in the treatment of brain disease. In *Nutrition and the Brain,* vol. 3, ed. R. J. Wurtman and J. J. Wurtman, pp. 117–181. New York: Raven Press.

Growden, J. H., E. L. Cohen, and R. J. Wurtman. 1977. Huntington's disease: Clinical and chemical effects of choline administration. *Annals of Neurology* 1: 418–422.

Growden, J. H., M. J. Hirsch, R. J. Wurtman, and W. Wiener. 1977. Oral choline administration to patients with tardive dyskinesia. *New England Journal of Medicine* 297:524–527.

Growden, J. H., A. J. Gelenberg, J. Doller, M. J. Hirsch, and R. J. Wurtman. 1978. Lecithin can suppress tardive dyskinesia. *New England Journal of Medicine* 298:1029–1030.

Hartman, E. and C. Spinweber. 1979. Sleep induced by l-tryptophan: Effects of dosages within normal dietary intake. *Journal of Nervous and Mental Disorders* 167:497–499.

Hartmann, E., C. Spinweber, and J. C. Ware. 1983. Effect of amino acids on quantified sleepiness. *Nutrition and Behavior* 1:179–183.

Hrboticky, N., L. A. Leiter, and G. H. Anderson. 1985. Effects of L-tryptophan on short-term food intake in lean men. *Nutrition Research* 5:595–600.

Jackson, I. V., E. A. Nuttall, and J. Perez-Cruet. 1979. Treatment of tardive dyskinesia with lecithin. *American Journal of Psychiatry* 136:1458–1459.

Jouvet, M. 1968. Insomnia and decrease of cerebral 5-hydroxytryptamine after destruction of the raphe system in the cat. *Advances in Pharmacology* 6:265–279.

Kanarek, R. B. 1987. Neuropharmacological approaches to studying diet selection. In *Amino Acids in Health and Disease: New Perspectives,* ed. S. Kaufman, pp. 383–401. New York: Alan R. Liss.

Leathwood, P. D. 1986. Neurotransmitter precursors: From animal experiments to human applications. *Nutrition Reviews* 44(Suppl.):193–204.

Medsger, T. A. 1990. Tryptophan-induced eosinophilia-myalgia syndrome. *New England Journal of Medicine* 322:926–927.

Nathan, C. and Y. Rolland. 1987. Pharmacological treatments that affect CNS activity: Serotonin. *Annals of the New York Academy of Sciences* 499:277–296.

Pollack, J. D. and N. Rowland. 1981. Peripherally administered serotonin decreases food intake in rats. *Pharmacology, Biochemistry and Behavior* 15:179–183.

Saminin, R. and S. Garattini. 1990. The pharmacology of serotoninergic drugs affecting appetite. In *Nutrition and the Brain,* vol. 8, ed. R. J. Wurtman and J. J. Wurtman, pp. 163–192. New York: Raven Press.

Silverstone, T. 1981. Clinical pharmacology of anorectic drugs. In *Anorectic Agents Mechanisms of Action,* ed. S. Garattini and R. Samanin, pp. 211–222. New York: Raven Press.

Silverstone, T. and E. Goodall. 1984. The clinical pharmacology of appetite suppressant drugs. *International Journal of Obesity* 8(Suppl. 1):23–33.

Spring, B. J., H. R. Lieberman, G. Swope, and G. S. Garfield. 1986. Effects of carbohydrates on mood and behavior. *Nutrition Reviews* 44(Suppl.):51–60.

Tarsy, D. 1983. History and definition of tardive dyskinesia. *Clinical Neuropharmacology* 6:91–99.

Wecker, L. 1990. Choline utilization by central cholinergic neurons. In *Nutrition and the Brain,* vol. 8, ed. R. J. Wurtman and J. J. Wurtman, pp. 147–162. New York: Raven Press.

Wells, B. G. and P. E. Hayes. 1989. Depressive illness. In *Pharmacotherapy: A Pathophysiological Approach,* ed. J. T. DiPiro et al., pp. 748–764. New York: Elsevier.

Wurtman, J. J. 1987. Excessive carbohydrate snack intake among a class of obese people. *New York Academy of Sciences* 499:197–202.

Wurtman, R. J. 1987. Nutrients affecting brain composition and behavior. *Integrative Psychiatry* 5:226–257.

Wurtman, R. J., F. Hefti, and E. Melamed. 1981. Precursor control of neurotransmitter synthesis. *Pharmacological Reviews* 32:315–335.

Wurtman, J. J. and R. J. Wurtman. 1984. D-fenfluramine selectively decreases carbohydrate but not protein intake in obese subjects. *International Journal of Obesity* 8(Suppl. 1):79–84.

Wurtman, R. J. and J. J. Wurtman. 1989. Carbohydrates and depression. *Scientific American* January:68–75.

Wyatt, R. J., K. Engelman, D. J. Kupfer, D. H. Fram, A. Sjoerdsma, and F. Snyder. 1970. Effects of l-tryptophan (a natural sedative) on human sleep. *Lancet* 2:842–846.

Yogman, M. W. 1986. Nutrients and newborn behavior: Neurotransmitters as mediators? *Nutrition Reviews* 44(Suppl. 1):74–77.

Yokogoshi, H. and R. J. Wurtman. 1986. Meal composition and plasma amino acid ratios: Effects of various proteins on carbohydrate, and of various protein concentrations. *Metabolism* 35:837–842.

13

Obesity

Awareness of the health risks of obesity goes back practically to the beginning of medical science. In the fourth century B.C., Hippocrates observed, "Sudden death is more common in those who are naturally fat than in the lean."

Today, obesity represents a major health problem in affluent Western societies. Excess body weight has been demonstrated to increase the risk of various diseases and is associated with a range of adverse psychological consequences. As a result of both the physiological and psychological sequelae of obesity, weight reduction has become a preoccupation for many people. This preoccupation is evident in the physician's office, in the media, in the grocery store, in bookstores, and in the ever-growing popularity of diet centers, health clubs, and exercise spas. Although some individuals do lose weight, maintaining weight loss over an extended period of time unfortunately has remained for many an impossible dream.

DEFINITION

Obesity may be defined as an excess accumulation of body fat, or adipose tissue, and is diagnosed when adipose tissue accounts for 25% or more of body weight in men and 30% or more in women.

Different techniques have been developed to differentiate obese individuals from those who are simply overweight due to increased lean body mass, such as athletes. Measurements of body density, which involve comparing the weight of subjects submerged in a water tank to their weight on land, provide an extremely accurate method for determining body fat. Because muscle is more dense than fat, it displaces more water than fat. Thus, a muscular individual will have a higher body density than an obese person.

Within the past decade a variety of other methods, including total body water determination, total body electrical conductivity, ultrasound, magnetic resonance imaging, and bioelectric impedance, have been developed to determine body fat content.

Although these techniques provide relatively accurate estimates of total fat and its distribution, their complexity and expense make them impractical for clinical use. Therefore, indirect measures of body fat, including skin-fold thickness and weight in relation to height, are more commonly used to ascertain obesity.

The classic method for indirectly assessing obesity is skin-fold thickness. Approximately half of the fat in the body is found under the skin. The thickness of this subcutaneous layer of fat at various sites, most commonly the biceps on the inside of the arm, the triceps on the outside back of the arm, and the subscapular and supra-iliac regions, is measured using an instrument known as the Harpenden caliper. An average of several measurements is then compared to standards for the individual's age and sex, or incorporated into formulas that provide an estimate of the percentage of total body fat. Although this method of calculating body fat is convenient, it requires substantial skill and training. Another difficulty is that there is no agreement on the number and location of fat sites that most accurately reflect actual body fat content. Moreover, because total body fat can increase with age in sites other than subcutaneous ones, the accumulation of fat in older people may not be taken into account using skin-fold measurements alone.

Although other techniques exist, the measurement of weight in relation to height remains the most frequently used method for assessing obesity. Using these measures, individuals whose body weight is in excess of 120% of their "desirable" weight are considered obese. Life insurance statistics provide the basis for desirable weight, which is defined as the weight, with respect to height and frame size, at which mortality rate is the lowest (Table 13-1). Although these data are usually used to determine obesity, they are inadequate in a number of ways. First, they only reflect data from individuals who can afford to buy insurance, that is, predominantly middle-class Caucasians. In addition, age is not considered a relevant variable. The data generally represent the weights of individuals in their early twenties and thus fail to reflect the fact that weight may gradually increase with age without detrimental effects on mortality rates. Further, these data represent the weight of individuals at the time insurance was purchased, not the weight at the time of death.

An alternative method for determining obesity using weight and height statistics is the body mass index (BMI), or Quetelet index. BMI is defined as body weight measured in kilograms, divided by the square of a person's height measured in meters: $BMI = kg/m^2$. The correlation between BMI and body fat as measured by body density is very high, ranging from 0.7 to 0.8. The normal range for BMI, which coincides with the lowest mortality rates, is between 20 and 24.9. Mortality rates and health risks of obesity begin to increase when the BMI becomes greater than 25 (Bray 1987; Garrow 1988; Pi-Sunyer 1988; Guthrie 1989).

TABLE 13-1. Metropolitan Life Insurance Company Height–Weight Data

Height (in)	Weight (lbs)	
	Men	Women
57		112 (99–128)
59		117 (101–134)
61	131 (123–145)	122 (105–140)
63	135 (127–151)	128 (111–148)
65	140 (131–159)	134 (117–156)
67	146 (135–167)	140 (123–164)
69	152 (139–175)	146 (129–170)
71	159 (145–183)	153 (135–176)
73	166 (150–192)	
75	174 (145–202)	

Source: Metropolitan Life 1983.
Note: Weights for height at which lowest mortality rates occur. The ranges are for all frame sizes (small, medium, and large). The number shown is the midpoint for individuals with medium frames.

PREVALENCE

Thirty-four million Americans, or 26% of the adult population, are at least 20% above their desirable weight. The incidence of obesity increases throughout adulthood, peaking for men in their mid 40s and early 50s, and women in their late 50s and early 60s. After these ages the prevalence of obesity decreases, perhaps because of the higher mortality rate among middle-aged obese adults (Bray 1987; Pi-Sunyer 1988).

Children and adolescents are not immune to obesity. Recent work indicates that obesity in children and adolescents in the United States has increased substantially over the past 20 years. Current estimates indicate that from 6% to 15% of school-age children, and 20% to 30% of adolescents, are overweight (Dietz 1987).

Childhood obesity as a predisposing factor in adult obesity has been widely studied. Although some studies suggest that childhood obesity does not lead to obesity in adulthood, results of other work have found that over 26% of obese infants and children were still obese 20 years later, compared with a rate of 15% that would statistically be expected by chance. It is also estimated that approximately 80% of obese adolescents become obese adults and tend to be fatter than individuals who became obese later in life (Dietz 1987).

PHYSIOLOGICAL ASPECTS

In 1985, a consensus conference convened by the National Institutes of Health (1985) concluded:

> The evidence is now overwhelming that obesity, defined as excessive storage of energy in the form of fat, has adverse effects on health and longevity. Obesity is clearly associated with hypertension, hypercholesterolemia, noninsulin-dependent diabetes mellitus, and excess of certain cancers and other medical problems. . . . Thirty-four million adult Americans have a body mass index greater than 27.8 (men) or 27.3 (women); at this level of obesity, which is very close to a weight increase of 20% above desirable, treatment is strongly advised. When diabetes, hypertension, or a family history for these disorders is present, treatment will lead to benefits even when lesser degrees of obesity are present.

The evidence that obesity can decrease life expectancy came first from life insurance statistics, which clearly indicated that excess weight is related to increased mortality for both men and women. The increase in mortality rate is not linear with increasing weight, but accelerates as people, particularly males, get heavier. Although a direct relationship between obesity and mortality is observed at a young age, this relationship lessens when weight is gained later in life. These findings suggest that it is continuous obesity over many years that adversely affects health and can lead to death (Bray 1987; Pi-Sunyer 1988).

Prospective studies examining the relationship between obesity and disease have explicitly demonstrated that excess weight is a risk factor for diabetes, cardiovascular disease, certain types of cancer, and gallbladder disease.

Diabetes

Obesity is considered the most important "environmental" risk factor in the development of noninsulin-dependent diabetes mellitus (NIDDM). Epidemiological studies encompassing many different geographic areas, races, and cultures have established a direct correlation between increased body weight and the prevalence of NIDDM. Obese individuals are more likely than their lean counterparts to demonstrate glucose intolerance, hyperinsulinemia, insulin resistance, and a decreased number of cellular insulin receptors. Weight reduction leads to normalization of glucose tolerance and insulin function, and its importance for the treatment of NIDDM cannot be emphasized too strongly (Kannel and Gordon 1979; Horton 1981; Olefsky and Kolterman 1981; Bray 1987; Pi-Sunyer 1988).

Cardiovascular Disease

Excess body weight is associated with an increase in many of the risk factors for cardiovascular disease, including hypertension, hypertriglyceridemia, and elevated plasma cholesterol levels. For example, a linear relationship between body weight and blood pressure has been observed in both men and women. Results of the Framingham study, which has followed 5,000 residents of Framingham, Massachusetts, for over three decades, indicate that for every 10% increment in relative weight, systolic blood pressure rises 6.5 mm. Weight loss in hypertensive patients reduces blood pressure, and weight regain elevates pressure.

Abnormalities in blood lipids, including hypertriglyceridemia, elevated plasma cholesterol levels, and an increase in the ratio of low-density lipoproteins to high-density lipoproteins, are frequent concomitants of increased adiposity.

Age may play a role in the relationship between obesity and cardiovascular disease. Obesity early in life (20 to 40 years) appears to have a greater influence on cardiovascular disease than late-onset obesity (Hubert et al. 1983; Bray 1987; Pi-Sunyer 1988; Manson et al. 1990).

The majority of prospective studies on obesity and coronary heart disease have included only men. The results of these studies have suggested that the risk of heart disease does not increase significantly until body weight reaches 20% or more above desirable weight. However, recent work examining the relationship between body weight and cardiovascular disease in 115,886 female American nurses from the ages of 30 to 55 demonstrates that even mild to moderate obesity elevates the risk of coronary heart disease. After adjustment for age and cigarette usage, the risk of both fatal coronary disease and nonfatal myocardial infarction was more than three times higher among women 30% or more above desirable weight than in women approximately 5% below desirable weight. The risk of coronary heart disease was approximately 1.5 times greater in mildly to moderately overweight women, or those 105% to 129% of desirable body weight, than in their leaner colleagues. In contrast to early research, in this study the current level of obesity was a more important determinant of present risk for heart disease than obesity in early adulthood. Further, weight gain during adulthood approximately doubled the risk of coronary disease. These results call into question the idea that a substantial increase in body weight is required before the risk of cardiovascular disease increases, as well as the wisdom of relaxing the standards of desirable weight for people as they age (Manson et al. 1990; VanItallie 1990).

Other Diseases

Obesity is a risk factor for several different types of cancer. Data from the Framingham study reveal that obese men have an elevated rate of colon, rectal, and prostate cancer, and obese women have an increased risk of cancer of the gallbladder, endometrium, cervix, ovaries, and breast (Lew and Garfinkel 1979; Hubert et al. 1983; Schapira et al. 1990).

An association between obesity and gallbladder disease has also been documented. In the Framingham study, the risk of developing gallbladder disease was approximately twice as great in individuals 20% or more above the median weight for their height than in those less than 90% of the median weight for their height. Moreover, obesity increased the risk of dying of gallbladder disease. It has been suggested that elevated cholesterol production and secretion may contribute to the heightened risk of gallbladder disease in the obese. Elevated cholesterol production increases cholesterol concentrations in bile, which enhances the risk of gallstones (Friedman, Kannel, and Dawber 1966; Bray 1987; Pi-Sunyer 1988).

Respiratory problems are also common in obese individuals. Alterations in pulmonary functioning are observed in the massively obese and those in whom obesity and other respiratory or cardiovascular problems are combined. As an individual gains weight, the muscular work required for ventilation increases. If the movement of the chest is sufficiently constricted, hypoventilation and carbon dioxide retention occurs. This condition can lead to lethargy and somnolence (Bray 1987; Pi-Sunyer 1988).

Obesity may also contribute to other health-related problems, including bone and joint disorders, sterility and pregnancy difficulties in women, and varicose veins. Obese people also are more accident prone and suffer a greater risk of complications during surgery.

Body Fat Distribution and the Health Risks of Obesity

The pattern of regional fat distribution may be a more significant factor in determining the health risks of obesity than total body fat. Distribution of fat in the abdominal or upper body region (android obesity) is more closely linked to many of the detrimental consequences of obesity than fat in the buttocks, thighs, or lower body region (gynoid obesity). Android obesity is due primarily to enlarged fat cells in the abdominal region. The size of these fat cells, as compared to fat cells in the gluteal or femoral region, is highly correlated with metabolic variables such as plasma insulin and triglyceride levels.

Men typically exhibit android obesity, whereas women may exhibit either an android or gynoid pattern of fat distribution. This sexual dimorphism in the expression of obesity has been related to the observation that moderately obese men are more likely to develop the metabolic aberrations associated with obesity than are moderately obese women. Moreover, obese women with an android pattern of fat distribution more frequently display metabolic abnormalities, including hyperglycemia and hyperinsulinemia, than those with a gynoid pattern.

One method used to infer body fat distribution is the waist-to-hip ratio (WHR). A high WHR is indicative of android obesity and has been directly related to hyperinsulinemia, impaired glucose tolerance, atherosclerosis, diabetes, and gout. A WHR greater than 1.0 for men and 0.9 for women has been associated with an increased risk of cardiovascular disease even when the body mass index is within the normal range. Recent work has also demonstrated that women with predominantly upper-body obesity have an increased risk of breast cancer when compared to women with lower-body obesity. (Bjorntorp 1987; Sjostrom 1987; Garrow 1988; Tarui et al. 1988; Leibel, Edens, and Fried 1989; Schapira et al. 1990; VanItallie 1990).

The connection between android obesity and the health risks associated with obesity are not yet known. One possible explanation is that abdominal fat, particularly that which accumulates around the visceral organs, may increase free fatty acid release, leading to hypertriglyceridemia, hyperinsulinemia, and insulin resistance. Evaluation for android obesity should be incorporated into regular medical exams. In addition, it should be stressed that caloric restriction, exercise, and consequent weight reduction, if permanently maintained, can decrease abdominal fat distribution and the risk of disease.

PSYCHOLOGICAL CONSEQUENCES

Not only do the obese suffer physiological complications related to excess weight, but they are also the victims of a fairly universal, ingrained disdain for their condition. In Western societies, prejudice against the obese is pervasive and cuts across age, sex, race, and socioeconomic status (Wadden and Stunkard 1987).

Empirical evidence indicates that the obese face discrimination in almost all facets of their lives, ranging from difficulties with admission to the college of their choice to later advancement in the job market. Canning and Mayer (1966), for example, found that obese high school students had lower acceptance rates to prestigious colleges than normal-weight students with equivalent IQ scores, grades, attendance records, and extracurricular activities. Obesity in these young adults was determined by pictures included with their applications and on their appearance at personal interviews.

Obese individuals also face discrimination both in seeking employment and on the job. They are viewed as less desirable than other employees with comparable skills. The extent of job-related discrimination against the obese is impossible to determine, perhaps in part because of the reluctance of employers to discuss their biases. In one study, however, Roe and Eickwort (1976) reported that 16% of employers surveyed stated that they would not hire an obese woman under any circumstances, and another 44% would not hire one under certain circumstances such as when direct contact with customers was required (Mayer 1968; Allon 1982; Wadden and Stunkard 1987).

The societal bias against overweight individuals starts early in life. When children as young as 4 years of age were asked to rate pictures of a normal child, a child with a brace, a child in a wheelchair, a child with a facial disfigurement, and a grossly obese child, they rated the obese child as least desirable. In other studies, children were shown silhouettes of a thin figure, a normal-weight figure, and an obese figure and asked to ascribe behavioral characteristics to each of them. Children consistently ascribed the characteristics such as friendly, kind, happy, and polite to the normal-weight figure. In contrast, the obese figure was described as being lazy, dirty, stupid, and ugly. In the preceding studies, the obese were judged most negatively because the children believed them to be responsible for their own condition. Often, the primary problem of the obese is perceived as being a lack of self-control, which has led to their depiction in the popular media as indiscriminate gluttons (Richardson et al. 1961; Goodman et al. 1963; Kirkpatrick and Saunders 1978).

Obese individuals may perceive their own bodies as grotesque and loathsome, and believe that others view them with contempt and hostility. Among particularly vulnerable groups, such as adolescent girls, even very slight increases in weight above some popular notion of the ideal may be associated with disturbances in body image and feelings of lack of self-worth (see chapter 14). Although the prevalence of obesity among adolescent girls is small, a number of surveys have revealed that a substantial proportion of young women in high school believe they are overweight and make frequent attempts to lose weight (Wadden and Stunkard 1987).

The idea that obesity is primarily the result of overindulgence and a lack of self-control has pervaded our feelings toward the obese for decades. Recent work suggests that obesity may not simply be the result of excess food intake, however, but also due to a variety of metabolic abnormalities. A better understanding of these metabolic parameters could lead to a lessening of the societal biases against the obese.

ETIOLOGY

The basic explanation for weight gain is that over an extended period of time an individual's energy intake exceeds his or her energy expenditure, resulting in energy being stored in the form of adipose tissue (energy storage = energy intake − energy expenditure).

Energy intake refers to food, or caloric, intake. Energy expenditure can be divided into three categories:

- *Basal metabolic rate* is the energy required for the basic maintenance of all the cells of the body. Basal metabolism provides the energy for protein synthesis, brain metabolism, and maintenance of ionic balance across cells, as well as for the contraction of the heart, gastrointestinal, and other continuously functioning muscle groups. Sex, age, body weight, physical condition, climate, and hormonal status influence basal energy expenditure. In addition, basal metabolism may differ by as much as 30% in individuals matched for age, sex, and body weight. This difference may help to explain the observation that at a given fixed energy intake, one person may gain weight while another does not.

- *Physical activity* includes the energy required by the muscles, plus a small amount of energy needed for the concomitant increase in heart rate and breathing that occurs during strenuous activity. The energy cost of physical work depends on body size, as well as the relative strenuousness and duration of the activity. Heavy people utilize more energy than lean ones for the same activity.

- The thermic effect of food, or diet-induced thermogenesis (DIT), refers to the production of heat that results from the ingestion, absorption, and digestion of food. Within one to three hours after consuming a meal, there is a rise in caloric expenditure representing 10% or more of the total calories consumed (Bray 1976; Pi-Sunyer 1988; Guthrie 1989).

Until recently, excess energy intake has been considered to be the primary cause of obesity. However, substantial evidence has accumulated to suggest that alterations in energy expenditure may also play an important role in the development of obesity.

Etiology in Experimental Animals

Studies with experimental animals have revealed many of the factors that can contribute to the development of obesity. In 1953, Jean Mayer divided these factors into three major categories which continue to be useful today:

- *Genetic*
  Single gene, dominant
    Yellow obese mouse
    Adipose mouse
  Single gene, recessive
    ob/ob mouse
    db/db mouse
    Zucker "fatty" rat (fa/fa)
  Polygenic, spontaneously obese
    New Zealand obese mouse
    Japanese mouse
    Wellesley mouse

Polygenic, obesity-prone
Osborne-Mendel rat
Sand rat (*Psammomys obesus*)
Spiny mouse (*Acomys cahirinus*)

- *Traumatic*
Neural
Ventromedial hypothalamic lesions
Paraventricular lesions
Midbrain lesions
Endocrine
Chronic insulin administration
Chronic glucocorticoid treatment

- *Environmental*
Physical restraint
Stress-induced
Nutritional
Force-feeding
Meal-feeding
High-fat diets
High-sugar diets
Cafeteria diets

Obesity can develop in experimental animals primarily as a consequence of genetic variables. Genetically obese rodents have been divided according to mode of inheritance into single gene, dominant; single gene, recessive; and polygenic strains. Among the genetic models, the greatest attention has been paid to the ob/ob mouse and the Zucker fatty rat. In both of these animals, obesity results from an abnormality in a single, recessive gene. Some characteristics of these animals are hyperphagia, hyperinsulinemia, adipocyte hypertrophy and hyperplasia, and abnormalities in lipid metabolism. Moreover, these animals display increased feed efficiency (weight gain per kilocalories consumed), and thus gain more weight than leaner rats, even when given equivalent amounts of food (Bray 1976).

Traumatic factors, including damage to the central nervous system, manipulations of the endocrine system, and pharmacological treatments, can also lead to obesity in experimental animals. Animals whose obesity is associated with destruction of the portion of the central nervous system known as the ventromedial hypothalamus (VMH) have dominated research. It has been hypothesized that the VMH normally acts to bring about cessation of food intake, and/or to set the upper limit for body weight. Damage to this area is accompanied by hyperphagia, increased feed efficiency, finicky eating behavior, adipocyte hypertrophy, hyperinsulinemia, and a reduction in dietary-induced thermogenesis (Bray 1976; Himms-Hagen 1989).

Environmental variables, including physical restraint, stress, and nutritional manipulations, can also produce obesity in experimental animals. Over the past decade, environmental models in which dietary factors promote excess energy intake and subsequent weight gain have caught the attention of many investigators. These models are particularly attractive because they are believed to mirror the human condition. Like humans, animals are sensitive to the obesity-promoting effects of certain foods and gain weight when offered diets high in fat or sugar, or an unlimited variety of highly palatable foods (cafeteria diets) (Kanarek and Marks-Kaufman 1988; Kanarek and Orthen-Gambill 1988).

Etiology of Human Obesity

FOOD INTAKE

For many years, gluttony was assumed to be the primary cause of obesity in humans. It was believed the obese suffered from inadequate self-control and that with additional will power they could lose weight. It was also proposed that the eating style of the obese differed from that of normal-weight individuals and that the obese could lose weight if taught to eat like the nonobese. The "obese eating style" was characterized by larger than normal meals, a rapid rate of food intake with large bites, decreased feelings of satiety, and an increased responsiveness to external food-related cues such as palatability.

Direct evidence for an obese eating style has proven to be very elusive. The original proposition that obesity was the consequence of maladaptive eating habits was based on clinical impressions rather than on experimental data. During the last twenty years, research has revealed that although some overweight people's eating habits are in accordance with an obese eating style, this is not universally the case. Indeed, researchers have been able to find very few, if any, undisputable differences between the eating patterns of obese and normal-weight individuals (Kanarek et al. 1984).

Although obesity certainly can result from overeating, metabolic factors also play an important role in the development of excess body fat. The first evidence for this finding came from studies comparing food intake in individuals with similar body weights and activity levels. In a study in England using this method, Rose and Williams (1961) found significant differences in caloric intakes between pairs of men matched on the basis of body weight and activity. In fact, in some pairs, the daily caloric intake necessary to maintain the normal body weight of one man was twice that of the other.

Further evidence of the variability in individuals' abilities to use calories comes from studies at the University of Vermont designed to produce experimental obesity in humans by overfeeding (Sims et al. 1973). Substantial differences in subjects' potential for weight gain were observed.

Some individuals easily gained weight when fed twice their normal daily caloric intake, and others, eating just as much, had difficulty gaining weight and never became obese.

These studies indicate that weight gain is not a necessary consequence of gastronomic indiscretion. The logical question that arises from these studies is, "What metabolic parameters might contribute to the development of obesity?" In the following sections, some of the metabolic parameters currently under investigation are reviewed.

DIET-INDUCED THERMOGENESIS

Recent studies have suggested that differences in DIT may contribute to the variability observed among individual capacities for weight gain. DIT includes two components: *obligatory thermogenesis,* which includes the energy needed to digest, absorb, and process or store nutrients; and *facultative thermogenesis,* which represents any additional energy expenditure not accounted for by obligatory thermogenesis.

Research with experimental animals indicates that facultative DIT occurs, at least in part, in brown adipose tissue (BAT), which is a specialized organ located primarily in the interscapular and paraspinal regions. BAT gets both its name and its characteristic brown color from its unusually large number of mitochondria, which have a high concentration of iron-containing cytochrome pigments. BAT is well suited for a role in thermogenesis, because these mitochondria are the major sites of heat production in the cell. In addition, BAT is richly supplied with blood vessels that are capable of extremely high rates of blood flow when stimulated, allowing heat produced by BAT to be rapidly conveyed to other organs of the body. Brown adipocytes are directly innervated by the sympathetic nervous system (Himms-Hagen 1989).

Initial evidence of BAT's role in the control of body weight came from studies demonstrating that rats fed a cafeteria diet outgained control animals given a standard laboratory diet, but did not gain as much weight as would be predicted from their excess caloric intake. Since the laws of thermodynamics have yet to be disproved, the excess calories that the cafeteria-fed rats did not store must have been expended as energy. Subsequent experiments revealed that BAT increased in size and metabolic activity in cafeteria-fed animals, leading to the hypothesis that the excess calories consumed by these animals were dissipated as heat in BAT (Rothwell and Stock 1979).

Further support for a role of BAT in the management of body weight has come from studies demonstrating deficits in DIT and BAT metabolism in a number of animals with experimental obesity. It has been proposed that the excess accumulation of body fat in these animals, which occurs even when they consume equivalent amounts of food to their normal-weight counterparts, may be associated with decreased functioning in BAT (Himms-Hagen 1989).

Intrigued by the preceding findings, experimenters have began to examine the role of DIT in human obesity. Although some studies suggest that a deficit in DIT may contribute to excess weight in humans, the results of other work do not support this conclusion. In 16 studies investigating the thermogenic response to a meal or single nutrient, 10 reported a decreased thermogenic response in obese subjects; however, 6 showed similar responses in normal-weight and obese subjects. These discrepant results suggest that there may be subgroups of obese individuals with a deficit in DIT, whereas other obese individuals may have a normal thermogenic response to food intake. Recent data suggest that obese individuals with marked insulin resistance are more likely to have a low thermogenic response than obese individuals who are not insulin-resistant (Jequier 1987).

The contribution of BAT to deficits in DIT in humans remains controversial. Although some investigators have argued that adult humans do not have sufficient amounts of BAT to produce excess heat, more recent work has demonstrated that BAT is present in humans of all ages. Additional work is now needed to determine the functional activity of BAT in adults and potential differences in BAT functioning between normal-weight and obese individuals (Himms-Hagen 1989).

LIPOPROTEIN LIPASE

Adipose tissue lipoprotein lipase (LPL) is an enzyme in adipose tissue that may be important for the regulation of body weight. LPL modulates the uptake of circulating plasma triglycerides by adipocytes. The enzyme enhances the breakdown of triglycerides to free fatty acids and glycerol phosphate. These smaller molecules can then be taken up by adipose cells and stored as triglycerides. Adipose tissue LPL is elevated in obesity. When LPL activity is measured per cell, it directly correlates with fat cell size and with percent of desirable weight.

Whether elevated LPL is a primary cause of obesity, or a consequence of the obese state, is unknown. Obese individuals could have increased LPL as a primary defect that amplifies their ability to "pull" triglycerides into adipose cells, or obesity could develop from some other cause with the enhanced LPL activity secondary to enlarged fat cells.

It has been hypothesized that if LPL is a causative factor in obesity, LPL activity should increase with weight loss and return to lower (although elevated) values with weight regain. The elevation of LPL with weight loss would enhance lipid clearance from the plasma and increase stored triglyceride levels in fat cells. Thus, the obese condition would be restored. Results of experiments testing this hypothesis have not been consistent. When LPL has been measured in obese subjects after fasting, an increase in the activity of the enzyme has consistently been observed. However, conflicting data have been obtained on the effects of weight loss on LPL activity. Some studies have shown an increase in LPL activity in fasting subjects who have lost weight, while others have found no change or a reduction in activity (Schwartz and Brunzell 1978; Eckel and Yost 1987; PiSunyer 1988; Kern et al. 1990).

LPL activity rapidly increases above prebaseline levels following refeeding in fasted subjects. This change may enhance the fat cells' capacity for storing circulating triglycerides. The rise in LPL activity may thus contribute to the efficient weight regain that occurs with refeeding in obese patients who were previously on a low-calorie diet (PiSunyer 1988).

Genetic Predisposition

It has long been hypothesized that genetic predisposition is a factor in the development of human obesity. Early as well as more recent studies have demonstrated that childhood obesity is much more common when one or both parents are obese than when both parents are lean (e.g., Angel 1949; Gurney 1936). More recently, Price and colleagues (1990) assessed the risk for obesity in 1,743 first-degree relatives (parents and siblings) of 566 obese individuals at three locations in the United States and one in Argentina. Adult patients whose obesity began in childhood had a greater number of obese first-degree relatives than those whose obesity began later in life. In addition, higher levels of obesity were associated with increased familial risk. These data were taken as evidence for a genetic predisposition toward obesity.

The problem with this type of data is, of course, that parents and children share not only genes, but also bed and board. Thus, it impossible to determine if the similarity in body weight between parents and children is attributable to heredity or environment.

Adoption studies have been used to help separate the effects of heredity from environmental factors. The rationale behind these studies is that the resemblance of adopted children to their biological parents can only be attributed to genetic variables, and the resemblance to their adopted parents can only be credited to environmental factors. Unfortunately, the results of adoption studies have not been consistent. Although some have demonstrated a higher correlation in body weight between biological parents and children than between adoptive parents and children, others have not (Foch and McClearn 1980).

Stunkard and co-workers (1986) have noted that these adoption studies have been handicapped by limited or nonexistent information on the weight status of the biological parents, and the failure to explore the entire range of body weight. To address these handicaps, Stunkard et al. (1986)

used the data base of the Danish Adoption Register, which contains extensive information about biological as well as adoptive parents. A questionnaire that included items on weight and height was mailed to over 4,600 adoptees, of which 3,580 provided complete responses. From this population, a sample of 540 adult adoptees were selected and divided into four weight classes: thin, medium-weight, overweight, and obese. A direct relation between the BMI and weight class of biologic parents and children was observed, while no relation between the BMI of adoptive parents and the weight class of adoptees was found. These results suggest that genetic influences are more important in determining degree of obesity than the family environment.

Confirmation of the role of genetic variables in obesity comes from studies comparing body weight in identical and fraternal twins reared together or apart. In the most complete study of this type, Stunkard et al. (1990) compared BMI in 154 pairs of identical twins reared together, 93 pairs of identical twins reared apart, 208 pairs of fraternal twins reared together, and 218 pairs of fraternal twins reared apart. The results of this study again provided strong evidence of the influence of heredity on BMI. The correlation in body weight of identical twins reared apart was extremely high, and only slightly lower than for twins reared together. The correlation of BMI between identical twins also was more than twice that of fraternal twins, regardless of whether the twins were reared together or apart.

The exact role of genetics in the development of obesity remains unknown. However, genetic differences in metabolic rate may be involved. For example, Griffith and Payne (1976) observed that normal-weight children of obese parents have a lower metabolic rate than normal-weight children of lean parents. In addition, other studies have demonstrated that metabolic rate at a young age predicts later BMI, and that metabolic rate is strongly familial (Bogardus et al. 1988; Ravussin et al. 1988; Roberts et al. 1988).

To further assess the possible role of genetics in response to overfeeding and the development of obesity, Bouchard and colleagues (1990) examined the effects of excess caloric intake on body weight and composition in 12 pairs of identical twins. After determining baseline caloric intake, subjects were overfed by 1,000 kcal per day for 84 days. During overfeeding, the similarity within each twin pair with respect to body weight, percentage of fat, and estimated subcutaneous fat was significant, but the similarity between pairs was not. Within-pair similarity was particularly evident with respect to changes in regional fat distribution and amount of abdominal visceral fat. Bouchard and co-workers (1990) concluded that an individual's genotype is an important determinant of adaptation to a sustained energy surplus.

Although the results of the preceding studies indicate a strong genetic component for obesity, they should not lead to pessimism about prevention and treatment of the disorder. Rather, this knowledge may foster better strategies for weight control and help to focus prevention efforts more specifically toward genetically vulnerable persons (Price et al. 1990).

TREATMENT

A 1990 Congressional report has determined that 65 million Americans spend $33 billion a year trying to lose weight. Diet foods, diet books, weight loss clinics, diet pills, and liquid diets are only some of the places our money goes. With all of these attempts at weight loss, however, 80% to 90% of those people who lose 25 pounds or more gain it back within two years. The following section discusses some of the treatments for obesity and their potential for success.

Surgery

Surgical treatment represents a radical form of therapy and generally is only recommended for the severely obese (100% or more overweight). Introduced in the early 1950s, surgery has significantly changed the potential for persons suffering from severe obesity to maintain large weight losses for extended periods of time (Bray 1976; Stunkard 1984; Hall et al. 1990).

The first extensively used surgical procedure for obesity was the *jejunoileal bypass,* in which the absorptive surface of the small intestine is reduced to approximately 18 inches. The rationale for this surgery was based on the idea that if the small intestine were reduced in length there would be decreased absorption of nutrients and therefore a reduction in body weight. Jejunoileal surgery proved to be very successful, with weight loss typically ranging from 70 to 200 pounds. It is interesting that weight loss following surgery resulted not only from a decrease in intestinal absorption of nutrients, but also from a reduction in food intake. It has been estimated that reduction of food intake accounted for 60% to 75% of the weight loss observed in patients with jejunoileal bypasses. Surgery also led to a normalization of eating patterns. Prior to surgery, many patients reported chaotic patterns of excessive food intake, but afterward, they showed marked changes in eating patterns; the number of meals per day decreased, as did binging, snacking, meal size, cravings for sweets, and eating in response to anger or depression. Moreover, the subjects reported an increased craving for fruits and vegetables. Further benefits of the surgery included amelioration of many of the medical complications of obesity and positive changes in psychosocial functioning, including improvements in mood, activity level, self-esteem, job status, and assertiveness (Mills and Stunkard 1976; Solow 1977; Bray 1980; Stunkard 1984).

While there were many positive aspects of intestinal bypass surgery, severe complications were not uncommon. Most significant, the overall mortality rate of the procedure ranged from 3% to 4%. The two main causes of mortality were pulmonary embolism, which generally occurred shortly after surgery, and liver disease, which tended to occur months to years subsequent to surgery. All patients who underwent jejunoileal bypass surgery experienced diarrhea, which was particularly severe during the early postoperative period and was frequently accompanied by loss of electrolytes through the stool. Potassium loss was marked and sometimes was associated with symptoms of weakness. If diarrhea was severe, loss of calcium and magnesium could also be significant, with tetany, or muscle spasms, reported in a number of patients. Other complications of this procedure included incisional hernias, pancreatitis, increased urinary stone formation, renal failure, gallstones, hypoproteinemia, and loss of bone mineral content (Bray 1980; Quaade 1981).

Because of these complications, intestinal bypass surgery has been replaced by a number of *gastric restriction* procedures, in which the size of the stomach is severely restricted so that only small amounts of food can be consumed at one time. In general, the volume of the stomach is reduced from 125 ml to approximately 25–50 ml, and the passageway from this restricted area of the stomach to the intestine is reduced from 5.0 cm to no more than 1.2 cm in diameter. These procedures result in substantial weight loss, with patients one year following surgery averaging a 30% to 35% decrease from their baseline weight. The smaller stomach and delay in gastric emptying resulting from these procedures is associated with a sensation of satiety after smaller than normal meals. Alterations in food preferences have also been noted following gastric restriction. Patients report significantly less liking for high-density fatty foods such as meats, butter, potato chips, and refined carbohydrates such as candies and sweetened drinks (Kenler, Brolin, and Cody 1990).

As with jejunoileal bypass, gastric restriction has been associated with positive changes in psychological functioning. Many patients experience increased feelings of self-confidence, as well as a sense of elation and well-being. Body image disturbances may also improve following gastric restriction. Before surgery, a majority of patients described their bodies as undesirable and loathsome, whereas subsequent to surgery, less than 5% reported severe negative body image.

Weight loss after gastric restriction also has beneficial effects on obesity-related conditions including diabetes, blood lipid levels, and respiratory difficulties.

Although gastric restriction is a more benign procedure than jejunoileal bypass, it is not without difficulties. Overall mortality is estimated to be approximately 1%. Complications include vomiting, reflux esophagitis, stomach ulcers, and anastomotic leaks with subsequent peritonitis (Halmi 1980; Halmi et al. 1981; Quaade 1981; Hall et al. 1990).

Another method used to reduce stomach volume has been the *intragastric balloon*. A balloon is inserted into the stomach and then inflated to reduce gastric capacity. While the balloon is inflated, food intake is reduced, and significant weight loss occurs; however, when the balloon is deflated, weight gain is typical. Numerous complications such as vomiting, nausea, ulcers, gastric perforations, and intestinal obstructions have been reported in patients with intragastric balloons. As a result the use of intragastric balloons has declined sharply. (Munro et al. 1987; Morrow and Mona 1990).

Jaw wiring has also been employed to prevent mastication, and therefore the ingestion of solid, but not liquid foods. Patients who undergo this procedure can be expected to lose approximately 2 kg per month after an initial rapid weight loss lasting for a month. Generally, jaw wiring for obesity continues for six to eight months. When the wires are removed, however, weight gain is not uncommon. Indeed, even with an extensive follow-up program including dietary counseling, behavior modification, and exercise, the overall weight loss of individuals who have undergone jaw wiring is no better than that achieved by those who did not experience surgery but otherwise received the same treatment program (Munro et al. 1987).

Lipectomy, or surgical removal of adipose tissue primarily from the abdominal region, and *liposuction,* which consists of suctioning off subcutaneous fat, have also been suggested as a potential treatment for obesity. However, these procedures do not remove enough adipose tissue to significantly reduce weight. In addition, the safety of these procedures has come into question.

Pharmacological Treatment

Throughout the years, many pharmacological approaches to the treatment of obesity have been tried. Most early pharmacological agents worked by reducing energy intake. Specifically, these drugs acted to reduce hunger, stimulate satiety, or block the absorption of calories. More recently, observations that abnormalities in energy expenditure may be associated with obesity have led to the development of drugs designed to stimulate energy expenditure in obese individuals (Table 13-2).

Several criteria have been proposed for the ideal anti-obesity drug:

1. A sustained loss of weight through a reduction in body fat with a sparing of body protein.

2. Maintenance of the weight loss once a desirable body weight has been achieved.

TABLE 13-2. Some Pharmacological Agents Proposed for the Treatment of Obesity

Drug	Trade Name	Mechanism of Action
Prescription		
D,L-amphetamine	Benzedrine℡	Appetite suppressant
D-amphetamine	Dexedrine℡	Appetite suppressant
Fenfluramine	Ponderal℡	Appetite suppressant
Mazindol	Sanorex℡	Appetite suppressant
Diethylpropion	Tenuate℡	Appetite suppressant
Clortermine	Voranil℡	Appetite suppressant
Over-the-counter		
Phenylpropanolamine (PPA)	Acutrim℡ Dexatrim℡	Appetite suppressant
Experimental		
Cholecystokinin (CCK)		Appetite suppressant
Opioid Antagonists		Appetite suppressant
Chlorocitric Acid		Appetite suppressant, inhibit gastric emptying
Acarbose		Inhibit dietary carbohydrate absorption
BRL 26830A		Stimulate energy expenditure
Ro 16-8714		Stimulate energy expenditure
LY 104119		Stimulate energy expenditure

3. Improved compliance with a weight reduction program of diet and exercise.

4. Absence of side effects or abuse liability when the drug is chronically administered.

Unfortunately, no pharmacological agent meets all of these criteria (Sullivan 1987).

The majority of drugs used in the treatment of obesity are appetite suppressants, which act to reduce hunger. The first widely marketed appetite suppressant, or anorectic drug, was amphetamine, a central nervous system stimulant that acts by increasing the activity of the neurotransmitters norepinephrine and dopamine.

Amphetamine's potential as a weight-reducing agent was first noted in 1937, when it was observed that patients treated with the drug for depression or narcolepsy lost weight. Initially, it was believed that amphetamine produced its effects on body weight by increasing activity, but it was soon demonstrated that its primary action with respect to weight control was to decrease food intake. Studies have indicated that amphetamine decreases subjective feelings of hunger and inhibits the onset of eating. On the basis of these findings, it has been proposed that the drug acts to decrease sensations of hunger (Silverstone 1981).

Although amphetamine can lead to substantial weight loss, it is far from being an ideal drug. It has a wide variety of side effects including restlessness, irritability, cardiovascular excitation, insomnia, and confusion, and chronic use may lead to panic states and paranoid delusions. Moreover, tolerance to its anorectic actions and physical dependence on amphetamine develop rapidly, and addiction to the drug is not uncommon. As a result, amphetamine is no longer a recommended treatment for obesity (Blundell 1980; Weintraub and Bray 1989).

Over the past two decades, a number of other drugs have been prescribed for the treatment of obesity (Table 13-3). One of the most well studied and currently widely promoted drugs is fenfluramine, which acts to increase the activity of the neurotransmitter serotonin. In comparison to patients given a placebo, patients taking fenfluramine displayed a significantly greater rate of weight loss, which was maintained for as long as three months. In contrast to amphetamine, which reduces feelings of hunger, fenfluramine is believed to enhance feelings of satiety. Following the administration of fenfluramine, subjects began to eat at the same time as controls, but stopped eating sooner. The drug may also decrease rate of eating, as well as snacking behavior (Nathan and Roland 1987).

In contrast to amphetamine, fenfluramine does not stimulate the central nervous system. It does, however, produce a number of side effects including drowsiness, lethargy, diarrhea, and depression. Although tolerance to the anorectic properties of fenfluramine has been reported, physical dependence and addiction to the drug have not been documented.

Recently a number of neuroendocrine substances have been examined for their usefulness in treating obesity. Most notable of these is cholecystokinin (CCK), a polypeptide that is released from the small intestine during the ingestion of a meal. Research with experimental animals, including mice, rats, pigs, sheep, and monkeys, has clearly demonstrated that CCK reduces food intake and elicits a behavioral state of satiety.

Studies of the effects of CCK on food intake in humans have proven promising. CCK reduces food intake in normal and moderately obese subjects without significant side effects. One of the more interesting aspects of CCK's effects on food intake in humans is that subjects did not appear to perceive that they had eaten less nor did they report that they were less satisfied with the test meal. In addition, after eating a smaller lunch-time meal following CCK administration, subjects did not snack more often in the afternoon and did not eat their evening meal sooner than after a normal sized meal.

Despite these encouraging results, significant obstacles to the therapeutic use of CCK include the shortage of data on the efficacy and safety of chronically administered CCK, and the lack of information on its ability to produce long-term weight loss in humans (Gibbs 1985; Smith and Gibbs 1988). In addition, CCK is not active when given orally and must be given by injection.

Recent work with experimental animals suggests that the endogenous opioid peptide system may be associated with the overeating and weight gain seen in some forms of experimental obesity. Evidence for this suggestion comes from the observations that drugs that mimic the activity of the endogenous opioids (opioid agonists) increase food intake, and those that block the actions of these compounds (opioid antagonists) inhibit feeding behavior. Moreover, opioid antagonists (e.g., naloxone and naltrexone) are more effective in reducing food intake in obese animals than in normal-weight controls (Kanarek and Marks-Kaufman 1990).

The action of opioid antagonists on food intake in experimental animals has led to the proposal that these agents might be useful in the treatment of human obesity. In support of this proposal, some investigators have reported that opioid antagonists do reduce food intake in lean and obese individuals. In addition, these drugs can decrease thinking about food and feelings of hunger (e.g., Atkinson 1982; Spiegel et al. 1987; Wolkowitz et al. 1988). Although these results suggest that opioid antagonists might be useful for the treatment of obesity, it should be noted that other researchers have failed to observe reductions in food intake following the administration of these drugs. Moreover, research assessing the chronic effects of opioid antagonists on body weight has found that they did not result in greater weight loss than a placebo. A further problem with these drugs is that on an acute basis, high doses can lead to nausea and abdominal cramps, while on a chronic basis, liver abnormalities develop in some patients (e.g., Atkinson et al. 1985; Maggio et al. 1985; Malcolm et al. 1985; Mitchell et al. 1987).

All of the pharmacological agents discussed thus far act primarily as appetite suppressants. As previously mentioned, recent evidence suggests that impairments in diet-induced thermogenesis may also contribute to the development of obesity. As a result, pharmacological stimulation of thermogenesis has become a target of research into anti-obesity agents. Three thermogenic agents have recently been developed. Still in the experimental stage, these drugs are known only by their code names, Ro 16-8714, BRL 26830A, and LY 104119. All three drugs stimulate BAT thermogenesis, enhance lipolysis, and promote weight loss in genetically obese rodents. Clinical evaluations have confirmed the thermogenic effects of Ro 16-8714 and BRL 26830A in human subjects; however, at doses of Ro 16-8714 that increased thermogenesis, heart rate became elevated. In addition, although administration of BRL 26830A resulted in weight loss in one study with obese humans, it failed to do so in a second study (Sullivan, Hogan, and Triscari 1987; Himms-Hagen 1989).

Although drugs may be useful in the treatment of obesity, it is important to remember that other therapies, such as diet, exercise, and modification of eating habits, must be used in conjunction with drugs. As with many of the treatments for obesity, long-term maintenance of weight loss with pharmacological agents has so far proven illusive.

Dietary Approaches

For the majority of obese and overweight individuals, dieting represents the primary strategy for weight loss. Dietary approaches to weight loss generally take one of three forms: starvation, very low-calorie diets, and conventional reducing diets. With starvation (fasting), 1.5 to 2.5 kg per week may be lost; however, there is a fundamental flaw in this approach. Excess weight is gained approximately in the proportion of 75% fat to 25% lean body mass. In contrast, weight loss by starvation is in the ratio of 50% fat to 50% lean body mass. Therefore, although individuals may return to normal weight by fasting, they will not return to a normal body composition. A second obvious problem with starvation diets is that they do not allow the individual to learn new eating habits. Once the starvation regime ceases, old patterns of eating resume, and the weight is regained (Stunkard 1984; Garrow 1988; Pi-Sunyer 1988).

Very low-calorie diets (VLCDs) have become a popular form of treatment for the moderately obese, or those 41% to 100% overweight. This dieting approach is an attempt to attain rapid weight loss without a change in body composition. There are two types: the protein-sparing modified fast, and the powdered protein formula diet. The protein-sparing modified fast provides from 400 to 700 calories a day, largely or exclusively protein in the form of lean meat, fish, or fowl. The formula diet consists of a protein source of high biological value, such as milk or eggs, carbohydrate, and the recommended daily allowances for vitamins and minerals. Each form of VLCD is proposed to have certain advantages. The protein-sparing modified fast is less disruptive of social eating and is associated with less hunger, and the formula diet is easier to prepare and removes the temptation of conventional foods.

In contrast to earlier liquid protein diets, which were associated with a number of fatalities, the VLCDs appear to be safe when carefully administered under medical supervision for periods of not more than three months.

On a short-term basis, VLCDs are very effective. Data from a number of studies indicate an average weight loss of 20 kg over 12 weeks. The long-term effectiveness of these diets is limited, however. It is becoming evident that few people who lose large amounts of weight on these diets are able to maintain the weight loss when they resume eating normal food.

Studies typically show that approximately two-thirds of the initial weight loss is regained over one year. Moreover, side effects such as orthostatic hypotension, hair loss, dry skin, fatigue, cold intolerance, and constipation have been reported. A final drawback is that because of the necessity of extensive medical supervision, VLCDs tend to be very expensive, ranging from $2,500 to $3,500 for a three-month period (Stunkard 1984; Apfelbaum, Fricker, and Igoin-Apfelbaum 1987; Bracciale 1988; Garrow 1988; Pi-Sunyer 1988; Wilson 1990).

VLCDs are not recommended for mildly obese persons; (20 to 40% overweight); instead, a diet containing from 800 to 1,200 kilocalories per day is more often prescribed. A cursory look at the nutrition section in bookstores and libraries, or at popular magazines, reveals an enormous number of diets from which to choose, and which vary substantially with respect to nutritional makeup and value. Many popular diets emphasize intake of one specific dietary constituent and thus may be nutritionally imbalanced. Other diets, based on counting calories, allow a wider range of foods, and are nutritionally more balanced; however, they may also be more difficult to follow because they require careful monitoring of portion size.

The following general criteria for a nutritionally adequate diet can lead to steady and reasonable weight loss, and a good possibility of long-term success (Stunkard 1984; Guthrie 1989). The diet must

- Be deficient in kilocalories, as determined by comparing its caloric value with an a estimate of the person's needs. A diet that is deficient in kilocalories for one person may not necessarily be deficient for another.
- Be adequate in all other nutrients except kilocalories.
- Have sufficient fat or bulk to provide for feelings of satiety.
- Be adaptable to family meals, and easily followed when eating out.
- Be reasonable in cost.
- Be able to be followed for a sufficient period of time to achieve the desired weight loss.
- Provide a new set of eating habits that can help maintain the weight loss over time.

In summary, a sensible dieting plan should be one that can be incorporated into the individual's life-style. Good diets emphasize changes in what, how much, and how often one eats, in addition to a regular program of physical activity. Although quick-fix diets with "magic" foods, pills, or devices may lead to rapid weight loss, these results are usually temporary and lead to an even faster rebound in weight gain.

YO-YO DIETING

Many dieters successfully lose weight, but few are able to maintain this loss for an extended period of time. It is estimated that 80% to 90% of people who lose weight will regain it within five years. The failure to maintain weight loss on a long-term basis is called "yo-yo dieting," that is, repeated cycles of weight loss and gain. Clinical observations and personal reports of people who have a pattern of yo-yo dieting indicate that weight loss may become more difficult with each successive diet. On the basis of these observations, it has been hypothesized that repeated dieting may lead to a metabolic slowdown that makes the body more efficient at fat utilization and storage over time.

The first study testing this hypothesis was conducted with experimental animals. Adult rats were fed a high-fat diet and became obese, and were then given a restricted amount of food until they returned to normal weight. This pattern of weight gain and loss was subsequently repeated. During the first cycle, it took obese rats 21 days to lose their excess weight. During the second cycle, it took them 46 days to lose the same amount of weight. Significant differences in weight gain were also noted. In the first cycle, the rats needed 45 days to reach their obese weight, whereas in the second cycle they regained the weight in only 14 days. Thus, weight loss was two times slower, and regain three times faster, during the second cycle of yo-yo diet than during the first (Brownell et al. 1986).

Recent work with human outpatients undergoing a protein-sparing modified fast for a second time has provided support for the idea that repeated dieting can alter metabolic efficiency. These patients had a slower rate of weight loss, 2.1 lbs per week, during their second dieting experience than during their first, when they lost 3.1 lbs per week. Similar results were observed in a group of hospitalized inpatients whose food intake was carefully controlled (Blackburn et al. 1989).

Additional evidence of the potentially detrimental effects of yo-yo dieting comes from work demonstrating a significant positive correlation between waist-to-hip ratio and frequency of cycles of weight loss and gain. These data suggest that the practice of yo-yo dieting may increase abdominal fat deposits and related health risks (Rodin et al. 1990).

Exercise and the Treatment of Obesity

Although obese individuals are not always less active than normal-weight people, inactivity is often associated with obesity. Studies of adolescent boys and girls at summer camp, for example, found that obese adolescents were significantly less active than other normal-weight campers (Stefanik, Heald, and Mayer 1959; Bullen, Reed, and Mayer 1964). Differences in activity levels between the lean and obese have also been noted in adults (Stern 1984).

The use of exercise as a treatment for obesity has been widely promoted. The rationale for this treatment is that if energy expenditure is augmented by increasing physical activity, and if energy intake is kept constant, weight loss will occur. Although this method for weight control may appear to be simple, several factors must be considered when assessing the value of exercise. First, significant amounts of physical activity are required to expend sufficient calories for weight loss. Second, although it has been suggested that exercise can inhibit food intake, this phenomenon has not been demonstrated conclusively. Most studies examining the relationship of exercise, food intake, and weight loss have not directly measured food intake, but rather have interpreted weight loss as a reflection of decreased food intake. In studies that have measured food intake among normal-weight subjects, increased energy expenditure is generally compensated for by increased food intake, and body weight is maintained. Studies with obese individuals have suggested that food intake is not necessarily linked to activity expenditure and thus may not increase with exercise. This inference indicates a potential benefit for exercise in the obese. A third problem with exercise programs is that only very motivated individuals may continue for sufficient periods of time for weight loss to occur.

Despite these difficulties, exercise is a valuable adjunct in a weight-reduction regimen. Caloric restriction (i.e., dieting) decreases basal metabolism, which can be overcome by exercise. In addition, exercise may have a beneficial effect on abnormalities in lipid metabolism associated with obesity. Finally, exercise can have positive psychological effects. Increased physical activity has been associated with improvements in self-image and increased feelings of self-control (Stern 1984; Pi-Sunyer 1987, 1988).

CONCLUSION

It has become obvious that obesity is a heterogeneous disorder that may result either from increased energy intake or decreased energy expenditure. One of the goals for the next decade of research should be a better understanding of the multiple determinants of obesity. It is also important that techniques for weight loss be critically evaluated, and that strategies for long-term maintenance of weight control be developed.

Finally, methods of preventing obesity should certainly be emphasized more than they have in the past. Education about the health risks of obesity should begin at a young age, with an emphasis on participation in appropriate physical activities.

REFERENCES

Allon, N. 1982. The stigma of obesity in everyday life. In *Psychological Aspects of Obesity: A Handbook,* ed. B. Wolman, pp. 130–174. New York: Van Nostrand Reinhold.

Angel, J. A. 1949. Constitution in female obesity. *American Journal of Physical Anthropology* 7:433–471.

Apfelbaum, M., J. Fricker, and L. Igoin-Apfelbaum. 1987. Low- and very low-calorie diets. *American Journal of Clinical Nutrition* 45:1126–1134.

Atkinson, R. L. 1982. Naloxone decreases food intake in obese humans. *Journal of Clinical Endocrinology and Metabolism* 55:196–198.

Atkinson, R. L., L. K. Berke, C. R. Drake, M. L. Bibbs, F. L. Williams, and D. L. Kaiser. 1985. Effects of long-term therapy with naltrexone on body weight in obesity. *Clinical Pharmacology and Therapeutics* 38:419–422.

Bjorntorp, P. 1987. Adipose tissue distribution and morbidity. In *Recent Advances in Obesity Research,* vol. 5, ed. E. M. Berry, S. H. Blondheim, H. E. Eliohou, and E. Shafrir, pp. 60–65. London: John Libbey.

Blackburn, G. L., G. T. Wilson, B. S. Kanders, L. J. Stein, P. T. Lavin, J. Adler, and K. D. Brownell. 1989. Weight cycling: The experience of human dieters. *American Journal of Clinical Nutrition* 49:1105–1109.

Blundell, J. E. 1980. Pharmacological adjustments of the mechanisms underlying feeding and obesity. In *Obesity,* ed. A. J. Stunkard, pp. 182–207. Philadelphia: W. B. Saunders.

Bogardus, C., S. Lillioja, S. Rasvussin, W. Abbott, J. K. Zawadzki, A. Young, W. Knowler, R. Jacobowitz, and P. P. Moll. 1988. Familial dependence on the resting metabolic rate. *New England Journal of Medicine* 318:462–472.

Bouchard, C., A. Tremblay, J.-P. Depres, A. Nadeau, P. J. Lupien, G. Theriault, J. Dussault, S. Moorjani, S. Pinault, and G. Fournier. 1990. The response to long-term overfeeding in identical twins. *New England Journal of Medicine* 322:1477–1482.

Bracciale, D. 1988. Optifast/medifast programs: Are they safe and effective? *American Council on Science and Health News & Views,* pp. 7–8.

Bray, G. A. 1976. *The Obese Patient.* Philadelphia: W. B. Saunders.

Bray, G. A. 1980. Jejunoileal bypass, jaw wiring, and vagotomy for massive obesity. In *Obesity,* ed. A. J. Stunkard, pp. 369–387. Philadelphia: W. B. Saunders.

Bray, G. A. 1987. Overweight is risking fate. Definition, classification, prevalence, and risks. *Annals of the New York Academy of Sciences* 499:14–28.

Brownell, K., M. R. C. Greenwood, E. Stellar, and E. E. Shrager. 1986. The effects of repeated cycles of weight loss and regain in rats. *Physiology and Behavior* 38:459–464.

Bullen, B. A., R. B. Reed, and J. Mayer. 1964. Physical activity of obese and nonobese adolescent girls appraised by motion picture sampling. *American Journal of Clinical Nutrition* 4:211–233.

Canning, H. and J. Mayer. 1966. Obesity: Its possible effects on college admissions. *New England Journal of Medicine* 275:1172–1174.

Dietz, W. H. 1987. Childhood obesity. *Annals of the New York Academy of Sciences* 499:47–54.

Eckel, R. H. and T. J. Yost. 1987. Weight reduction increases adipose tissue lipoprotein responsiveness in obese women. *Journal of Clinical Investigation* 80:992–997.

Foch, T. F. and G. E. McClearn. 1980. Genetics, body weight and obesity. In *Obesity,* ed. A. J. Stunkard, pp. 48–71. Philadelphia: W. B. Saunders.

Friedman, G. D., W. B. Kannel, and R. R. Dawber. 1966. The epidemiology of gallbladder disease: Observations in Framingham Study. *Journal of Chronic Diseases* 19:273–292.

Garrow, J. S. 1988. *Obesity and Related Diseases.* Edinburgh: Churchill Livingstone.

Gibbs, J. 1985. Gut peptides in obesity: Can we use them to learn and to treat? In *Dietary Treatment and Prevention of Obesity,* ed. R. T. Frankle, J. Dwyer, L. Morgane, and A. Owen, pp. 97–104. London: John Libbey.

Goodman, N., S. A. Richardson, S. M. Dornbush, and A. H. Hastorf. 1963. Variant reaction to physical disability. *American Sociological Review* 28:429–435.

Griffith, M. and P. R. Payne. 1976. Energy expenditure in small children of obese and non-obese parents. *Nature* 260:698–700.

Gurney, R. 1936. Hereditary factor in obesity. *Archives of Internal Medicine* 12:1797–1803.

Guthrie, H. A. 1989. *Introductory Nutrition.* St. Louis: Times Mirror/Mosby.

Hall, J. C., J. McK. Watts, P. E. O'Brien, R. E. Dunstan, J. F. Walsh, A. H. Slovotinek, and R. G. Emlsie. 1990. Gastric surgery for morbid obesity. *Annals of Surgery* 211:419–427.

Halmi, K. 1980. Gastric bypass for massive obesity. In *Obesity,* ed. A. J. Stunkard, pp. 388–394. Philadelphia: W. B. Saunders.

Halmi, K., E. Mason, J. Falk, and A. J. Stunkard. 1981. Appetitive behavior after gastric bypass for obesity. *International Journal of Obesity* 5:457–464.

Himms-Hagen, J. 1989. Brown adipose tissue thermogenesis and obesity. *Progress in Lipid Research* 28:67–115.

Horton, E. S. 1981. Effects of altered caloric intake and composition of the diet on insulin resistance in obesity. In *Recent Advances in Obesity Research,* vol. 3, ed. P. Bjorntorp, M. Cairella, and A. N. Howard, pp. 248–253. London: John Libbey.

Hubert, H. B., N. Feinlieb, P. McNamara, and W. Castelli. 1983. Obesity as an independent risk factor for cardiovascular disease: A 26-year follow-up of participants in the Framingham Heart Study. *Circulation* 67:968–977.

Jequier, E. 1987. Energy utilization in human obesity. *Annals of the New York Academy of Sciences* 499:73–83.

Kanarek, R. B. and R. Marks-Kaufman. 1988. Animal models of appetitive behavior: Interaction of nutritional factors and drug-seeking behavior. In *Control of Appetite*, ed. M. Winick, pp. 1–25. New York: Wiley.

Kanarek, R. B. and R. Marks-Kaufman. 1991. Opioid peptides: Food intake, nutrient selection and food preferences. In *Neuropharmacology of Appetite*, ed. S. J. Cooper and J. M. Lieberman. London: Oxford University Press.

Kanarek, R. B. and N. Orthen-Gambill. 1988. Dietary-induced obesity in experimental animals. In *Use of Animal Models for Research in Human Nutrition*, ed. A. C. Beynen and C. E. West, pp. 83–110. New York: Krager.

Kanarek, R. B., N. Orthen-Gambill, R. Marks-Kaufman, and J. Mayer. 1984. Obesity: Possible psychological and metabolic determinants. In *Nutrition and Behavior*, ed. J. R. Galler, pp. 339–396. New York: Plenum.

Kannel, W. B. and T. Gordon. 1979. Physiological and medical concomitants of obesity: The Framingham study. In *Obesity in America*, ed. G. A. Bray, pp. 125–160 (NIH Publication No. 79-359). Washington, DC: U.S. Department of Health, Education and Welfare.

Kenler, H. A., R. E. Brolin, and R. P. Cody. 1990. Changes in eating behavior after horizontal gastroplasty and Roux-en-Y gastric bypass. *American Journal of Clinical Nutrition* 52:87–92.

Kern, P. A., J. M. Ong, B. Saffari, and J. Carty. 1990. The effects of weight loss on the activity and expression of adipose tissue lipoprotein lipase in very obese humans. *New England Journal of Medicine* 322:1053–1059.

Kirkpatrick, S. W. and D. M. Saunders. 1978. Body image stereotypes: A developmental comparison. *Journal of Genetic Psychology* 1132:87–95.

Lew, E. A. and L. Garfinkel. 1979. Variations in mortality by weight among 750,000 men and women. *Journal of Chronic Diseases* 32:563–576.

Liebel, R. L., N. K. Edens, and S. K. Fried. 1989. Physiological basis for the control of body fat distribution in humans. *Annual Review of Nutrition* 9:417–443.

Maggio, C. A., E. Presta, E. P. Bracco, J. R. Vasselli, H. R. Kissileff, and S. A. Hashim. 1985. Naltrexone and human eating behavior: A dose-ranging inpatient trial in moderately obese men. *Brain Research Bulletin* 14:657–661.

Malcolm, R., P. M. O'Neil, J. D. Sexauer, F. E. Riddle, H. S. Currey, and C. Counts. 1985. A controlled trial of naltrexone in obese humans. *International Journal of Obesity* 9:347–353.

Manson, J. E., G. A. Colditz, M. J. Stampfer, W. D. Willett, B. Rosner, R. R.

Monson, F. E. Speizer, and C. H. Hennekens. 1990. A prospective study of obesity and risk of coronary heart disease in women. *New England Journal of Medicine* 322:882–889.

Mayer, J. 1953. Genetic, traumatic, and environmental factors in the etiology of obesity. *Physiological Reviews* 33:472–508.

Mayer, J. 1968. *Overweight, Causes, Costs, and Control.* Englewood Cliffs, NJ: Prentice Hall.

Mills, M. J. and A. J. Stunkard. 1976. Behavioral changes following surgery for obesity. *American Journal of Psychiatry* 133:527–531.

Mitchell, J. E., J. E. Morley, A. S. Levine, D. Haksukami, M. Gannon, and D. Pfohl. 1987. High-dose naltrexone therapy and dietary counseling for obesity. *Biological Psychiatry* 22:35–42.

Morrow, S. R. and L. K. Mona. 1990. Effect of gastric balloons on nutrient intake and weight loss in obese subjects. *Journal of the American Dietetic Association* 90:717–718.

Munro, J. F, I. C. Stewart, P. H. Seidelin, H. S. Mackenzie, and N. G. Dewhurst. 1987. Mechanical treatment for obesity. *Annals of the New York Academy of Sciences* 499:305–312.

Nathan, C. and Y. Rolland. 1987. Pharmacological treatments that affect CNS activity: Serotonin. *Annals of the New York Academy of Sciences* 499:277–296.

National Institutes of Health. 1985. Consensus development panel on the health implications of obesity: Conference statement. *Annals of Internal Medicine* 103:1073–1077.

Olefsky, J. M. and O. G. Kolterman. 1981. In vivo studies of insulin resistance in human obesity. In *Recent Advances in Obesity Research,* vol. 3, ed. P. Bjorntorp, M. Cairella, and A. N. Howard, pp. 254–267. London: John Libbey.

Pi-Sunyer, F. X. 1987. Exercise effects on caloric intake. *Annals of the New York Academy of Sciences* 499:94–103.

Pi-Sunyer, F. X. 1988. Obesity. In *Modern Nutrition in Health and Disease,* ed. M. E. Shils and V. N. Young, pp. 795–816. Philadelphia: Lea & Febiger.

Price, R. A., A. J. Stunkard, R. Ness, T. Wadden, S. Heshka, B. Kanders, and A. Cormillot. 1990. Childhood onset (age < 10) obesity has high familial risk. *International Journal of Obesity* 14:185–195.

Quaade, F. 1981. Surgical treatment of obesity. In *Recent Advances in Obesity Research,* vol. 3, ed. P. Bjorntorp, M Cairella, and A. N. Howard, pp. 318–329. London: John Libbey.

Rasvussin, E., S. Lillioja, W. C. Knowler, L. Christin, D. Freymond, W. G. H. Abbott, V. Boyce, B. V. Howard, and C. Bogardus. 1988. Reduced rate of energy expenditure as a risk factor for body weight gain. *New England Journal of Medicine* 318:467–472.

Richardson, S., N. Goodman, A. Hastorf, and S. Dornbush. 1961. Cultural uniformity and reaction to physical disability. *American Sociological Review* 26:241–247.

Roberts, S. B., B. A. Savage, W. A. Coward, B. Chew, and A. Lucas. 1988. Energy expenditure and intake in infants born to lean and overweight mothers. *New England Journal of Medicine* 318:461–466.

Rodin, J., N. Radke-Sharpe, M. Rebuffe-Scrive, and M. R. C. Greenwood. 1990. Weight cycling and fat distribution. *International Journal of Obesity* 14:303–310.

Roe, D. A. and K. R. Eickwort. 1976. Relationships between obesity and associated health factors with unemployment among low-income women. *Journal of the American Medical Women's Association* 31:193–194ff.

Rose, G. A. and R. T. Williams. 1961. Metabolic studies on large and small eaters. *British Journal of Nutrition* 15:1–9.

Rothwell, N. J. and Stock, M. J. 1979. A role for brown adipose tissue in diet-induced thermogenesis. *Nature* 281:31–35.

Schapira, D. V., N. B. Kuman, G. H. Lyman, and C. E. Cox. 1990. Abdominal obesity and breast cancer risk. *Annals of Internal Medicine* 112:182–186.

Schwartz, R. S. and J. D. Brunzell. 1978. Increased adipose tissue lipoprotein-lipase activity in moderately obese men after weight reduction. *Lancet* 1:1230–1231.

Silverstone, T. 1981. Clinical pharmacology of anorectic drugs. In *Anorectic Agents: Mechanisms of Action and Tolerance,* ed. S. Garratini and R. Saminin, pp. 211–222. New York: Raven Press.

Sims, E. A. H., E. Danforth, E. S. Horton, G. A. Bray, T. A. Glennon, and L. B. Salans. 1973. Endocrine and metabolic effects of experimental obesity in man. *Recent Progress in Hormone Research* 29:457–469.

Sjostrom, L. 1987. New aspects of weight-for-height indices and adipose tissue distribution in relation to cardiovascular risk and total adipose tissue volume. In *Recent Advances in Obesity Research,* vol. 5, ed. E. M. Berry, S. H. Blondheim, H. E. Eliohou, and F. Shafrir, pp. 66–76. London: John Libbey.

Smith, G. P. and J. Gibbs. 1988. The satiating effect of cholecystokinin. In *Control of Appetite,* ed. M. Winick, pp. 35–40. New York: Wiley.

Solow, C. 1977. Psychosocial aspects of intestinal bypass surgery for massive obesity: Current status. *American Journal of Clinical Nutrition* 30:103–108.

Spiegel, T. A., A. J. Stunkard, E. E. Shrager, C. P. O'Brien, M. F. Morrison, and E. Stellar. 1987. Effect of naltrexone on food intake, hunger and satiety in obese men. *Physiology and Behavior* 40:135–141.

Stefanik, P. A., F. P. Heald, Jr., and J. Mayer. 1959. Caloric intake in relation to energy output of obese and non-obese adolescent boys. *American Journal of Clinical Nutrition* 7:55–62.

Stern, J. S. 1984. Is obesity a disease of inactivity? In *Eating and Its Disorders*, ed. A. J. Stunkard and E. Stellar, pp. 131–139. New York: Raven Press.

Stunkard, A. J. 1984. The current status of treatment for obesity in adults. In *Eating and Its Disorders*, ed. A. J. Stunkard and E. Stellar, pp. 157–173. New York: Raven Press.

Stunkard, A. J., J. R. Harris, N. L. Pedersen, and G. E. McClearn. 1990. The body-mass index of twins who have been reared apart. *New England Journal of Medicine* 322:1483–1487.

Stunkard, A. J., T. I. A. Sorensen, C. Hanis, T. W. Teasdale, R. Chakraborty, W. J. Schull, and F. Schulsinger. 1986. An adoption study of human obesity. *New England Journal of Medicine* 314:193–198.

Sullivan, A. C. 1987. Drug treatment of obesity: A perspective. In *Recent Advances in Obesity Research*, vol. 5, ed. E. M. Berry, S. H. Blondheim, E. Eliohou, and E. Shafrir, pp. 293–299. London: John Libbey.

Sullivan, A. C., S. Hogan, and J. Triscari. 1987. New developments in pharmacological treatments for obesity. *Annals of the New York Academy of Medicine* 499:269–276.

Tarui, S., S. Fujioka, K. Tokunaga, and Y. Matsuzawa. 1988. Comparison of pathophysiology between subcutaneous-type and visceral type obesity. In *Diet and Obesity*, ed. G. A. Bray, pp. 143–152. New York: S. Krager.

VanItallie, T. B. 1990. The perils of obesity in middle-aged women. *New England Journal of Medicine* 322:928–929.

Wadden, T. A. and A. J. Stunkard. 1987. Psychopathology and obesity. *Annals of the New York Academy of Sciences* 499:55–65.

Weintraub, M. and G. A. Bray. 1989. Drug treatment of obesity. *Medical Clinics of North America* 73:237–249.

Wilson, M. A. 1990. Southwestern internal medicine conference: Treatment of obesity. *American Journal of Medical Science* 299:62–68.

Wolkowitz, O. M., A. R. Doran, M. R. Cohen, R. M. Cohen, T. N. Wise, and D. Pickar. 1988. Single-dose naloxone acutely reduces eating in obese humans: Behavioral and biochemical effects. *Biological Psychiatry* 24:483–487.

14

Eating Disorders

The past two decades have witnessed a striking increase in the eating disorders, anorexia nervosa and bulimia. Both of these disorders occur most frequently, but not exclusively, in young women. It has been hypothesized that one of the primary reasons for the increase in the prevalence of these eating disorders is our culture's recent obsession with thinness and a stigma against obesity.

Anorexia nervosa is characterized by severe weight loss as a result of deliberate self-starvation. This behavior is associated with a fear of fatness. An intense fear of weight gain is also a concomitant of bulimia. While the anorexic starves, however, the bulimic typically gorges and then vomits. More specifically, bulimia has been defined as recurrent episodes of compulsive overeating, followed by attempts to avoid the caloric consequences of the binge by self-induced vomiting, the use of laxatives or diuretics, or strenuous activity (Andersen 1984).

This chapter explores the factors that may lead to the development of these two eating disorders and their physiological and psychological correlates. Additionally, treatment strategies for these potentially life-threatening conditions will be examined.

ANOREXIA NERVOSA

Anorexia nervosa frequently begins with a young woman's initial intent to "lose a few pounds." She may cut out sweets and snacks, and then receive praise from family and friends for being "more in control." As she reaches her weight goal, the young woman may still feel overweight and thus continues to restrict her eating. By the time anyone notices that there is something wrong, she may be consuming only 600 to 800 calories a day. Calorically dense foods and those high in refined carbohydrates are typically avoided. Her diet may be become limited to fruits, vegetables, and cottage cheese and be controlled by rigid, self-imposed rules. When confronted with her consequent extreme weight loss, the young woman may complain that she is still too heavy or that a particular part of her body is too large.

Anorexia nervosa is an unusual disorder. Although individuals suffering from it have many of the same physiological and behavioral symptoms seen in other forms of starvation, they have one unique characteristic: deliberate, self-imposed hunger. The disorder presents a paradox, for it is most often seen in young well-to-do women, starving in the midst of plenty. The term "anorexia nervosa" even appears to be inappropriate, for "anorexia" suggests a loss of appetite. However, individuals with this disorder do not suffer from a lack of hunger, but rather from an intense fear of gaining weight. Individuals with anorexia nervosa frequently are preoccupied with eating and thoughts of food (Pirke and Ploog 1986; Halmi 1987; Halmi 1989).

History

The first clinical description of anorexia nervosa has been attributed to Dr. Richard Morton, who believed the condition was the result of "Sadness and Anxious Cares." In a report published in 1689 under the title "A Nervous Consumption," Morton described the case of Mr. Duke's daughter of St. Mary Axe, England, who became ill at the age of eighteen (Bruch 1973):

> In the month of July she fell into a total suppression of her Monthly Courses from a multitude of Cares and Passions of her Mind, but without any symptoms of the Green-Sickness following upon it. From which time her Appetite began to abate and her Digestion to be bad; her flesh also began to be flaccid and pale. . . . she was wont by her studying at Night, and continual pouring upon Books, to expose herself both Day and Night to the injuries of the Air. . . . I do not remember that I did ever see in all my practice, one that was conversant with the living so much wasted with the greatest degree of a Consumption (like a Skeleton only clad with Skin) yet there was no fever, but on the contrary a coldness of the Whole Body. . . . only her Appetite was diminished, and her Digestion uneasie, with Fainting Fits, which did frequently return upon her (as quoted in Bruch 1973).

Mr. Duke's daughter rejected medication and died three months after Morton described her condition. It is interesting to note that if Dr. Morton's report were translated into more modern terms, it would be a very clinically accurate description of anorexia nervosa in its most dramatic form.

The first modern descriptions of anorexia were offered in the early 1870s by Sir William Gull in England and by Dr. Charles Lasegue in France. In 1874, Gull, who was the first to use the term anorexia nervosa, provided a detailed clinical portrait of the disorder:

> In an address on medicine delivered at Oxford in the Autumn of 1868, I referred to a peculiar form of disease occurring mostly in young women and characterized by extreme emaciation. . . . The subjects of this affection are mostly of the

female sex and chiefly between the ages of 16 and 23. I have occasionally seen it in males at the same age. . . . The condition was one of simple starvation. . . . The want of appetite is, I believe, due to a morbid mental state. . . . We might call the state hysterical, . . . I prefer however the more general term "nervosa" since the disease occurs in males as well as females and is probably central rather than peripheral. (Gull 1874)

Gull's and Lasegue's descriptions of anorexia led to a substantial increase in medical awareness of the disease. With the advent of Freudian thinking in the first half of the twentieth century, a psychoanalytic perspective dominated researchers' ideas about the disorder. It was hypothesized that anorexia was rooted in faulty psychosexual development. Specifically, it was proposed that "fear of oral impregnation" resulted in the decrease in food intake observed in anorectic patients. Although these ideas seem somewhat archaic today, they represent the first serious attempts to understand the etiology of the disease (Bruch 1973; Andersen 1984; Russell and Treasure 1989).

The modern era of interest in anorexia nervosa began in the 1950s, when Hilda Bruch, a psychoanalyst, began to study young anorectic women. Bruch suggested that the rigid behavior associated with eating represented a "struggle for control" (Bruch 1973, 1977, 1979). She found these young women to be "outstandingly good and quiet children, obedient, clean, eager to please, helpful at home, precociously dependable and excelling in school work. . . . When they got to adolescence and were supposed to be self-reliantly independent, they couldn't come to terms with their childhood robot obedience" (Bruch 1977). These children could be characterized as overcompliant, oversubmissive, and lacking an age-appropriate sense of autonomy. Bruch viewed the excessive concern with body size and the rigid control of eating as symptoms of the "youngster's desperate fight against feeling enslaved and exploited and not competent to lead a life of their own" (Bruch 1977). Bruch proposed that strict limitation of food intake might be one of the only ways the anorectic could feel in control of her own life.

In the 1970s, evidence that anorexia nervosa was increasing in prevalence led to a dramatic rise in both medical and public interest in the disorder. Medical researchers began exploring not only etiological factors in the development of anorexia, but also its physiological and psychological correlates. At the same time, public interest was stimulated by an abundance of reports about anorexia nervosa in the popular press and on radio and television.

Diagnostic Criteria

In 1972, one of the first clear guidelines for diagnosing anorexia nervosa was proposed by Feighner and colleagues (Feighner et al. 1972). These guidelines, which have continued to be used in many research and treatment centers, include

- Age of onset prior to 25 years
- Loss of at least 25% of original body weight
- Active refusal of the patient to eat enough to maintain a normal body weight; sustained efforts to prevent food from being absorbed
- Intense fear of becoming obese which does not decrease as weight loss progresses
- Body image disturbances
- No known medical or psychiatric illness to account for the disorder
- At least two of the following features: amenorrhea, lanugo, bradycardia, periods of overactivity, or episodes of bulimia and vomiting.

The American Psychiatric Association has recognized the disorder for many years and in 1987 revised its diagnostic criteria, reflecting increased awareness of the symptoms and prevalence of anorexia.

Diagnostic Criteria for Anorexia Nervosa

A. Refusal to maintain body weight over a minimal normal weight for age and height, e.g., weight loss leading to maintenance of body weight 15% below that expected; or failure to make expected weight gain during period of growth, leading to body weight 15% below that expected.
B. Intense fear of gaining weight or becoming fat, even though underweight.
C. Disturbance in the way in which one's body weight, size, or shape is experienced; e.g., the person claims to "feel fat" even when emaciated, believes that one area of the body is "too fat" even when obviously underweight.
D. In females, absence of at least three consecutive menstrual cycles when otherwise expected to occur (primary or secondary amenorrhea). A woman is considered to have amenorrhea if her periods occur only following hormone, e.g., estrogen, administration. (From American Psychiatric Association 1987, p. 67)

In contrast to earlier criteria that concentrated on reduced food intake, the most recent ones focus more on fear of gaining weight and disturbances in body image.

Many individuals with anorexia nervosa also binge-eat, but maintain their weight loss by purging. It has been suggested that they differ from anorexics who maintain their weight loss solely by caloric restriction (Gilbert 1986). These individuals will be discussed in the section on bulimia.

Prevalence

Anorexia nervosa occurs most frequently in adolescent girls (85% to 95% of the reported cases), with the remainder of the cases reported in prepubertal boys and older women. Prevalence has been estimated to range from 0.5% to 1.0% in women between the ages of 14 and 25 (Bemis 1978; Casper 1986; Halmi, Schneider, and Cooper 1989). Anorexia is rarely seen in lower socioeconomic classes and has been only infrequently reported in underdeveloped countries. In a study done in England, it was found that one in 200 young women in private schools were afflicted with this disorder, while only one case in 3,000 was reported in young women in the general population (Bruch 1979; Garner, Garfinkel, and Olmsted 1983; Andersen 1984; Farmer, Treasure, and Szmukler 1986).

A number of subgroups who may be particularly vulnerable to anorexia nervosa have been identified. These subgroups are characterized as placing a high positive value on slimness and a negative one on obesity. For example, Garner and Garfinkel (1980) reported a high incidence of anorexia nervosa among professional dance and modeling students. Other subgroups with increased vulnerability include jockeys, gymnasts, and entertainers, all of whom are intensely pressured toward being slim as a professional requirement (Andersen 1984).

Etiology

It has become clear that there is no single cause of anorexia nervosa. Rather, the disorder must be considered the result of several predisposing factors. Not everyone predisposed to anorexia nervosa develops the disorder; and of those who do develop it, the precise interaction of predisposing factors varies from individual to individual. The etiology of anorexia nervosa may be divided into three major categories: those occurring within the individual, family, and culture (Garfinkel and Garner 1983).

INDIVIDUAL FACTORS

Difficulties in autonomous functioning and in developing a sense of personal identity leading to an impaired ability to function separately from one's family may predispose a young woman to anorexia (Garfinkel and Garner 1983). Hilda Bruch hypothesized that fundamental ego deficits in autonomy and mastery over one's body, which she described as an overall sense of "personal ineffectiveness," may bias an individual toward anorexia nervosa. Similar ideas about the importance of feelings of ineffectiveness in the development of anorexia have been expressed by Selvini-Palazzoli (1970), who suggested that these feelings derive from early interactions with parents.

Problems with autonomy and feelings of ineffectiveness are certainly not limited to individuals with anorexia nervosa, but rather are important issues for adolescents in general. It is thus obvious that other factors must interact with these feelings to produce anorexia nervosa. It also has been proposed that obsessional or hysterical traits are common characteristics of anorectic individuals. Bruch and others have described anorexics as compliant, perfectionistic, obedient, eager to please, oversubmissive, and lacking in responsiveness to inner needs (e.g., Bruch 1973; Halmi 1974; Garfinkel and Garner 1983). These characteristics suggest that anorexics may have extremely high personal expectations and need to please others in order to maintain their sense of self-worth.

Several researchers have noted that premorbid obesity is common in girls who later develop anorexia (Crisp et al. 1977; Garfinkel and Garner 1983). It has also been reported that anorectic patients generally weigh more at birth than their siblings, leading some to suggest that an early heightened nutritional state may be associated with earlier prepubertal growth and sexual development (Crisp 1970; Halmi 1974). This earlier development may require a premature confrontation with adolescent demands for autonomy or sexuality, for which the potential anorectic is unprepared. Additionally, a young woman who has previously experienced obesity may be very aware of past humiliations. This awareness could serve as an especially powerful factor in the predisposition to inflexible dieting, particularly if the individual's self-worth is largely determined by appearance (Garfinkel and Garner 1983).

There is now good evidence for a genetic predisposition for anorexia nervosa. The disease is more prevalent in siblings of individuals with the disorder (6%) than in the general population (0.5% to 1.0%) (Garfinkel and Garner 1983). Moreover, recent studies have demonstrated a much higher concordance rate for anorexia in monozygotic (identical) than dizygotic (fraternal) twins. In a study of 30 female twin pairs, if one twin had anorexia nervosa, the second twin was more likely to develop the disorder if the twins were monozygotic (9 out of 16) than if they were dizygotic (1 out of 14) (Holland et al. 1984). Subsequent studies have confirmed these findings (Russell and Treasure 1989). It has been hypothesized that genetic vulnerability to anorexia nervosa may represent a defect in the homeostatic mechanisms that normally ensure weight gain after a period of weight loss. Such a hypothesis would lead to the prediction that in a society where dieting is common and weight reduction promoted, those with the proposed genetic deficit in body weight regulation would be the most likely to develop anorexia nervosa (Russell and Treasure 1989).

FAMILIAL FACTORS

Familial interactions may also play a role in predisposing an individual to anorexia nervosa. Anecdotal reports suggest that families of anorexics can be characterized as intrusive. Such families may show little concern for individual privacy, and there may be excessive togetherness. Values of cohesion and protection within the family may take precedence over autonomy and individual self-realization. It is hypothesized that mutual concern may become overprotectiveness, with the parents guarding the children, and the children in turn developing into "parent watchers." When the child faces the adolescent tasks of individuation and separation, she falters, and the overt expression of her needs for self-control, autonomy, and self-definition may be diverted into covert or self-destructive channels. These family characteristics may interfere with the development of autonomy and thereby produce a vulnerability to anorexia (Rosman et al. 1977; Rakoff 1983).

There is substantial evidence that the families of anorexics may also have excessive concerns about appearance including weight, eating, and fitness and heavily rely on external standards for determining self-worth and success. Associated with these concerns is the repeated observation that parents of anorexics tend to be from the higher economic classes and older than average when their children were born (Garfinkel and Garner 1983).

An increased degree of psychiatric illness and symptomology in the families of anorexics has also been reported. Although not universally observed, some studies have found a greater than normal incidence of affective disorders including depression and manic-depressive illness in these families. A relatively high rate of alcoholism also has been observed in family members of anorexics. Estimates indicate that from 12% to 19% of the fathers of anorexics may suffer from alcoholism compared to approximately 9% in the general population (Hall 1978; Winokur, March, and Mendels 1980; Rakoff 1983; Devlin and Walsh 1989). Finally, an association between psychosomatic illness and anorexia has been noted. For example, Kalucy and colleagues reported that 30% of the mothers of anorexics examined in their research suffered from migraine headaches (Kalucy, Crisp, and Harding 1977).

SOCIOCULTURAL FACTORS

The role of social and cultural factors in the development of anorexia has been well documented by Garner and co-workers (Garner, Garfinkel, and Olmsted 1983). The increasing prevalence of anorexia nervosa and related eating disorders has been taken by many investigators as compelling evidence that such factors have a role in the development of the disorder. Improved diagnosis due to greater medical and public awareness accounts only partially for the reported increase in anorexia nervosa.

One of the reasons for the rising incidence of anorexia nervosa may be the overwhelming emphasis placed on thinness in today's society. The fashion industry and news media have clearly encouraged the association between thinness and such positive attributes as beauty, success, wealth, and happiness. To more directly document and quantify the shift in the cultural image of the ideal female shape, Garner and colleagues (1980) collected data from several sources, including *Playboy* magazine centerfolds and Miss America pageant contestants, over a 20-year period.

Data from both of these sources revealed that the preferred female shape had apparently shifted toward a thinner ideal.

To obtain the societal goal of thinness, dieting has become a way of life for many in our culture, particularly young women. A recent study of nearly 500 schoolgirls in the San Francisco area revealed that almost half of the 9-year-olds and 80% of the 10- and 11-year-olds said they were dieting. Eighty-nine percent of the 17-year-old girls questioned reported that they were dieting. Only 17% of all of the girls were actually overweight (Lehrman 1987).

Cultural pressure for women to meet a thinner standard for physical attractiveness and the subsequent impetus for dieting may be predisposing factors for anorexia, but they cannot be viewed as the primary cause of the disease. Many young women are confronted with these pressures, but only a few develop anorexia. Thus, we must conclude that there is as yet an unestablished interaction among individual, familial, and cultural factors that results in the disease.

Physiological Consequences

There are a vast number of medical complications associated with anorexia nervosa. The disorder affects almost every organ system, including the endocrine, cardiovascular, gastrointestinal, pulmonary, dermatological, renal, neurological, and hematological systems (see Table 14-1). Many of the medical complications are similar to those which occur in other forms of starvation. However, some complications do appear to be specific manifestations of anorexia. The severity of the physiological changes that occur in anorexia nervosa varies directly as a function of the duration and magnitude of reduced food intake and the percentage of body weight loss.

ENDOCRINE SYSTEM

Endocrine abnormalities are very pronounced in anorexia. The hypothalamic–pituitary–gonadal axis appears to be one of the first systems affected. Amenorrhea (the loss of the menstrual period) is a fundamental component of anorexia nervosa. In younger women, amenorrhea is frequently accompanied by growth retardation and delayed onset of puberty. It has been proposed that starvation and weight loss are solely responsible for amenorrhea; however, others have argued to the contrary. In support of the latter argument, up to one-third of the patients who eventually developed anorexia nervosa reported the loss of their menstrual periods prior to the loss of any weight. This amenorrhea was most likely due to both early dietary changes and stress.

Low plasma levels of the gonadotropic hormones, luteinizing hormone (LH) and follicle-stimulating hormone (FSH), which are produced by the

TABLE 14-1. Physiological Consequences of Anorexia Nervosa

Organ System	Consequences
Endocrine	Amenorrhea and infertility
	Low plasma LH and FSH levels
	Infantile or pubertal pattern of LH secretion
	Low plasma estradiol and progesterone levels
	Decreased LH and FSH response to gonadotropin-releasing hormone
	Decreased conversion of T4 to T3 within the thyroid gland
	Symptoms of hypothyroidism including cold intolerance and decreased basal metabolic rate
	Increased plasma cortisol values
	Increased secretion of growth hormone
Cardiovascular	Decreased heart rate
	Low blood pressure
	Electrocardiographic abnormalities
	Congestive heart failure
Gastrointestinal	Decreased gastric motility and delayed gastric emptying
	Superior mesentery artery syndrome
	Gastric dilation and rupture
	Abdominal pain
Dermatological	Hair loss
	Lanugo or baby-fine hair on the face and back
	Dry skin and brittle hair and nails
Renal	Decreased urine concentration leading to polyuria
Pulmonary	Subcutaneous emphysema
Neurological	Pseudoatrophy of the brain
	Enlarged inner and outer cerebrospinal fluid space
	Abnormal daytime electroencephalogram
	Sleep disturbances
	Alterations in functioning of the sympathetic nervous system
Metabolic	Decreased body fat
	Increased plasma free fatty acid levels
	Increased plasma cholesterol
	Zinc and trace mineral deficiencies
	Vitamin A deficiency
Other	Osteoporosis
	Impaired thermoregulation
	Anemia
	Edema

Adapted from Pirke and Ploog 1986; Casper 1986; and Pomeroy and Mitchell 1989.

pituitary gland and are critical for normal ovarian function, are common in anorexia nervosa. Additionally, estrogen and progesterone levels are decreased. Women with anorexia nervosa typically display an immature response (resembling that of prepubertal girls) when LH and FSH secretion are stimulated by administration of the gonadotropin-releasing hormones. In general, levels of LH and FSH return to normal with weight gain. However, this is not always the case. There is evidence suggesting that the time needed for gonadotropin secretion patterns to return to normal increases with age of the patients and the duration of the disease (Drossman, Ontjes, and Heizer 1979; Andersen 1984; Pirke and Ploog 1986; Pomeroy and Mitchell 1989; Russell and Treasure 1989).

The hypothalamic–pituitary–thyroid axis is also altered. Anorectic individuals tend to exhibit hypothyroidism. Thyroid function tests are often abnormal. Clinically, these abnormalities are evidenced by hypothermia, cold intolerance, and a decrease in basal metabolic rate (Casper 1986; Pirke and Ploog 1986; Pomeroy and Mitchell 1989).

Finally, alterations in the hypothalamic–pituitary–adrenal axis are also observed in anorexia. Plasma levels of cortisol, a hormone important in the regulation of fat, carbohydrate, and protein metabolism, are frequently increased as a result of both increased production and slowed metabolism of the hormone. When starving subjects or anorectic patients resume eating, cortisol secretion and metabolism rapidly normalize, suggesting that elevated cortisol secretion is an adaptation to starvation. It is assumed that cortisol stimulates gluconeogenesis, which is significantly decreased in starvation (Pirke and Ploog 1986; Pomeroy and Mitchell 1989).

CARDIOVASCULAR SYSTEM

Cardiovascular changes in anorexia nervosa range from low heart rate, low blood pressure, and electrocardiographic abnormalities to congestive heart failure and sudden cardiac death. When anorectic patients are challenged with exercise, increases in blood pressure and pulse rate are lower than in normal controls. It has been suggested that these results are indicative of impaired sympathetic nervous system functioning. Many of the changes in the cardiovascular system may be due to restrictions in fluid intake which can accompany reduced food intake in anorexia nervosa (Silverman 1983; Casper 1986; Pirke and Ploog 1986; Pomeroy and Mitchell 1989).

GASTROINTESTINAL SYSTEM

Gastric functioning is also altered in anorexia nervosa. Anorectic patients frequently complain of excessive feelings of fullness after eating. Recent work suggests that decreased gastric motility associated with delayed gastric emptying may be at least partially responsible for this symptom. Delayed gastric emptying appears to be a direct result of the severe reduction in food intake that accompanies anorexia. Once a pattern of starvation has been established, delayed gastric emptying may contribute to its persistence by producing increased feelings of satiety when food is consumed (Robinson 1989).

Patients with anorexia are also at risk for superior mesenteric artery syndrome, which involves compression of blood vessels serving the distal portion of the duodenum and can lead to abdominal pain and vomiting (Casper 1986; Pomeroy and Mitchell 1989).

METABOLIC ALTERATIONS

The metabolic changes associated with anorexia nervosa are similar to those seen in starvation. When an individual eats fewer calories than required for the body's energy needs, body tissue is consumed to supply the deficit calories. Initially, glycogen reserves are depleted, followed by the use of muscle tissue for energy. Finally, fat is utilized. Fat mobilization results in the release of free fatty acids. Plasma free fatty acid levels are often elevated in patients with anorexia nervosa. Other metabolic problems identified with this disorder include an inability to concentrate urine, with a concomitant reduction in intracellular water. Although rare, zinc and other trace mineral deficiencies and hypovitaminosis A have been observed in anorectic patients (Pirke and Ploog 1986; Pomeroy and Mitchell 1989).

OTHER PHYSIOLOGICAL ALTERATIONS

Dermatological abnormalities in anorexia nervosa include hair loss, development of lanugo-like hair (fine, silky hair on the back and face), dry skin, and brittle nails. Osteoporosis and several hematological abnormalities have also been documented (Casper 1986; Pomeroy and Mitchell 1989).

The majority of alterations in physiological functioning that occur in anorexia nervosa return to normal when the patient gains back the weight that was lost.

Psychological Characteristics

Anorexics exhibit many of the psychological disturbances that are seen in other forms of starvation. Bizarre eating habits, preoccupation with food, irritability, emotional lability, depression, and sexual disinterest appear as common psychological features of both anorexia nervosa and starvation (Keys et al. 1950; Bemis 1978). In anorexia, bizarre eating habits may include refusing to eat when others are present or taking an extremely long time to eat a small amount of food. Preoccupation with food may manifest itself by attending cooking classes, collecting recipes, insisting on feeding members of the family, or taking courses in nutrition (Gilbert 1986).

While many of the psychological changes observed in anorexia are similar to those seen in starvation, there are several differences that make the disorder unique. First, anorexics tend to display a severe disturbance in body image. They typically misperceive their body size and report themselves to be larger than they actually are. In other instances, they may accurately perceive their overall body size, but insist that one feature is either unattractive or larger than it should be. This distortion is not affected by scales or reports of trusted others.

A second difference is that anorexics frequently misinterpret both internal and external stimuli. Most pronounced are inaccuracies in the way in which internal cues for hunger are perceived. Instead of being a signal to eat, the sensation of hunger can become a positive reinforcement. After just a few bits of food, the anorectic patient will often report feeling full. This feeling may be associated with the delay in gastric emptying mentioned previously. Anorexics also demonstrate a lack of appropriate responsiveness to such external stimuli as cold, fatigue, and sexual stimulation (Bruch 1973; Robinson 1989; Halmi and Sunday 1991).

Third, in contrast to starving individuals who typically avoid physical activity and become easily fatigued, anorexics are often hyperactive and deny feelings of fatigue (Bruch 1973; Kron et al. 1978). Patients with anorexia may increase activity as a further means of reducing body weight.

A fourth distinction between starving individuals and those with anorexia nervosa is that anorexics frequently display an extreme fear of loss of control. A common thought may be, "If I take one bite, I won't be able to stop." There is inordinate self-discipline which may include obsessive rituals centered on food.

Finally, many anorexics may experience "a paralyzing sense of ineffectiveness." The world seems beyond their control, and they feel helpless and unable to change anything in their lives. The one thing they can control is their eating (Bruch 1973, 1977, 1979; Casper 1986; Gilbert 1986).

Treatment

There is no question that anorexia nervosa can be a life-threatening disease. It has been estimated that between 10% and 15% of all victims die. Death has been associated with inanition, suicide, infection, and cardiopulmonary disease (Drossman, Ontjes, and Heizer 1979; Pirke and Ploog 1986; Libnickey 1987).

The high mortality rate and the other detrimental consequences of anorexia nervosa make early detection and treatment of the disease critical. Because of the complexity of the disorder, a multidimensional treatment approach should be attempted.

The first step in the medical management of anorectic patients is to correctly diagnose the disorder. A careful medical history including inquiries about dietary habits, weight history, and menstrual irregularities should be taken, followed by a physical examination that includes blood tests, thyroid function tests, an electrocardiogram, and renal function tests. Additionally, individual and family psychiatric assessments should be undertaken (Pomeroy and Mitchell 1989; Yager 1989).

Once the diagnosis of anorexia nervosa is confirmed, treatment can be initiated. The first and most essential step is nutritional rehabilitation. The experience of many clinicians is that without correcting the starvation state and the starvation-induced emotional and cognitive states, the patient cannot benefit from psychological treatment. Correction of body weight can pose a substantial challenge to the clinician. Weight restoration requires the patient's cooperation, which may be difficult to obtain. One method that has been used successfully is to negotiate a treatment contract with the patient and her family before treatment begins. This procedure allows patients to determine what is tolerable and enlists their collaboration by leaving some control in their hands (Casper 1986; Pirke and Ploog 1986; Pomeroy and Mitchell 1989; Yager 1989).

A variety of techniques have been suggested for nutritional rehabilitation. Tube feeding and total parenteral nutrition are recommended only for severe cases of emaciation. For most patients, nutritional rehabilitation is done on an inpatient basis and begins gradually, with the individual given 1,400 to 1,800 calories a day. As the patient adjusts to this feeding regimen, caloric intake is slowly increased. One of the most critical features of effective nutritional management is a good nursing staff that can provide the patient with encouragement and support in her efforts to confront her ambivalence and compulsions. The nutritional program may include behavioral modification techniques such as requiring bed rest until a stable pattern of weight gain is evident, informational feedback about calories and weight, and gradual assumption of control of eating by the patient. Once the patient begins to gain weight and appears motivated, psychological treatment can be instituted (Casper 1986; Pirke and Ploog 1986; Yager 1989).

PSYCHOLOGICAL TREATMENT

No one type of psychotherapy is ideal for anorexia nervosa. Rather, psychotherapeutic strategies must be tailored to the cognitive styles, and psychological and developmental levels, of the participants. It has been recommended that some combination of individual and family therapy may be the most useful treatment plan (Yager 1989).

A number of types of psychotherapy have been used in anorexia. Initial treatment used psychoanalytic techniques that were based on the belief that anorexia is primarily the the result of impaired psychosexual development. Although some success was achieved using psychoanalytic methods, recognition of the multidetermined nature of anorexia has resulted in a decrease in the use of this approach.

Behavior therapy has frequently been employed in the treatment of anorexia. It has been demonstrated that both positive reinforcers, such as praise or the opportunity to engage in a favored activity, and negative reinforcers, such as enforced bed rest or denial of privileges, can influence the rate at which patients eat and gain weight. Providing the patient with knowledge about caloric intake and weight gain may increase the success of behavior therapy programs (Agras 1987; Yager 1989). Behavior therapy appears to be an effective treatment, but not all professionals agree on its long-term benefits. It has been proposed that behavior therapy may cause problems because it treats the symptoms rather than the cause of this disorder. Some have claimed that anorectic patients gaining weight as a result of behavior therapy could feel that they were then losing even more control over their own lives. This feeling could have devastating psychological effects (Bruch 1977). However, this claim has not been fully substantiated.

Based on the realization that anorexia nervosa may reflect difficulties in the family relationship, family therapy is often recommended. Rosman et al. (1977) have identified four characteristic patterns of functioning in families of anorectic patients: enmeshment, overprotectiveness, rigidity, and lack of conflict resolution. The patient is viewed as being involved in the parental conflict in a way as to control, detour, avoid, or suppress it. The family members are seen together in therapy. Treatment is initially directed at symptom removal, such as altering eating patterns using family resources. Later treatment focuses on issues within the family such as marital or parental problems.

PHARMACOLOGICAL TREATMENT

One of the more controversial treatments for anorexia is the use of psychoactive drugs. Much of the initial interest in drug therapies grew out of attempts to treat certain target symptoms with drugs that had originally been developed for other diagnoses. For example, antipsychotic drugs were proposed to treat the delusional beliefs of anorexics concerning body weight and body image. More recently, drug treatments have been derived from basic research findings on the mechanisms that control food intake and the regulation of body weight. A number of drug therapies have been employed, with varying degrees of success. These include the administration of antipsychotic agents: L-dopa; delta-9-tetrahydrocannabinol, the active ingredient in marijuana; and lithium carbonate (Johanson and Knorr 1977; Drossman, Ontjes, and Heizer 1979; Mitchell 1989).

Based on the findings that symptoms of depression are frequent in anorexia, a number of researchers have investigated the effects of antidepressants in the treatment of the disorder. Several studies have reported beneficial outcomes with the use of antidepressants including relatively rapid weight gain, positive alterations in ideas about food, and improved social relationships. However, other studies have not observed significant advantages for antidepressants over placebos (Mitchell 1989).

It has also been suggested that cyproheptadine, a serotonin and histamine antagonist that stimulates appetite and weight gain in patients given the drug for asthma and other allergic conditions, might be useful in the treatment of anorexia. Initial studies (Vigersky and Loriaux 1977) did not find cyproheptadine to be an effective. More recent work, however, using larger doses of the drug, has demonstrated that anorectic patients taking cyproheptadine gain weight more rapidly than those given a placebo (Halmi et al. 1986).

OUTCOME OF TREATMENT PROGRAMS

The best outcomes of treatment programs have generally been observed in patients with high educational achievement, early age of onset, and improvement in body image after weight gain. Poor prognosis is associated with later age of onset, continual overestimation of body size after weight gain, premorbid obesity, lower weight at time of admission, long duration of illness, self-induced vomiting, laxative abuse, disturbed parental relationships, marked depression, obsessional behavior, or somatic complaints. It is also interesting to note that males generally have a poorer prognosis than females (Morgan and Russell 1975; Crisp et al. 1977; Drossman, Ontjes, and Heizer 1979; Anderson 1984).

It should be emphasized that regardless of the treatment modality, the majority of patients will not be cured of anorexia upon release from the hospital and/or after several months of psychotherapy. Continued therapy and support may be needed for some time to prevent relapses and worsening of symptoms.

BULIMIA

Bulimia is an eating disorder characterized by a binge-purge cycle of food intake. Bulimia denotes a ravenous appetite; literally, "ox hunger." Bulimia is observed in normal-weight and overweight individuals, as well as up to half of the patients diagnosed with anorexia nervosa. Bulimia, like anorexia nervosa, occurs primarily in women, with the female to male ratio estimated to be approximately 8 : 1 (Lipscomb 1987). While many women with bulimia also have anorexia, distinctions have been made between individuals with these two disorders. In general, bulimics tend to be heavier, older, and more outgoing than anorexics. In contrast to anorexics, individuals with bulimia are less likely to suffer from amenorrhea and more likely to engage in sexual behavior. Bulimics also display more symptoms of depression, show greater lability of mood, and are thought to be at a higher risk for suicide than anorexics (Andersen 1984; Devlin and Walsh 1989).

Bulimic individuals may rarely eat normal meals. When forced by circumstances (e.g., social occasions or parental pressure), most consume very little food. In contrast, during a binge episode large amounts of foods are rapidly ingested. The size of a binge can vary greatly, ranging from 1,000 to 20,000 calories. Foods consumed during a binge tend to be high in fat and carbohydrate and are frequently those that are avoided during dieting: cake, ice cream, doughnuts, chocolate, bread and butter, cookies, and candy. Most binge eating is done in the evening and at night and often in secrecy. Binge eating can be precipitated by a variety of conditions including anxiety and tension, boredom, frustration, depression, or simply the sight of food (Casper 1986; Walsh 1988; Drewnowski 1989).

Following a binge, there are often feelings of anxiety, depression, and guilt. The bulimic may feel a sense of humiliation for having lost control and thus seek to undo the overeating, most frequently by regurgitating the ingested food. Vomiting eventually can become tied to binge eating. Many bulimics overeat with the forethought of vomiting afterward. For some bulimics, purging is accomplished by the use of large amounts of laxatives and/or diuretics. In either situation, the patient is aware of the abnormal nature of her behavior and attempts to hide it from family and friends (Andersen 1984; Casper 1986).

History and Diagnosis

Clinical reports of bulimia were published as early as the late 1800s. Although bulimic behavior was usually associated with anorexia, it was also observed in individuals with diabetes mellitus and malaria, and among young girls living in boarding schools. It was not until the 1940s, however, that detailed reports of compulsive overeating and purging behavior began appearing in the medical literature. Although the majority of reports identified these behaviors in anorexics, descriptions of bulimic behavior in nonanorectic populations were also presented.

In the 1950s, binge eating was recognized among some obese individuals. This behavior was characterized by consumption of large quantities of food in extended binges. Frequently, these episodes were precipitated by upsetting life events and were often followed by self-condemnation. In general, however, obese individuals were not reported to engage in purging behavior (Stunkard 1959).

It was not until the mid-1970s that reports of bulimic behavior among normal-weight individuals became prevalent. In 1979, Gerald Russell was the first to use the term "bulimia nervosa" in an article that described a group of 30 patients who displayed symptoms of bulimia (Russell 1979). In addition to providing a detailed portrayal of these individuals, Russell also offered criteria for diagnosing the disorder including powerful and intractable urges to overeat, avoidance of the fattening effects of food by inducing vomiting or abusing purgatives or both, and a morbid fear of becoming fat.

With the growing awareness that bulimic behavior is not restricted to individuals with anorexia nervosa and that it represents a distinct type of eating disorder, in 1980 the American Psychiatric Association published criteria for the diagnosis of the disorder in the third edition of the Diagnostic and Statistical Manual of Mental Disorders (DSM-III). Although these criteria helped to define bulimia, investigators studying the disorder felt that there were several problems with the diagnostic guidelines. First, individuals with a any history of anorexia were eliminated. Research comparing anorexics with no history of bulimic episodes to those with such a history, and to patients with no history of anorexia but demonstrated bulimic behavior, indicated the groups reporting bulimic symptoms were more similar to each other than to the anorectic group who did not display bulimia (e.g., Norman and Herzog 1983; Garner, Garfinkel, and O'Shaughnessy 1985). A second problem with the original criteria was that frequency of binge eating was not stipulated. To remedy these problems the diagnostic criteria for bulimia were revised in the latest edition of DSM-IIIR (American Psychiatric Association 1987). In this revision, any criteria related to weight have been eliminated, and the frequency of binge eating is stipulated (Johnson and Conners 1987):

Diagnostic Criteria for Bulimia Nervosa

A. Recurrent episodes of binge eating (rapid consumption of a large amount of food in a discrete time period).
B. A feeling of lack of control over eating behavior during the eating binges.
C. The person regularly engages in either self-induced vomiting, use of laxatives or diuretics, strict dieting or fasting, or vigorous exercise in order to prevent weight gain.
D. A minimum average of two binge-eating episodes a week for at least three months.
E. Persistent overconcern with body shape and weight. (From American Psychiatric Association 1987, pp. 68–69)

Prevalence

A large number of reports on the prevalence of bulimia have appeared in the last decade (e.g., Halmi, Falk, and Schwartz 1981; Pope et al. 1984; Gray and Ford 1985; Nevo 1985). Unfortunately, estimates of frequency vary substantially among these reports. Numerous factors can account for the discrepancies. First, the studies have differed widely in their subject populations and included college-age and high-school students, women interviewed while shopping, and women seeking medical or family planning advice. A second problem is that the majority of studies investigating the prevalence of bulimia used self-report questionnaires. Across the studies, the questionnaires differed substantially with respect to the criteria used to define binging and purging behavior. Additionally, some questionnaires inquired only about current behavior, and others asked about prior behavior. Finally, a number of studies required students to fill out questionnaires in class where the "mind set" of students as they answered questions could have had a large impact (Johnson and Connors 1987).

Despite the variety of results we can conclude from studies that binge eating is a relatively common occurrence, ranging from 26% to 61% in females and from 28% to 42% in males. However, when more restrictive criteria are employed, such as a minimum binge frequency of once a week and the routine use of purging, the estimates of the frequency of bulimia drop significantly. The incidence of bulimia in young women is presently estimated to range from 1% to 8% (Johnson and Connors 1987; Walsh 1988; Halmi, Schneider, and Cooper 1989).

Etiology

Why do some individuals get caught in a binge-purge cycle of eating? As for anorexia nervosa, a single cause for bulimia cannot be isolated; rather, there are a variety of factors that contribute to the behavior (Farmer, Treasure, and Szmukler 1986; Lipscomb 1987; Shapiro 1988). Personality variables certainly play a role in the development of the disorder. It has been hypothesized, for example, that bulimia may be closely tied to depressive disorders. Several lines of evidence support this hypothesis (Walsh et al. 1985; Hudson et al. 1987a, 1987b; Johnson and Connors 1987; Devlin and Walsh 1989).

- Many bulimic patients display symptoms that are characteristic of depression.
- There is a high degree of affective disorders among relatives of bulimics.
- Similar biological abnormalities (e.g., a blunted response to thyroid-stimulating hormone) have been found in depression and bulimia.
- Antidepressant medication has been found to be an effective therapy for some bulimic patients.

In general, women with bulimia have been characterized as high-achievers from high-achieving families; however, they also tend to be dependent, passive, and unassertive. They may be self-conscious and have difficulties expressing their feelings. Moreover, bulimics are extremely vulnerable to rejection and failure and may have problems with impulse control. Bulimic behavior has been associated with other behaviors indicative of abnormal impulse control including shoplifting and over-consumption of alcohol and drugs (Casper 1986; Lipscomb 1987).

Familial factors also contribute to the development of bulimia. The family environment of bulimic patients can be described as chaotic, conflicted, and neglectful. Family members may be deficient in problem-solving skills, use indirect and contradictory methods of communication, and be nonsupportive of independent behavior. These family characteristics can make children feel insecure, disorganized, disconnected, and anxious (Johnson and Connors 1987).

As in anorexia, social and cultural values may also encourage bulimic behavior in vulnerable individuals. As previously mentioned, the pursuit of thinness and chronic dieting have become norms in our society. In support of the idea that dieting behavior may lead to the development of bulimia, many patients report that their abnormal eating behavior began at a time when they were dieting (Walsh 1988).

The changing roles of women in today's society may also favor the development of bulimic behavior. Women now face multiple, ambiguous, and often contradictory role expectations, such as accommodating traditional feminine roles with more recent standards for professional and personal achievement. It has been suggested that the wider range of choices available to women in contemporary society may provide personal freedom for those who are psychologically healthy, but for women who feel insecure, depressed, and not in control of their lives, these choices may be particularly unsettling and lead to abnormal eating behavior (Garner, Garfinkel, and Olmsted 1983).

Physiological Consequences

The physiological consequences of bulimia are not as well characterized as those of anorexia, because until recently the disorder was not recognized as a separate clinical entity. The physical complications of bulimia affect almost every system of the body and range from minor problems, such as abrasions on the knuckles from continual use of the hand to induce vomiting, to severe and life-threatening difficulties such as electrolyte disturbances resulting from continual purging (Table 14-2).

Many of the medical complications of bulimia are also side effects of disordered eating behavior. The rapid consumption of large amounts of food can lead to acute gastric dilation with consequent pain and nausea. Inflammation of the pancreas with fever, severe abdominal pain, abdominal distention, and increased heart rate may develop as a consequence of abrupt pancreatic stimulation during frequent binge-eating episodes.

Many bulimic patients vomit regularly after a binge episode in an attempt to remove the food from their stomach. Recurrent vomiting of acidic stomach contents can result in erosion of the esophagus. Forceful vomiting can tear the esophagus, which can be a life-threatening event. Vomiting can also lead to fluid loss and dehydration. As a result, the body responds by retaining excess water, and edema can result. Bulimic patients may experience excessive thirst, decreased urinary output, and dizziness.

Vomiting also removes electrolytes that are important in maintaining the integrity of many systems in the body. Loss of potassium, sodium, and chloride from the body can lead to a variety of cardiac symptoms ranging from irregular heart beat and palpitations to congestive heart failure.

TABLE 14-2. Physiological Consequences of Bulimia

Organ System	Consequences
Endocrine	Menstrual abnormalities
	Abnormal response to growth hormone and thyroid-stimulating hormone
	Hypoglycemia
	Elevated prolactin levels
Cardiovascular	Bradycardia
	Arrhythmias
	Hypotension
	Electrocardiographic abnormalities
	Congestive heart failure
	Sudden cardiac arrest
Gastrointestinal	Esophagitis
	Esophageal perforations
	Gastric dilation and rupture
	Pancreatitis
	Constipation
	Impaired colon function
	Abnormal liver function
	Abdominal cramps
Oral	Gum disease
	Enamel erosion
	Tooth decay
	Enlargement of the salivary gland
Dermatological	Bruises and lacerations over knuckles
Renal	Decreased glomerular filtration rate
	Kidney damage
	Polyuria and polydipsia
	Elevated blood urea nitrogen
Fluid and Electrolytes	Dehydration
	Hypokalemia
	Hyponatremia
	Hypochloremia
	Metabolic alkalosis
	Metabolic acidosis (usually secondary to laxative abuse)
Neurological	Abnormalities in the electroencephalogram
Other	Impaired thermoregulation

Adapted from Casper 1986; Pomeroy and Mitchell 1989.

Dental decay, gum problems, and swelling of the salivary glands are also common consequences of vomiting.

It was recently suggested that purging behavior may also lead to taste disturbances in bulimia. Relative to controls, bulimic individuals demonstrated a decreased ability to taste salty, sweet, acid, or bitter solutions when taste receptors on their palate were stimulated. The palate may be particularly sensitive to purging behavior, because vomit is directed toward the roof of the mouth where palate receptors are located. The acid in vomit may damage these receptors. It has further been proposed that damage to palate receptors could contribute to the maintenance of bulimic behavior as a result of a decreased sensitivity to the taste of vomit (Rodin et al. 1990).

Laxative and diuretic abuse is also common in bulimia. Reports indicate that 38% to 75% of individuals with eating disorders use laxatives or diuretics as a method of weight control. Laxative and diuretic use can become an addictive behavior, with bulimic patients developing tolerance to their effects and thus using increasing amounts. Chronic use of laxatives can result in the loss of normal colon function, which may become so severe that colonic resection is necessary. Additionally, laxative and diuretic abuse can lead to shifts in fluid balance, dehydration, malabsorption, abdominal cramping, electrolyte imbalances, and muscle cramps.

Although not as well documented as in anorexia nervosa, recent work indicates that abnormalities in endocrine functioning also occur in bulimia. Menstrual abnormalities including oligomenorrhea, dysmenorrhea, and irregular menstruation are common. Elevated prolactin levels and abnormal responses to growth hormone and thyroid-stimulating hormone also have been found in a small number of subjects with bulimia (Andersen 1984; Casper 1986; Halmi 1987; Johnson and Connors 1987; Pomeroy and Mitchell 1989).

Treatment

Treatment of bulimia is initially aimed at interrupting the cycle of overeating and purging, in an attempt to normalize eating patterns. A variety of different approaches have been used including behavioral therapy, group therapy, psychotherapy, and pharmacological treatments.

As with anorexia nervosa, treatment of bulimia should begin with a comprehensive multidimensional assessment. This assessment should incorporate a complete psychiatric history of the individual and her family; detailed information regarding eating habits, attitudes toward food, and body image disturbances; and a physical examination (Yager 1989). Once this assessment is complete, treatment can begin.

PSYCHOLOGICAL TREATMENT

One method of psychotherapy receiving increasing attention is cognitive behavior therapy (Fairburn 1984; Johnson and Connors 1987). In this approach, the therapist's role is to be informative and supportive. Treatment is done on an outpatient basis and usually lasts from four to six months. This type of therapy is considered problem-oriented, with both specific goals and specific means to achieve those goals stated. The bulimic patient is made responsible for the changes that are to be made, thus providing her with the sense that she is in control of her eating behavior.

In the initial stages of treatment, the goal is to disrupt the binge-purge cycle by self-monitoring, in which patients maintain a detailed record of all the food they consume. Not only must they record what they ate, but also where the food was eaten, and if binging, why it was eaten. In addition, a record is kept of purging behavior, any laxative abuse, and daily weight. Patients are also educated about weight regulation, dieting, and the dangers of purging and of laxative and diuretic abuse.

The second stage of treatment concentrates on cognitive restructuring, identifying and trying to alter the maladaptive and irrational self-beliefs that maintain and reinforce bulimic behavior. In an attempt to break the binge-purge cycle, the patient may be told to restrict food intake to three or four meals and two snacks a day, whether or not she is hungry. Strategies such as the introduction of previously forbidden food into the patient's diet, and providing alternative behaviors in place of binging, may also be included.

The final stage of therapy focuses on sustaining the progress which has been made by careful monitoring of eating behavior. Relapses are prevented by preparing patients to deal with stressful events that might evoke prior bulimic patterns. Short-term success rates of cognitive behavior therapy have been relatively high, with 60% to 80% of patients reporting significant reductions in both binging and purging behavior (Fairburn 1984; Johnson and Connors 1987; Yager 1989).

Group therapy may also be successful in the treatment of bulimia. Like individual therapy, group therapy incorporates the keeping of detailed dietary records, goal setting, education about weight regulation, and cognitive restructuring of eating behavior. Group feedback and support, relaxation techniques, and assertiveness training also may be included. Success rates for group therapy vary substantially, with 50% to 90% of participants reporting reductions in binging and purging (Yager 1989).

Because most relapses occur within six months after an individual has initially ceased binging, follow-up for a year is generally recommended in both individual and group therapy (Yager 1989).

PHARMACOLOGICAL TREATMENT

In the early 1980s, studies of the efficacy of antidepressant medications in bulimia were initiated. The initial rationale for these studies grew from the observations that symptoms of depression were common in bulimia and might partly account for the alterations in feeding behavior observed. In general, antidepressants have proved superior to placebos in decreasing the frequency of binging and purging, and in ameliorating depression and anxiety in bulimic patients. However, while some patients respond well to antidepressants, others do not. For example, some patients report a number of side effects including hypotension and insomnia (e.g., Pope and Hudson 1982; Pope et al. 1983; Mitchell and Groat 1984; Mitchell 1989;

Pope and Hudson 1989; McCann and Agras 1990). Additionally, in a recent study comparing the effects of antidepressant treatment and group psychotherapy, it was found that group therapy, with or without drug treatment, was superior to drug treatment alone. These results raise questions about the use of antidepressants in the treatment of bulimia. Although these drugs are helpful for some patients, there is a question as to whether they should be used as the sole treatment, because certain forms of psychotherapy may be more beneficial (Mitchell 1989).

A number of other drugs, including anticonvulsants and opioid antagonists, have been investigated for the treatment of bulimia. Of these other agents, the opioid antagonist naltrexone appears most promising. Administration of large doses of naltrexone has been associated with a reduction in bulimic symptoms in some patients (Jones and Gold 1986; Mitchell 1989). However, gastrointestinal side effects can occur as a result of naltrexone administration, and recent work has indicated that large doses of the drug may be toxic to the liver. Thus, the feasibility of using this drug in the treatment of bulimia is questionable.

OUTCOME OF TREATMENT FOR BULIMIA NERVOSA

Long-term outcome in bulimia has been less well studied than in anorexia nervosa. Predictors of good outcomes in bulimia have been contradictory, but there is some agreement on poor outcome being associated with alcohol abuse, suicide attempts, and increased depression on follow-up visits (Herzog, Keller, and Lavori 1988). Bulimia tends to follow a pattern of remissions and relapses, and at least one-third of patients are still found to be bulimic several years after their initial diagnosis.

CONCLUSION

Given the serious consequences of both anorexia and bulimia, it is somewhat surprising that more attention has not been paid to the area of prevention of these eating disorders. Parents, teachers, and health care educators and workers can play an important role in prevention. One of the most critical features in a prevention program is the provision of accurate information about the causes and consequences of both disorders. Facts about current knowledge of food intake and body weight regulation should be presented. Discussions with young adults about the role of the media in promoting a generally false association between thinness and happiness or success, and the dangers of social pressure, could also be beneficial.

As previously mentioned, one important component in the development of both anorexia nervosa and bulimia is an apparent lack of self-esteem in individuals with these disorders. Activities that enhance self-image could be useful as a preventive measure. Further, realistic concepts of self should be stressed.

TABLE 14-3. Early Warning Signs of Anorexia Nervosa and Bulimia

Anorexia	Bulimia
Preoccupation with appearance	Frequent weight fluctuations
Disturbances in body image	Secretive behavior
Denial of substantial weight loss	Depression
Increased activity	Mood lability
Obsessions with food	Tooth decay
Decreased food intake	Swollen salivary glands
Declining performance in school	Abdominal pain and bowel problems
Withdrawal from friends and normal	Frequent sore throats
activities	Dehydration
Cold intolerance	
Amenorrhea	
Depression	

Finally, parents, teachers, and health care workers should also be aware of the signs of eating disorders so that early intervention can occur (Table 14-3). The earlier treatment is initiated, the more successful it may be.

With appropriate preventive strategies, we can hope for a reduction in the potentially devastating outcomes of anorexia and bulimia.

REFERENCES

Agras, W. S. 1987. *Eating Disorders: Management of Obesity, Bulimia and Anorexia Nervosa.* Elmsford, NY: Pergamon Press.

American Psychiatric Association. 1987. *Diagnostic and Statistical Manual of Mental Disorders,* Washington, D.C.: American Psychiatric Association.

Andersen, A. E. 1984. Anorexia nervosa and bulimia: Biological, psychological, and sociocultural aspects. In *Nutrition and Behavior,* ed. J. R. Galler, pp. 305–338. New York: Plenum.

Bemis, K. W. 1978. Current approaches to the etiology and treatment of anorexia nervosa. *Psychological Bulletin* 85:593–617.

Bruch, H. 1973. *Eating Disorders* New York: Basic Books.

Bruch, H. 1977. Psychological antecedents of anorexia nervosa. In *Anorexia Nervosa,* ed. R. A. Vigersky, pp. 1–10. New York: Raven Press.

Bruch, H. 1979. *The Golden Cage.* New York: Vintage Books.

Casper, R. C. 1986. The pathophysiology of anorexia nervosa and bulimia nervosa. *Annual Review of Nutrition* 6:299–316.

Crisp, A. H. 1970. Premorbid factors in adult disorders of weight, with particular reference to primary anorexia nervosa (weight phobia): A literature review. *Journal of Psychosomatic Research* 14:1–22.

Crisp, A. H., Kalucy, R. S., Lacey, J. H., and Harding, B. 1977. The long-term prognosis in anorexia nervosa: Some factors predictive of outcome. In *Anorexia Nervosa,* ed. R. A. Vigersky, pp. 55–65. New York: Raven Press.

Devlin, M. J. and Walsh, B. T. 1989. Eating disorders and depression. *Psychiatric Annals* 19:473–476.

Drewnowski, A. 1989. Taste responsiveness in eating disorders. *Annals of the New York Academy of Sciences* 575:399–409.

Drossman, D. A., Ontjes, D. A., and Heizer, W. D. 1979. Clinical conference: Anorexia nervosa. *Gastroenterology* 77:1115–1131.

Fairburn, C. G. 1984. Bulimia: Its epidemiology and management. In *Eating and Its Disorders,* ed. A. J. Stunkard and E. Stellar, pp. 235–258. New York: Raven Press.

Farmer, A., Treasure, J., and Szmukler, G. 1986. Eating disorders: A review of recent research. *Digestive Diseases* 4:13–25.

Feighner, J. P., Robins, E., Guze, S. B., Woodruff, R. A., Winokur, G., and Munoz, R. 1972. Diagnostic criteria for use in psychiatric research. *Archives of General Psychiatry* 26:57–63.

Garfinkel, P. E. and Garner, D. M. 1983. The multidetermined nature of anorexia nervosa. In *Anorexia Nervosa: Recent Developments in Research,* ed. P. L. Darby et al., pp. 3–14. New York: Alan R. Liss.

Garner, D. M. and Garfinkel, P. E. 1980. Sociocultural factors in the development of anorexia nervosa. *Psychological Medicine* 10:647–656.

Garner, D. M., Garfinkel, P. E., and Olmsted, M. P. 1983. An overview of sociocultural factors in the development of anorexia nervosa. In *Anorexia Nervosa: Recent Developments in Research,* ed. P. L. Darby et al., pp. 65–82. New York: Alan R. Liss.

Garner, D. M., Garfinkel, P. E., and O'Shaughnessy, A. 1985. The validity of the distinction between bulimics with and without anorexia nervosa. *American Journal of Psychiatry* 142:581–587.

Garner, D. M., Garfinkel, P. E., Schwartz, D., and Thompson, M. 1980. Cultural expectations of thinness in women. *Psychological Reports* 47:483–491.

Gilbert, S. 1986. *Pathology of Eating: Psychology and Treatment.* London: Routledge & Kegan Paul.

Gray, J. J. and Ford, K. 1985. The incidence of bulimia in a college sample. *International Journal of Eating Disorders* 4:210–215.

Gull, W. W. 1874. Anorexia nervosa. *Lancet* 1868:22–28.

Hall, A. 1978. Family structure and relationships of 50 female anorexia nervosa patients. *Australian and New Zealand Journal of Psychiatry* 50:381–395.

Halmi, K. A. 1974. Anorexia nervosa: Demographic and clinical features in 94 cases. *Psychosomatic Medicine* 36:18–25.

Halmi, K. A. 1987. Anorexia nervosa and bulimia. *Annual Review of Medicine* 38:373–380.

Halmi, K. A., Eckert, E., Ladu, T., and Cohen, J. 1986. Anorexia nervosa: Treatment efficacy of cyproheptadine and amitriptyline. *Archives of General Psychiatry* 43:177–181.

Halmi, K. A., Falk, J. R., and Schwartz, E. 1981. Binge eating and vomiting: A survey of a college population. *Journal of Psychological Medicine* 11:697–706.

Halmi, K., Schneider, L., and Cooper, S. J. 1989. Preface. *Annals of the New York Academy of Sciences* 517:xi–xii.

Halmi, K. A. and Sunday S. R. 1991. Temporal patterns of hunger and fullness ratings and related cognitions in anorexia and bulimia. *Appetite,* in press in *Appetite.*

Herzog, D. B., Keller, M. B., and Lavori, P. W. 1988. Outcome in anorexia nervosa and bulimia nervosa: A review of the literature. *Journal of Nervous and Mental Diseases* 176:131–143.

Holland, A. J., Hall, A., Murray, R., Russell, G. F. M., and Crisp, A. H. 1984. Anorexia nervosa: A study of 34 twin pairs and one set of triplets. *British Journal of Psychiatry* 145:414–419.

Hudson, J. I., Pope, H. G., Jonas, J. M., Yurgelun-Todd, D., and Frankenburg, F. R. 1987a. A controlled family history study of bulimia. *Psychological Medicine* 17:883–890.

Hudson, J. I., Pope, H. G., Yurgelun-Todd, D., Jonas, J. M., and Frankenburg, F. R. 1987b. A controlled study of the lifetime prevalence of affective and other psychiatric disorders in bulimic outpatients. *American Journal of Psychiatry* 144:1283–1287.

Johanson, A. J. and Knorr, N. J. 1977. L-dopa as treatment for anorexia nervosa. In *Anorexia Nervosa,* ed. R. A. Vigersky, pp. 363–372. New York: Raven Press.

Johnson, C. and Connors, M. E. 1987. *The Etiology and Treatment of Bulimia Nervosa.* New York: Basic Books.

Jones, J. M. and Gold, M. S. 1986. Naltrexone reverses bulimic symptoms. *Lancet* 1:807.

Kalucy, R. S., Crisp, A. H., and Harding, B. 1977. A study of 56 families with anorexia nervosa. *British Journal of Medical Psychology* 50:381–395.

Keys, A., Brozek, J., Henschel, A., Mickelson, O., and Taylor, H. L. 1950. *The Biology of Human Starvation.* Minneapolis: University of Minnesota Press.

Kron, L., Katz, J. L., Gorzynski, G., and Weiner, H. 1978. Hyperactivity in anorexia nervosa: A fundamental clinical feature. *Comprehensive Psychiatry* 19:433–440.

Lehrman, K. 1987. Anorexia and bulimia: Causes and cures. *Consumers' Research* September:29–32.

Libnickey, S. C. 1987. Beyond dieting: A preventive perspective on eating disorders. *Health Values* January/February:27–35.

Lipscomb, P. A. 1987. Bulimia: Diagnosis and management in the primary care setting. *Journal of Family Practice* 24:187–194.

McCann, U. D. and Agras W. S. 1990. Successful treatment of nonpurging bulimia nervosa with desipramine: a double-blind, placebo-controlled study. *American Journal of Psychiatry* 147:1509–1513.

Mitchell, J. E. 1989. Psychopharmacology of eating disorders. *Annals of the New York Academy of Sciences* 517:41–48.

Mitchell, J. E. and Groat, R. 1984. A placebo-controlled double-blind trial of amitriptyline in bulimia. *Journal for Clinical Psychopharmacology* 4:186–193.

Morgan, H. G. and Russell, G. F. M. 1975. Value of family background and clinical features as predictors of long-term outcome in anorexia nervosa. *Psychological Medicine* 5:355–371.

Nevo, S. 1985. Bulimic symptoms: Prevalence and ethnic differences among college women. *International Journal of Eating Disorders* 4:151–168.

Norman, D. K. and Herzog, D. B. 1983. Bulimia, anorexia nervosa, and anorexia nervosa with bulimia: A comparative analysis of MMPI profiles. *International Journal of Eating Disorders* 2:43–52.

Pirke, K. M. and Ploog, D. 1986. Psychobiology of anorexia nervosa. In *Nutrition and the Brain,* vol. 7, ed. R. J. Wurtman and J. J. Wurtman, pp. 167–198. New York: Raven Press.

Pomeroy, C. and Mitchell, J. E. 1989. Medical complications and management of eating disorders. *Psychiatric Annals* 19:488–493.

Pope, H. G. and Hudson, J. I. 1982. Treatment of bulimia with antidepressants. *Psychopharmacology* 78:176–179.

Pope, H. G. and Hudson, J. I. 1989. Pharmacological treatment of bulimia nervosa: Research findings and practical suggestions. *Psychiatric Annals* 19:438–485.

Pope, H. G., Hudson, J. I., Jonas, J. M., and Yurgelun-Todd, D. 1983. Bulimia treated with imipramine: A placebo-controlled double-blind study. *American Journal of Psychiatry* 140:554–558.

Pope, H. G., Hudson, J. I., Yurgelun-Todd, D., and Hudson, M. S. 1984. Prevalence of anorexia nervosa and bulimia in three student populations. *International Journal of Eating Disorders* 3:45–51.

Rakoff, V. 1983. Multiple determinants of family dynamics in anorexia nervosa. In *Anorexia Nervosa: Recent Developments in Research,* ed. P. L. Darby et al., pp. 29–40. New York: Alan R. Liss.

Robinson, P. H. 1989. Gastric function in eating disorders. *Annals of the New York Academy of Sciences* 517:456–465.

Rodin, J., Bartoshuk, L., Peterson, C., and Schank, D. 1990. Bulimia and taste: Possible interactions. *Journal of Abnormal Psychology* 99:32–39.

Rosman, B. L., Minuchin, S., Baker, L., and Liebman, R. 1977. A family approach to anorexia nervosa: Study, treatment and outcome. In *Anorexia Nervosa,* ed. R. A. Vigersky, pp. 341–356. New York: Raven Press.

Russell, G. F. M. 1979. Bulimia nervosa: An ominous variant of anorexia nervosa. *Psychological Medicine* 9:429–448.

Russell, G. F. M. and Treasure, J. 1989. The modern history of anorexia nervosa: An interpretation of why the illness has changed. *Annals of the New York Academy of Sciences* 575:13–27.

Selvini-Palazzoli, M. D. 1970. Anorexia nervosa. In *The World Biennial of Psychiatry and Psychotherapy,* ed. S. Arieti, pp. 197–218. New York: Basic Books.

Shapiro, S. 1988. Bulimia: An entity in search of definition. *Journal of Clinical Psychology* 44:491–498.

Silverman, J. A. 1983. Medical consequences of starvation; the malnutrition of anorexia nervosa: Caveat medicus. In *Anorexia Nervosa: Recent Developments in Research,* ed. P. L. Darby et al., pp. 293–299. New York: Alan R. Liss.

Stunkard, A. J. 1959. Eating patterns and obesity. *Psychiatric Quarterly* 33:284–292.

Vigersky, R. A. and Loriaux, D. L. 1977. The effect of cyproheptadine in anorexia nervosa: A double-blind trial. In *Anorexia Nervosa,* ed. R. A. Vigersky, pp. 349–356. New York: Raven Press.

Walsh, B. T. 1988. Appetite regulation in bulimia. In *Control of Appetite,* ed. M. Winick, pp. 137–149. New York: Wiley.

Walsh, B. T., Roose, S. P., Glassman, A. H., Gladis, M., and Sadik, C. 1985. Bulimia and depression. *Psychosomatic Medicine* 47:123–131.

Winokur, A., March V., and Mendels, J. 1980. Primary affective disorder in relatives of patients with anorexia nervosa. *American Journal of Psychiatry* 137:695–698.

Yager, J. 1989. Psychological treatments for eating disorders. *Psychiatric Annals* 19:477–482.

Index